# the new
# KNITTING
# STITCH
## dictionary

# *the new* KNITTING STITCH *dictionary*

## 500 PATTERNS
### for Textures, Lace, Aran Cables, Colorwork, Motifs, Edgings
### AND MORE

Lydia Klös

Stackpole
Books
Essex, Connecticut
Blue Ridge Summit, Pennsylvania

## THANK YOU!

We would like to thank company MEZ GmbH (www.mezcrafts.com) for providing yarn support for this book: www.mezcrafts.com

## STACKPOLE BOOKS

An imprint of Globe Pequot, the trade division of The Rowman & Littlefield Publishing Group, Inc.
4501 Forbes Blvd., Ste. 200
Lanham, MD 20706
www.rowman.com

Distributed by NATIONAL BOOK NETWORK
800-462-6420

The original German edition was published as *Strickmuster—Die Sammlung*

Copyright © 2021 frechverlag GmbH, Stuttgart, Germany (www.top-kreativ.de)
This edition is published by arrangement with Anja Endemann, ae Rights Agency, Calvinstr. 23,
10557 Berlin, Germany
Photos: frechverlag GmbH, 70499 Stuttgart, Germany; lichtpunkt, Michael Ruder, Stuttgart, Germany
Product management: Franziska Schmidt
Editing: Christine Schlitt, Worms, Germany; Karen Lee Luick, Esslingen, Germany
Graphic design: Petra Theilfarth
Translation: Katharina Sokiran

British Library Cataloguing in Publication Information available

**Library of Congress Cataloging-in-Publication Data available**

Names: Klos, Lydia, author.
Title: The new knitting stitch dictionary : 500 patterns for textures,
    lace, aran cables, colorwork, motifs, edgings and more / Lydia Klös.
Other titles: Strickmuster. English
Description: Lanham, MD : Rowman & Littlefield Publishing Group, [2023] |
    "The original German edition was published as Strickmuster-Die Sammlung
    Copyright © 2021 frechverlag GmbH, Stuttgart, Germany." | Summary: "This
    book features 500 innovative knitting stitch patterns. The stitches are
    divided into sections by type of stitch: texture, lace, cables, flower
    and leaf patterns, bobbles, lifted stitches, Fair Isle, intarsia,
    borders, and more"— Provided by publisher.
Identifiers: LCCN 2022039799 (print) | LCCN 2022039800 (ebook) | ISBN
    9780811771986 (paperback) | ISBN 9780811771993 (epub)
Subjects: LCSH: Knitting—Patterns.
Classification: LCC TT825 .K61613 2023  (print) | LCC TT825  (ebook) | DDC
    746.43/2041—dc23/eng/20220826
LC record available at https://lccn.loc.gov/2022039799
LC ebook record available at https://lccn.loc.gov/2022039800

Printed in India

First Edition

If you have been drawn in by the ENTHRALLING HOBBY OF KNITTING, you've chosen just the right book! Using only a few basic stitches, a multitude of fascinating stitch patterns has been compiled for you, waiting to be turned into FABULOUS KNITTING PROJECTS by your creativity and imagination.

This collection contains 500 STITCH PATTERNS, providing wonderful pattern suggestions for simple knitting projects as well as challenging and sophisticated ideas for master knitters.

The book is divided into 13 CHAPTERS—11 stitch pattern chapters, 1 chapter of KNITTING BASICS (also refer here for stitch abbreviations and symbol explanations), and a final chapter providing you with INSPIRATION for designing your own projects, using the stitch patterns from this book.

To classify the different stitch pattern types and make ORIENTATION WITHIN THE BOOK easier, every stitch pattern chapter is presented in its own color scheme.

Well-known classics and traditional stitch patterns are supplemented by many newly created stitch patterns. Feel inspired by this INDISPENS-ABLE REFERENCE WORK to plan your upcoming projects and create your very own knitting design.

# CONTENTS

# KNIT-PURL PATTERNS

## 001 SEED STITCH

➡ [multiple of 2 + 2 selv sts]

Shown are both RS and WS rows. Begin with the selv st before the pattern repeat, rep the marked pattern repeat (2 sts wide) widthwise continuously, and end with the selv st after the pattern repeat. Repeat Rows 1 and 2 heightwise.

Pattern
Repeat =
2 stitches

**Stitch Key**

● = 1 selvedge stitch

■ = Knit 1 stitch

— = Purl 1 stitch

## 002 SEED STITCH RIBBING

[multiple of 3 + 2 sts + 2 selv sts]

Only RS rows are shown; in WS rows, purl all sts. Begin with the selv st before the pattern repeat, rep the marked pattern repeat (3 sts wide) widthwise continuously, and end with the sts after the pattern repeat. Repeat Rows 1 and 2 heightwise.

Pattern
Repeat =
3 stitches

**Stitch Key**

● = 1 selvedge stitch

■ = Knit 1 stitch

— = Purl 1 stitch

## 003 SAND PATTERN

[multiple of 2 + 2 selv sts]

Shown are both RS and WS rows. Begin with the selv st before the pattern repeat, rep the marked pattern repeat (2 sts wide) widthwise continuously, and end with the selv st after the pattern repeat. Repeat Rows 1 and 2 heightwise.

Pattern
Repeat =
2 stitches

**Stitch Key**

● = 1 selvedge stitch

■ = Knit 1 stitch

— = Purl 1 stitch

## 004 ANDALUSIAN STITCH

[multiple of 2 + 1 st + 2 selv sts]

Only RS rows are shown; in WS rows, purl all sts. Begin with the selv st before the pattern repeat, rep the marked pattern repeat (2 sts wide) widthwise continuously, and end with the sts after the pattern repeat. Repeat Rows 1–4 heightwise.

Pattern
Repeat =
2 stitches

**Stitch Key**

● = 1 selvedge stitch

■ = Knit 1 stitch

— = Purl 1 stitch

## 005  SMALL BASKETWEAVE PATTERN    [multiple of 6 + 2 selv sts]

Shown are both RS and WS rows. Begin with the selv st before the pattern repeat, rep the marked pattern repeat (6 sts wide) widthwise continuously, and end with the selv st after the pattern repeat. Repeat Rows 1–8 heightwise.

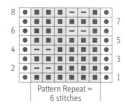

Pattern Repeat = 6 stitches

### Stitch Key

● = 1 selvedge stitch

■ = Knit 1 stitch

— = Purl 1 stitch

## 006  SMALL TRIANGLE PATTERN    ➡ [multiple of 6 + 2 selv sts]

Shown are both RS and WS rows. Begin with the selv st before the pattern repeat, rep the marked pattern repeat (6 sts wide) widthwise continuously, and end with the selv st after the pattern repeat. Repeat Rows 1–6 heightwise.

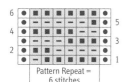

Pattern Repeat = 6 stitches

### Stitch Key

● = 1 selvedge stitch

■ = Knit 1 stitch

— = Purl 1 stitch

Front

Back

## 007  SMALL GARTER STITCH SQUARES  [multiple of 6 + 1 st + 2 selv sts]

Shown are both RS and WS rows. Begin with the selv st before the pattern repeat, rep the marked pattern repeat (6 sts wide) widthwise continuously, and end with the sts after the pattern repeat. Repeat Rows 1–12 heightwise.

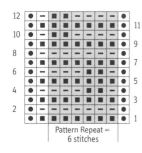

Pattern Repeat = 6 stitches

### Stitch Key

● = 1 selvedge stitch

■ = Knit 1 stitch

— = Purl 1 stitch

## 008 EMBOSSED LATTICE

[multiple of 10 + 3 sts + 2 selv sts]

Shown are both RS and WS rows. Begin with the selv st before the pattern repeat, rep the marked pattern repeat (10 sts wide) widthwise continuously, and end with the sts after the pattern repeat. Repeat Rows 1–10 heightwise.

Pattern Repeat = 10 stitches

### Stitch Key

● = 1 selvedge stitch

■ = Knit 1 stitch

– = Purl 1 stitch

## 009 DIMENSIONAL RIBBING

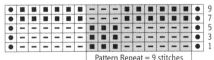 [multiple of 12 + 1 st + 2 selv sts]

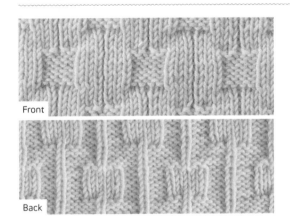

Front

Back

Only RS rows are shown; in WS rows, purl all sts. Begin with the selv st before the pattern repeat, rep the marked pattern repeat (12 sts wide) widthwise continuously, and end with the sts after the pattern repeat. Repeat Rows 1–20 heightwise.

Pattern Repeat = 12 stitches

### Stitch Key

● = 1 selvedge stitch

■ = Knit 1 stitch

– = Purl 1 stitch

## 010 LARGE BASKETWEAVE PATTERN

➡ [multiple of 9 + 6 sts + 2 selv sts]

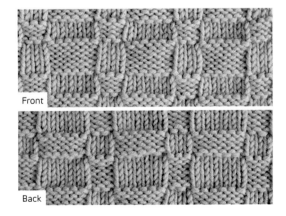

Front

Back

Only RS rows are shown; in WS rows, knit the knits, and purl the purls. Begin with the selv st before the pattern repeat, rep the marked pattern repeat (9 sts wide) widthwise continuously, and end with the sts after the pattern repeat. Repeat Rows 1–10 heightwise.

Pattern Repeat = 9 stitches

### Stitch Key

● = 1 selvedge stitch

■ = Knit 1 stitch

– = Purl 1 stitch

## 011 VERTICAL ZIGZAG PATTERN

[multiple of 7 + 2 selv sts]

Only RS rows are shown; in WS rows, purl all sts. Begin with the selv st before the pattern repeat, rep the marked pattern repeat (7 sts wide) widthwise continuously, and end with the selv st after the pattern repeat. Repeat Rows 1–16 heightwise.

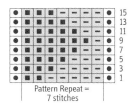

Pattern Repeat =
7 stitches

### Stitch Key

● = 1 selvedge stitch

■ = Knit 1 stitch

— = Purl 1 stitch

## 012 EMBOSSED BROKEN RIBBING

[multiple of 10 + 2 selv sts]

Shown are both RS and WS rows. Begin with the selv st before the pattern repeat, rep the marked pattern repeat (10 sts wide) widthwise continuously, and end with the selv st after the pattern repeat. Repeat Rows 1–4 heightwise.

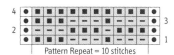

Pattern Repeat = 10 stitches

### Stitch Key

● = 1 selvedge stitch

■ = Knit 1 stitch

— = Purl 1 stitch

## 013 STAIR PATTERN

[multiple of 8 + 2 sts + 2 selv sts]

Only RS rows are shown; in WS rows, knit the knits, and purl the purls. Begin with the selv st before the pattern repeat, rep the marked pattern repeat (8 sts wide) widthwise continuously, and end with the sts after the pattern repeat. Repeat Rows 1–16 heightwise.

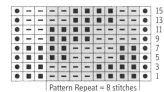

Pattern Repeat = 8 stitches

### Stitch Key

● = 1 selvedge stitch

■ = Knit 1 stitch

— = Purl 1 stitch

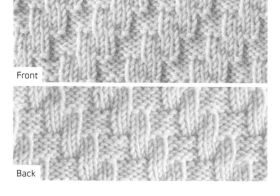

Front

Back

## 014 CHECKERBOARD PATTERN

[multiple of 8 + 2 selv sts]

Only RS rows are shown; in WS rows, knit the knits, and purl the purls. Begin with the selv st before the pattern repeat, rep the marked pattern repeat (8 sts wide) width-wise continuously, and end with the selv st after the pattern repeat. Repeat Rows 1–12 heightwise.

Pattern Repeat = 8 stitches

**Stitch Key**

● = 1 selvedge stitch

■ = Knit 1 stitch

▬ = Purl 1 stitch

## 015 TILE PATTERN

[multiple of 5 + 1 st + 2 selv sts]

Only WS rows are shown; in RS rows, knit all sts. Begin with the selv st before the pattern repeat, rep the marked pattern repeat (5 sts wide) widthwise continuously, and end with the sts after the pattern repeat. Repeat Rows 1–8 heightwise.

Pattern Repeat = 5 stitches

**Stitch Key**

● = 1 selvedge stitch

■ = Knit 1 stitch

▬ = Purl 1 stitch

## 016 LATTICE PATTERN

[multiple of 8 + 1 st + 2 selv sts]

Shown are both RS and WS rows. Begin with the selv st before the pattern repeat, rep the marked pattern repeat (8 sts wide) widthwise continuously, and end with the sts after the pattern repeat. Repeat Rows 1–8 heightwise.

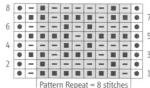

Pattern Repeat = 8 stitches

**Stitch Key**

● = 1 selvedge stitch

■ = Knit 1 stitch

▬ = Purl 1 stitch

## 017 WAVY LINE PATTERN

[multiple of 6 + 5 sts + 2 selv sts]

Shown are both RS and WS rows. Begin with the selv st before the pattern repeat, rep the marked pattern repeat (6 sts wide) widthwise continuously, and end with the sts after the pattern repeat. Repeat Rows 1–6 heightwise.

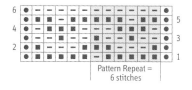

Pattern Repeat = 6 stitches

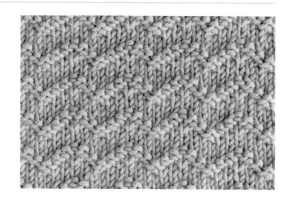

**Stitch Key**

● = 1 selvedge stitch

■ = Knit 1 stitch

— = Purl 1 stitch

## 018 ZIGZAG SEED STITCH PATTERN

[multiple of 10 + 2 selv sts]

Shown are both RS and WS rows. Begin with the selv st before the pattern repeat, rep the marked pattern repeat (10 sts wide) widthwise continuously, and end with the selv st after the pattern repeat. Repeat Rows 1–10 heightwise.

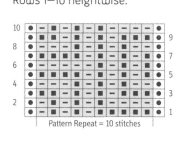

Pattern Repeat = 10 stitches

**Stitch Key**

● = 1 selvedge stitch

■ = Knit 1 stitch

— = Purl 1 stitch

## 019 LARGE LADDER PATTERN

➡ [multiple of 14 + 2 selv sts]

Shown are both RS and WS rows. Begin with the selv st before the pattern repeat, rep the marked pattern repeat (14 sts wide) widthwise continuously, and end with the selv st after the pattern repeat. Repeat Rows 1–16 heightwise.

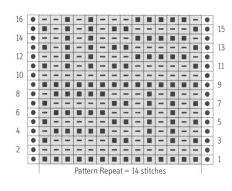

Pattern Repeat = 14 stitches

Front

Back

**Stitch Key**

● = 1 selvedge stitch

■ = Knit 1 stitch

— = Purl 1 stitch

## 020 HORIZONTAL RIDGE PATTERN [multiple of 1 + 2 selv sts]

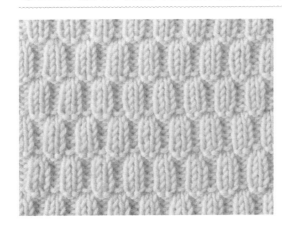

Shown are both RS and WS rows. Begin with the selv st before the pattern repeat, rep the marked pattern repeat (1 st wide) widthwise continuously, and end with the selv st after the pattern repeat. Repeat Rows 1–4 heightwise.

**Stitch Key**

● = 1 selvedge stitch

■ = Knit 1 stitch

– = Purl 1 stitch

Pattern Repeat = 1 stitch

## 021 SHIFTED RIBBING PATTERN  [multiple of 4 + 2 selv sts]

Shown are both RS and WS rows. Begin with the selv st before the pattern repeat, rep the marked pattern repeat (4 sts wide) widthwise continuously, and end with the selv st after the pattern repeat. Repeat Rows 1–12 heightwise.

**Stitch Key**

● = 1 selvedge stitch

■ = Knit 1 stitch

– = Purl 1 stitch

Pattern Repeat = 4 stitches

## 022 MOSS STITCH PATTERN  [multiple of 2 + 2 selv sts]

Shown are both RS and WS rows. Begin with the selv st before the pattern repeat, rep the marked pattern repeat (2 sts wide) widthwise continuously, and end with the selv st after the pattern repeat. Repeat Rows 1–4 heightwise.

**Stitch Key**

● = 1 selvedge stitch

■ = Knit 1 stitch

– = Purl 1 stitch

Pattern Repeat = 2 stitches

## 023 TRELLIS PATTERN

[multiple of 2 + 2 selv sts]

Shown are both RS and WS rows. Begin with the selv st before the pattern repeat, rep the marked pattern repeat (2 sts wide) widthwise continuously, and end with the selv st after the pattern repeat. Repeat Rows 1–6 heightwise.

Pattern Repeat = 2 stitches

### Stitch Key

● = 1 selvedge stitch

■ = Knit 1 stitch

— = Purl 1 stitch

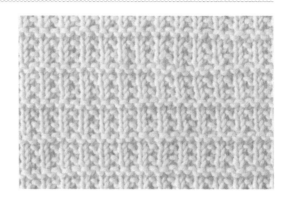

## 024 WAFFLE PATTERN

[multiple of 3 + 1 st + 2 selv sts]

Shown are both RS and WS rows. Begin with the selv st before the pattern repeat, rep the marked pattern repeat (3 sts wide) widthwise continuously, and end with the sts after the pattern repeat. Repeat Rows 1–4 heightwise.

Pattern Repeat = 3 stitches

### Stitch Key

● = 1 selvedge stitch

■ = Knit 1 stitch

— = Purl 1 stitch

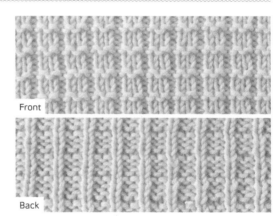

Front

Back

## 025 BIAS RIBBING PATTERN

[multiple of 4 + 2 selv sts]

Only RS rows are shown; in WS rows, knit the knits, and purl the purls. Begin with the selv st before the pattern repeat, rep the marked pattern repeat (4 sts wide) widthwise continuously, and end with the selv st after the pattern repeat. Repeat Rows 1–8 heightwise.

Pattern Repeat = 4 stitches

### Stitch Key

● = 1 selvedge stitch

■ = Knit 1 stitch

— = Purl 1 stitch

Front

Back

## 026 DIAMOND COLUMN PATTERN

[multiple of 8 + 1 st + 2 selv sts]

Shown are both RS and WS rows. Begin with the selv st before the pattern repeat, rep the marked pattern repeat (8 sts wide) widthwise continuously, and end with the sts after the pattern repeat. Repeat Rows 1–8 heightwise.

Pattern Repeat = 8 stitches

### Stitch Key

● = 1 selvedge stitch

■ = Knit 1 stitch

– = Purl 1 stitch

## 027 ZIGZAG LINE PATTERN

[multiple of 8 + 2 selv sts]

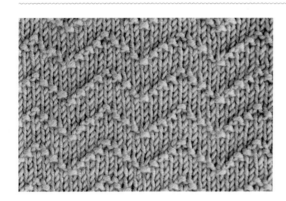

Shown are both RS and WS rows. Begin with the selv st before the pattern repeat, rep the marked pattern repeat (8 sts wide) widthwise continuously, and end with the selv st after the pattern repeat. Repeat Rows 1–6 heightwise.

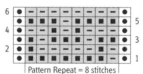

Pattern Repeat = 8 stitches

### Stitch Key

● = 1 selvedge stitch

■ = Knit 1 stitch

– = Purl 1 stitch

## 028 LOZENGE STRIPS

➡ [multiple of 8 + 1 st + 2 selv sts]

Front

Back

Only WS rows are shown. In RS rows, knit the knits, and purl the purls. Begin with the selv st before the pattern repeat, rep the marked pattern repeat (8 sts wide) widthwise continuously, and end with the sts after the pattern repeat. Repeat Rows 1–10 heightwise.

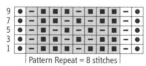

Pattern Repeat = 8 stitches

### Stitch Key

● = 1 selvedge stitch

■ = Knit 1 stitch

– = Purl 1 stitch

## 029 RHOMBOID PATTERN

➡ [multiple of 9 + 2 selv sts]

Shown are both RS and WS rows. Begin with the selv st before the pattern repeat, rep the marked pattern repeat (9 sts wide) widthwise continuously, and end with the selv st after the pattern repeat. Repeat Rows 1–8 heightwise.

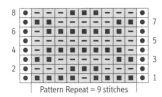

Pattern Repeat = 9 stitches

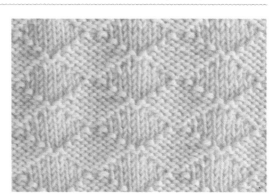

**Stitch Key**

● = 1 selvedge stitch

■ = Knit 1 stitch

▬ = Purl 1 stitch

## 030 BASKETWEAVE PATTERN

[multiple of 6 + 2 selv sts]

Only RS rows are shown; in WS rows, knit the knits, and purl the purls. Begin with the selv st before the pattern repeat, rep the marked pattern repeat (6 sts wide) widthwise continuously, and end with the selv st after the pattern repeat. Repeat Rows 1–12 heightwise.

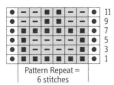

Pattern Repeat = 6 stitches

**Stitch Key**

● = 1 selvedge stitch

■ = Knit 1 stitch

▬ = Purl 1 stitch

## 031 TRIANGLE PATTERN

➡ [multiple of 7 + 2 selv sts]

Shown are both RS and WS rows. Begin with the selv st before the pattern repeat, rep the marked pattern repeat (7 sts wide) widthwise continuously, and end with the selv st after the pattern repeat. Repeat Rows 1–12 heightwise.

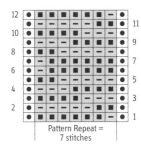

Pattern Repeat = 7 stitches

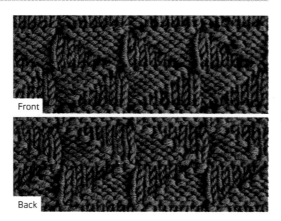

Front

Back

**Stitch Key**

● = 1 selvedge stitch

■ = Knit 1 stitch

▬ = Purl 1 stitch

## 032 KNIT-PURL ZIGZAG PATTERN

➡ [multiple of 12 + 2 selv sts]

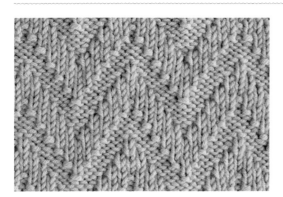

Only RS rows are shown; in WS rows, knit the knits, and purl the purls. Begin with the selv st before the pattern repeat, rep the marked pattern repeat (12 sts wide) widthwise continuously, and end with the sts after the pattern repeat. Repeat Rows 1–12 heightwise.

Pattern Repeat = 12 stitches

11
9
7
5
3
1

**Stitch Key**

● = 1 selvedge stitch

■ = Knit 1 stitch

— = Purl 1 stitch

## 033 CHAIN-LINK FENCE PATTERN

[multiple of 14 + 2 selv sts]

Shown are both RS and WS rows. Begin with the selv st before the pattern repeat, rep the marked pattern repeat (14 sts wide) widthwise continuously, and end with the selv st after the pattern repeat. Repeat Rows 1–12 heightwise.

Pattern Repeat = 14 stitches

12
11
10
9
8
7
6
5
4
3
2
1

**Stitch Key**

● = 1 selvedge stitch

■ = Knit 1 stitch

— = Purl 1 stitch

## 034 SMALL LADDER PATTERN

➡ [multiple of 8 + 5 sts + 2 selv sts]

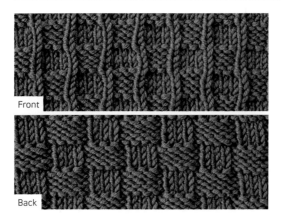

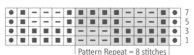

Front

Back

Only RS rows are shown; in WS rows, knit the knits, and purl the purls. Begin with the selv st before the pattern repeat, rep the marked pattern repeat (8 sts wide) widthwise continuously, and end with the sts after the pattern repeat. Repeat Rows 1–8 heightwise.

Pattern Repeat = 8 stitches

7
5
3
1

**Stitch Key**

● = 1 selvedge stitch

■ = Knit 1 stitch

— = Purl 1 stitch

## 035 POINTY CHEVRON PATTERN

[multiple of 18 + 1 st + 2 selv sts]

Only RS rows are shown; in WS rows, knit the knits, and purl the purls. Begin with the selv st before the pattern repeat, rep the marked pattern repeat (18 sts wide) widthwise continuously, and end with the sts after the pattern repeat. Repeat Rows 1–16 heightwise.

**Stitch Key**

● = 1 selvedge stitch

■ = Knit 1 stitch

− = Purl 1 stitch

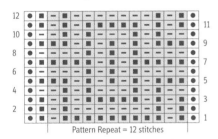

Pattern Repeat = 18 stitches

## 036 KING CHARLES BROCADE

[multiple of 12 + 1 st + 2 selv sts]

Shown are both RS and WS rows. Begin with the selv st before the pattern repeat, rep the marked pattern repeat (12 sts wide) widthwise continuously, and end with the sts after the pattern repeat. Repeat Rows 1–12 heightwise.

**Stitch Key**

● = 1 selvedge stitch

■ = Knit 1 stitch

− = Purl 1 stitch

Pattern Repeat = 12 stitches

## 037 SLANTED RHOMBOID PATTERN

[multiple of 8 + 2 selv sts]

Shown are both RS and WS rows. Begin with the selv st before the pattern repeat, rep the marked pattern repeat (8 sts wide) widthwise continuously, and end with the selv st after the pattern repeat. Repeat Rows 1–14 heightwise.

**Stitch Key**

● = 1 selvedge stitch

■ = Knit 1 stitch

− = Purl 1 stitch

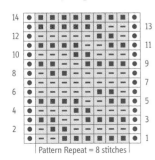

Pattern Repeat = 8 stitches

## 038 RIBBING WITH ZIGZAGS [multiple of 14 + 1 st + 2 selv sts]

Only WS rows are shown; in RS rows, knit all sts. Begin with the selv st before the pattern repeat, rep the marked pattern repeat (14 sts wide) widthwise continuously, and end with the sts after the pattern repeat. Repeat Rows 1–18 heightwise.

Pattern Repeat = 14 stitches

### Stitch Key

- ● = 1 selvedge stitch
- ■ = Knit 1 stitch
- – = Purl 1 stitch

## 039 BRICK PATTERN ➡ [multiple of 8 + 2 selv sts]

Only RS rows are shown; in WS rows, knit the knits, and purl the purls. Begin with the selv st before the pattern repeat, rep the marked pattern repeat (8 sts wide) widthwise continuously, and end with the selv st after the pattern repeat. Repeat Rows 1–8 heightwise.

Pattern Repeat = 8 stitches

### Stitch Key

- ● = 1 selvedge stitch
- ■ = Knit 1 stitch
- – = Purl 1 stitch

## 040 ARGYLE-AND-FLOWER-BUD GRID ➡ [multiple of 12 + 1 st + 2 selv sts]

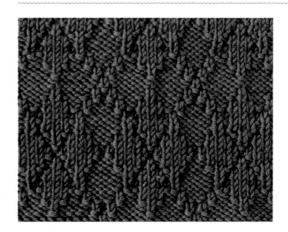

Only RS rows are shown; in WS rows, knit the knits, and purl the purls. Begin with the selv st before the pattern repeat, rep the marked pattern repeat (12 sts wide) widthwise continuously, and end with the sts after the pattern repeat. Repeat Rows 1–24 heightwise.

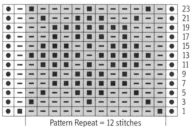

Pattern Repeat = 12 stitches

### Stitch Key

- ● = 1 selvedge stitch
- ■ = Knit 1 stitch
- – = Purl 1 stitch

# 041 ARGYLE COMBINATION

➡ [multiple of 18 + 1 st + 2 selv sts]

Only RS rows are shown; in WS rows, knit the knits, and purl the purls. Begin with the selv st before the pattern repeat, rep the marked pattern repeat (18 sts wide) widthwise continuously, and end with the sts after the pattern repeat. Repeat Rows 1–32 heightwise.

Front

Back

Pattern Repeat = 18 stitches

## Stitch Key

● = 1 selvedge stitch    ■ = Knit 1 stitch    – = Purl 1 stitch

# 042 STAGGERED HEARTS

➡ [multiple of 14 + 2 selv sts]

Shown are both RS and WS rows. Begin with the selv st before the pattern repeat, rep the marked pattern repeat (14 sts wide) widthwise continuously, and end with the selv st after the pattern repeat. Repeat Rows 1–24 heightwise.

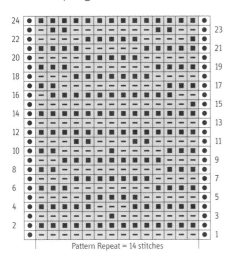

Pattern Repeat = 14 stitches

## Stitch Key

● = 1 selvedge stitch

■ = Knit 1 stitch

– = Purl 1 stitch

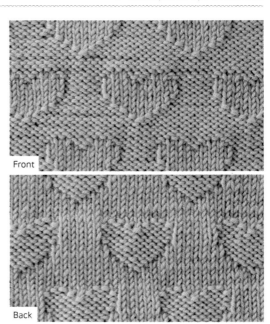

Front

Back

## 043 SMALL HEARTS

➡ [multiple of 14 + 2 selv sts]

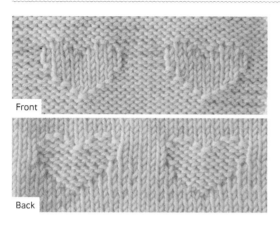

Front

Back

Shown are both RS and WS rows. Begin with the selv st before the pattern repeat, rep the marked pattern repeat (14 sts wide) widthwise continuously, and end with the selv st after the pattern repeat. Repeat Rows 1–14 heightwise.

Pattern Repeat = 14 stitches

### Stitch Key

● = 1 selvedge stitch

■ = Knit 1 stitch

— = Purl 1 stitch

## 044 DIAMOND PATTERN

➡ [multiple of 14 + 1 st + 2 selv sts]

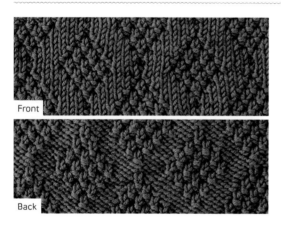

Front

Back

Only RS rows are shown; in WS rows, knit the knits, and purl the purls. Begin with the selv st before the pattern repeat, rep the marked pattern repeat (14 sts wide) widthwise continuously, and end with the sts after the pattern repeat. Repeat Rows 1–16 heightwise.

Pattern Repeat = 14 stitches

### Stitch Key

● = 1 selvedge stitch

■ = Knit 1 stitch

— = Purl 1 stitch

## 045 WIDE BROKEN RIBBING

[multiple of 12 + 2 sts + 2 selv sts]

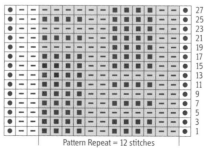

Only RS rows are shown; in WS rows, knit the knits, and purl the purls. Begin with the selv st before the pattern repeat, rep the marked pattern repeat (12 sts wide) widthwise continuously, and end with the sts after the pattern repeat. Repeat Rows 1–28 heightwise.

Pattern Repeat = 12 stitches

### Stitch Key

● = 1 selvedge stitch

■ = Knit 1 stitch

— = Purl 1 stitch

## 046 BASKETWEAVE RIBBING

[multiple of 8 + 5 sts + 2 selv sts]

Only WS rows are shown; in RS rows, knit all sts. Begin with the selv st before the pattern repeat, rep the marked pattern repeat (8 sts wide) widthwise continuously, and end with the sts after the pattern repeat. Repeat Rows 1–18 heightwise.

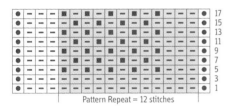

Pattern Repeat = 8 stitches

### Stitch Key

● = 1 selvedge stitch

■ = Knit 1 stitch

– = Purl 1 stitch

## 047 MOSS STITCH SQUARES

➡ [multiple of 12 + 3 sts + 2 selv sts]

Only RS rows are shown; in WS rows, knit the knits, and purl the purls. Begin with the selv st before the pattern repeat, rep the marked pattern repeat (12 sts wide) widthwise continuously, and end with the sts after the pattern repeat. Repeat Rows 1–18 heightwise, ending with a Row 4 of the pattern to complete.

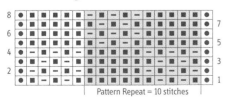

Pattern Repeat = 12 stitches

### Stitch Key

● = 1 selvedge stitch

■ = Knit 1 stitch

– = Purl 1 stitch

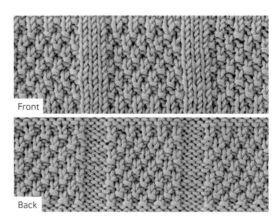

Front

Back

## 048 SMALL BASKETWEAVE PATTERN

➡ [multiple of 10 + 5 sts + 2 selv sts]

Shown are both RS and WS rows. Begin with the selv st before the pattern repeat, rep the marked pattern repeat (10 sts wide) widthwise continuously, and end with the sts after the pattern repeat. Repeat Rows 1–8 heightwise.

Pattern Repeat = 10 stitches

### Stitch Key

● = 1 selvedge stitch

■ = Knit 1 stitch

– = Purl 1 stitch

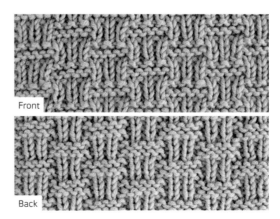

Front

Back

## 049 LARGE STAIR PATTERN

➡ [multiple of 18 + 2 selv sts]

Front

Back

Only RS rows are shown; in WS rows, knit the knits, and purl the purls. Begin with the selv st before the pattern repeat, rep the marked pattern repeat (18 sts wide) widthwise continuously, and end with the selv st after the pattern repeat. Repeat Rows 1–24 heightwise.

Pattern Repeat = 18 stitches

### Stitch Key

● = 1 selvedge stitch

■ = Knit 1 stitch

– = Purl 1 stitch

## 050 FILLED LOZENGE PATTERN

➡ [multiple of 18 + 1 st + 2 selv sts]

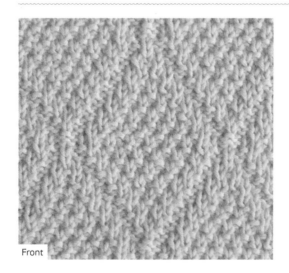

Front

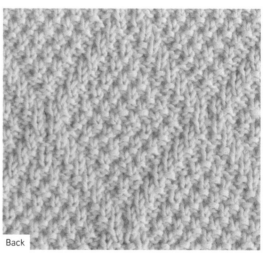

Back

Pattern Repeat = 18 stitches

Only RS rows are shown; in WS rows, knit the knits, and purl the purls. Begin with the selv st before the pattern repeat, rep the marked pattern repeat (18 sts wide) widthwise continuously, and end with the sts after the pattern repeat. Repeat Rows 1–32 heightwise.

### Stitch Key

● = 1 selvedge stitch

■ = Knit 1 stitch

– = Purl 1 stitch

# 051 PENNANT PATTERN

➡ [multiple of 11 + 2 selv sts]

Shown are both RS and WS rows. Begin with the selv st before the pattern repeat, rep the marked pattern repeat (11 sts wide) widthwise continuously, and end with the selv st after the pattern repeat. Repeat Rows 1–22 heightwise.

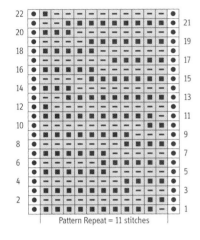

Pattern Repeat = 11 stitches

### Stitch Key

● = 1 selvedge stitch

■ = Knit 1 stitch

– = Purl 1 stitch

Front

Back

# 052 LARGE BASKETWEAVE PATTERN

➡ [multiple of 18 + 10 sts + 2 selv sts]

Shown are both RS and WS rows. Begin with the selv st before the pattern repeat, rep the marked pattern repeat (18 sts wide) widthwise continuously, and end with the sts after the pattern repeat. Repeat Rows 1–18 heightwise.

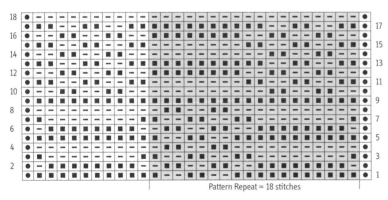

Pattern Repeat = 18 stitches

### Stitch Key

● = 1 selvedge stitch     ■ = Knit 1 stitch     – = Purl 1 stitch

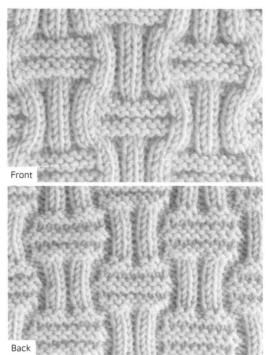

Front

Back

28

## 053 ALTERNATING RHOMBOIDS

[multiple of 8 + 2 selv sts]

Shown are both RS and WS rows. Begin with the selv st before the pattern repeat, rep the marked pattern repeat (8 sts wide) widthwise continuously, and end with the selv st after the pattern repeat. Repeat Rows 1–16 heightwise.

### Stitch Key

● = 1 selvedge stitch

■ = Knit 1 stitch

— = Purl 1 stitch

Pattern Repeat = 8 stitches

## 054 SQUARE PATTERN

[multiple of 13 + 2 sts + 2 selv sts]

Front

Back

Shown are both RS and WS rows. Begin with the selv st before the pattern repeat, rep the marked pattern repeat (13 sts wide) widthwise continuously, and end with the sts after the pattern repeat. Repeat Rows 1–20 heightwise, ending with a Row 4 of the pattern to complete.

### Stitch Key

● = 1 selvedge stitch

■ = Knit 1 stitch

— = Purl 1 stitch

Pattern Repeat = 13 stitches

## 055 STAGGERED DOT PATTERN

[multiple of 4 + 2 selv sts]

Only RS rows are shown; in WS rows, purl all sts. Begin with the selv st before the pattern repeat, rep the marked pattern repeat (4 sts wide) widthwise continuously, and end with the selv st after the pattern repeat. Repeat Rows 1–8 heightwise.

Pattern Repeat = 4 stitches

### Stitch Key

⬤ = 1 selvedge stitch

◼ = Knit 1 stitch

— = Purl 1 stitch

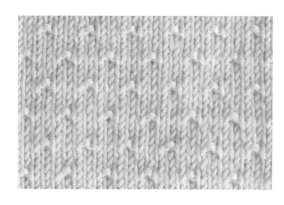

## 056 BASKETWEAVE PATTERN

[multiple of 14 + 9 sts + 2 selv sts]

Only RS rows are shown; in WS rows, knit the knits, and purl the purls. Begin with the selv st before the pattern repeat, rep the marked pattern repeat (14 sts wide) widthwise continuously, and end with the sts after the pattern repeat. Repeat Rows 1–16 heightwise.

### Stitch Key

⬤ = 1 selvedge stitch

◼ = Knit 1 stitch

— = Purl 1 stitch

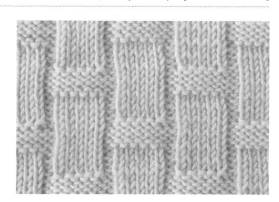

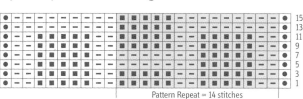

Pattern Repeat = 14 stitches

## 057 ROPE PATTERN

[multiple of 18 + 4 sts + 2 selv sts]

Shown are both RS and WS rows. Begin with the selv st before the pattern repeat, rep the marked pattern repeat (18 sts wide) widthwise continuously, and end with the sts after the pattern repeat. Repeat Rows 1–16 heightwise.

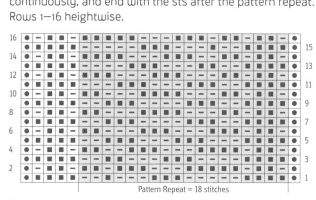

Pattern Repeat = 18 stitches

### Stitch Key

⬤ = 1 selvedge stitch       ◼ = Knit 1 stitch       — = Purl 1 stitch

# CABLE PATTERNS

# TRAVELING-STITCH PATTERNS

# Individual Cables and Cable Pattern Columns

## 058 SIMPLE CABLE OVER 6 STITCHES

[multiple of 9 + 2 selv sts]

Only RS rows are shown; in WS rows, knit the knits, and purl the purls. Begin with the sts before the pattern repeat, rep the marked pattern repeat (9 sts wide) widthwise either once for a single vertical pattern column or continuously for an all-over pattern, and end with the sts after the pattern repeat. Repeat Rows 1–6 heightwise.

Pattern Repeat = 9 stitches

**Stitch Key**

⊡ = 1 selvedge stitch

■ = Knit 1 stitch

– = Purl 1 stitch

= Hold 3 stitches on a cable needle in front of work, knit 3 stitches, then knit the 3 stitches from the cable needle

## 059 SIMPLE CABLE OVER 2 AND 6 STITCHES

[multiple of 14 + 2 selv sts]

Only RS rows are shown; in WS rows, knit the knits, and purl the purls. Begin with the sts before the pattern repeat, rep the marked pattern repeat (14 sts wide) widthwise either once for a single vertical pattern column or continuously for an all-over pattern, and end with the sts after the pattern repeat. Repeat Rows 1–6 heightwise.

Pattern Repeat = 14 stitches

**Stitch Key**

⊡ = 1 selvedge stitch

■ = Knit 1 stitch

– = Purl 1 stitch

= Hold 1 stitch on a cable needle behind work, knit the next stitch, then knit the stitch from the cable needle

= Hold 3 stitches on a cable needle behind work, knit 3 stitches, then knit the 3 stitches from the cable needle

## 060 PLAITED CABLE OVER 6 STITCHES

[multiple of 9 + 2 selv sts]

Only RS rows are shown; in WS rows, knit the knits, and purl the purls. Begin with the sts before the pattern repeat, rep the marked pattern repeat (9 sts wide) widthwise either once for a single vertical pattern column or continuously for an all-over pattern, and end with the sts after the pattern repeat. Repeat Rows 1–6 heightwise.

Pattern Repeat = 9 stitches

**Stitch Key**

⊡ = 1 selvedge stitch

■ = Knit 1 stitch

– = Purl 1 stitch

= Hold 2 stitches on a cable needle behind work, knit 2 stitches, then knit the 2 stitches from the cable needle

= Hold 2 stitches on a cable needle in front of work, knit 2 stitches, then knit the 2 stitches from the cable needle

## 062 PLAITED CABLE OVER 9 STITCHES

[multiple of 12 + 9 sts + 2 selv sts]

Only RS rows are shown; in WS rows, knit the knits, and purl the purls. Begin with the sts before the pattern repeat, rep the marked pattern repeat (12 sts wide) widthwise either once for a single vertical pattern column or continuously for an all-over pattern, and end with the sts after the pattern repeat. Repeat Rows 1–10 heightwise.

Pattern Repeat = 12 stitches

### Stitch Key

● = 1 selvedge stitch

■ = Knit 1 stitch

− = Purl 1 stitch

= Hold 3 stitches on a cable needle in front of work, knit 3 stitches, then knit the 3 stitches from the cable needle

= Hold 3 stitches on a cable needle behind work, knit 3 stitches, then knit the 3 stitches from the cable needle

## 062 PLAITED CABLE OVER 12 STITCHES

[multiple of 15 + 9 sts + 2 selv sts]

Only RS rows are shown; in WS rows, knit the knits, and purl the purls. Begin with the sts before the pattern repeat, rep the marked pattern repeat (15 sts wide) widthwise either once for a single vertical pattern column or continuously for an all-over pattern, and end with the sts after the pattern repeat. Repeat Rows 1–10 heightwise.

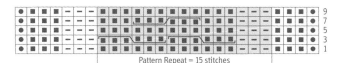

Pattern Repeat = 15 stitches

### Stitch Key

● = 1 selvedge stitch

■ = Knit 1 stitch

− = Purl 1 stitch

= Hold 3 stitches on a cable needle in front of work, knit 3 stitches, then knit the 3 stitches from the cable needle

= Hold 3 stitches on a cable needle behind work, knit 3 stitches, then knit the 3 stitches from the cable needle

## 063 STAGHORN CABLE OVER 8 STITCHES [multiple of 11 + 9 sts + 2 selv sts]

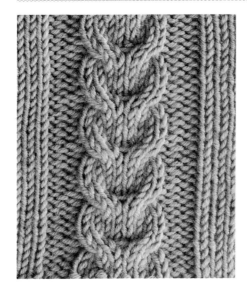

Only RS rows are shown; in WS rows, knit the knits, and purl the purls. Begin with the sts before the pattern repeat, rep the marked pattern repeat (11 sts wide) widthwise either once for a single vertical pattern column or continuously for an all-over pattern, and end with the sts after the pattern repeat. Repeat Rows 1–6 heightwise.

Pattern Repeat = 11 stitches

### Stitch Key

- ● = 1 selvedge stitch
- ■ = Knit 1 stitch
- – = Purl 1 stitch
- = Hold 2 stitches on a cable needle in front of work, knit 2 stitches, then knit the 2 stitches from the cable needle
- = Hold 2 stitches on a cable needle behind work, knit 2 stitches, then knit the 2 stitches from the cable needle

## 064 STAGHORN CABLE OVER 12 STITCHES [multiple of 15 + 9 sts + 2 selv sts]

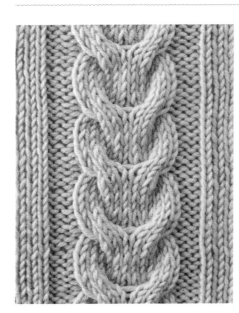

Only RS rows are shown; in WS rows, knit the knits, and purl the purls. Begin with the sts before the pattern repeat, rep the marked pattern repeat (15 sts wide) widthwise either once for a single vertical pattern column or continuously for an all-over pattern, and end with the sts after the pattern repeat. Repeat Rows 1–8 heightwise.

Pattern Repeat = 15 stitches

### Stitch Key

- ● = 1 selvedge stitch
- ■ = Knit 1 stitch
- – = Purl 1 stitch
- = Hold 3 stitches on a cable needle in front of work, knit 3 stitches, then knit the 3 stitches from the cable needle
- = Hold 3 stitches on a cable needle behind work, knit 3 stitches, then knit the 3 stitches from the cable needle

## FOUR-STRAND CABLE OVER 18 STITCHES

[multiple of 21 + 9 sts + 2 selv sts]

Only RS rows are shown; in WS rows, knit the knits, and purl the purls. Begin with the sts before the pattern repeat, rep the marked pattern repeat (21 sts wide) widthwise either once for a single vertical pattern column or continuously for an all-over pattern, and end with the sts after the pattern repeat. Repeat Rows 1–8 heightwise.

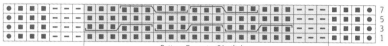

Pattern Repeat = 21 stitches

### Stitch Key

 = 1 selvedge stitch

■ = Knit 1 stitch

– = Purl 1 stitch

= Hold 3 stitches on a cable needle in front of work, knit 3 stitches, then knit the 3 stitches from the cable needle

= Hold 3 stitches on a cable needle behind work, knit 3 stitches, then knit the 3 stitches from the cable needle

## PLAITED SIX-STRAND CABLE

[multiple of 27 + 8 sts + 2 selv sts]

Only RS rows are shown; in WS rows, knit the knits, and purl the purls. Begin with the sts before the pattern repeat, rep the marked pattern repeat (27 sts wide) widthwise either once for a single vertical pattern column or continuously for an all-over pattern, and end with the sts after the pattern repeat. Repeat Rows 1–16 heightwise.

### Stitch Key

● = 1 selvedge stitch

■ = Knit 1 stitch

– = Purl 1 stitch

= Hold 3 stitches on a cable needle in front of work, hold 1 stitch on a second cable needle behind work, knit 3 stitches, then purl the stitch from the second cable needle, then knit the 3 stitches from the first cable needle

= Hold 4 stitches on a cable needle behind work, knit 3 stitches, then transfer the 4th stitch from the cable needle to the left needle and purl it, then knit the 1st, 2nd, and 3rd stitch from the cable needle

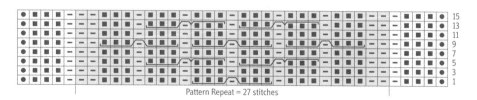

Pattern Repeat = 27 stitches

## 067 CHAIN-LINK CABLE

[multiple of 14 + 6 sts + 2 selv sts]

Only RS rows are shown; in WS rows, knit the knits, and purl the purls. Begin with the sts before the pattern repeat, rep the marked pattern repeat (14 sts wide) widthwise either once for a single vertical pattern column or continuously for an all-over pattern, and end with the sts after the pattern repeat. Repeat Rows 1–24 heightwise.

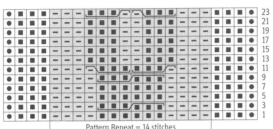

Pattern Repeat = 14 stitches

### Stitch Key

⬤ = 1 selvedge stitch

■ = Knit 1 stitch

— = Purl 1 stitch

■■■/■■■ = Hold 3 stitches on a cable needle behind work, knit 3 stitches, then knit the 3 stitches from the cable needle

—■■■ = Hold 3 stitches on a cable needle in front of work, purl 1 stitch, then knit the 3 stitches from the cable needle

■■■/— = Hold 1 stitch on a cable needle behind work, knit 3 stitches, then purl the stitch from the cable needle

## 068 CELTIC CABLE

[multiple of 10 + 9 sts + 2 selv sts]

Only RS rows are shown; in WS rows, knit the knits, and purl the purls. Begin with the sts before the pattern repeat, rep the marked pattern repeat (10 sts wide) widthwise either once for a single vertical pattern column or continuously for an all-over pattern, and end with the sts after the pattern repeat. Repeat Rows 1–10 heightwise.

### Stitch Key

⬤ = 1 selvedge stitch

■ = Knit 1 stitch

— = Purl 1 stitch

■■■\■■■ = Hold 3 stitches on a cable needle in front of work, knit 3 stitches, then knit the 3 stitches from the cable needle

■■■/■■■ = Hold 3 stitches on a cable needle behind work, knit 3 stitches, then knit the 3 stitches from the cable needle

——\■■■ = Hold 3 stitches on a cable needle in front of work, purl 2 stitches, then knit the 3 stitches from the cable needle

■■■/—— = Hold 2 stitches on a cable needle behind work, knit 3 stitches, then purl the 2 stitches from the cable needle

Pattern Repeat = 10 stitches

## CROWN PATTERN

[multiple of 18 + 2 selv sts]

Shown are both RS and WS rows. Begin with the selv st before the pattern repeat, rep the marked pattern repeat (18 sts wide) widthwise either once for a single vertical pattern column or continuously for an all-over pattern, and end with the selv st after the pattern repeat. Repeat Rows 1–28 heightwise.

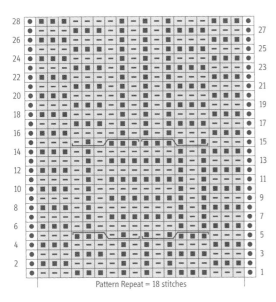

Pattern Repeat = 18 stitches

### Stitch Key

● = 1 selvedge stitch

■ = Knit 1 stitch

— = Purl 1 stitch

= Hold 3 stitches on a cable needle in front of work, knit 3 stitches, then work the 3 stitches from the cable needle as (knit 1 stitch, purl 1 stitch, and knit 1 stitch)

= Hold 3 stitches on a cable needle behind work, purl 1 stitch, knit 1 stitch, and purl 1 stitch, then knit the 3 stitches from the cable needle

= Hold 3 stitches on a cable needle in front of work, knit 3 stitches, then work the 3 stitches from the cable needle as (purl 1 stitch, knit 1 stitch, and purl 1 stitch)

= Hold 3 stitches on a cable needle behind work, knit 1 stitch, purl 1 stitch, and knit the next stitch, then knit the 3 stitches from the cable needle

## ANTLER CABLE

[multiple of 19 + 9 sts + 2 selv sts]

Only RS rows are shown; in WS rows, knit the knits, and purl the purls. Begin with the sts before the pattern repeat, rep the marked pattern repeat (19 sts wide) widthwise either once for a single vertical pattern column or continuously for an all-over pattern, and end with the sts after the pattern repeat. Repeat Rows 1–6 heightwise.

### Stitch Key

● = 1 selvedge stitch

■ = Knit 1 stitch

— = Purl 1 stitch

= Hold 2 stitches on a cable needle in front of work, knit 2 stitches, then knit the 2 stitches from the cable needle

= Hold 2 stitches on a cable needle behind work, knit 2 stitches, then knit the 2 stitches from the cable needle

Pattern Repeat = 19 stitches

## 071 CABLE COLUMN OVER 32 STITCHES

[multiple of 38 + 2 selv sts]

Only RS rows are shown; in WS rows, knit the knits, and purl the purls. Begin with the selv st before the pattern repeat, rep the marked pattern repeat (38 sts wide) widthwise either once for a single vertical pattern column or continuously for an all-over pattern, and end with the selv st after the pattern repeat. Repeat Rows 1–20 heightwise.

### Stitch Key

● = 1 selvedge stitch

■ = Knit 1 stitch

– = Purl 1 stitch

= Hold 2 stitches on a cable needle in front of work, knit 2 stitches, then knit the 2 stitches from the cable needle

= Hold 4 stitches on a cable needle in front of work, purl 1 stitch, then knit the 4 stitches from the cable needle

= Hold 1 stitch on a cable needle behind work, knit 4 stitches, then purl the stitch from the cable needle

= Hold 4 stitches on a cable needle in front of work, knit 4 stitches, then knit the 4 stitches from the cable needle

= Hold 4 stitches on a cable needle behind work, knit 4 stitches, then knit the 4 stitches from the cable needle

Pattern Repeat = 38 stitches

19 17 15 13 11 9 7 5 3 1

## 072 HONEYCOMB CABLE

[multiple of 15 + 9 sts + 2 selv sts]

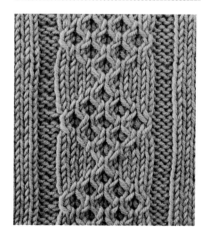

Only RS rows are shown; in WS rows, knit the knits, and purl the purls. Begin with the sts before the pattern repeat, rep the marked pattern repeat (15 sts wide) widthwise either once for a single vertical pattern column or continuously for an all-over pattern, and end with the sts after the pattern repeat. Repeat Rows 1–12 heightwise.

Pattern Repeat = 15 stitches

11 9 7 5 3 1

### Stitch Key

● = 1 selvedge stitch

■ = Knit 1 stitch

– = Purl 1 stitch

= Hold 1 stitch on a cable needle in front of work, knit the next stitch, then knit the stitch from the cable needle

= Hold 1 stitch on a cable needle behind work, knit the next stitch, then knit the stitch from the cable needle

## CABLE COLUMN OVER 21 STITCHES

[multiple of 22 + 11 st + 2 selv sts]

Only RS rows are shown; in WS rows, knit the knits, and purl the purls. Begin with the sts before the pattern repeat, rep the marked pattern repeat (22 sts wide) widthwise either once for a single vertical pattern column or continuously for an all-over pattern, and end with the sts after the pattern repeat. Repeat Rows 1–32 heightwise.

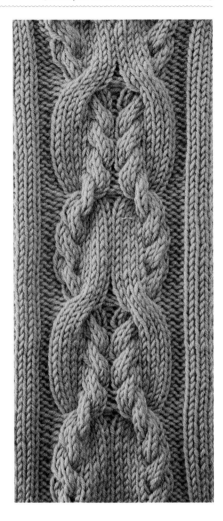

Pattern Repeat = 22 stitches

### Stitch Key

● = 1 selvedge stitch

■ = Knit 1 stitch

– = Purl 1 stitch

= Hold 3 stitches on a cable needle in front of work, knit 3 stitches, then knit the 3 stitches from the cable needle

= Hold 3 stitches on a cable needle behind work, knit 3 stitches, then knit the 3 stitches from the cable needle

= Hold 4 stitches on a cable needle behind work, hold 3 stitches on a cable needle in front of work, knit 3 stitches, then knit the 3 stitches from the second cable needle, then knit the 4 stitches from the first cable needle

= Hold 6 stitches on a cable needle in front of work, knit 4 stitches, then place the 1st, 2nd, and 3rd stitch from the cable needle onto a second cable needle, and hold behind work, knit the 4th, 5th, and 6th stitch from the first cable needle, then knit the 3 stitches from the second cable needle

= Hold 4 stitches on a cable needle in front of work, knit 6 stitches, then knit the 4 stitches from the cable needle

= Hold 6 stitches on a cable needle behind work, knit 4 stitches, then knit the 6 stitches from the cable needle

## 074 OWL CABLE OVER 4 STITCHES

[multiple of 6 + 2 sts + 2 selv sts]

Shown are both RS and WS rows. Begin with the sts before the pattern repeat, rep the marked pattern repeat (6 sts wide) widthwise either once for a single owl motif or continuously for an all-over pattern, and end with the sts after the pattern repeat. Repeat Rows 1–22 heightwise either once for a single owl motif or continuously for an all-over owl pattern.

Pattern Repeat = 6 stitches

### Stitch Key

⬤ = 1 selvedge stitch

■ = Knit 1 stitch

– = Purl 1 stitch

⟋ = Purl 2 stitches together

V = Make 2 stitches from 1 (kfb): first, knit 1 stitch, but leave it on the left needle, then knit the same stitch again through the back loop

☐ = No stitch, for better overview only

= Hold 1 stitch on a cable needle in front of work, knit the next stitch, then knit the stitch from the cable needle

= Hold 1 stitch on a cable needle behind work, knit the next stitch, then knit the stitch from the cable needle

= Hold 1 stitch on a cable needle in front of work, purl the next stitch, then knit the stitch from the cable needle

= Hold 1 stitch on a cable needle behind work, knit the next stitch, then purl the stitch from the cable needle

## 075 OWL CABLE OVER 8 STITCHES

[multiple of 9 + 8 sts + 2 selv sts]

Shown are both RS and WS rows. Begin with the sts before the pattern repeat, rep the marked pattern repeat (9 sts wide) widthwise either once for a single owl motif or continuously for an all-over pattern, and end with the sts after the pattern repeat. Repeat Rows 1–28 heightwise either once for a single owl motif or continuously for an all-over owl pattern.

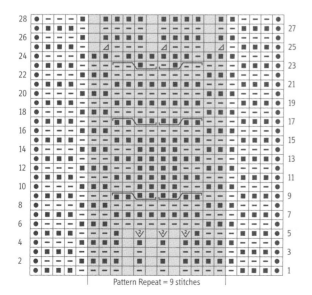

Pattern Repeat = 9 stitches

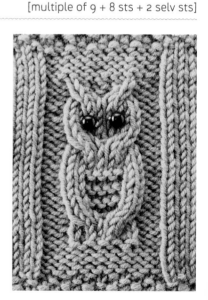

### Stitch Key

⬤ = 1 selvedge stitch

■ = Knit 1 stitch

– = Purl 1 stitch

⟋ = Purl 2 stitches together

V = Make 2 stitches from 1 (kfb): first, knit 1 stitch, but leave it on the left needle, then knit the same stitch again through the back loop

☐ = No stitch, for better overview only

= Hold 2 stitches on a cable needle in front of work, knit 2 stitches, then knit the 2 stitches from the cable needle

= Hold 2 stitches on a cable needle behind work, knit 2 stitches, then knit the 2 stitches from the cable needle

= Hold 2 stitches on a cable needle in front of work, purl 2 stitches, then work the 2 stitches from the cable needle as (purl 1 stitch and knit 1 stitch)

= Hold 2 stitches on a cable needle behind work, knit 1 stitch, and purl 1 stitch, then purl the 2 stitches from the cable needle

## 076 OWL CABLE OVER 12 STITCHES

[multiple of 12 + 8 sts + 2 selv sts]

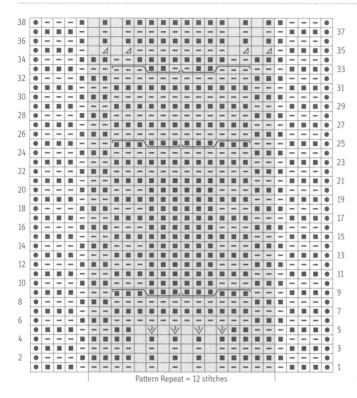

Pattern Repeat = 12 stitches

### Stitch Key

● = 1 selvedge stitch

■ = Knit 1 stitch

– = Purl 1 stitch

⊿ = Purl 2 stitches together

⋁ = Make 2 stitches from 1 (kfb): first, knit 1 stitch, but leave it on the left needle, then knit the same stitch again through the back loop

☐ = No stitch, for better overview only

= Hold 3 stitches on a cable needle in front of work, knit 3 stitches, then knit the 3 stitches from the cable needle

= Hold 3 stitches on a cable needle behind work, knit 3 stitches, then knit the 3 stitches from the cable needle

= Hold 3 stitches on a cable needle in front of work, purl 3 stitches, then work the 3 stitches from the cable needle as (purl 1 stitch, and knit 2 stitches)

= Hold 3 stitches on a cable needle behind work, knit 2 stitches, and purl 1 stitch, then purl the 3 stitches from the cable needle

Shown are both RS and WS rows. Begin with the sts before the pattern repeat, rep the marked pattern repeat (12 sts wide) widthwise either once for a single owl motif or continuously for an all-over owl pattern, and end with the sts after the pattern repeat. Repeat Rows 1–38 heightwise either once for a single owl motif or continuously for an all-over owl pattern.

## 077 OWL CABLE OVER 16 STITCHES

[multiple of 16 + 6 sts + 2 selv sts]

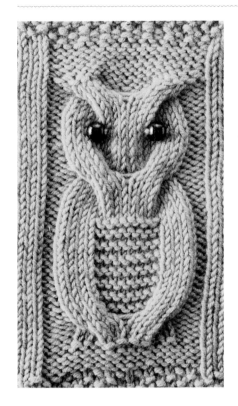

Shown are both RS and WS rows. Begin with the sts before the pattern repeat, rep the marked pattern repeat (16 sts wide) widthwise either once for a single owl motif or continuously for an all-over owl pattern, and end with the sts after the pattern repeat. Repeat Rows 1–50 heightwise either once for a single owl motif or continuously for an all-over pattern.

### Stitch Key

■ = 1 selvedge stitch

■ = Knit 1 stitch

– = Purl 1 stitch

⟋ = Purl 2 stitches together

V = Make 2 stitches from 1 (kfb): first, knit 1 stitch, but leave it on the left needle, then knit the same stitch again through the back loop

☐ = No stitch, for better overview only

= Hold 4 stitches on a cable needle in front of work, knit 4 stitches, then knit the 4 stitches from the cable needle

= Hold 4 stitches on a cable needle behind work, knit 4 stitches, then knit the 4 stitches from the cable needle

= Hold 4 stitches on a cable needle in front of work, purl 4 stitches, then work the 4 stitches from the cable needle as (purl 1 stitch and knit 3 stitches)

= Hold 4 stitches on a cable needle behind work, knit 3 stitches, and purl 1 stitch, then purl the 4 stitches from the cable needle

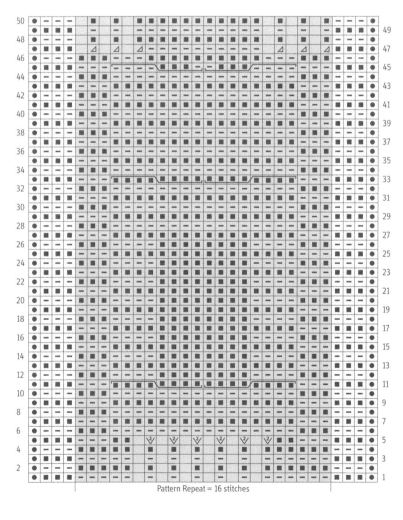

Pattern Repeat = 16 stitches

# All-over Cable Patterns

## SIMPLE CABLE OVER 4 STITCHES

[multiple of 7 + 3 sts + 2 selv sts]

Only RS rows are shown; in WS rows, knit the knits, and purl the purls. Begin with the selv st before the pattern repeat, rep the marked pattern repeat (7 sts wide) width-wise either once for a single vertical pattern column or continuously for an all-over pattern, and end with the sts after the pattern repeat. Repeat Rows 1–6 heightwise.

### Stitch Key

- ● = 1 selvedge stitch
- ■ = Knit 1 stitch
- ─ = Purl 1 stitch
- = Hold 2 stitches on a cable needle in front of work, knit 2 stitches, then knit the 2 stitches from the cable needle

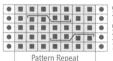

Pattern Repeat
= 7 stitches

## SHIFTING SAND

[multiple of 7 + 2 selv sts]

Only RS rows are shown; in WS rows, purl all sts. Begin with the selv st before the pattern repeat, rep the marked pattern repeat (7 sts wide) widthwise continuously, and end with the selv st after the pattern repeat. Repeat Rows 1–10 heightwise.

Pattern Repeat
= 7 stitches

### Stitch Key

- ● = 1 selvedge stitch
- ■ = Knit 1 stitch
- = Hold 2 stitches on a cable needle behind work, knit 2 stitches, then knit the 2 stitches from the cable needle
- = Hold 2 stitches on a cable needle in front of work, knit 2 stitches, then knit the 2 stitches from the cable needle

## CABLE WAVES

[multiple of 6 + 2 selv sts]

Only RS rows are shown; in WS rows, knit the knits, and purl the purls. Begin with the selv st before the pattern repeat, rep the marked pattern repeat (6 sts wide) widthwise continuously, and end with the selv st after the pattern repeat. Repeat Rows 1–16 heightwise.

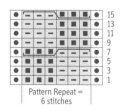

Pattern Repeat =
6 stitches

### Stitch Key

- ● = 1 selvedge stitch
- ■ = Knit 1 stitch
- ─ = Purl 1 stitch
- = Hold 3 stitches on a cable needle in front of work, purl 3 stitches, then knit the 3 stitches from the cable needle
- = Hold 3 stitches on a cable needle behind work, knit 3 stitches, then purl the 3 stitches from the cable needle

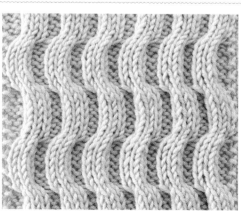

## 081 CABLE COLUMN WITH RIDGES [multiple of 17 + 7 sts + 2 selv sts]

Only RS rows are shown; in WS rows, knit the knits, and purl the purls. Begin with the selv st before the pattern repeat, rep the marked pattern repeat (17 sts wide) widthwise either once for a single vertical pattern column or continuously for an all-over pattern, and end with the sts after the pattern repeat. Repeat Rows 1–4 heightwise.

Pattern Repeat = 17 stitches

### Stitch Key

● = 1 selvedge stitch

■ = Knit 1 stitch

− = Purl 1 stitch

= Hold 1 stitch on a cable needle behind work, knit the next stitch, then knit the stitch from the cable needle

= Hold 1 stitch on a cable needle in front of work, knit the next stitch, then knit the stitch from the cable needle

= Hold 2 stitches on a cable needle in front of work, knit the next stitch, then knit the 2 stitches from the cable needle

## 082 WIDE CABLE RIBBING [multiple of 20 + 2 sts + 2 selv sts]

Only RS rows are shown; in WS rows, knit the knits, and purl the purls. Begin with the selv st before the pattern repeat, rep the marked pattern repeat (20 sts wide) widthwise either once for a single vertical pattern column or continuously for an all-over pattern, and end with the sts after the pattern repeat. Repeat Rows 1–24 heightwise.

Pattern Repeat = 20 stitches

### Stitch Key

● = 1 selvedge stitch

■ = Knit 1 stitch

− = Purl 1 stitch

= Hold 2 stitches on a cable needle in front of work, knit 2 stitches, then knit the 2 stitches from the cable needle

## DOUBLE SNAKES

[multiple of 8 + 6 sts + 2 selv sts]

Only RS rows are shown; in WS rows, knit the knits, and purl the purls. Begin with the sts before the pattern repeat, rep the marked pattern repeat (8 sts wide) widthwise either once for a single vertical pattern column or continuously for an all-over pattern, and end with the sts after the pattern repeat. Repeat Rows 1–8 heightwise.

**Stitch Key**

● = 1 selvedge stitch

■ = Knit 1 stitch

− = Purl 1 stitch

= Hold 2 stitches on a cable needle in front of work, knit 2 stitches, then knit the 2 stitches from the cable needle

= Hold 2 stitches on a cable needle behind work, knit 2 stitches, then knit the 2 stitches from the cable needle

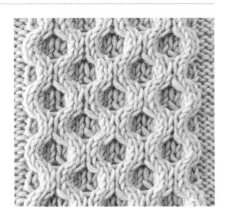

Pattern Repeat = 8 stitches

## FRENCH BRAID CABLES

[multiple of 14 + 1 st + 2 selv sts]

Only RS rows are shown; in WS rows, knit the knits, and purl the purls. Begin with the selv st before the pattern repeat, rep the marked pattern repeat (14 sts wide) widthwise either once for a single vertical pattern column or continuously for an all-over pattern, and end with the sts after the pattern repeat. Repeat Rows 1–12 heightwise.

**Stitch Key**

● = 1 selvedge stitch

■ = Knit 1 stitch

− = Purl 1 stitch

= Hold 1 stitch on a cable needle in front of work, knit 2 stitches, then knit the stitch from the cable needle

= Hold 2 stitches on a cable needle behind work, knit the next stitch, then knit the 2 stitches from the cable needle

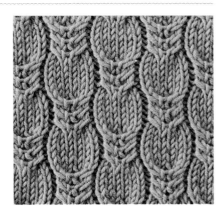

Pattern Repeat = 14 stitches

## SAND WIND

[multiple of 12 + 2 selv sts]

Only RS rows are shown; in WS rows, purl all sts. Begin with the selv st before the pattern repeat, rep the marked pattern repeat (12 sts wide) widthwise continuously, and end with the selv st after the pattern repeat. Repeat Rows 1–8 heightwise.

**Stitch Key**

● = 1 selvedge stitch

■ = Knit 1 stitch

= Hold 3 stitches on a cable needle in front of work, knit 3 stitches, then knit the 3 stitches from the cable needle

= Hold 3 stitches on a cable needle behind work, knit 3 stitches, then knit the 3 stitches from the cable needle

Pattern Repeat = 12 stitches

## 086 COLUMNS WITH CABLE BORDER [multiple of 18 + 6 sts + 2 selv sts]

Only RS rows are shown; in WS rows, knit the knits, and purl the purls. Begin with the selv st before the pattern repeat, rep the marked pattern repeat (18 sts wide) widthwise either once for a single vertical pattern column or continuously for an all-over pattern, and end with the sts after the pattern repeat. Repeat Rows 1–4 heightwise.

Pattern Repeat = 18 stitches

### Stitch Key

● = 1 selvedge stitch

■ = Knit 1 stitch

– = Purl 1 stitch

= Hold 1 stitch on a cable needle in front of work, knit the next stitch, then knit the stitch from the cable needle

= Hold 2 stitches on a cable needle in front of work, knit 2 stitches, then knit the 2 stitches from the cable needle

= Hold 2 stitches on a cable needle behind work, knit 2 stitches, then knit the 2 stitches from the cable needle

## 087 STAGGERED CHAIN-LINK PATTERN [multiple of 16 + 10 sts + 2 selv sts]

Only RS rows are shown; in WS rows, knit the knits, and purl the purls. Begin with the sts before the pattern repeat, rep the marked pattern repeat (16 sts wide) widthwise continuously, and end with the sts after the pattern repeat. Repeat Rows 1–16 heightwise.

Pattern Repeat = 16 stitches

### Stitch Key

● = 1 selvedge stitch

■ = Knit 1 stitch

– = Purl 1 stitch

= Hold 2 stitches on a cable needle in front of work, hold 2 stitches on a second cable needle behind work, knit 2 stitches, then knit the stitches from the second cable needle, then knit the stitches from the first cable needle

= Hold 2 stitches on a cable needle in front of work, hold 2 stitches on a second cable needle behind work, knit 2 stitches, then purl the stitches from the second cable needle, then knit the stitches from the first cable needle

## CABLED RHOMBOIDS [multiple of 9 + 1 st + 2 selv sts]

Only RS rows are shown; in WS rows, knit the knits, and purl the purls. Begin with the selv st before the pattern repeat, rep the marked pattern repeat (9 sts wide) width-wise continuously, and end with the sts after the pattern repeat. Repeat Rows 1–24 heightwise.

### Stitch Key

$\boxed{\bullet}$ = 1 selvedge stitch

$\boxed{\blacksquare}$ = Knit 1 stitch

$\boxed{-}$ = Purl 1 stitch

$\boxed{\blacksquare\blacksquare\blacksquare/\blacksquare\blacksquare\blacksquare}$ = Hold 3 stitches on a cable needle behind work, knit 3 stitches, then knit the 3 stitches from the cable needle

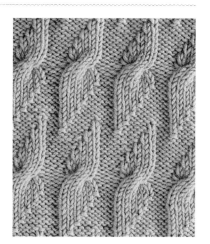

Pattern Repeat = 9 stitches

## CABLE VARIATION OVER 16 STITCHES [multiple of 36 + 2 sts + 2 selv sts]

Only RS rows are shown; in WS rows, knit the knits, and purl the purls. For an all-over pattern, begin with the sts before the pattern repeat, rep the marked pattern repeat (36 sts wide) widthwise continuously, and end with the sts after the pattern repeat. For a single vertical pattern column, work only the first 18 sts of the pattern repeat. Repeat Rows 1–36 heightwise.

### Stitch Key

$\boxed{\bullet}$ = 1 selvedge stitch

$\boxed{\blacksquare}$ = Knit 1 stitch

$\boxed{-}$ = Purl 1 stitch

$\boxed{\blacksquare\blacksquare\blacksquare\blacksquare\backslash\blacksquare\blacksquare\blacksquare\blacksquare}$ = Hold 4 stitches on a cable needle in front of work, knit 4 stitches, then knit the 4 stitches from the cable needle

$\boxed{\blacksquare\blacksquare\blacksquare\blacksquare/\blacksquare\blacksquare\blacksquare\blacksquare}$ = Hold 4 stitches on a cable needle behind work, knit 4 stitches, then knit the 4 stitches from the cable needle

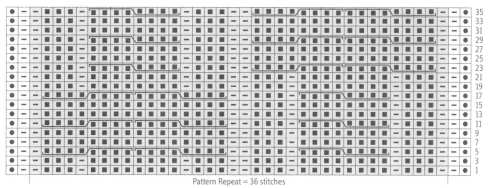

Pattern Repeat = 36 stitches

## 090 CABLE-AND-SQUARE PATTERN

[multiple of 18 + 1 st + 2 selv sts]

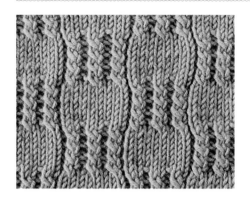

Only RS rows are shown; in WS rows, knit the knits, and purl the purls. Begin with the selv st before the pattern repeat, rep the marked pattern repeat (18 sts wide) widthwise continuously, and end with the sts after the pattern repeat. Repeat Rows 1–16 heightwise.

**Stitch Key**

● = 1 selvedge stitch

■ = Knit 1 stitch

– = Purl 1 stitch

= Hold 1 stitch on a cable needle in front of work, knit the next stitch, then knit the stitch from the cable needle

Pattern Repeat = 18 stitches

## 091 PEARL NECKLACE PATTERN

[multiple of 12 + 7 sts + 2 selv sts]

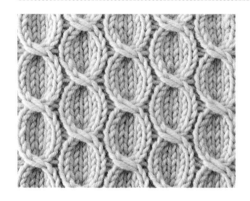

Only RS rows are shown; in WS rows, knit the knits, and purl the purls. Begin with the selv st before the pattern repeat, rep the marked pattern repeat (12 sts wide) widthwise continuously, and end with the sts after the pattern repeat. Repeat Rows 1–8 heightwise.

**Stitch Key**

● = 1 selvedge stitch

■ = Knit 1 stitch

– = Purl 1 stitch

= Hold 1 stitch on a cable needle in front of work, hold 3 stitches on a second cable needle behind work, knit the next stitch, then knit the stitches from the second cable needle, then knit the stitch from the first cable needle

Pattern Repeat = 12 stitches

## 092 CABLE CHAINS

[multiple of 10 + 1 st + 2 selv sts]

Only RS rows are shown; in WS rows, knit the knits, and purl the purls. Begin with the selv st before the pattern repeat, rep the marked pattern repeat (10 sts wide) widthwise continuously, and end with the sts after the pattern repeat. Repeat Rows 1–16 heightwise.

Pattern Repeat = 10 stitches

**Stitch Key**

● = 1 selvedge stitch

■ = Knit 1 stitch

– = Purl 1 stitch

= Hold 2 stitches on a cable needle behind work, knit 2 stitches, then knit the 2 stitches from the cable needle

## 093 BUTTERFLY CABLES

[multiple of 16 + 1 st + 2 selv sts]

Only RS rows are shown; in WS rows, knit the knits, purl the purls, and purl those stitches through the back loop that had been knitted through the back loop in the RS row. Begin with the selv st before the pattern repeat, rep the marked pattern repeat (16 sts wide) widthwise continuously, and end with the sts after the pattern repeat. Repeat Rows 1–48 heightwise.

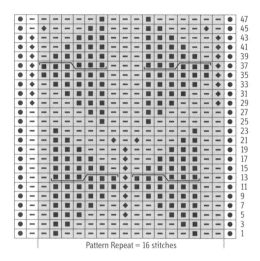

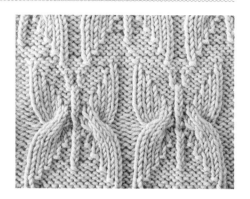

Pattern Repeat = 16 stitches

### Stitch Key

● = 1 selvedge stitch

■ = Knit 1 stitch

– = Purl 1 stitch

◆ = Knit 1 stitch through the back loop

= Hold 3 stitches on a cable needle in front of work, knit 3 stitches, then knit the 3 stitches from the cable needle

= Hold 3 stitches on a cable needle behind work, knit 3 stitches, then knit the 3 stitches from the cable needle

## 094 BASKETWEAVE WITH CABLES

[multiple of 18 + 1 st + 2 selv sts]

Shown are both RS and WS rows. Begin with the selv st before the pattern repeat, rep the marked pattern repeat (18 sts wide) widthwise continuously, and end with the sts after the pattern repeat. Repeat Rows 1–24 heightwise.

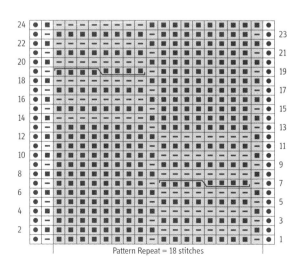

Pattern Repeat = 18 stitches

### Stitch Key

● = 1 selvedge stitch

■ = Knit 1 stitch

– = Purl 1 stitch

= Hold 4 stitches on a cable needle in front of work, knit 4 stitches, then knit the 4 stitches from the cable needle

50

## 095 WOVEN CABLE STITCH
[multiple of 4 + 2 selv sts]

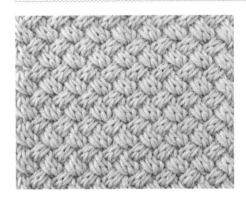

Only RS rows are shown; in WS rows, purl all sts. Begin with the sts before the pattern repeat, rep the marked pattern repeat (4 sts wide) widthwise continuously, and end with the sts after the pattern repeat. Repeat Rows 1–4 heightwise.

Pattern
Repeat =
4 stitches

**Stitch Key**

● = 1 selvedge stitch

■ = Knit 1 stitch

= Hold 2 stitches on a cable needle in front of work, knit 2 stitches, then knit the 2 stitches from the cable needle

= Hold 2 stitches on a cable needle behind work, knit 2 stitches, then knit the 2 stitches from the cable needle

## 096 HONEYCOMB PATTERN
[multiple of 4 + 2 selv sts]

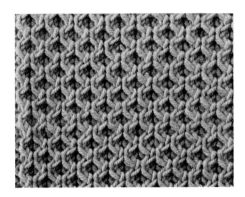

Only RS rows are shown; in WS rows, purl all sts. Begin with the selv st before the pattern repeat, rep the marked pattern repeat (4 sts wide) widthwise continuously, and end with the selv st after the pattern repeat. Repeat Rows 1–4 heightwise.

Pattern
Repeat =
4 stitches

**Stitch Key**

● = 1 selvedge stitch

= Hold 1 stitch on a cable needle in front of work, knit the next stitch, then knit the stitch from the cable needle

= Hold 1 stitch on a cable needle behind work, knit the next stitch, then knit the stitch from the cable needle

## 097 STAGGERED TWIN CABLE PATTERN
[multiple of 12 + 2 selv sts]

Only RS rows are shown; in WS rows, purl all sts. Begin with the selv st before the pattern repeat, rep the marked pattern repeat (12 sts wide) widthwise continuously, and end with the selv st after the pattern repeat. Repeat Rows 1–16 heightwise.

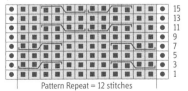

Pattern Repeat = 12 stitches

**Stitch Key**

● = 1 selvedge stitch

■ = Knit 1 stitch

= Hold 2 stitches on a cable needle in front of work, knit 2 stitches, then knit the 2 stitches from the cable needle

= Hold 2 stitches on a cable needle behind work, knit 2 stitches, then knit the 2 stitches from the cable needle

## CABLE VARIATION OVER 10 STITCHES

[multiple of 26 + 3 sts + 2 selv sts]

Only RS rows are shown; in WS rows, knit the knits, and purl the purls. For an all-over pattern, begin with the selv st before the pattern repeat, rep the marked pattern repeat (26 sts wide) widthwise continuously, and end with the sts after the pattern repeat. For a single vertical pattern column, work only the first 16 sts of the pattern repeat. Repeat Rows 1–20 heightwise.

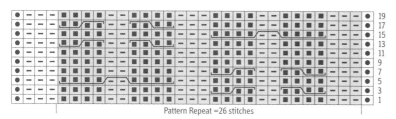

Pattern Repeat =26 stitches

### Stitch Key

● = 1 selvedge stitch

■ = Knit 1 stitch

– = Purl 1 stitch

= Hold 2 stitches on a cable needle in front of work, knit 2 stitches, then knit the 2 stitches from the cable needle

= Hold 2 stitches on a cable needle behind work, knit 2 stitches, then knit the 2 stitches from the cable needle

= Hold 4 stitches on a cable needle in front of work, hold 2 stitches on a second cable needle behind work, knit 4 stitches, then purl the stitches from the second cable needle, then knit the stitches from the first cable needle

## CABLE MOTIFS

[multiple of 14 + 1 st + 2 selv sts]

Only RS rows are shown; in WS rows, knit the knits, and purl the purls. Begin with the sts before the pattern repeat, rep the marked pattern repeat (14 sts wide) widthwise continuously, and end with the sts after the pattern repeat. Repeat Rows 1–32 heightwise.

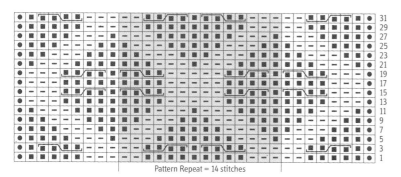

Pattern Repeat = 14 stitches

### Stitch Key

● = 1 selvedge stitch

■ = Knit 1 stitch

– = Purl 1 stitch

= Hold 2 stitches on a cable needle in front of work, knit 2 stitches, then knit the 2 stitches from the cable needle

= Hold 2 stitches on a cable needle behind work, knit 2 stitches, then knit the 2 stitches from the cable needle

## 100 CABLE VARIATION OVER 8 STITCHES [multiple of 14 + 6 sts + 2 selv sts]

Only RS rows are shown; in WS rows, knit the knits, and purl the purls. Begin with the selv st before the pattern repeat, rep the marked pattern repeat (14 sts wide) widthwise either once for a single vertical pattern column or continuously for an all-over pattern, and end with the sts after the pattern repeat. Repeat Rows 1–18 heightwise.

Pattern Repeat = 14 stitches

### Stitch Key

⬤ = 1 selvedge stitch

◼ = Knit 1 stitch

➖ = Purl 1 stitch

= Hold 1 stitch on a cable needle in front of work, knit the next stitch, then knit the stitch from the cable needle

= Hold 2 stitches on a cable needle in front of work, knit 2 stitches, then knit the 2 stitches from the cable needle

= Hold 2 stitches on a cable needle behind work, knit 2 stitches, then knit the 2 stitches from the cable needle

## 101 CABLE VARIATION OVER 15 STITCHES [multiple of 15 + 3 sts + 2 selv sts]

Shown are both RS and WS rows. Begin with the selv st before the pattern repeat, rep the marked pattern repeat (15 sts wide) widthwise either once for a single vertical pattern column or continuously for an all-over pattern, and end with the sts after the pattern repeat. Repeat Rows 1–12 heightwise.

Pattern Repeat = 15 stitches

### Stitch Key

⬤ = 1 selvedge stitch

◼ = Knit 1 stitch

➖ = Purl 1 stitch

◆ = Knit 1 stitch through the back loop

◇ = Purl 1 stitch through the back loop

= Hold 1 stitch on a cable needle behind work, purl 2 stitches through the back loop, then knit the stitch from the cable needle

= Hold 2 stitches on a cable needle in front of work, knit the next stitch, then purl the 2 stitches from the cable needle through the back loop

= Hold 2 stitches on a cable needle behind work, knit 2 stitches through the back loop, then knit the 2 stitches from the cable needle through the back loop

## REVERSIBLE CABLE PATTERN ➡ [multiple of 12 + 6 sts + 2 selv sts]

Shown are both RS and WS rows. Begin with the selv st before the pattern repeat, rep the marked pattern repeat (12 sts wide) widthwise continuously, and end with the sts after the pattern repeat. Repeat Rows 1–12 heightwise.

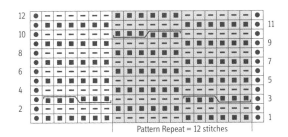

Pattern Repeat = 12 stitches

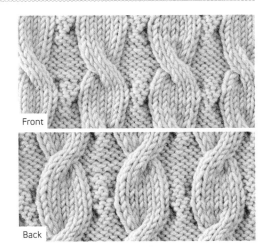

Front

Back

### Stitch Key

⬤ = 1 selvedge stitch

◼ = Knit 1 stitch

– = Purl 1 stitch

= Hold 3 stitches on a cable needle in front of work, knit 3 stitches, then knit the 3 stitches from the cable needle

= Hold 3 stitches on a cable needle behind work, knit 3 stitches, then knit the 3 stitches from the cable needle

---

## CABLED DIAMONDS [multiple of 8 + 2 sts + 2 selv sts]

Only RS rows are shown; in WS rows, knit the knits, and purl the purls. Begin with the sts before the pattern repeat, rep the marked pattern repeat (8 sts wide) widthwise continuously, and end with the sts after the pattern repeat. Repeat Rows 1–14 heightwise.

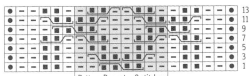

Pattern Repeat = 8 stitches

### Stitch Key

⬤ = 1 selvedge stitch

◼ = Knit 1 stitch

– = Purl 1 stitch

= Hold 2 stitches on a cable needle in front of work, knit 2 stitches, then knit the 2 stitches from the cable needle

= Hold 2 stitches on a cable needle in front of work, purl 1 stitch, then knit the 2 stitches from the cable needle

= Hold 1 stitch on a cable needle behind work, knit 2 stitches, then purl the stitch from the cable needle

## 104 SMALL CABLE TRIANGLES

[multiple of 10 + 3 sts + 2 selv sts]

Only RS rows are shown; in WS rows, knit the knits, and purl the purls. Begin with the sts before the pattern repeat, rep the marked pattern repeat (10 sts wide) widthwise continuously, and end with the sts after the pattern repeat. Repeat Rows 1–24 heightwise.

Pattern Repeat = 10 stitches

### Stitch Key

● = 1 selvedge stitch

■ = Knit 1 stitch

– = Purl 1 stitch

= Hold 4 stitches on a cable needle in front of work, knit 3 stitches, then knit the 4 stitches from the cable needle

## 105 CABLED CIRCLES

[multiple of 8 + 4 sts + 2 selv sts]

Only RS rows are shown; in WS rows, knit the knits, and purl the purls. Begin with the sts before the pattern repeat, rep the marked pattern repeat (8 sts wide) widthwise continuously, and end with the sts after the pattern repeat. Repeat Rows 1–16 heightwise.

Pattern Repeat = 8 stitches

### Stitch Key

● = 1 selvedge stitch

■ = Knit 1 stitch

– = Purl 1 stitch

= Hold 2 stitches on a cable needle in front of work, knit 2 stitches, then knit the 2 stitches from the cable needle

= Hold 2 stitches on a cable needle in front of work, purl 2 stitches, then knit the 2 stitches from the cable needle

= Hold 2 stitches on a cable needle behind work, knit 2 stitches, then purl the 2 stitches from the cable needle

## 106 CLASSIC DIAMONDS

[multiple of 20 + 2 selv sts]

### Stitch Key

● = 1 selvedge stitch

■ = Knit 1 stitch

= Hold 1 stitch on a cable needle in front of work, knit the next stitch, then slip the stitch from the cable needle purlwise, with working yarn in back of work

= Hold 1 stitch on a cable needle behind work, slip 1 stitch purlwise, with working yarn in back of work, then knit the stitch from the cable needle

= Hold 1 stitch on a cable needle behind work, slip 1 stitch purlwise, with working yarn in back of work, then slip the stitch from the cable needle purlwise, with working yarn in back of work

= Hold 3 stitches on a cable needle in front of work, knit the next stitch, then knit the 3 stitches from the cable needle

= Hold 1 stitch on a cable needle behind work, knit 3 stitches, then knit the stitch from the cable needle

= Hold 3 stitches on a cable needle in front of work, slip 1 stitch purlwise, with working yarn in back of work, then knit the 3 stitches from the cable needle

= Hold 1 stitch on a cable needle behind work, knit 3 stitches, then slip the stitch from the cable needle purlwise with working yarn in back of work

Only RS rows are shown; in WS rows, purl all sts. Begin with the sts before the pattern repeat, rep the marked pattern repeat (20 sts wide) widthwise continuously, and end with the sts after the pattern repeat. Repeat Rows 1–32 heightwise.

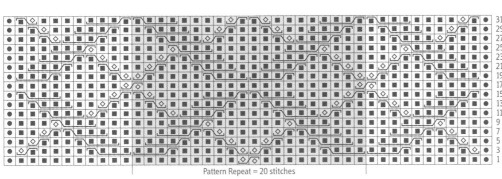

Pattern Repeat = 20 stitches

# 107 CABLE CIRCLES

[multiple of 20 + 2 sts + 2 selv sts]

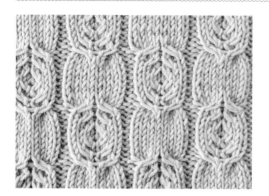

Only RS rows are shown; in WS rows, knit the knits, and purl the purls. Begin with the sts before the pattern repeat, rep the marked pattern repeat (20 sts wide) widthwise continuously, and end with the sts after the pattern repeat. Repeat Rows 1–20 heightwise.

Pattern Repeat = 20 stitches

## Stitch Key

● = 1 selvedge stitch

■ = Knit 1 stitch

– = Purl 1 stitch

= Hold 1 stitch on a cable needle in front of work, knit the next stitch, then knit the stitch from the cable needle

= Hold 1 stitch on a cable needle behind work, knit the next stitch, then knit the stitch from the cable needle

= Hold 2 stitches on a cable needle behind work, knit the next stitch, then knit the 2 stitches from the cable needle

= Hold 1 stitch on a cable needle in front of work, knit 2 stitches, then knit the stitch from the cable needle

= Hold 3 stitches on a cable needle behind work, knit the next stitch, then knit the 3 stitches from the cable needle

= Hold 1 stitch on a cable needle in front of work, knit 3 stitches, then knit the stitch from the cable needle

# 108 INTERWOVEN CABLE PATTERN

[multiple of 6 + 2 selv sts]

Only RS rows are shown; in WS rows, knit the knits, and purl the purls. Begin with the sts before the pattern repeat, rep the marked pattern repeat (6 sts wide) widthwise continuously, and end with the sts after the pattern repeat. Repeat Rows 1–8 heightwise.

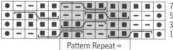

Pattern Repeat = 6 stitches

## Stitch Key

● = 1 selvedge stitch

■ = Knit 1 stitch

– = Purl 1 stitch

= Hold 2 stitches on a cable needle in front of work, knit 2 stitches, then knit the 2 stitches from the cable needle

= Hold 2 stitches on a cable needle behind work, knit 2 stitches, then knit the 2 stitches from the cable needle

= Hold 2 stitches on a cable needle in front of work, purl 2 stitches, then knit the 2 stitches from the cable needle

= Hold 2 stitches on a cable needle behind work, knit 2 stitches, then purl the 2 stitches from the cable needle

## 109 ZIGZAGGING CABLE GARLAND

[multiple of 9 + 2 selv sts]

Only RS rows are shown; in WS rows, knit the knits, and purl the purls. Begin with the selv st before the pattern repeat, rep the marked pattern repeat (9 sts wide) widthwise continuously, and end with the selv st after the pattern repeat. Repeat Rows 1–36 heightwise.

### Stitch Key

● = 1 selvedge stitch

■ = Knit 1 stitch

− = Purl 1 stitch

= Hold 2 stitches on a cable needle in front of work, knit 2 stitches, then knit the 2 stitches from the cable needle

= Hold 2 stitches on a cable needle behind work, knit 2 stitches, then knit the 2 stitches from the cable needle

Pattern Repeat = 9 stitches

## 110 INTERTWINED LOZENGES

[multiple of 8 + 2 selv sts]

### Stitch Key

● = 1 selvedge stitch

■ = Knit 1 stitch

− = Purl 1 stitch

= Hold 2 stitches on a cable needle in front of work, knit 2 stitches, then knit the 2 stitches from the cable needle

= Hold 2 stitches on a cable needle in front of work, purl 1 stitch, then knit the 2 stitches from the cable needle

= Hold 1 stitch on a cable needle behind work, knit 2 stitches, then purl the stitch from the cable needle

Pattern Repeat = 8 stitches

Only RS rows are shown; in WS rows, knit the knits, and purl the purls. Begin with the sts before the pattern repeat, rep the marked pattern repeat (8 sts wide) widthwise either once for a single vertical pattern column or continuously for an all-over pattern, and end with the sts after the pattern repeat. Repeat Rows 1–28 heightwise.

# Two-color Cable Patterns

## 111 CABLES ON A TWO-COLOR BACKGROUND

[multiple of 10 + 2 selv sts]

Shown are both RS and WS rows. Begin with the selv st before the pattern repeat, rep the marked pattern repeat (10 sts wide) width-wise continuously, and end with the selv st after the pattern repeat. Repeat Rows 1–6 heightwise.

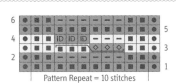

Pattern Repeat = 10 stitches

### Stitch Key

■ = Knit 1 stitch in color A

■ = Knit 1 stitch in color B

– = Purl 1 stitch in color A

– = Purl 1 stitch in color B

● = 1 selvedge stitch in color A

● = 1 selvedge stitch in color B

ID = Slip 1 stitch in color B purlwise, with working yarn in front of work

= Hold 3 stitches in color B on a cable needle in front of work, knit 3 stitches in color A, then slip the 3 stitches from the cable needle purlwise to the right needle with working yarn in back of work

## 112 DOUBLE CABLE ON A TWO-COLOR BACKGROUND

[multiple of 12 + 2 selv sts]

Shown are both RS and WS rows. Begin with the selv st before the pattern repeat, rep the marked pattern repeat (12 sts wide) width-wise continuously, and end with the selv st after the pattern repeat. Repeat Rows 1–6 heightwise.

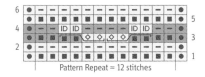

Pattern Repeat = 12 stitches

### Stitch Key

■ = Knit 1 stitch in color A

■ = Knit 1 stitch in color B

– = Purl 1 stitch in color A

– = Purl 1 stitch in color B

● = 1 selvedge stitch in color A

● = 1 selvedge stitch in color B

ID = Slip 1 stitch in color A purlwise, with working yarn in front of work

= Hold 2 stitches in color A on a cable needle in front of work, knit 2 stitches in color B, then slip the 2 stitches from the cable needle purlwise, with working yarn in back of work

= Hold 2 stitches on a cable needle behind work, slip 2 stitches in color A purlwise, with working yarn in back of work, then knit the 2 stitches from the cable needle in color B

# 113 TWO-COLOR DOUBLE CABLE

[multiple of 12 + 2 selv sts]

Shown are both RS and WS rows. Begin with the selv st before the pattern repeat, rep the marked pattern repeat (12 sts wide) widthwise continuously, and end with the selv st after the pattern repeat. Repeat Rows 1–12 heightwise.

## Stitch Key

■ = Knit 1 stitch in color A

■ = Knit 1 stitch in color B

− = Purl 1 stitch in color A

− = Purl 1 stitch in color B

● = 1 selvedge stitch in color A

● = 1 selvedge stitch in color B

⊡ = Slip 1 stitch in color A purlwise, with working yarn in back of work

ID = Slip 1 stitch in color A purlwise, with working yarn in front of work

⊡ = Slip 1 stitch in color B purlwise, with working yarn in back of work

ID = Slip 1 stitch in color B purlwise, with working yarn in front of work

■ ■ ◇ ◇ = Hold 2 stitches in color A on a cable needle behind work, knit 2 stitches in color B, then slip the 2 stitches from the cable needle purlwise, with working yarn in back of work

◇ ◇ ■ ■ = Hold 2 stitches on a cable needle in front of work, slip 2 stitches in color A purlwise, with working yarn in back of work, then knit the 2 stitches from the cable needle in color B

■ ■ ◇ ◇ = Hold 2 stitches in color B on a cable needle behind work, knit 2 stitches in color A, then slip the 2 stitches from the cable needle purlwise, with working yarn in back of work

◇ ◇ ■ ■ = Hold 2 stitches on a cable needle in front of work, slip 2 stitches in color B purlwise, with working yarn in back of work, then knit the 2 stitches from the cable needle in color A

# 114 TWO-COLOR CABLE RIBBING

[multiple of 12 + 2 selv sts]

## Stitch Key

■ = Knit 1 stitch in color A

■ = Knit 1 stitch in color B

− = Purl 1 stitch in color A

− = Purl 1 stitch in color B

● = 1 selvedge stitch in color A

● = 1 selvedge stitch in color B

ID = Slip 1 stitch in color A purlwise, with working yarn in front of work

ID = Slip 1 stitch in color B purlwise, with working yarn in front of work

◇ ■ = Hold 1 stitch on a cable needle behind work, slip 1 stitch in color A purlwise, with working yarn in back of work, then knit the stitch from the cable needle in color B

◇ ■ = Hold 1 stitch on a cable needle behind work, slip 1 stitch in color B purlwise, with working yarn in back of work, then knit the stitch from the cable needle in color A

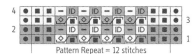

Pattern Repeat = 12 stitches

Shown are both RS and WS rows. Begin with the selv st before the pattern repeat, rep the marked pattern repeat (12 sts wide) widthwise continuously, and end with the selv st after the pattern repeat. Repeat Rows 1–4 heightwise.

## 115 TWO-COLOR CABLE ON A TWO-COLOR BACKGROUND [multiple of 9 + 1 st + 2 selv sts]

Shown are both RS and WS rows. Begin with the selv st before the pattern repeat, rep the marked pattern repeat (9 sts wide) widthwise continuously, and end with the sts after the pattern repeat. Repeat Rows 1—12 heightwise.

### Stitch Key

■ = Knit 1 stitch in color B

■ = Knit 1 stitch in color A

– = Purl 1 stitch in color B

– = Purl 1 stitch in color A

● = 1 selvedge stitch in color B

● = 1 selvedge stitch in color A

QI = Slip 1 stitch in color B purl-wise, with working yarn in back of work

ID = Slip 1 stitch in color B purl-wise, with working yarn in front of work

QI = Slip 1 stitch in color A purl-wise, with working yarn in back of work

ID = Slip 1 stitch in color A purl-wise, with working yarn in front of work

◇◇■■ = Hold 2 stitches on a cable needle in front of work, slip 2 stitches in color B purlwise, with working yarn in back of work, then knit the 2 stitches from the cable needle in color A

◇◇■■ = Hold 2 stitches on a cable needle in front of work, slip 2 stitches in color A purlwise, with working yarn in back of work, then knit the 2 stitches from the cable needle in color B

Pattern Repeat = 9 stitches

## 116 LOZENGES ON A CONTRASTING COLOR BACKGROUND [multiple of 12 + 2 selv sts]

Each row is worked using two colors. Only RS rows are shown; in WS rows, purl all stitches in the appropriate color. Begin with the sts before the pattern repeat, rep the marked pattern repeat (12 sts wide) widthwise continuously, and end with the sts after the pattern repeat. Repeat Rows 1—24 heightwise.

### Stitch Key

■ = Knit 1 stitch in color A

■ = Knit 1 stitch in color B

● = 1 selvedge stitch in color B

■■■■■■ = Hold 3 stitches on a cable needle in front of work, knit 3 stitches in color A, then knit the 3 stitches from the cable needle in color A

■■■■■ = Hold 1 stitch on a cable needle behind work, knit 3 stitches in color A, then knit the stitch from the cable needle in color B

■■■■■ = Hold 3 stitches on a cable needle in front of work, knit 1 stitch in color B, then knit the 3 stitches from the cable needle in color A

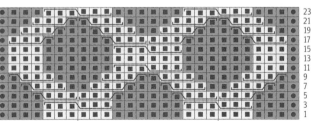

Pattern Repeat = 12 stitches

## TWO-COLOR INTERWOVEN PATTERN [multiple of 4 + 2 selv sts]

Each row is worked using two colors. Only RS rows are shown; in WS rows, purl all stitches in the appropriate color. Begin with the sts before the pattern repeat, rep the marked pattern repeat (4 sts wide) widthwise continuously, and end with the sts after the pattern repeat. Repeat Rows 1–4 heightwise.

### Stitch Key

■ = Knit 1 stitch in color A

■ = Knit 1 stitch in color B

● = 1 selvedge stitch in color A

● = 1 selvedge stitch in color B

▣▣/◨ = Hold 2 stitches on a cable needle behind work, knit 2 stitches in color B, then knit the 2 stitches from the cable needle in color A

▣▣◨◨ = Hold 2 stitches on a cable needle in front of work, knit 2 stitches in color B, then knit the 2 stitches from the cable needle in color A

Pattern Repeat = 4 stitches

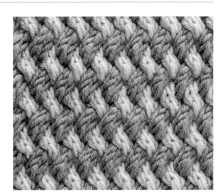

## DIAMONDS ON A TWO-COLOR BACKGROUND [multiple of 8 + 4 sts + 2 selv sts]

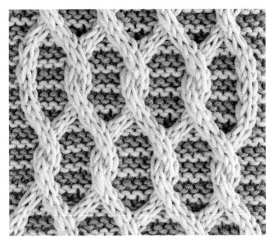

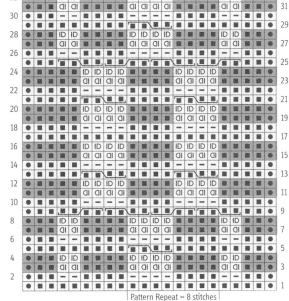

Pattern Repeat = 8 stitches

Shown are both RS and WS rows. Begin with the sts before the pattern repeat, rep the marked pattern repeat (8 sts wide) widthwise continuously, and end with the sts after the pattern repeat. Repeat Rows 1–32 heightwise.

### Stitch Key

■ = Knit 1 stitch in color A

■ = Knit 1 stitch in color B

─ = Purl 1 stitch in color A

● = 1 selvedge stitch in color A

● = 1 selvedge stitch in color B

⧄ = Slip 1 stitch in color A purlwise, with working yarn in back of work

ID = Slip 1 stitch in color A purlwise, with working yarn in front of work

▣▣◨◨ = Hold 2 stitches on a cable needle in front of work, knit 2 stitches in color A, then knit the 2 stitches from the cable needle in color A

▣▣/◨ = Hold 2 stitches on a cable needle behind work, knit 2 stitches in color A, then knit the 2 stitches from the cable needle in color A

# Traveling-Stitch Patterns

## 119 RHOMBOID PATTERN

[multiple of 8 + 2 sts + 2 selv sts]

Only RS rows are shown; in WS rows, knit the knits, and purl the purls. Begin with the sts before the pattern repeat, rep the marked pattern repeat (8 sts wide) widthwise continuously, and end with the sts after the pattern repeat. Repeat Rows 1–14 heightwise.

| Pattern Repeat = 8 stitches |

### Stitch Key

● = 1 selvedge stitch

■ = Knit 1 stitch

− = Purl 1 stitch

= Hold 1 stitch on a cable needle in front of work, knit the next stitch, then knit the stitch from the cable needle

= Hold 1 stitch on a cable needle behind work, knit the next stitch, then knit the stitch from the cable needle

= Hold 1 stitch on a cable needle in front of work, purl the next stitch, then knit the stitch from the cable needle

= Hold 1 stitch on a cable needle behind work, knit the next stitch, then purl the stitch from the cable needle

## 120 FOUR-STRAND CABLE

[multiple of 10 + 2 sts + 2 selv sts]

Shown are both RS and WS rows. Begin with the sts before the pattern repeat, rep the marked pattern repeat (10 sts wide) widthwise continuously, and end with the sts after the pattern repeat. Repeat Rows 1–8 heightwise.

| Pattern Repeat = 10 stitches |

### Stitch Key

● = 1 selvedge stitch

■ = Knit 1 stitch

− = Purl 1 stitch

◆ = Knit 1 stitch through the back loop

◇ = Purl 1 stitch through the back loop

= Hold 1 stitch on a cable needle behind work, knit 1 stitch through the back loop, then knit the stitch from the cable needle through the back loop

= Hold 1 stitch on a cable needle in front of work, knit 1 stitch through the back loop, then knit the stitch from the cable needle through the back loop

= Hold 1 stitch on a cable needle in front of work, knit the next stitch, then purl the stitch from the cable needle through the back loop

= Hold 1 stitch on a cable needle behind work, purl 1 stitch through the back loop, then knit the stitch from the cable needle

## 121 SMALL LATTICE PATTERN

[multiple of 6 + 2 sts + 2 selv sts]

Only RS rows are shown; in WS rows, purl all sts. Begin with the sts before the pattern repeat, rep the marked pattern repeat (6 sts wide) widthwise continuously, and end with the sts after the pattern repeat. Repeat Rows 1–12 heightwise.

### Stitch Key

■ = 1 selvedge stitch

■ = Knit 1 stitch

▆▆ = Hold 1 stitch on a cable needle in front of work, knit the next stitch, then knit the stitch from the cable needle

▆▆ = Hold 1 stitch on a cable needle behind work, knit the next stitch, then knit the stitch from the cable needle

Pattern Repeat = 6 stitches

## 122 DIAMOND PATTERN

[multiple of 4 + 2 sts + 2 selv sts]

Only RS rows are shown; in WS rows, purl all sts. Begin with the sts before the pattern repeat, rep the marked pattern repeat (4 sts wide) widthwise continuously, and end with the sts after the pattern repeat. Repeat Rows 1–8 heightwise.

### Stitch Key

● = 1 selvedge stitch

– = Purl 1 stitch

▆▆ = Hold 1 stitch on a cable needle in front of work, knit the next stitch, then knit the stitch from the cable needle

▆▆ = Hold 1 stitch on a cable needle in front of work, purl the next stitch, then knit the stitch from the cable needle

▆▆ = Hold 1 stitch on a cable needle behind work, knit the next stitch, then purl the stitch from the cable needle

Pattern Repeat = 4 stitches

## 123 ZIGZAG COLUMN PATTERN

[multiple of 16 + 1 st + 2 selv sts]

Only RS rows are shown; in WS rows, knit the knits, and purl the purls through the back loop. Begin with the selv st before the pattern repeat, rep the marked pattern repeat (16 sts wide) widthwise continuously, and end with the sts after the pattern repeat. Repeat Rows 1–16 heightwise.

### Stitch Key

● = 1 selvedge stitch

– = Purl 1 stitch

◆ = Knit 1 stitch through the back loop

◆/– = Hold 1 stitch on a cable needle behind work, knit 1 stitch through the back loop, then purl the stitch from the cable needle

–◆ = Hold 1 stitch on a cable needle in front of work, purl 1 stitch, then knit the stitch from the cable needle through the back loop

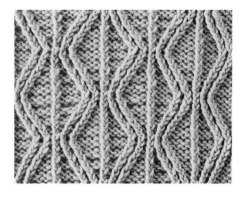

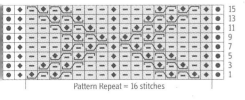

Pattern Repeat = 16 stitches

## 124 SMALL LOZENGE STRANDS

[multiple of 12 + 10 sts + 2 selv sts]

### Stitch Key

■ = 1 selvedge stitch

■ = Knit 1 stitch

– = Purl 1 stitch

= Hold 1 stitch on a cable needle in front of work, knit the next stitch, then knit the stitch from the cable needle

= Hold 1 stitch on a cable needle behind work, knit the next stitch, then knit the stitch from the cable needle

= Hold 1 stitch on a cable needle in front of work, purl the next stitch, then knit the stitch from the cable needle

= Hold 1 stitch on a cable needle behind work, knit the next stitch, then purl the stitch from the cable needle

Only RS rows are shown; in WS rows, knit the knits, and purl the purls. Begin with the sts before the pattern repeat, rep the marked pattern repeat (12 sts wide) widthwise continuously, and end with the sts after the pattern repeat. Repeat Rows 1–24 heightwise.

Pattern Repeat = 12 stitches

## 125 FOLDED BANDS

[multiple of 16 + 2 sts + 2 selv sts]

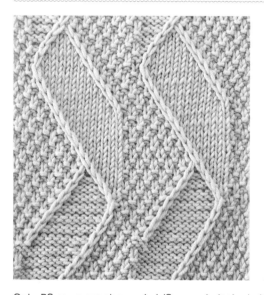

Pattern Repeat = 16 stitches

### Stitch Key

■ = 1 selvedge stitch

■ = Knit 1 stitch

– = Purl 1 stitch

= Hold 1 stitch on a cable needle behind work, slip 1 stitch purlwise, with working yarn in back of work, then purl the stitch from the cable needle

= Hold 1 stitch on a cable needle in front of work, knit the next stitch, then slip the stitch from the cable needle purlwise, with working yarn in back of work

= Hold 1 stitch on a cable needle in front of work, purl 1 stitch, then slip the stitch from the cable needle purlwise, with working yarn in back of work

Only RS rows are shown; in WS rows, knit the knits, purl the purls, and purl stitches that had been slipped on the RS. Begin with the selv st before the pattern repeat, rep the marked pattern repeat (16 sts wide) widthwise continuously, and end with the sts after the pattern repeat. Repeat Rows 1–52 heightwise.

## 126 HEART MOTIF

[multiple of 17 + 1 st + 2 selv sts]

Only RS rows are shown; in WS rows, knit the knits, and purl the purls. Begin with the selv st before the pattern repeat, rep the marked pattern repeat (17 sts wide) either once for a single heart motif or continuously for an all-over pattern, and end with the sts after the pattern repeat. Work Rows 1–24 heightwise either once for a single heart motif or continuously for an all-over pattern.

### Stitch Key

- ● = 1 selvedge stitch
- ■ = Knit 1 stitch
- − = Purl 1 stitch
- = Hold 1 stitch on a cable needle in front of work, knit the next stitch, then knit the stitch from the cable needle
- = Hold 1 stitch on a cable needle behind work, knit the next stitch, then knit the stitch from the cable needle
- = Hold 1 stitch on a cable needle in front of work, purl the next stitch, then knit the stitch from the cable needle
- = Hold 1 stitch on a cable needle behind work, knit the next stitch, then purl the stitch from the cable needle

Pattern Repeat = 17 stitches

## 127 INTERTWINED CIRCLES

[multiple of 8 + 1 st + 2 selv sts]

Shown are both RS and WS rows. Begin with the sts before the pattern repeat, rep the marked pattern repeat (8 sts wide) widthwise either once for a single vertical pattern column or continuously for an all-over pattern, and end with the sts after the pattern repeat. Repeat Rows 1–18 heightwise.

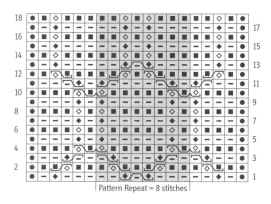

Pattern Repeat = 8 stitches

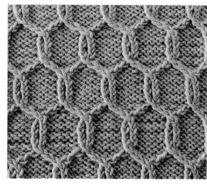

### Stitch Key

- ● = 1 selvedge stitch
- ■ = Knit 1 stitch
- − = Purl 1 stitch
- ◆ = Knit 1 stitch through the back loop
- ◇ = Purl 1 stitch through the back loop
- = Hold 1 stitch on a cable needle behind work, knit 1 stitch through the back loop, then purl the stitch from the cable needle

- = Hold 1 stitch on a cable needle in front of work, purl 1 stitch, then knit the stitch from the cable needle through the back loop
- = Hold 1 stitch on a cable needle behind work, knit the next stitch, then purl the stitch from the cable needle through the back loop
- = Hold 1 stitch on a cable needle in front of work, purl 1 stitch through the back loop, then knit the stitch from the cable needle

- = Hold 1 stitch on a cable needle in front of work, hold 1 stitch on a second cable needle behind work, knit 1 stitch through the back loop, then purl the stitch from the second cable needle, then knit the stitch from the first cable needle through the back loop
- = Hold 2 stitches on a cable needle in front of work, purl 1 stitch through the back loop, then place the second stitch from the cable needle onto the left needle, and hold the cable needle bearing the 1st stitch behind work, then knit the stitch on the left needle, then purl the stitch from the cable needle through the back loop

## 128 INTERTWINED CHAIN-LINK CABLES

[multiple of 15 + 7 sts + 2 selv sts]

Shown are both RS and WS rows. Begin with the sts before the pattern repeat, rep the marked pattern repeat (15 sts wide) widthwise either once for a single vertical pattern column or continuously for an all-over pattern, and end with the sts after the pattern repeat. Repeat Rows 1–20 heightwise.

Pattern Repeat = 15 stitches

### Stitch Key

⬤ = 1 selvedge stitch

■ = Knit 1 stitch

− = Purl 1 stitch

= Hold 1 stitch on a cable needle behind work, knit 1 stitch through the back loop, then purl the stitch from the cable needle

= Hold 1 stitch on a cable needle in front of work, purl 1 stitch, then knit the stitch from the cable needle through the back loop

= Hold 1 stitch on a cable needle behind work, purl 1 stitch through the back loop, then purl the stitch from the cable needle through the back loop

= Hold 1 stitch on a cable needle in front of work, purl 1 stitch through the back loop, then purl the stitch from the cable needle through the back loop

## 129 PATTERN VARIATION

[multiple of 6 + 2 sts + 2 selv sts]

Only RS rows are shown; in WS rows, knit the knits, and purl the purls through the back loop. Begin with the sts before the pattern repeat, rep the marked pattern repeat (6 sts wide) widthwise continuously, and end with the sts after the pattern repeat. Repeat Rows 1–18 heightwise.

### Stitch Key

⬤ = 1 selvedge stitch

− = Purl 1 stitch

◆ = Knit 1 stitch through the back loop

= Hold 1 stitch on a cable needle in front of work, hold 2 stitches on a second cable needle behind work, knit 1 stitch through the back loop, then purl the stitches from the second cable needle, then knit the stitch from the first cable needle through the back loop

Pattern Repeat = 6 stitches

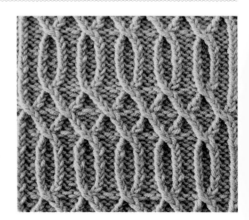

## 130 TRIANGLE ORNAMENTS  [multiple of 14 + 7 sts + 2 selv sts]

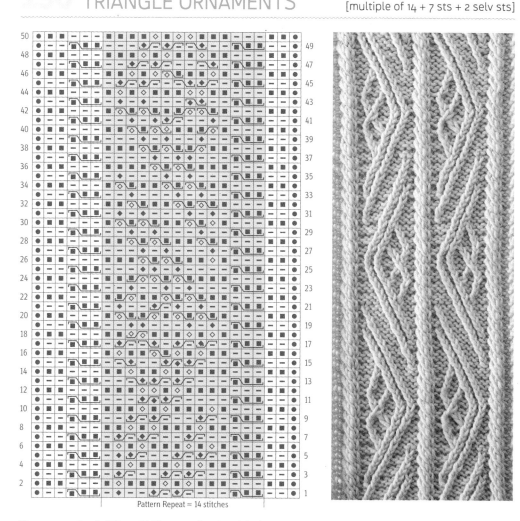

Pattern Repeat = 14 stitches

Shown are both RS and WS rows. Begin with the sts before the pattern repeat, rep the marked pattern repeat (14 sts wide) widthwise either once for a single vertical pattern column or continuously for an all-over pattern, and end with the sts after the pattern repeat. Repeat Rows 1–50 heightwise.

### Stitch Key

**●** = 1 selvedge stitch

**■** = Knit 1 stitch

**–** = Purl 1 stitch

**◆** = Knit 1 stitch through the back loop

**◇** = Purl 1 stitch through the back loop

**◆/–** = Hold 1 stitch on a cable needle behind work, knit 1 stitch through the back loop, then purl the stitch from the cable needle

**–/◆** = Hold 1 stitch on a cable needle in front of work, purl 1 stitch, then knit the stitch from the cable needle through the back loop

**◇/■** = Hold 1 stitch on a cable needle in front of work, purl 1 stitch through the back loop, then knit the stitch from the cable needle

**■/◇** = Hold 1 stitch on a cable needle behind work, knit the next stitch, then purl the stitch from the cable needle through the back loop

**◆/◆** = Hold 1 stitch on a cable needle behind work, knit 1 stitch through the back loop, then knit the stitch from the cable needle through the back loop

**◇/◆** = Hold 1 stitch on a cable needle in front of work, knit 1 stitch through the back loop, then knit the

stitch from the cable needle through the back loop

**◇/◇** = Hold 1 stitch on a cable needle behind work, purl 1 stitch through the back loop, then purl the stitch from the cable needle through the back loop

**◇\◇** = Hold 1 stitch on a cable needle in front of work, purl 1 stitch through the back loop, then purl the stitch from the cable needle through the back loop

**■■/■** = Hold 2 stitches on a cable needle in front of work, knit the next stitch, then knit the 2 stitches from the cable needle

## 131 TRAVELING-STITCH TRIANGLES

[multiple of 14 + 9 sts + 2 selv sts]

### Stitch Key

- ● = 1 selvedge stitch
- ■ = Knit 1 stitch
- – = Purl 1 stitch
- ◆ = Knit 1 stitch through the back loop
- ◇ = Purl 1 stitch through the back loop
- ⬥ = Knit 2 stitches together left-leaning (ssk)
- ⬧ = Purl 2 stitches together left-leaning (ssp)
- + = Increase 1 stitch twisted from the bar between stitches
- ✕ = Increase 1 stitch purlwise twisted from the bar between stitches

◆╱◆ = Hold 1 stitch on a cable needle behind work, knit 1 stitch through the back loop, then knit the stitch from the cable needle through the back loop

◆╲◆ = Hold 1 stitch on a cable needle in front of work, knit 1 stitch through the back loop, then knit the stitch from the cable needle through the back loop

◇╱◇ = Hold 1 stitch on a cable needle behind work, purl 1 stitch through the back loop, then purl the stitch from the cable needle through the back loop

◇╲◇ = Hold 1 stitch on a cable needle in front of work, purl 1 stitch through the back loop, then purl the stitch from the cable needle through the back loop

◆╱– = Hold 1 stitch on a cable needle behind work, knit 1 stitch through the back loop, then purl the stitch from the cable needle

–╲◆ = Hold 1 stitch on a cable needle in front of work, purl 1 stitch, then knit the stitch from the cable needle through the back loop

◇╲■ = Hold 1 stitch on a cable needle in front of work, purl 1 stitch through the back loop, then knit the stitch from the cable needle

Shown are both RS and WS rows. Begin with the sts before the pattern repeat, rep the marked pattern repeat (14 sts wide) widthwise either once for a single vertical pattern column or continuously for an all-over pattern, and end with the sts after the pattern repeat. Repeat Rows 1–38 heightwise.

Pattern Repeat = 14 stitches

■╱◇ = Hold 1 stitch on a cable needle behind work, knit the next stitch, then purl the stitch from the cable needle through the back loop

◆╱– = Hold 1 stitch on a cable needle behind work, knit 2 stitches through the back loop, then purl the stitch from the cable needle

–╲◆ = Hold 2 stitches on a cable needle in front of work, purl 1 stitch, then knit the 2 stitches from the cable needle through the back loop

◇╲■ = Hold 1 stitch on a cable needle in front of work, purl 2 stitches through the back loop, then knit the stitch from the cable needle

■╱◇ = Hold 2 stitches on a cable needle behind work, knit the next stitch, then purl the 2 stitches from the cable needle through the back loop

◆╲◆ = Hold 1 stitch on a cable needle behind work, knit 2 stitches through the back loop, then knit the stitch from the cable needle through the back loop

◆╲◆ = Hold 2 stitches on a cable needle in front of work, knit 1 stitch through the back loop, then knit the 2 stitches from the cable needle through the back loop

◇╲◇ = Hold 1 stitch on a cable needle in front of work, purl 2 stitches through the back loop, then purl the stitch from the cable needle through the back loop

◇╱◇ = Hold 2 stitches on a cable needle behind work, purl 1 stitch through the back loop, then purl the 2 stitches from the cable needle through the back loop

## 132 TRAVELING-STITCH CIRCLES

[multiple of 17 + 11 st + 2 selv sts]

Shown are both RS and WS rows. Begin with the sts before the pattern repeat, rep the marked pattern repeat (17 sts wide) widthwise either once for a single vertical pattern column or continuously for an all-over pattern, and end with the sts after the pattern repeat. Repeat Rows 1–12 heightwise.

Pattern Repeat = 17 stitches

### Stitch Key

⬤ = 1 selvedge stitch

◼ = Knit 1 stitch

— = Purl 1 stitch

◆ = Knit 1 stitch through the back loop

◇ = Purl 1 stitch through the back loop

◆◣◆ = Hold 1 stitch on a cable needle in front of work, knit 1 stitch through the back loop, then knit the stitch from the cable needle through the back loop

◇◢◇ = Hold 1 stitch on a cable needle behind work, purl 1 stitch through the back loop, then purl the stitch from the cable needle through the back loop

◼◢◇ = Hold 1 stitch on a cable needle behind work, knit the next stitch, then purl the stitch from the cable needle through the back loop

◇◣◼ = Hold 1 stitch on a cable needle in front of work, purl 1 stitch through the back loop, then knit the stitch from the cable needle

◆◢— = Hold 1 stitch on a cable needle behind work, knit 1 stitch through the back loop, then purl the stitch from the cable needle

—◣◆ = Hold 1 stitch on a cable needle in front of work, purl 1 stitch, then knit the stitch from the cable needle through the back loop

# ARAN PATTERNS

# ALPINE PATTERNS

# CELTIC PATTERNS

## 133 CABLE PATTERN WITH HEART MOTIF GARLAND

[multiple of 41 + 23 sts + 2 selv sts]

**❱ Chart on page 311**

Only RS rows are shown; in WS rows, knit the knits, and purl the purls. Begin with the sts before the pattern repeat, rep the marked pattern repeat (41 sts wide) widthwise, and end with the sts after the pattern repeat. Repeat Rows 1–20 heightwise.

## 134 NORDIC CABLE PATTERN

↔ [multiple of 73 sts + 2 selv sts]

**WIDENING THE STITCH PATTERN**

**Widening the stitch pattern in the middle:** Rep Pattern Repeat 2 (= 12 sts) and Pattern Repeat 3 (= 12 sts) each, either once or multiple times.
**Widening the stitch pattern at the outside edges:** Rep Pattern Repeat 1 (= 1 st) and Pattern Repeat 4 (= 1 st) each, either once or multiple times.

**❱ Chart on page 313**

Only RS rows are shown; in WS rows, knit the knits, and purl the purls. Begin with the selv st before Pattern Repeat 1, work Pattern Repeat 1 (1 st wide) according to the desired width of the pattern either once or multiple times, then work up to the beginning of Pattern Repeat 2. Work Pattern Repeat 2 (12 sts wide) according to the desired width of the pattern either once or multiple times, then work up to the beginning of Pattern Repeat 3, and work Pattern Repeat 3 (12 sts wide) according to the desired width of the pattern either once or multiple times. Afterward, continue to the beginning of Pattern Repeat 4, work Pattern Repeat 4 (1 st wide) according to the desired width of the pattern either once or multiple times, and end with the selv st after Pattern Repeat 4. Repeat Rows 1–30 heightwise.

# 135 ALPINE PATTERN WITH TRAVELING STITCHES

↔ [multiple of 2 + 84 sts + 2 selv sts]

**❯ Chart on page 316**

Only RS rows are shown; in WS rows, knit the knits, and purl the purls through the back loop. Begin with the selv st before Pattern Repeat 1, work Pattern Repeat 1 (1 st wide) according to the desired width of the pattern either once or multiple times. Then work the stitches up to the beginning of Pattern Repeat 2, work Pattern Repeat 2 (1 st wide) according to the desired width of the pattern either once or multiple times, and end with the selv st after Pattern Repeat 2. Repeat Rows 1–20 heightwise.

**WIDENING THE STITCH PATTERN**

**Widening the stitch pattern at the outside edges:** Rep Pattern Repeats 1 (= 1 st) and 2 (= 1 st) each, either once or multiple times.

# 136 TEXTURED CABLE PATTERN

↔ [multiple of 4 + 69 sts + 2 selv sts]

**❯ Chart on page 312**

Only RS rows are shown; in WS rows, knit the knits, and purl the purls. Begin with the selv st before Pattern Repeat 1, and work Pattern Repeat 1 (2 sts wide) as often as needed for the desired width of the pattern. Then work the pattern panel (69 sts wide), work Pattern Repeat 2 (2 sts wide) as often as needed for the desired width of the pattern, and end with the selv st after Pattern Repeat 2. Repeat Rows 1–26 heightwise.

**WIDENING THE STITCH PATTERN**

**Adjusting the width of the pattern:** Rep Pattern Repeats 1 and 2 continuously until the desired stitch count has been reached.

## 137 LAID-BACK CABLE DIAMONDS [multiple of 40 + 19 sts + 2 selv sts]

**》 Chart on page 312**
Only RS rows are shown; in WS rows, knit the knits, and purl the purls. Begin with the selv st before the pattern repeat, rep the pattern repeat (40 sts wide) continuously, and end with the sts after the pattern repeat. Repeat Rows 1–24 heightwise.

## 138 ELEGANT CABLE COMBINATION [multiple of 39 + 6 sts + 2 selv sts]

Only RS rows are shown; in WS rows, knit the knits, and purl the purls. Begin with the selv st before the pattern repeat, rep the pattern repeat (39 sts wide) continuously, and end with the sts after the pattern repeat. Repeat Rows 1–12 heightwise.

Pattern Repeat = 39 stitches

### Stitch Key

● = 1 selvedge stitch

■ = Knit 1 stitch

— = Purl 1 stitch

= Hold 1 stitch on a cable needle behind work, knit the next stitch, then knit the stitch from the cable needle

= Hold 1 stitch on a cable needle in front of work, knit 2 stitches, then knit the stitch from the cable needle

= Hold 2 stitches on a cable needle behind work, knit the next stitch, then knit the 2 stitches from the cable needle

= Hold 2 stitches on a cable needle in front of work, knit 2 stitches, then knit the 2 stitches from the cable needle

= Hold 2 stitches on a cable needle behind work, knit 2 stitches, then knit the 2 stitches from the cable needle

= Hold 3 stitches on a cable needle in front of work, hold 1 stitch on a second cable needle behind work, knit 1 stitch, purl 1 stitch, and knit the next stitch, then purl the stitch from the second cable needle, then work the stitches from the first cable needle as (knit 1 stitch, purl 1 stitch, and knit 1 stitch)

## 139 TRADITIONAL ARAN PATTERN  ↔ [multiple of 62 sts + 2 selv sts]

**❱ Chart on page 310**

Only RS rows are shown; in WS rows, knit the knits, and purl the purls. Begin with the sts before Pattern Repeat 1, work Pattern Repeat 1 (1 st wide) according to the desired width of the pattern either once or multiple times. Then work the stitches up to the beginning of Pattern Repeat 2, and work Pattern Repeat 2 (8 sts wide) according to the desired width of the pattern either once or multiple times (photo = 3 times). After this, work the stitches up to the beginning of Pattern Repeat 3, work Pattern Repeat 3 (1 st wide) according to the desired width of the pattern either once or multiple times, and end with the sts after Pattern Repeat 3. Repeat Rows 1–24 heightwise.

**WIDENING THE STITCH PATTERN**

**Widening the stitch pattern in the middle:** Rep Pattern Repeat 2 (= 8 sts) either once or multiple times consecutively.
**Widening the stitch pattern at the outside edges:** Rep Pattern Repeats 1 (= 1 st) and 3 (= 1 st) each, either once or multiple times.

## 140 TRAVELING-STITCH COMBINATION  ↔ [multiple of 70 sts + 2 selv sts]

**❱ Chart on page 311**

Only RS rows are shown; in WS rows, knit the knits, and purl the purls through the back loop. Begin with the sts before Pattern Repeat 1, work Pattern Repeat 1 (2 sts wide) according to the desired width of the pattern either once or multiple times. Then work the stitches up to the beginning of Pattern Repeat 2, and work Pattern Repeat 2 (4 sts wide) according to the desired width of the pattern either once or multiple times (photo = 5 times). After this, work the stitches up to the beginning of Pattern Repeat 3, work Pattern Repeat 3 (2 sts wide) according to the desired width of the pattern either once or multiple times, and end with the sts after Pattern Repeat 3. Repeat Rows 1–16 heightwise.

**WIDENING THE STITCH PATTERN**

**Widening the stitch pattern in the middle:** Rep Pattern Repeat 2 (= 4 sts) either once or multiple times consecutively.
**Widening the stitch pattern at the outside edges:** Rep Pattern Repeats 1 (= 2 sts) and 3 (= 2 sts) each, either once or multiple times.

## 141 CELTIC SYMBOL

↔ [multiple of 4 + 27 st + 2 selv sts]

Only RS rows are shown; in WS rows, knit the knits, and purl the purls. Begin with the selv st before Pattern Repeat 1, work Pattern Repeat 1 (2 sts wide) according to the desired width of the pattern either once or multiple times. Then work the stitches up to the beginning of Pattern Repeat 2, work Pattern Repeat 2 (2 sts wide) according to the desired width of the pattern either once or multiple times, and end with the selv st after Pattern Repeat 2. Repeat Rows 1–68 heightwise either once for a single motif or continuously for an all-over pattern.

**WIDENING THE STITCH PATTERN**

Widening the stitch pattern at the outside edges:
Rep Pattern Repeats 1 (= 2 sts) and 2 (= 2 sts) each, either once or multiple times.

## 142 CELTIC ORNAMENT

↔ [multiple of 2 + 43 sts + 2 selv sts]

❱ Chart on page 314

Only RS rows are shown; in WS rows, knit the knits, and purl the purls. Begin with the selv st before Pattern Repeat 1, work Pattern Repeat 1 (1 st wide) according to the desired width of the pattern either once or multiple times. Then work the stitches up to the beginning of Pattern Repeat 2, work Pattern Repeat 2 (1 st wide) according to the desired width of the pattern either once or multiple times, and end with the selv st after Pattern Repeat 2. Repeat Rows 1–36 heightwise either once for a single motif or continuously for an all-over pattern.

**WIDENING THE STITCH PATTERN**

Widening the stitch pattern at the outside edges: Rep Pattern Repeats 1 (= 1 st) and 2 (= 1 st) each, either once or multiple times.

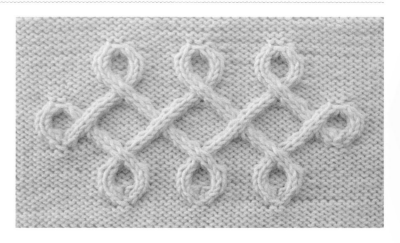

# CELTIC SYMBOL

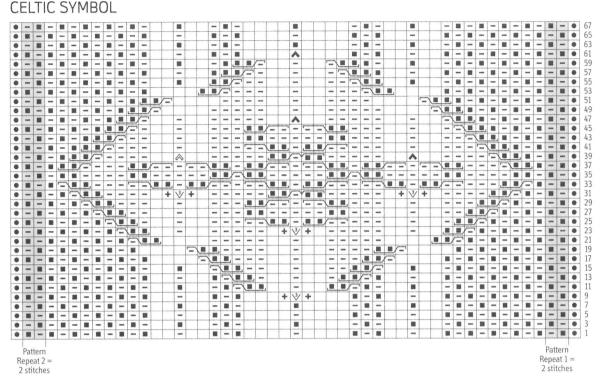

Pattern
Repeat 2 =
2 stitches

Pattern
Repeat 1 =
2 stitches

## Stitch Key

⬤ = 1 selvedge stitch

■ = Knit 1 stitch

— = Purl 1 stitch

+ = Increase 1 stitch twisted from the bar between stitches

☐ = No stitch, for better overview only

Λ = Quadruple passing-over, starting at left: Slip 2 stitches purl-wise to the right needle. * On the left needle, pass the second stitch over the first stitch. Slip the first stitch on the left needle purlwise to the right needle, and on the right needle, pass the second stitch (counted from the tip of the needle) over the first stitch (counted from the tip of the needle). Now, return the first stitch to the left needle. Repeat from * once, then purl the stitch.

◬ = Quadruple passing-over, starting at right: Slip 3 stitches purl-wise to the right needle. * On the right needle, pass the second stitch (counted from the tip of the needle) over the first stitch (counted from the tip of the needle). Then slip the first stitch from the right needle purlwise to the left needle; there, pass the second stitch over the first stitch. Now, return the first stitch to the right needle. Repeat from * once. Then return the stitch to the left needle, and purl it.

V = Into the following stitch, work a total of 3 stitches (knit 1 stitch, knit 1 stitch through the back loop, knit 1 stitch)

⬛⬛⬛ = Hold 2 stitches on a cable needle in front of work, purl 1 stitch, then knit the 2 stitches from the cable needle

⬛⬛⬛ = Hold 1 stitch on a cable needle behind work, knit 2 stitches, then purl the stitch from the cable needle

⬛⬛⬛ = Hold 2 stitches on a cable needle in front of work, purl 2 stitches, then knit the 2 stitches from the cable needle

⬛⬛⬛ = Hold 2 stitches on a cable needle behind work, knit 2 stitches, then purl the 2 stitches from the cable needle

⬛⬛⬛⬛ = Hold 2 stitches on a cable needle in front of work, hold 1 stitch on a second cable needle behind work, knit 2 stitches, then purl the stitch from the second cable needle, then knit the 2 stitches from the first cable needle

⬛⬛⬛⬛ = Hold 3 stitches on the first cable needle behind work, knit 2 stitches, then place the first and second stitch from the first cable needle onto a second cable needle, and hold in front of work. Purl the remaining stitch from the first cable needle, then knit the 2 stitches from the second cable needle.

# 143 QUAINT HEART PATTERN

[multiple of 28 + 17 sts + 2 selv sts]

Only RS rows are shown; in WS rows, knit the knits, and purl the purls. Begin with the selv st before the pattern repeat, repeat the pattern repeat (28 sts wide) continuously, and end with the sts after the pattern repeat. Repeat Rows 1–24 heightwise.

Pattern Repeat = 28 stitches

23
21
19
17
15
13
11
9
7
5
3
1

## Stitch Key

● = 1 selvedge stitch

■ = Knit 1 stitch

– = Purl 1 stitch

+ = Increase 1 stitch twisted from the bar between stitches

☐ = No stitch, for better overview only

= Hold 1 stitch on a cable needle in front of work, knit the next stitch, then knit the stitch from the cable needle

= Hold 1 stitch on a cable needle behind work, knit the next stitch, then knit the stitch from the cable needle

= Hold 1 stitch on a cable needle in front of work, purl the next stitch, then knit the stitch from the cable needle

= Hold 1 stitch on a cable needle behind work, knit the next stitch, then purl the stitch from the cable needle

= Hold 2 stitches on a cable needle behind work, knit the next stitch, then knit the 2 stitches from the cable needle

= Hold 2 stitches on a cable needle in front of work, knit the next stitch, then knit the 2 stitches from the cable needle

= Hold 1 stitch on a cable needle behind work, knit 2 stitches, then knit the stitch from the cable needle

= Hold 2 stitches on a cable needle in front of work, purl 1 stitch, then knit the 2 stitches from the cable needle

= Hold 1 stitch on a cable needle behind work, knit 2 stitches, then purl the stitch from the cable needle

N = Make 1 nupp: into the following stitch, work a total of 3 stitches (alternating [knit 1 stitch, knit 1 stitch through the back loop]), turn work, purl 3 stitches, turn work, slip 2 stitches knitwise, knit 1 stitch, and pass the slipped stitches over

▲ = Quadruple passing-over, starting at left: Slip 2 stitches purlwise to the right needle. On the left needle, pass the second stitch over the first stitch. Slip the first stitch on the left needle purlwise to the right needle, and on the right needle, pass the second stitch (counted from the tip of the needle) over the first stitch (counted from the tip of the needle). Now, return the first stitch to the left needle, and again, pass the second stitch over the first stitch. Return the first stitch to the right needle, and once again, pass the second stitch over the first stitch. Place the first stitch back onto the left needle, then purl it.

△ = Quadruple passing-over, starting at right: Slip 3 stitches purlwise to the right needle; there, pass the second stitch (counted from the tip of the needle) over the first stitch (counted from tip of the needle). Now, slip the first stitch from the right needle purlwise onto the left needle. On the left needle, pass the second stitch over the first stitch, then slip the first stitch back to the right needle. There, again, pass the second stitch over the first stitch, and slip the first stitch back to the left needle. On the left needle, once more, pass the second stitch over the first stitch, then purl the stitch.

## 144 FESTIVE ALPINE PATTERN

↔ [multiple of 2 + 91 st + 2 selv sts]

**❱ Chart on page 320**

Only RS rows are shown; in WS rows, knit the knits, purl the purls, and purl stitches through the back loop that had been knitted through the back loop in RS rows. Begin with the selv st before Pattern Repeat 1, work Pattern Repeat 1 (1 st wide) according to the desired width of the pattern either once or multiple times. Then work the stitches up to the beginning of Pattern Repeat 2, work Pattern Repeat 2 (1 st wide) according to the desired width of the pattern either once or multiple times, and end with the selv st after Pattern Repeat 2. Repeat Rows 1–18 heightwise.

**WIDENING THE STITCH PATTERN**

**Widening the stitch pattern at the outside edges:** Rep Pattern Repeats 1 (= 1 st) and 2 (= 1 st) each, either once or multiple times.

## 145 CABLE-AND-NUPP PATTERN

↔ [multiple of 16 + 80 sts + 2 selv sts]

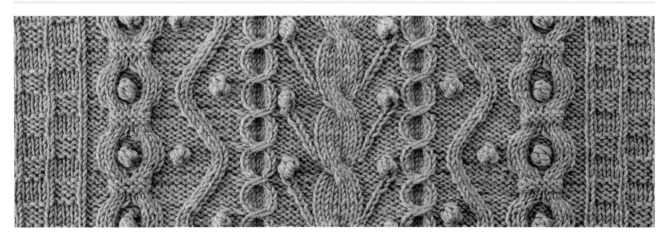

**❱ Chart on page 320**

Only RS rows are shown; in WS rows, knit the knits, and purl the purls. Begin with the selv st before Pattern Repeat 1, work Pattern Repeat 1 (8 sts wide) according to the desired width of the pattern either once or multiple times. Then work the stitches up to the beginning of Pattern Repeat 2, work Pattern Repeat 2 (8 sts wide) according to the desired width of the pattern either once or multiple times, and end with the selv st after Pattern Repeat 2. Repeat Rows 1–24 heightwise.

**WIDENING THE STITCH PATTERN**

**Widening the stitch pattern at the outside edges:** Rep Pattern Repeats 1 (= 8 sts) and 2 (= 8 sts) each, either once or multiple times.

## 146 IRISH PATTERN COMBINATION

↔ [multiple of 67 sts + 2 selv sts]

❭ Chart on page 310

Only RS rows are shown; in WS rows, knit the knits, and purl the purls. Begin with the sts before Pattern Repeat 1, work Pattern Repeat 1 (14 sts wide) according to the desired width of the pattern either once or multiple times. Then work the stitches up to the beginning of Pattern Repeat 2, and work Pattern Repeat 2 (10 sts wide) according to the desired width of the pattern either once or multiple times. After this, work the stitches up to the beginning of Pattern Repeat 3, work Pattern Repeat 3 (14 sts wide) according to the desired width of the pattern either once or multiple times, and end with the sts after Pattern Repeat 3. Work Rows 1–10 once heightwise, then repeat only Rows 3–10 continuously.

### WIDENING THE STITCH PATTERN

**Widening the stitch pattern in the middle:** Rep Pattern Repeat 2 (= 10 sts) either once or multiple times consecutively.
**Widening the stitch pattern at the outside edges:** Rep Pattern Repeats 1 (= 14 sts) and 3 (= 14 sts) each, either once or multiple times.

## 147 ARAN-AND-CABLE PATTERN

[multiple of 32 + 12 sts + 2 selv sts]

Only RS rows are shown; in WS rows, knit the knits, and purl the purls. Begin with the selv st before the pattern repeat, repeat the pattern repeat (32 sts wide) continuously, and end with the sts after the pattern repeat. Work Rows 1–18 once heightwise, then repeat only Rows 3–18 continuously.

Pattern Repeat = 32 stitches

### Stitch Key

● = 1 selvedge stitch

■ = Knit 1 stitch

– = Purl 1 stitch

⬛⬛⬛ = Hold 2 stitches on a cable needle in front of work, knit 2 stitches, then knit the 2 stitches from the cable needle

⬛⬛⬛ = Hold 2 stitches on a cable needle behind work, knit 2 stitches, then knit the 2 stitches from the cable needle

⬛⬛⬛ = Hold 2 stitches on a cable needle in front of work, purl 2 stitches, then knit the 2 stitches from the cable needle

⬛⬛⬛ = Hold 2 stitches on a cable needle behind work, knit 2 stitches, then purl the 2 stitches from the cable needle

## 148 CLASSIC ARAN PATTERN

↔ [multiple of 8 + 92 sts + 2 selv sts]

**❯ Chart on pages 318—319**

Only RS rows are shown; in WS rows, knit the knits, and purl the purls. Begin with the selv st before Pattern Repeat 1, work Pattern Repeat 1 (4 sts wide) according to the desired width of the pattern either once or multiple times. Then work the stitches up to the beginning of Pattern Repeat 2, work Pattern Repeat 2 (4 sts wide) according to the desired width of the pattern either once or multiple times, and end with the selv st after Pattern Repeat 2. Repeat Rows 1—16 heightwise.

**WIDENING THE STITCH PATTERN**

**Widening the stitch pattern at the outside edges:** Rep Pattern Repeats 1 (= 4 sts) and 2 (= 4 sts) each, either once or multiple times.

## 149 LEAF PATTERN COMBINATION

↔ [multiple of 86 sts + 2 selv sts]

**❯ Chart on pages 316—317**

Only RS rows are shown; in WS rows, knit the knits, and purl the purls. Begin with the selv st before Pattern Repeat 1, work Pattern Repeat 1 (4 sts wide) according to the desired width of the pattern either once or multiple times, then work up to the beginning of Pattern Repeat 2. Work Pattern Repeat 2 (19 sts wide) according to the desired width of the pattern either once or multiple times, then work up to the beginning of Pattern Repeat 3, and work Pattern Repeat 3 (19 sts wide) according to the desired width of the pattern either once or multiple times. Afterward, continue to the beginning of Pattern Repeat 4, work Pattern Repeat 4 (4 sts wide) according to the desired width of the pattern either once or multiple times, and end with the selv st after Pattern Repeat 4. Repeat Rows 1—32 heightwise.

**WIDENING THE STITCH PATTERN**

**Widening the stitch pattern at the outside edges:** Rep Pattern Repeats 2 (= 19 sts) and 3 (= 19 sts) each, either once or multiple times.

**Widening the stitch pattern at the outside edges:** Rep Pattern Repeats 1 (= 4 sts) and 4 (= 4 sts) each, either once or multiple times.

## 150 CELTIC KNOT  ↔↕ [multiple of 4 + 39 sts + 2 selv sts]

❯ **Chart on page 309**

Only RS rows are shown; in WS rows, knit the knits, and purl the purls. Begin with the selv st before Pattern Repeat 1, work Pattern Repeat 1 (2 sts wide) according to the desired width of the pattern either once or multiple times. Then work the stitches up to the beginning of Pattern Repeat 2, work Pattern Repeat 2 (2 sts wide) according to the desired width of the pattern either once or multiple times, and end with the selv st after Pattern Repeat 2. Work Rows 1–4 according to the desired height of the pattern either once or multiple times, then work Rows 5–52 once, then work Rows 53–56 according to the desired height of the pattern either once or multiple times.

### WIDENING THE STITCH PATTERN

**Widening the pattern frame at the sides:** Rep Pattern Repeats 1 (= 2 sts) and 2 (= 2 sts) each, either once or multiple times.
**Enlarging the pattern frame at the bottom and top:** Rep Rows 1–4, and Rows 53–56 according to the desired height of the pattern each, either once or multiple times.

## 151 QUADRUPLE KNOT  ↔↕ [multiple of 8 + 30 sts + 2 selv sts]

❯ **Chart on page 315**

Only RS rows are shown; in WS rows, knit the knits, and purl the purls. Begin with the selv st before Pattern Repeat 1, work Pattern Repeat 1 (4 sts wide) according to the desired width of the pattern either once or multiple times. Then work the stitches up to the beginning of Pattern Repeat 2, work Pattern Repeat 2 (4 sts wide) according to the desired width of the pattern either once or multiple times, and end with the selv st after Pattern Repeat 2. Work Rows 1–4 according to the desired height of the pattern either once or multiple times, then work Rows 5–44 once, then work Rows 45–48 according to the desired height of the pattern either once or multiple times.

### WIDENING THE STITCH PATTERN

**Widening the pattern frame at the sides:** Rep Pattern Repeats 1 (= 4 sts) and 2 (= 4 sts) each, either once or multiple times.
**Enlarging the pattern frame at the bottom and top:** Rep Rows 1–4, and Rows 45–48 according to the desired height of the pattern each, either once or multiple times.

## 152 CLASSIC ALPINE PATTERN

↔ [multiple of 90 sts + 2 selv sts]

**❱ Chart on pages 318–319**

Only RS rows are shown; in WS rows, knit the knits, and purl the purls. Begin with the selv st before Pattern Repeat 1, work Pattern Repeat 1 (1 st wide) according to the desired width of the pattern either once or multiple times. Then work the stitches up to the beginning of Pattern Repeat 2, and work Pattern Repeat 2 (8 sts wide) according to the desired width of the pattern either once or multiple times. After this, work the stitches up to the beginning of Pattern Repeat 3, work Pattern Repeat 3 (1 st wide) according to the desired width of the pattern either once or multiple times, and end with the selv st after Pattern Repeat 3. Repeat Rows 1–16 heightwise.

**WIDENING THE STITCH PATTERN**

**Widening the stitch pattern in the middle:** Rep Pattern Repeat 2 (= 8 sts) either once or multiple times consecutively.

**Widening the stitch pattern at the outside edges:** Rep Pattern Repeats 1 (= 1 st) and 3 (= 1 st) each, either once or multiple times.

## 153 CABLE PATTERN COMBINATION

↔ [multiple of 86 sts + 2 selv sts]

**❱ Chart on pages 318–319**

Only RS rows are shown; in WS rows, knit the knits, and purl the purls. Begin with the selv st before Pattern Repeat 1, work Pattern Repeat 1 (3 sts wide) according to the desired width of the pattern either once or multiple times. Then work the stitches up to the beginning of Pattern Repeat 2, and work Pattern Repeat 2 (8 sts wide) according to the desired width of the pattern either once or multiple times (photo = 3 times). After this, work the stitches up to the beginning of Pattern Repeat 3, work Pattern Repeat 3 (3 sts wide) according to the desired width of the pattern either once or multiple times, and end with the selv st after Pattern Repeat 3. Repeat Rows 1–16 heightwise.

**WIDENING THE STITCH PATTERN**

**Widening the stitch pattern in the middle:** Rep Pattern Repeat 2 (= 8 sts) either once or multiple times consecutively.

**Widening the stitch pattern at the outside edges:** Rep Pattern Repeats 1 (= 3 sts) and 3 (= 3 sts) each, either once or multiple times.

## 154 ENDLESS KNOT

↔↕ [multiple of 2 + 37 sts + 2 selv sts]

Only RS rows are shown; in WS rows, knit the knits, and purl the purls. Begin with the selv st before Pattern Repeat 1, work Pattern Repeat 1 (1 st wide) according to the desired width of the pattern either once or multiple times. Then work the stitches up to the beginning of Pattern Repeat 2, work Pattern Repeat 2 (1 st wide) according to the desired width of the pattern either once or multiple times, and end with the selv st after Pattern Repeat 2. Work Rows 1 and 2 according to the desired height of the pattern either once or multiple times, then work Rows 3–60 once, then work Rows 61–62 according to the desired height of the pattern either once or multiple times.

### WIDENING THE STITCH PATTERN

**Widening the pattern frame at the sides:** Rep Pattern Repeats 1 (= 1 st) and 2 (= 1 st) each, either once or multiple times.
**Enlarging the pattern frame at the bottom and top:** Rep Rows 1 and 2, and Rows 61 and 62 according to the desired height of the pattern each, either once or multiple times.

## 155 MAGIC KNOT

↔↕ [multiple of 8 + 32 sts + 2 selv sts]

❱ **Chart on page 308**
Only RS rows are shown; in WS rows, knit the knits, and purl the purls. Begin with the selv st before Pattern Repeat 1, work Pattern Repeat 1 (4 sts wide) according to the desired width of the pattern either once or multiple times. Then work the stitches up to the beginning of Pattern Repeat 2, work Pattern Repeat 2 (4 sts wide) according to the desired width of the pattern either once or multiple times, and end with the selv st after Pattern Repeat 2. Work Rows 1–4 according to the desired height of the pattern either once or multiple times, then work Rows 5–82 once, then repeat Rows 83–86 according to the desired height of the pattern either once or multiple times.

### WIDENING THE STITCH PATTERN

**Widening the frame pattern at the sides:** Rep Pattern Repeats 1 (= 4 sts) and 2 (= 4 sts) each, either once or multiple times.
**Widening the frame pattern at the bottom and top:** Rep Rows 1–4, and Rows 83–86 according to the desired height of the pattern each, either once or multiple times.

# ENDLESS KNOT

Row numbers (right side, top to bottom): 61, 59, 57, 55, 53, 51, 49, 47, 45, 43, 41, 39, 37, 35, 31, 29, 27, 25, 23, 21, 19, 17, 15, 13, 11, 9, 7, 5, 3, 1

Pattern Repeat 2 = 2 stitches

Pattern Repeat 1 = 1 stitch

## Stitch Key

● = 1 selvedge stitch

■ = Knit 1 stitch

– = Purl 1 stitch

+ = Increase 1 stitch twisted from the bar between stitches

☐ = No stitch, for better overview only

⋀ = Quadruple passing-over, starting at left: Slip 2 stitches purlwise to the right needle. * On the left needle, pass the second stitch over the first stitch. Slip the first stitch on the left needle purlwise to the right needle, and on the right needle, pass the second stitch (counted from the tip of the needle) over the first stitch (counted from the tip of the needle). Now, return the first stitch to the left needle. Repeat from * once, then purl the stitch.

⋀ = Quadruple passing-over, starting at right: Slip 3 stitches purlwise to the right needle. * On the right needle, pass the second stitch (counted from the tip of the needle) over the first stitch (counted from the tip of the needle). Then slip the first stitch from the right needle purlwise to the left needle; there, pass the second stitch over the first stitch. Now, return the first stitch to the right needle. Repeat from * once. Then return the stitch to the left needle, and purl it.

◖ = Sextuple passing-over, starting at left: Slip 3 stitches purlwise to the right needle. * On the left needle, pass the second stitch over the first stitch. Slip the first stitch on the left needle purlwise to the right needle, and on the right needle, pass the second stitch (counted from the tip of the needle) over the first stitch (counted from the tip of the needle). Now, return the first stitch to the left needle. Repeat from * twice more, then purl the stitches.

⦸ (V³) = Into the following stitch, work a total of 3 stitches (knit 1 stitch, knit 1 stitch through the back loop, knit 1 stitch)

⦸ (V⁵) = Into the following stitch, work a total of 5 stitches (alternating "knit 1 stitch, knit 1 stitch through the back loop")

☐☐■■ = Hold 2 stitches on a cable needle in front of work, purl 1 stitch, then knit the 2 stitches from the cable needle

■■☐ = Hold 1 stitch on a cable needle behind work, knit 2 stitches, then purl the stitch from the cable needle

☐☐■■ = Hold 2 stitches on a cable needle in front of work, purl 2 stitches, then knit the 2 stitches from the cable needle

■■☐☐ = Hold 2 stitches on a cable needle behind work, knit 2 stitches, then purl the 2 stitches from the cable needle

■■■■ = Hold 2 stitches on a cable needle in front of work, knit 2 stitches, then knit the 2 stitches from the cable needle

■■☐■■ = Hold 3 stitches on the first cable needle behind work, knit 2 stitches, then place the first and second stitch from the first cable needle onto a second cable needle, and hold in front of work. Purl the remaining stitch from the first cable needle, then knit the 2 stitches from the second cable needle.

☐☐■■ = Hold 3 stitches on a cable needle in front of work, purl 2 stitches, then knit the 3 stitches from the cable needle

■■■☐☐ = Hold 2 stitches on a cable needle behind work, knit 3 stitches, then purl the 2 stitches from the cable needle

■■■■■ = Hold 3 stitches on a cable needle in front of work, knit 2 stitches, then knit the 3 stitches from the cable needle

■■■■■ = Hold 2 stitches on a cable needle in front of work, knit 3 stitches, then knit the 2 stitches from the cable needle

■■■☐■■ = Hold 3 stitches on the first cable needle behind work, knit 3 stitches, then place the 1st and 2nd stitches from the first cable onto a second cable needle, and hold in front of work. Purl the remaining stitch from the first cable needle, then knit the 2 stitches from the second cable needle.

■■☐■■■ = Hold 4 stitches on the first cable needle behind work, knit 2 stitches, then place the 1st, 2nd, and 3rd stitches from the first cable needle onto a second cable needle, and hold in front of work. Purl the remaining stitch from the first cable needle, then knit the 3 stitches from the second cable needle.

Stitch
pattern 162

# LACE-AND-CABLE PATTERNS

## 156 CABLE TRIANGLES [multiple of 10 + 5 sts + 2 selv sts]

Only RS rows are shown; in WS rows, purl all stitches and yarn overs. Begin with the sts before the pattern repeat, rep the marked pattern repeat (10 sts wide) widthwise continuously, and end with the sts after the pattern repeat. Repeat Rows 1–12 heightwise.

### Stitch Key

● = 1 selvedge stitch

■ = Knit 1 stitch

O = Make 1 yarn over

◢ = Knit 2 stitches together

◣ = Knit 2 stitches together left-leaning with passing over (skp): slip 1 stitch knitwise, knit the next stitch, and pass the slipped stitch over

▲ = Double left-leaning decrease with passing over (sk2p): slip 1 stitch knitwise, knit 2 stitches together, pass the slipped stitch over

= Hold 4 stitches on a cable needle behind work, knit 3 stitches, then knit the 4 stitches from the cable needle

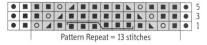

Pattern Repeat = 10 stitches

## 157 CHEVRON PATTERN WITH CABLES [multiple of 13 + 1 st + 2 selv sts]

Only RS rows are shown; in WS rows, purl all stitches and yarn overs. Begin with the selv st before the pattern repeat, rep the marked pattern repeat (13 sts wide) widthwise continuously, and end with the sts after the pattern repeat. Repeat Rows 1–6 heightwise.

### Stitch Key

● = 1 selvedge stitch

■ = Knit 1 stitch

O = Make 1 yarn over

◢ = Knit 2 stitches together

◣ = Knit 2 stitches together left-leaning with passing over (skp): slip 1 stitch knitwise, knit the next stitch, and pass the slipped stitch over

= Hold 3 stitches on a cable needle in front of work, knit 3 stitches, then knit the 3 stitches from the cable needle

Pattern Repeat = 13 stitches

## 158 CABLE-AND-ARC PATTERN

[multiple of 15 + 8 sts + 2 selv sts]

Pattern Repeat = 15 stitches

### Stitch Key

● = 1 selvedge stitch

■ = Knit 1 stitch

O = Make 1 yarn over

△ = Double left-leaning decrease with passing over (sk2p): slip 1

stitch knitwise, knit 2 stitches together, pass the slipped stitch over

■■■■■■■ = Hold 3 stitches on a cable needle in front of work, knit 3 stitches, then knit the 3 stitches from the cable needle

Only RS rows are shown; in WS rows, purl all stitches and yarn overs. Begin with the sts before the pattern repeat, rep the marked pattern repeat (15 sts wide) widthwise continuously, and end with the sts after the pattern repeat. Repeat Rows 1–8 heightwise.

## 159 EYELET-AND-CABLE PATTERN

[multiple of 20 + 2 sts + 2 selv sts]

### Stitch Key

● = 1 selvedge stitch

■ = Knit 1 stitch

— = Purl 1 stitch

O = Make 1 yarn over

◢ = Knit 2 stitches together

◣ = Knit 2 stitches together left-leaning with passing over

(skp): slip 1 stitch knitwise, knit the next stitch, and pass the slipped stitch over

■■■■■■■■■ = Hold 4 stitches on a cable needle in front of work, knit 4 stitches, then knit the 4 stitches from the cable needle

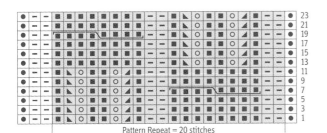

Pattern Repeat = 20 stitches

Only RS rows are shown; in WS rows, knit the knits, and purl the purls and the yarn overs. Begin with the selv st before the pattern repeat, rep the marked pattern repeat (20 sts wide) widthwise continuously, and end with the stitches after the pattern repeat. Repeat Rows 1–24 heightwise.

## 160 LACE PATTERN WITH DOUBLE CABLE [multiple of 11 + 7 sts + 2 selv sts]

Only RS rows are shown; in WS rows, purl all stitches and yarn overs. Begin with the sts before the pattern repeat, rep the marked pattern repeat (11 sts wide) widthwise continuously, and end with the sts after the pattern repeat. Repeat Rows 1–8 heightwise.

### Stitch Key

● = 1 selvedge stitch

■ = Knit 1 stitch

O = Make 1 yarn over

◢ = Knit 2 stitches together

◤ = Knit 2 stitches together left-leaning with passing over (skp): slip 1 stitch knitwise, knit the next stitch, and pass the slipped stitch over

△ = Double left-leaning decrease with passing over (sk2p): slip 1 stitch knitwise, knit 2 stitches together, pass the slipped stitch over

▨▨▨/▨▨▨ = Hold 3 stitches on a cable needle behind work, knit 3 stitches, then knit the 3 stitches from the cable needle

Pattern Repeat = 11 stitches

## 161 LACE PATTERN WITH TRIPLE CABLE [multiple of 18 + 3 sts + 2 selv sts]

### Stitch Key

● = 1 selvedge stitch

■ = Knit 1 stitch

O = Make 1 yarn over

◢ = Knit 2 stitches together

◤ = Knit 2 stitches together left-leaning with passing over (skp): slip 1 stitch knitwise, knit the next stitch, and pass the slipped stitch over

▨▨▨/▨▨▨ = Hold 3 stitches on a cable needle behind work, knit 3 stitches, then knit the 3 stitches from the cable needle

▨▨▨\▨▨▨ = Hold 3 stitches on a cable needle in front of work, knit 3 stitches, then knit the 3 stitches from the cable needle

Only RS rows are shown; in WS rows, purl all stitches and yarn overs. Begin with the sts before the pattern repeat, rep the marked pattern repeat (18 sts wide) widthwise continuously, and end with the sts after the pattern repeat. Repeat Rows 1–8 heightwise.

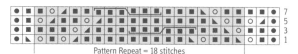

Pattern Repeat = 18 stitches

## 162 CABLE-AND-EYELET PATTERN

[multiple of 8 + 2 sts + 2 selv sts]

Only RS rows are shown; in WS rows, purl all stitches and yarn overs. Begin with the sts before the pattern repeat, rep the marked pattern repeat (8 sts wide) widthwise continuously, and end with the sts after the pattern repeat. Repeat Rows 1–8 heightwise.

### Stitch Key

● = 1 selvedge stitch

■ = Knit 1 stitch

○ = Make 1 yarn over

◢ = Knit 2 stitches together

◥ = Knit 2 stitches together left-leaning with passing over (skp): slip 1 stitch knitwise, knit the next stitch, and pass the slipped stitch over

= Hold 3 stitches on a cable needle in front of work, knit 3 stitches, then knit the 3 stitches from the cable needle

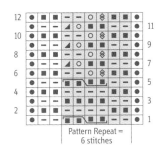

Pattern Repeat = 8 stitches

## 163 SMALL LACE CABLES

[multiple of 6 + 2 sts + 2 selv sts]

Shown are both RS and WS rows. Begin with the selv st before the pattern repeat, rep the marked pattern repeat (6 sts wide) widthwise continuously, and end with the sts after the pattern repeat. Repeat Rows 1–12 heightwise.

Pattern Repeat = 6 stitches

### Stitch Key

● = 1 selvedge stitch

■ = Knit 1 stitch

− = Purl 1 stitch

○ = Make 1 yarn over

◢ = Knit 2 stitches together

◈ = Purl 2 sts together left-leaning (ssp)

= Hold 2 stitches on a cable needle in front of work, knit 2 stitches, then knit the 2 stitches from the cable needle

## 164 STAGGERED SMALL LACE CABLES [multiple of 12 + 2 sts + 2 selv sts]

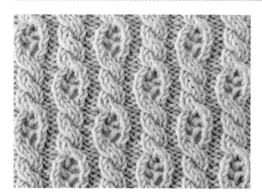

Pattern Repeat = 12 stitches

### Stitch Key

● = 1 selvedge stitch

■ = Knit 1 stitch

– = Purl 1 stitch

○ = Make 1 yarn over

◢ = Knit 2 stitches together

⊗ = Purl 2 stitches together left-leaning (ssp)

⊞⊞⊞⊞ = Hold 2 stitches on a cable needle in front of work, knit 2 stitches, then knit the 2 stitches from the cable needle

Shown are both RS and WS rows. Begin with the selv st before the pattern repeat, rep the marked pattern repeat (12 sts wide) widthwise continuously, and end with the sts after the pattern repeat. Repeat Rows 1–16 heightwise.

## 165 CABLE-FILLED LOZENGES [multiple of 12 + 1 st + 2 selv sts]

Only RS rows are shown; in WS rows, purl all stitches and yarn overs. Begin with the sts before the pattern repeat, rep the marked pattern repeat (12 sts wide) widthwise continuously, and end with the sts after the pattern repeat. Repeat Rows 1–20 heightwise.

Pattern Repeat = 12 stitches

### Stitch Key

● = 1 selvedge stitch

■ = Knit 1 stitch

○ = Make 1 yarn over

◢ = Knit 2 stitches together

◥ = Knit 2 stitches together left-leaning with passing over (skp): slip 1 stitch knitwise, knit the next stitch, and pass the slipped stitch over

△ = Double left-leaning decrease with passing over (sk2p): slip 1 stitch knitwise, knit 2 stitches together, pass the slipped stitch over

⊞⊞⊞⊞⊞ = Hold 3 stitches on a cable needle in front of work, knit 4 stitches, then knit the 3 stitches from the cable needle

⊞⊞⊞⊞⊞ = Hold 4 stitches on a cable needle behind work, knit 3 stitches, then knit the 4 stitches from the cable needle

## 166 LARGE STAGGERED EYELET CABLES [multiple of 20 + 2 sts + 2 selv sts]

### Stitch Key

● = 1 selvedge stitch

■ = Knit 1 stitch

– = Purl 1 stitch

○ = Make 1 yarn over

◢ = Knit 2 stitches together

▬▬▬▬▬ = Hold 4 stitches on a cable needle in front of work, knit 4 stitches, then knit the 4 stitches from the cable needle

Only RS rows are shown; in WS rows, knit the knits, and purl the purls and yarn overs. Begin with the selv st before the pattern repeat, rep the marked pattern repeat (20 sts wide) widthwise continuously, and end with the sts after the pattern repeat. Repeat Rows 1–32 heightwise.

Pattern Repeat = 20 stitches

## 167 BIAS CABLE-AND-EYELET PATTERN COLUMNS

[multiple of 36 + 10 sts + 2 selv sts]

Only RS rows are shown; in WS rows, knit the knits, and purl the purls and yarn overs. Begin with the selv st before the pattern repeat, rep the marked pattern repeat (36 sts wide) either once for a single vertical pattern column or continuously for an all-over pattern, and end with the sts after the pattern repeat. Repeat Rows 1–6 heightwise.

### Stitch Key

● = 1 selvedge stitch

■ = Knit 1 stitch

– = Purl 1 stitch

○ = Make 1 yarn over

◢ = Knit 2 stitches together

◣ = Knit 2 stitches together left-leaning with passing over (skp): slip 1 stitch knitwise, knit the next stitch, and pass the slipped stitch over

▬▬▬▬ = Hold 3 stitches on a cable needle in front of work, knit 3 stitches, then knit the 3 stitches from the cable needle

Pattern Repeat = 36 stitches

## 168 ALL-OVER LACE-AND-CABLE PATTERN

[multiple of 12 + 2 sts + 2 selv sts]

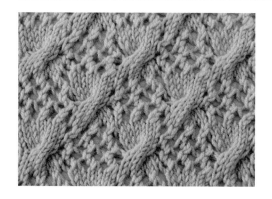

Only RS rows are shown; in WS rows, purl all stitches and yarn overs. Begin with the sts before the pattern repeat, rep the marked pattern repeat (12 sts wide) widthwise continuously, and end with the sts after the pattern repeat. Repeat Rows 1–20 heightwise.

### Stitch Key

● = 1 selvedge stitch

■ = Knit 1 stitch

○ = Make 1 yarn over

◢ = Knit 2 stitches together

= Hold 3 stitches on a cable needle behind work, knit 3 stitches, then knit the 3 stitches from the cable needle

Pattern Repeat =12 stitches

## 169 ALL-OVER CABLE-AND-DIAMOND PATTERN

[multiple of 22 + 11 st + 2 selv sts]

Only RS rows are shown; in WS rows, knit the knits, and purl the purls and yarn overs. Begin with the selv st before the pattern repeat, rep the marked pattern repeat (22 sts wide) widthwise continuously, and end with the sts after the pattern repeat. Repeat Rows 1–24 heightwise.

### Stitch Key

● = 1 selvedge stitch

■ = Knit 1 stitch

− = Purl 1 stitch

○ = Make 1 yarn over

◢ = Knit 2 stitches together

◣ = Knit 2 stitches together left-leaning with passing over (skp): slip 1 stitch knitwise, knit the next stitch, and pass the slipped stitch over

◿ = Purl 2 stitches together

◺ = Purl 2 stitches together left-leaning (ssp): slip 2 stitches individually knitwise, return them to the left needle, then purl them together through the back loop

▲ = Knit 3 stitches together

= Hold 2 stitches on a cable needle behind work, knit 2 stitches, then knit the 2 stitches from the cable needle

= Hold 2 stitches on a cable needle in front of work, knit 2 stitches, then knit the 2 stitches from the cable needle

Pattern Repeat = 22 stitches

## 170 SMALL DECORATIVE CABLES

[multiple of 8 + 2 sts + 2 selv sts]

Only RS rows are shown; in WS rows, knit the knits, and purl the purls and yarn overs. Begin with the selv st before the pattern repeat, rep the marked pattern repeat (8 sts wide) widthwise either once for a single vertical pattern column or continuously for an all-over pattern, and end with the sts after the pattern repeat. Repeat Rows 1–12 heightwise.

### Stitch Key

⬤ = 1 selvedge stitch

■ = Knit 1 stitch

– = Purl 1 stitch

○ = Make 1 yarn over

◢ = Knit 2 stitches together

◣ = Knit 2 stitches together left-leaning with passing over (skp): slip 1 stitch knitwise, knit the next stitch, and pass the slipped stitch over

= Hold 1 stitch on a cable needle in front of work, knit the next stitch, then knit the stitch from the cable needle

= Hold 1 stitch on a cable needle in front of work, knit 2 stitches, then knit the stitch from the cable needle

= Hold 2 stitches on a cable needle behind work, knit the next stitch, then knit the 2 stitches from the cable needle

Pattern Repeat = 8 stitches

## 171 STAGGERED LACE-AND-CABLE PATTERN

[multiple of 8 + 5 sts + 2 selv sts]

Only RS rows are shown; in WS rows, purl all stitches and yarn overs. Begin with the sts before the pattern repeat, rep the marked pattern repeat (8 sts wide) widthwise continuously, and end with the sts after the pattern repeat. Repeat Rows 1–24 heightwise.

### Stitch Key

⬤ = 1 selvedge stitch

■ = Knit 1 stitch

○ = Make 1 yarn over

⋂ = Knit 3 stitches together with center stitch on top (cdd): slip 2 stitches together knitwise, knit the next stitch, and pass the slipped stitches over

= Hold 3 stitches on a cable needle in front of work, knit 2 stitches, then knit the 3 stitches from the cable needle

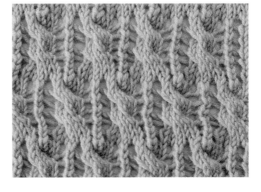

Pattern Repeat = 8 stitches

## 172 SMALL CABLED BUTTERFLIES
[multiple of 22 + 3 sts + 2 selv sts]

### Stitch Key

● = 1 selvedge stitch

■ = Knit 1 stitch

○ = Make 1 yarn over

◢ = Knit 2 stitches together

◣ = Knit 2 stitches together left-leaning with passing over (skp): slip 1 stitch knitwise, knit the next stitch, and pass the slipped stitch over

∩ = Knit 3 stitches together with center stitch on top (cdd): slip 2 stitches together knitwise, knit the next stitch, and pass the slipped stitches over

= Hold 3 stitches on a cable needle behind work, knit 4 stitches, then knit the 3 stitches from the cable needle

Only RS rows are shown; in WS rows, purl all stitches and yarn overs. Begin with the sts before the pattern repeat, rep the marked pattern repeat (22 sts wide) widthwise continuously, and end with the sts after the pattern repeat. Repeat Rows 1–20 heightwise.

Pattern Repeat = 22 stitches

## 173 OPENWORK CABLE-AND-DIAMOND PATTERN
[multiple of 12 + 1 st + 2 selv sts]

Only RS rows are shown; in WS rows, knit the knits, and purl the purls and yarn overs. Begin with the sts before the pattern repeat, rep the marked pattern repeat (12 sts wide) widthwise continuously, and end with the sts after the pattern repeat. Repeat Rows 1–28 heightwise.

Pattern Repeat = 12 stitches

### Stitch Key

● = 1 selvedge stitch

■ = Knit 1 stitch

— = Purl 1 stitch

○ = Make 1 yarn over

◢ = Knit 2 stitches together

◣ = Knit 2 stitches together left-leaning with passing over (skp): slip 1 stitch knitwise, knit the next stitch, and pass the slipped stitch over

◿ = Purl 2 stitches together

◺ = Purl 2 stitches together left-leaning (ssp): slip 2 stitches individually knitwise, return them to the left needle, then purl them together through the back loop

△ = Double left-leaning decrease with passing over (sk2p): slip 1 stitch knitwise, knit 2 stitches together, pass the slipped stitch over

= Hold 3 stitches on a cable needle in front of work, knit 2 stitches, then knit the 3 stitches from the cable needle

# 174 OPENWORK CABLE PATTERN [multiple of 12 + 4 sts + 2 selv sts]

Only RS rows are shown; in WS rows, knit the knits, and purl the purls and yarn overs. Begin with the selv st before the pattern repeat, rep the marked pattern repeat (12 sts wide) widthwise either once for a single vertical pattern column or continuously for an all-over pattern, and end with the sts after the pattern repeat. Repeat Rows 1–20 heightwise.

### Stitch Key

| ● | = 1 selvedge stitch |
| ■ | = Knit 1 stitch |
| – | = Purl 1 stitch |
| ○ | = Make 1 yarn over |
| ◢ | = Knit 2 stitches together |
| ◣ | = Knit 2 stitches together left-leaning with passing over (skp): slip 1 stitch knitwise, knit the next stitch, and pass the slipped stitch over |

= Hold 4 stitches on a cable needle in front of work, knit 4 stitches, then knit the 4 stitches from the cable needle

Pattern Repeat = 12 stitches

# 175 LACE-AND-CABLE COLUMNS [multiple of 7 + 4 sts + 2 selv sts]

Only RS rows are shown; in WS rows, purl all stitches and yarn overs. Begin with the selv st before the pattern repeat, rep the marked pattern repeat (7 sts wide) widthwise continuously, and end with the sts after the pattern repeat. Repeat Rows 1–4 heightwise.

### Stitch Key

| ● | = 1 selvedge stitch |
| ■ | = Knit 1 stitch |
| ○ | = Make 1 yarn over |
| ∩ | = Knit 3 stitches together with center stitch on top (cdd): slip 2 stitches together knitwise, knit the next stitch, and pass the slipped stitches over |

= Hold 2 stitches on a cable needle in front of work, knit 2 stitches, then knit the 2 stitches from the cable needle

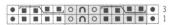

Pattern Repeat = 7 stitches

## 176 CABLE-AND-ZIGZAG PATTERN

[multiple of 10 + 4 sts + 2 selv sts]

Only RS rows are shown; in WS rows, knit the knits, and purl the purls and yarn overs. Begin with the sts before the pattern repeat, rep the marked pattern repeat (10 sts wide) widthwise continuously, and end with the sts after the pattern repeat. Repeat Rows 1–24 heightwise.

Pattern Repeat = 10 stitches

### Stitch Key

● = 1 selvedge stitch

■ = Knit 1 stitch

− = Purl 1 stitch

○ = Make 1 yarn over

◢ = Knit 2 stitches together

◣ = Knit 2 stitches together left-leaning with passing over (skp): slip 1 stitch knitwise, knit the next stitch, and pass the slipped stitch over

= Hold 2 stitches on a cable needle in front of work, knit 2 stitches, then knit the 2 stitches from the cable needle

## 177 CABLE-AND-DIAMOND BORDER

[multiple of 17 + 6 sts + 2 selv sts]

Only RS rows are shown; in WS rows, knit the knits, and purl the purls and yarn overs. Begin with the selv st before the pattern repeat, rep the marked pattern repeat (17 sts wide) widthwise either once for a single vertical pattern column or continuously for an all-over pattern, and end with the sts after the pattern repeat. Repeat Rows 1–12 heightwise.

Pattern Repeat = 17 stitches

### Stitch Key

● = 1 selvedge stitch

■ = Knit 1 stitch

− = Purl 1 stitch

○ = Make 1 yarn over

◢ = Knit 2 stitches together

◣ = Knit 2 stitches together left-leaning with passing over (skp): slip 1 stitch knitwise, knit the next stitch, and pass the slipped stitch over

△ = Double left-leaning decrease with passing over (sk2p): slip 1 stitch knitwise, knit 2 stitches together, pass the slipped stitch over

= Hold 2 stitches on a cable needle in front of work, knit 2 stitches, then knit the 2 stitches from the cable needle

## 178 VERTICAL CABLE-AND-ZIGZAG PATTERN [multiple of 8 + 2 sts + 2 selv sts]

Only RS rows are shown; in WS rows, purl all stitches and yarn overs. Begin with the sts before the pattern repeat, rep the marked pattern repeat (8 sts wide) widthwise continuously, and end with the sts after the pattern repeat. Repeat Rows 1–16 heightwise.

### Stitch Key

● = 1 selvedge stitch

■ = Knit 1 stitch

○ = Make 1 yarn over

◢ = Knit 2 stitches together

◤ = Knit 2 stitches together left-leaning with passing over (skp): slip 1 stitch knitwise, knit the next stitch, and pass the slipped stitch over

▣▣◢▣ = Hold 2 stitches on a cable needle behind work, knit 2 stitches, then knit the 2 stitches from the cable needle

▣▣◤▣ = Hold 2 stitches on a cable needle in front of work, knit 2 stitches, then knit the 2 stitches from the cable needle

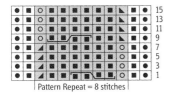

Pattern Repeat = 8 stitches

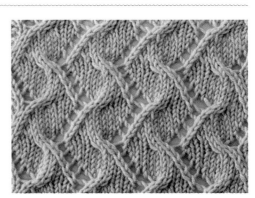

## 179 VERTICAL LACE-AND-CABLE WAVES [multiple of 10 + 3 sts + 2 selv sts]

### Stitch Key

● = 1 selvedge stitch

■ = Knit 1 stitch

○ = Make 1 yarn over

∩ = Knit 3 stitches together with center stitch on top (cdd): slip 2 stitches together knitwise, knit the next stitch, and pass the slipped stitches over

▣▣◤▣ = Hold 2 stitches on a cable needle in front of work, knit the next stitch, then knit the 2 stitches from the cable needle

Only RS rows are shown; in WS rows, purl all stitches and yarn overs. Begin with the selv st before the pattern repeat, rep the marked pattern repeat (10 sts wide) widthwise continuously, and end with the sts after the pattern repeat. Repeat Rows 1–16 heightwise.

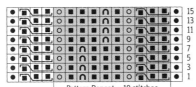

Pattern Repeat = 10 stitches

## 180 ZIGZAG EYELET-AND-CABLE PATTERN BORDER

[multiple of 34 + 24 sts + 2 selv sts]

**❯ Chart on page 322**

Only RS rows are shown; in WS rows, knit the knits, and purl the purls and yarn overs. Begin with the sts before the pattern repeat, repeat the pattern repeat (34 sts wide) continuously, and end with the sts after the pattern repeat. Alternatively, work the first 19 sts, and the last 7 sts (= 26 sts) as a separate border. Repeat Rows 1–16 heightwise.

## 181 EYELET-AND-CABLE PATTERN LOZENGES [multiple of 16 + 1 st + 2 selv sts]

Only RS rows are shown; in WS rows, knit the knits, and purl the purls and yarn overs. Begin with the sts before the pattern repeat, rep the marked pattern repeat (16 sts wide) widthwise continuously, and end with the sts after the pattern repeat. Repeat Rows 1–36 heightwise.

### Stitch Key

⬤ = 1 selvedge stitch

■ = Knit 1 stitch

– = Purl 1 stitch

○ = Make 1 yarn over

◢ = Knit 2 stitches together

◣ = Knit 2 stitches together left-leaning with passing over (skp): slip 1 stitch knitwise, knit the next stitch, and pass the slipped stitch over

◿ = Purl 2 stitches together

▲ = Double left-leaning decrease with passing over (sk2p): slip 1 stitch knitwise, knit 2 stitches together, pass the slipped stitch over

⬛⬛╱⬛⬛ = Hold 2 stitches on a cable needle behind work, knit 2 stitches, then knit the 2 stitches from the cable needle

⬛⬛╲⬛⬛ = Hold 2 stitches on a cable needle in front of work, knit 2 stitches, then knit the 2 stitches from the cable needle

Pattern Repeat = 16 stitches

## 182 ZIGZAG EYELET-AND-CABLE PATTERN [multiple of 16 + 1 st + 2 selv sts]

Only RS rows are shown; in WS rows, knit the knits, and purl the purls and yarn overs. Begin with the selv st before the pattern repeat, rep the marked pattern repeat (16 sts wide) widthwise continuously, and end with the sts after the pattern repeat. Repeat Rows 1–18 heightwise.

### Stitch Key

● = 1 selvedge stitch

■ = Knit 1 stitch

− = Purl 1 stitch

○ = Make 1 yarn over

◢ = Knit 2 stitches together

◣ = Knit 2 stitches together left-leaning with passing over (skp): slip 1 stitch knitwise, knit the next stitch, and pass the slipped stitch over

◿ = Purl 2 stitches together

△ = Purl 3 stitches together

■■◢ = Hold 1 stitch on a cable needle behind work, knit 2 stitches, then knit the stitch from the cable needle

◥■■■ = Hold 2 stitches on a cable needle in front of work, knit the next stitch, then knit the 2 stitches from the cable needle

Pattern Repeat = 16 stitches

## 183 LACE PATTERN WITH CENTER CABLE [multiple of 18 + 2 selv sts]

Only RS rows are shown; in WS rows, knit the knits, and purl the purls and yarn overs. Begin with the selv st before the pattern repeat, rep the marked pattern repeat (18 sts wide) widthwise either once for a single vertical pattern column or continuously for an all-over pattern, and end with the selv st after the pattern repeat. Repeat Rows 1–8 heightwise.

### Stitch Key

● = 1 selvedge stitch

■ = Knit 1 stitch

− = Purl 1 stitch

○ = Make 1 yarn over

◢ = Knit 2 stitches together

◣ = Knit 2 stitches together left-leaning with passing over (skp): slip 1 stitch knitwise, knit the next stitch, and pass the slipped stitch over

■■◥■■ = Hold 2 stitches on a cable needle in front of work, knit 2 stitches, then knit the 2 stitches from the cable needle

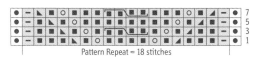

Pattern Repeat = 18 stitches

## 184 LACE-AND-CABLE COLUMNS [multiple of 12 + 4 sts + 2 selv sts]

Only RS rows are shown; in WS rows, knit the knits, and purl the purls and single yarn overs, work (purl 1, purl 1 through the back loop) into the double yarn overs. Begin with the selv st before the pattern repeat, rep the marked pattern repeat (12 sts wide) widthwise either once for a single vertical pattern column or continuously for an all-over pattern, and end with the sts after the pattern repeat. Repeat Rows 1—10 heightwise.

Pattern Repeat = 12 stitches

### Stitch Key

● = 1 selvedge stitch

■ = Knit 1 stitch

– = Purl 1 stitch

○ = Make 1 yarn over

◢ = Knit 2 stitches together

◣ = Knit 2 stitches together left-leaning with passing over (skp): slip 1 stitch knitwise, knit the next stitch, and pass the slipped stitch over

⬚/⬚ = Hold 1 stitch on a cable needle behind work, knit the next stitch, then knit the stitch from the cable needle

⬚⬚⬚⬚⬚⬚ = Hold 3 stitches on a cable needle in front of work, knit 3 stitches, then knit the 3 stitches from the cable needle

## 185 LACE BORDER WITH DOUBLE CABLES [multiple of 23 + 2 selv sts]

Only RS rows are shown; in WS rows, knit the knits, and purl the purls and yarn overs. Begin with the selv st before the pattern repeat, rep the marked pattern repeat (23 sts wide) widthwise continuously, and end with the selv st after the pattern repeat. Repeat Rows 1—8 heightwise.

Pattern Repeat = 23 stitches

### Stitch Key

● = 1 selvedge stitch

■ = Knit 1 stitch

○ = Make 1 yarn over

◢ = Knit 2 stitches together

◣ = Knit 2 stitches together left-leaning with passing over (skp): slip 1 stitch knitwise, knit the next stitch, and pass the slipped stitch over

◿ = Purl 2 stitches together

⬚⬚/⬚⬚ = Hold 2 stitches on a cable needle behind work, knit 2 stitches, then knit the 2 stitches from the cable needle

⬚⬚⬚⬚ = Hold 2 stitches on a cable needle in front of work, knit 2 stitches, then knit the 2 stitches from the cable needle

## 186 TEXTURED EYELET-AND-CABLE PATTERN
[multiple of 14 + 5 sts + 2 selv sts]

Only RS rows are shown; in WS rows, knit the knits, and purl the purls and yarn overs. Begin with the selv st before the pattern repeat, rep the marked pattern repeat (14 sts wide) widthwise either once for a single vertical pattern column or continuously for an all-over pattern, and end with the sts after the pattern repeat. Repeat Rows 1–24 heightwise.

### Stitch Key

● = 1 selvedge stitch

■ = Knit 1 stitch

– = Purl 1 stitch

O = Make 1 yarn over

◢ = Knit 2 stitches together

◣ = Knit 2 stitches together left-leaning with passing over (skp): slip 1 stitch knitwise, knit the next stitch, and pass the slipped stitch over

▐◣■■▐ = Hold 2 stitches on a cable needle in front of work, knit the next stitch, then knit the 2 stitches from the cable needle

Pattern Repeat = 14 stitches

## 187 FANNING-OUT CABLE PATTERN
[multiple of 36 + 2 selv sts]

Only RS rows are shown; in WS rows, knit the knits, and purl the purls and yarn overs. Begin with the selv st before the pattern repeat, rep the marked pattern repeat (36 sts wide) widthwise continuously, and end with the selv st after the pattern repeat. Repeat Rows 1–28 heightwise.

### Stitch Key

● = 1 selvedge stitch

■ = Knit 1 stitch

– = Purl 1 stitch

O = Make 1 yarn over

◢ = Knit 2 stitches together

◣ = Knit 2 stitches together left-leaning with passing over (skp): slip 1 stitch knitwise, knit the next stitch, and pass the slipped stitch over

■■■■■◣■■■■■ = Hold 5 stitches on a cable needle in front of work, knit 5 stitches, then knit the 5 stitches from the cable needle

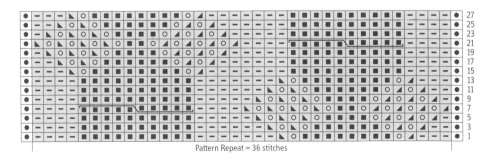

Pattern Repeat = 36 stitches

## 188 LACE-AND-CABLE PATTERN COMBINATION [multiple of 15 + 6 sts + 2 selv sts]

Only RS rows are shown; in WS rows, knit the knits, and purl the purls and yarn overs. Begin with the selv st before the pattern repeat, rep the marked pattern repeat (15 sts wide) widthwise either once for a single vertical pattern column or continuously for an all-over pattern, and end with the sts after the pattern repeat. Repeat Rows 1–4 heightwise.

### Stitch Key

● = 1 selvedge stitch

■ = Knit 1 stitch

– = Purl 1 stitch

○ = Make 1 yarn over

∩ = Knit 3 stitches together with center stitch on top (cdd): slip 2 stitches together knitwise, knit the next stitch, and pass the slipped stitches over

= Hold 1 stitch on a cable needle behind work, knit the next stitch, then knit the stitch from the cable needle

= Hold 1 stitch on a cable needle in front of work, knit the next stitch, then knit the stitch from the cable needle

Pattern Repeat = 15 stitches

## 189 LACE-AND-CABLE PATTERN ORNAMENTS [multiple of 18 + 2 selv sts]

Only RS rows are shown; in WS rows, knit the knits, and purl the purls and single yarn overs, work (purl 1, purl 1 through the back loop) into the double yarn overs. Begin with the sts before the pattern repeat, rep the marked pattern repeat (18 sts wide) widthwise continuously, and end with the sts after the pattern repeat. Repeat Rows 1–20 heightwise.

### Stitch Key

● = 1 selvedge stitch

■ = Knit 1 stitch

– = Purl 1 stitch

○ = Make 1 yarn over

◢ = Knit 2 stitches together

◣ = Knit 2 stitches together left-leaning with passing over (skp): slip 1 stitch knitwise, knit the next stitch, and pass the slipped stitch over

= Hold 2 stitches on a cable needle in front of work, knit 2 stitches, then knit the 2 stitches from the cable needle

Pattern Repeat = 18 stitches

# 190 LACE-AND-CABLE PATTERN OVALS [multiple of 18 + 1 st + 2 selv sts]

Only RS rows are shown; in WS rows, knit the knits, and purl the purls and single yarn overs, work (purl 1, purl 1 through the back loop) into the double yarn overs. Begin with the selv st before the pattern repeat, rep the marked pattern repeat (18 sts wide) widthwise continuously, and end with the sts after the pattern repeat. Repeat Rows 1–16 heightwise.

Pattern Repeat = 18 stitches

## Stitch Key

● = 1 selvedge stitch

■ = Knit 1 stitch

– = Purl 1 stitch

○ = Make 1 yarn over

◢ = Knit 2 stitches together

◤ = Knit 2 stitches together left-leaning with passing over (skp): slip 1 stitch knitwise, knit the next stitch, and pass the slipped stitch over

▨⁄–◤◇◇◢–▨ = Hold 1 stitch on a cable needle in front of work, hold 6 stitches on a second cable needle behind work, and knit 1 stitch. Then work the 6 stitches from the second cable needle as (purl 1 stitch, knit 2 stitches together, make 2 yarn overs, knit 2 stitches together with passing over, and purl 1 stitch). After this, knit the stitch from the first cable needle.

# LACE
# PATTERNS

# DROPPED-
# STITCH
# PATTERNS

# **Lace** Patterns

## 191 MESH PATTERN

[multiple of 2 + 3 sts + 2 selv sts]

Only RS rows are shown; in WS rows, knit all stitches and yarn overs. Begin with the sts before the pattern repeat, rep the marked pattern repeat (2 sts wide) widthwise continuously, and end with the sts after the pattern repeat. Repeat Rows 1–8 heightwise.

**Stitch Key**

- = 1 selvedge stitch
- = Knit 1 stitch
- = Make 1 yarn over
- = Knit 2 stitches together

Pattern Repeat = 2 stitches

## 192 BROAD EYELET COLUMNS

[multiple of 8 + 2 selv sts]

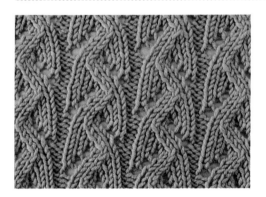

Only RS rows are shown; in WS rows, knit the knits, and purl the purls and yarn overs. Begin with the selv st before the pattern repeat, rep the marked pattern repeat (8 sts wide) widthwise continuously, and end with the selv st after the pattern repeat. Repeat Rows 1–12 heightwise.

**Stitch Key**

- = 1 selvedge stitch
- = Knit 1 stitch
- = Purl 1 stitch
- = Make 1 yarn over
- = Knit 2 stitches together
- = Knit 2 stitches together left-leaning with passing over (skp): slip 1 stitch knitwise, knit the next stitch, and pass the slipped stitch over

Pattern Repeat = 8 stitches

## 193 SMALL VINE PATTERN

[multiple of 12 + 1 st + 2 selv sts]

Only RS rows are shown; in WS rows, knit the knits, and purl the purls and yarn overs. Begin with the selv st before the pattern repeat, rep the marked pattern repeat (12 sts wide) widthwise continuously, and end with the sts after the pattern repeat. Repeat Rows 1–8 heightwise.

**Stitch Key**

- = 1 selvedge stitch
- = Knit 1 stitch
- = Purl 1 stitch
- = Make 1 yarn over
- = Knit 2 stitches together
- = Knit 2 stitches together left-leaning with passing over (skp): slip 1 stitch knitwise, knit the next stitch, and pass the slipped stitch over

Pattern Repeat = 12 stitches

## 194 VERTICAL EYELET PATTERN

[multiple of 4 + 1 st + 2 selv sts]

Only RS rows are shown; in WS rows, purl all stitches and yarn overs. Begin with the selv st before the pattern repeat, rep the marked pattern repeat (4 sts wide) width-wise continuously, and end with the sts after the pattern repeat. Repeat Rows 1–8 heightwise.

### Stitch Key

- ● = 1 selvedge stitch
- ■ = Knit 1 stitch
- ○ = Make 1 yarn over
- ◢ = Knit 2 stitches together
- ◣ = Knit 2 stitches together left-leaning with passing over (skp): slip 1 stitch knitwise, knit the next stitch, and pass the slipped stitch over

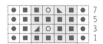

Pattern Repeat = 4 stitches

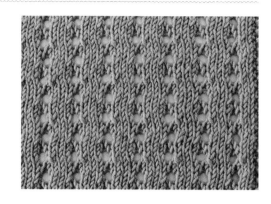

## 195 BROAD EYELET COLUMNS

[multiple of 11 + 1 st + 2 selv sts]

Only RS rows are shown; in WS rows, purl all stitches and yarn overs. Begin with the selv st before the pattern repeat, rep the marked pattern repeat (11 sts wide) width-wise continuously, and end with the sts after the pattern repeat. Repeat Rows 1 and 2 heightwise.

### Stitch Key

- ● = 1 selvedge stitch
- ■ = Knit 1 stitch
- ○ = Make 1 yarn over
- ◢ = Knit 2 stitches together
- ◣ = Knit 2 stitches together left-leaning with passing over (skp): slip 1 stitch knitwise, knit the next stitch, and pass the slipped stitch over

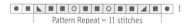

Pattern Repeat = 11 stitches

## 196 VERTICAL EYELET COLUMNS

[multiple of 5 + 2 selv sts]

Only RS rows are shown; in WS rows, purl all stitches and yarn overs. Begin with the selv st before the pattern repeat, rep the marked pattern repeat (5 sts wide) width-wise continuously, and end with the selv st after the pattern repeat. Repeat Rows 1 and 2 heightwise.

### Stitch Key

- ● = 1 selvedge stitch
- ■ = Knit 1 stitch
- ○ = Make 1 yarn over
- ◢ = Knit 2 stitches together
- ◣ = Knit 2 stitches together left-leaning with passing over (skp): slip 1 stitch knitwise, knit the next stitch, and pass the slipped stitch over

Pattern Repeat = 5 stitches

## 197 EYELET PATTERN WITH PASSED-OVER STITCHES

[multiple of 3 + 2 selv sts]

Only RS rows are shown; in WS rows, purl all stitches and yarn overs. Begin with the selv st before the pattern repeat, rep the marked pattern repeat (3 sts wide) width-wise continuously, and end with the selv st after the pattern repeat. Repeat Rows 1–4 heightwise.

Pattern Repeat = 3 stitches

**Stitch Key**

● = 1 selvedge stitch

■ = Knit 1 stitch

O = Make 1 yarn over

■■■ = Knit 3 stitches, and pass the first stitch over the two following stitches

## 198 EASY MESH PATTERN

[multiple of 2 + 2 selv sts]

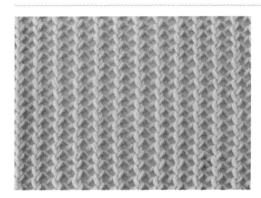

Shown are both RS and WS rows. Begin with the selv st before the pattern repeat, rep the marked pattern repeat (2 sts wide) width-wise continuously, and end with the selv st after the pattern repeat. Repeat Rows 1 and 2 heightwise.

Pattern Repeat = 2 stitches

**Stitch Key**

● = 1 selvedge stitch

O = Make 1 yarn over

◿ = Purl 2 stitches together

◣ = Knit 2 stitches together left-leaning with passing over (skp): slip 1 stitch knitwise, knit the next stitch, and pass the slipped stitch over

## 199 ENGLISH EYELET PATTERN

[multiple of 2 + 2 selv sts]

Shown are both RS and WS rows. Begin with the selv st before the pattern repeat, rep the marked pattern repeat (2 sts wide) width-wise continuously, and end with the selv st after the pattern repeat. Repeat Rows 1–4 heightwise.

Pattern Repeat = 2 stitches

**Stitch Key**

● = 1 selvedge stitch

– = Purl 1 stitch

O = Make 1 yarn over

◣ = Knit 2 stitches together left-leaning with passing over (skp): slip 1 stitch knitwise, knit the next stitch, and pass the slipped stitch over

## 200 EYELET-AND-LATTICE PATTERN

[multiple of 7 + 2 selv sts]

Shown are both RS and WS rows. Begin with the selv st before the pattern repeat, rep the marked pattern repeat (7 sts wide) widthwise continuously, and end with the selv st after the pattern repeat. Repeat Rows 1–8 heightwise.

### Stitch Key

⬤ = 1 selvedge stitch

◼ = Knit 1 stitch

− = Purl 1 stitch

◯ = Make 1 yarn over

◢ = Knit 2 stitches together

◣ = Knit 2 stitches together left-leaning with passing over (skp): slip 1 stitch knitwise, knit the next stitch, and pass the slipped stitch over

◿ = Purl 2 stitches together

⧄ = Purl 2 stitches together left-leaning (ssp)

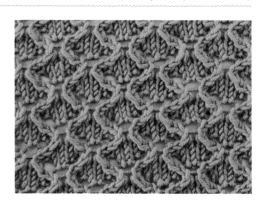

Pattern Repeat = 7 stitches

## 201 LACE PATTERN COLUMNS

[multiple of 12 + 5 sts + 2 selv sts]

Only RS rows are shown; in WS rows, purl all stitches and yarn overs. Begin with the selv st before the pattern repeat, rep the marked pattern repeat (12 sts wide) widthwise continuously, and end with the sts after the pattern repeat. Repeat Rows 1–6 heightwise.

### Stitch Key

⬤ = 1 selvedge stitch

◼ = Knit 1 stitch

◯ = Make 1 yarn over

◢ = Knit 2 stitches together

◣ = Knit 2 stitches together left-leaning with passing over (skp): slip 1 stitch knitwise, knit the next stitch, and pass the slipped stitch over

Pattern Repeat = 12 stitches

## 202 HORIZONTAL LACE PATTERN

[multiple of 2 + 2 selv sts]

Shown are both RS and WS rows. Begin with the selv st before the pattern repeat, rep the marked pattern repeat (2 sts wide) widthwise continuously, and end with the selv st after the pattern repeat. Repeat Rows 1–10 heightwise.

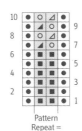

Pattern Repeat = 2 stitches

### Stitch Key

⬤ = 1 selvedge stitch

◼ = Knit 1 stitch

◯ = Make 1 yarn over

◢ = Knit 2 stitches together

◿ = Purl 2 stitches together

## 203 BELL PATTERN

[multiple of 5 + 2 sts + 2 selv sts]

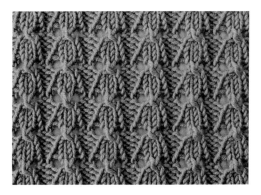

Only RS rows are shown; in WS rows, knit the knits, and purl the purls and yarn overs. Begin with the selv st before the pattern repeat, rep the marked pattern repeat (5 sts wide) widthwise continuously, and end with the sts after the pattern repeat. Repeat Rows 1–6 heightwise.

Pattern Repeat = 5 stitches

### Stitch Key

● = 1 selvedge stitch

■ = Knit 1 stitch

– = Purl 1 stitch

○ = Make 1 yarn over

▲ = Double left-leaning decrease with passing over (sk2p): slip 1 stitch knitwise, knit 2 stitches together, pass the slipped stitch over

## 204 SHIFTED BELLS

[multiple of 6 + 2 sts + 2 selv sts]

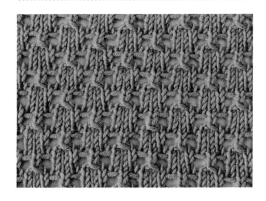

Only RS rows are shown; in WS rows, purl the stitches, and knit the yarn overs. Begin with the sts before the pattern repeat, rep the marked pattern repeat (6 sts wide) widthwise continuously, and end with the sts after the pattern repeat. Repeat Rows 1–8 heightwise.

Pattern Repeat = 6 stitches

### Stitch Key

● = 1 selvedge stitch

■ = Knit 1 stitch

○ = Make 1 yarn over

▲ = Double left-leaning decrease with passing over (sk2p): slip 1 stitch knitwise, knit 2 stitches together, pass the slipped stitch over

## 205 POINTED ARCHES

[multiple of 10 + 1 st + 2 selv sts]

Only RS rows are shown; in WS rows, purl all stitches and yarn overs. Begin with the selv st before the pattern repeat, rep the marked pattern repeat (10 sts wide) widthwise continuously, and end with the sts after the pattern repeat. Repeat Rows 1–8 heightwise.

Pattern Repeat = 10 stitches

### Stitch Key

● = 1 selvedge stitch

■ = Knit 1 stitch

○ = Make 1 yarn over

▲ = Double left-leaning decrease with passing over (sk2p): slip 1 stitch knitwise, knit 2 stitches together, pass the slipped stitch over

## 206 GROMMET PATTERN

[multiple of 6 + 2 selv sts]

Shown are both RS and WS rows. Begin with the selv st before the pattern repeat, rep the marked pattern repeat (6 sts wide) width-wise continuously, and end with the selv st after the pattern repeat. Repeat Rows 1–4 heightwise.

**Stitch Key**

● = 1 selvedge stitch

■ = Knit 1 stitch

− = Purl 1 stitch

○ = Make 1 yarn over

◿ = Purl 2 stitches together

☐ = No stitch, for better overview only

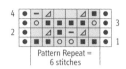

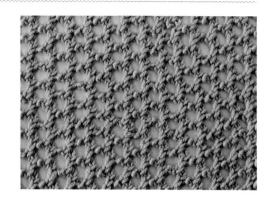

## 207 OPENWORK PATTERN

[multiple of 3 + 1 st + 2 selv sts]

Shown are both RS and WS rows. Begin with the selv st before the pattern repeat, rep the marked pattern repeat (3 sts wide) width-wise continuously, and end with the sts after the pattern repeat. Repeat Rows 1–4 heightwise.

**Stitch Key**

● = 1 selvedge stitch

■ = Knit 1 stitch

− = Purl 1 stitch

○ = Make 1 yarn over

◢ = Knit 2 stitches together

## 208 LACE-AND-RIBBING PATTERN

[multiple of 7 + 2 sts + 2 selv sts]

Only RS rows are shown; in WS rows, knit the knits, and purl the purls and yarn overs. Begin with the selv st before the pattern re-peat, rep the marked pattern repeat (7 sts wide) widthwise continu-ously, and end with the sts after the pattern repeat. Repeat Rows 1–4 heightwise.

**Stitch Key**

● = 1 selvedge stitch

■ = Knit 1 stitch

− = Purl 1 stitch

○ = Make 1 yarn over

◢ = Knit 2 stitches to-gether

◤ = Knit 2 stitches to-gether left-leaning with passing over (skp): slip 1 stitch knitwise, knit the next stitch, and pass the slipped stitch over

## 209 FILIGREE COLUMN PATTERN [multiple of 9 + 2 selv sts]

Only RS rows are shown; in WS rows, purl all stitches and yarn overs. Begin with the selv st before the pattern repeat, rep the marked pattern repeat (9 sts wide) widthwise continuously, and end with the selv st after the pattern repeat. Repeat Rows 1–8 heightwise.

Pattern Repeat = 9 stitches

### Stitch Key

● = 1 selvedge stitch

■ = Knit 1 stitch

○ = Make 1 yarn over

◢ = Knit 2 stitches together

◣ = Knit 2 stitches together left-leaning with passing over (skp): slip 1 stitch knitwise, knit the next stitch, and pass the slipped stitch over

## 210 COLUMNS WITH PASSED-OVER STITCHES [multiple of 3 + 2 selv sts]

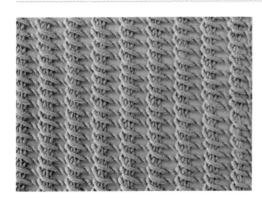

Only RS rows are shown; in WS rows, purl all stitches and yarn overs. Begin with the selv st before the pattern repeat, rep the marked pattern repeat (3 sts wide) widthwise continuously, and end with the selv st after the pattern repeat. Repeat Rows 1 and 2 heightwise.

Pattern Repeat = 3 stitches

### Stitch Key

● = 1 selvedge stitch

○ = Make 1 yarn over

▷▷ = Slip 1 stitch purlwise, knit 2 stitches, and pass the slipped stitch over

## 211 EYELET PATTERN WITH VERTICAL RIDGES [multiple of 4 + 2 selv sts]

Shown are both RS and WS rows. Begin with the selv st before the pattern repeat, rep the marked pattern repeat (4 sts wide) widthwise continuously, and end with the selv st after the pattern repeat. Repeat Rows 1 and 2 heightwise.

Pattern Repeat = 4 stitches

### Stitch Key

● = 1 selvedge stitch

■ = Knit 1 stitch

— = Purl 1 stitch

○ = Make 1 yarn over

◣ = Knit 2 stitches together left-leaning with passing over (skp): slip 1 stitch knitwise, knit the next stitch, and pass the slipped stitch over

◢ = Purl 2 stitches together

# BROKEN BOX PATTERN

[multiple of 2 + 2 selv sts]

In this stitch pattern, RS and WS rows are worked using two different needle sizes: RS on needle size 5.0 mm [US 8], and WS rows on needle size 2.0 mm [US 0].

Shown are both RS and WS rows. Begin with the selv st before the pattern repeat, rep the marked pattern repeat (2 sts wide) widthwise continuously, and end with the selv st after the pattern repeat. Repeat Rows 1 and 2 heightwise.

### Stitch Key

● = 1 selvedge stitch

■ = Knit 1 stitch

– = Purl 1 stitch

◆ = Knit 1 stitch through the back loop

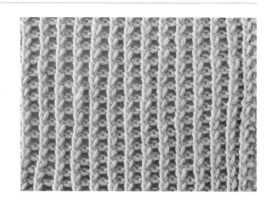

Pattern
Repeat =
2 stitches

# ALTERNATING SPIKES

[multiple of 10 + 2 selv sts]

Only RS rows are shown; in WS rows, purl all stitches and yarn overs. Begin with the selv st before the pattern repeat, rep the marked pattern repeat (10 sts wide) widthwise continuously, and end with the selv st after the pattern repeat. Repeat Rows 1–12 heightwise.

### Stitch Key

● = 1 selvedge stitch

■ = Knit 1 stitch

○ = Make 1 yarn over

◢ = Knit 2 stitches together

◣ = Knit 2 stitches together left-leaning with passing over (skp): slip 1 stitch knitwise, knit the next stitch, and pass the slipped stitch over

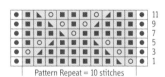

Pattern Repeat = 10 stitches

# OPENWORK DIAMOND PATTERN

[multiple of 10 + 2 selv sts]

Only RS rows are shown; in WS rows, purl all stitches and single yarn overs, work (purl 1, knit 1) into the double yarn overs. Begin with the selv st before the pattern repeat, rep the marked pattern repeat (10 sts wide) widthwise continuously, and end with the selv st after the pattern repeat. Repeat Rows 1–16 heightwise.

### Stitch Key

● = 1 selvedge stitch

■ = Knit 1 stitch

○ = Make 1 yarn over

◢ = Knit 2 stitches together

◣ = Knit 2 stitches together left-leaning with passing over (skp): slip 1 stitch knitwise, knit the next stitch, and pass the slipped stitch over

Pattern Repeat = 10 stitches

## 215 CAT'S PAWS
[multiple of 8 + 1 st + 2 selv sts]

Only RS rows are shown; in WS rows, purl all stitches and yarn overs. Begin with the selv st before the pattern repeat, rep the marked pattern repeat (8 sts wide) widthwise continuously, and end with the sts after the pattern repeat. Repeat Rows 1–8 heightwise.

Pattern Repeat = 8 stitches

### Stitch Key

| Symbol | Meaning |
| --- | --- |
| ● | = 1 selvedge stitch |
| ■ | = Knit 1 stitch |
| O | = Make 1 yarn over |
| ◤ | = Knit 2 stitches together |
| ◥ | = Knit 2 stitches together left-leaning with passing over (skp): slip 1 stitch knitwise, knit the next stitch, and pass the slipped stitch over |

## 216 STAGGERED FLOWERS
[multiple of 10 + 7 sts + 2 selv sts]

Only RS rows are shown; in WS rows, purl all stitches and yarn overs. Begin with the sts before the pattern repeat, rep the marked pattern repeat (10 sts wide) widthwise continuously, and end with the sts after the pattern repeat. Repeat Rows 1–20 heightwise.

Pattern Repeat = 10 stitches

### Stitch Key

| Symbol | Meaning |
| --- | --- |
| ● | = 1 selvedge stitch |
| ■ | = Knit 1 stitch |
| O | = Make 1 yarn over |
| ◤ | = Knit 2 stitches together |
| ◥ | = Knit 2 stitches together left-leaning with passing over (skp): slip 1 stitch knitwise, knit the next stitch, and pass the slipped stitch over |

## 217 BUTTERFLY PATTERN
[multiple of 10 + 2 selv sts]

Shown are both RS and WS rows. Begin with the selv st before the pattern repeat, rep the marked pattern repeat (10 sts wide) widthwise continuously, and end with the selv st after the pattern repeat. Repeat Rows 1–12 heightwise.

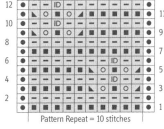

Pattern Repeat = 10 stitches

### Stitch Key

| Symbol | Meaning |
| --- | --- |
| ● | = 1 selvedge stitch |
| ■ | = Knit 1 stitch |
| ◤ | = Knit 2 stitches together |
| – | = Purl 1 stitch |
| O | = Make 1 yarn over |
| ◥ | = Knit 2 stitches together left-leaning with passing over (skp): slip 1 stitch knitwise, knit the next stitch, and pass the slipped stitch over |
| ID | = Slip 1 stitch purlwise, with working yarn in front of work |

## 218 STAGGERED ROSEBUDS

[multiple of 12 + 7 sts + 2 selv sts]

Pattern Repeat = 12 stitches

### Stitch Key

● = 1 selvedge stitch

■ = Knit 1 stitch

O = Make 1 yarn over

◢ = Knit 2 stitches together

◣ = Knit 2 stitches together left-leaning with passing over (skp): slip 1 stitch knitwise, knit the next stitch, and pass the slipped stitch over

△ = Double left-leaning decrease with passing over (sk2p): slip 1 stitch knitwise, knit 2 stitches together, pass the slipped stitch over

Only RS rows are shown; in WS rows, purl all stitches and yarn overs. Begin with the sts before the pattern repeat, rep the marked pattern repeat (12 sts wide) widthwise continuously, and end with the sts after the pattern repeat. Repeat Rows 1–12 heightwise.

## 219 TURTLE PATTERN

[multiple of 6 + 1 st + 2 selv sts]

Only RS rows are shown; in WS rows, purl all stitches and yarn overs. Begin with the sts before the pattern repeat, rep the marked pattern repeat (6 sts wide) widthwise continuously, and end with the sts after the pattern repeat. Repeat Rows 1–12 heightwise.

### Stitch Key

● = 1 selvedge stitch

■ = Knit 1 stitch

O = Make 1 yarn over

◢ = Knit 2 stitches together

◣ = Knit 2 stitches together left-leaning with passing over (skp): slip 1 stitch knitwise, knit the next stitch, and pass the slipped stitch over

△ = Double left-leaning decrease with passing over (sk2p): slip 1 stitch knitwise, knit 2 stitches together, pass the slipped stitch over

☐ = No stitch, for better overview only

Pattern Repeat = 6 stitches

## 220 STAGGERED BLOSSOMS

[multiple of 12 + 8 sts + 2 selv sts]

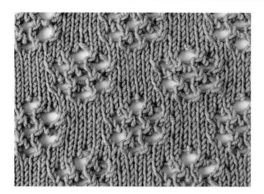

Pattern Repeat = 12 stitches

Only RS rows are shown; in WS rows, purl all stitches, work (purl 1, knit 1) into the double yarn overs. Begin with the sts before the pattern repeat, rep the marked pattern repeat (12 sts wide) widthwise continuously, and end with the sts after the pattern repeat. Repeat Rows 1–20 heightwise.

### Stitch Key

- ● = 1 selvedge stitch
- ■ = Knit 1 stitch
- ○ = Make 1 yarn over
- ◢ = Knit 2 stitches together
- ◥ = Knit 2 stitches together left-leaning with passing over (skp): slip 1 stitch knitwise, knit the next stitch, and pass the slipped stitch over

## 221 CROCUS PATTERN

[multiple of 11 + 9 sts + 2 selv sts]

Pattern Repeat = 11 stitches

Only RS rows are shown; in WS rows, purl all stitches and yarn overs. Begin with the sts before the pattern repeat, rep the marked pattern repeat (11 sts wide) widthwise continuously, and end with the sts after the pattern repeat. Repeat Rows 1–32 heightwise.

### Stitch Key

- ● = 1 selvedge stitch
- ■ = Knit 1 stitch
- ○ = Make 1 yarn over
- ◢ = Knit 2 stitches together
- ◥ = Knit 2 stitches together left-leaning with passing over (skp): slip 1 stitch knitwise, knit the next stitch, and pass the slipped stitch over
- △ = Double left-leaning decrease with passing over (sk2p): slip 1 stitch knitwise, knit 2 stitches together, pass the slipped stitch over

## GRAPEVINE PATTERN

[multiple of 8 + 2 selv sts]

Shown are both RS and WS rows. Begin with the selv st before the pattern repeat, rep the marked pattern repeat (8 sts wide) width-wise continuously, and end with the selv st after the pattern repeat. Repeat Rows 1–12 heightwise.

### Stitch Key

● = 1 selvedge stitch

■ = Knit 1 stitch

– = Purl 1 stitch

◆ = Knit 1 stitch through the back loop

○ = Make 1 yarn over

☐ = No stitch, for better overview only

◢ = Knit 2 stitches together

◣ = Knit 2 stitches together left-leaning with passing over (skp): slip 1 stitch knitwise, knit the next stitch, and pass the slipped stitch over

◿ = Purl 2 stitches together

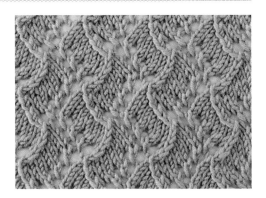

◺ = Purl 2 stitches together left-leaning (ssp): slip 2 stitches individually knitwise, return them to the left needle, then purl them together through the back loop

Pattern Repeat = 8 stitches

## LITTLE HOUSES

[multiple of 10 + 1 st + 2 selv sts]

Begin with Row 1 (WS), and in WS rows (= odd-numbered rows), purl all stitches and yarn overs. Only RS (= even-numbered) rows are shown. Begin with the selv st before the pattern repeat, rep the marked pattern repeat (10 sts wide) widthwise continuously, and end with the sts after the pattern repeat. Repeat Rows 1–14 heightwise.

### Stitch Key

● = 1 selvedge stitch

■ = Knit 1 stitch

○ = Make 1 yarn over

◢ = Knit 2 stitches together

◣ = Knit 2 stitches together left-leaning with passing over (skp): slip 1 stitch knitwise, knit the next stitch, and pass the slipped stitch over

▲ = Double left-leaning decrease with passing over (sk2p): slip 1 stitch knitwise, knit 2 stitches together, pass the slipped stitch over

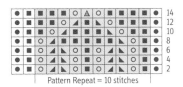

Pattern Repeat = 10 stitches

## 224 DELICATE LACE PATTERN COLUMNS

[multiple of 4 + 1 st + 2 selv sts]

Only RS rows are shown; in WS rows, purl all stitches and yarn overs. Begin with the selv st before the pattern repeat, rep the marked pattern repeat (4 sts wide) widthwise continuously, and end with the sts after the pattern repeat. Repeat Rows 1–4 heightwise.

Pattern Repeat = 4 stitches

### Stitch Key

● = 1 selvedge stitch

■ = Knit 1 stitch

○ = Make 1 yarn over

◬ = Double left-leaning decrease with passing over (sk2p): slip 1 stitch knitwise, knit 2 stitches together, pass the slipped stitch over

☐ = No stitch, for better overview only

## 225 UNDULATING LACE COLUMNS

[multiple of 9 + 2 sts + 2 selv sts]

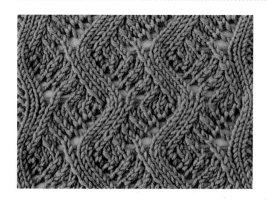

Only RS rows are shown; in WS rows, purl all stitches and yarn overs. Begin with the selv st before the pattern repeat, rep the marked pattern repeat (9 sts wide) widthwise continuously, and end with the sts after the pattern repeat. Repeat Rows 1–20 heightwise.

Pattern Repeat = 9 stitches

### Stitch Key

● = 1 selvedge stitch

■ = Knit 1 stitch

○ = Make 1 yarn over

◢ = Knit 2 stitches together

◤ = Knit 2 stitches together left-leaning with passing over (skp): slip 1 stitch knitwise, knit the next stitch, and pass the slipped stitch over

## 226 ARCHED PEAKS

[multiple of 10 + 1 st + 2 selv sts]

Only RS rows are shown; in WS rows, purl all stitches and yarn overs. Begin with the selv st before the pattern repeat, rep the marked pattern repeat (10 sts wide) widthwise continuously, and end with the sts after the pattern repeat. Repeat Rows 1–16 heightwise.

Pattern Repeat = 10 stitches

### Stitch Key

● = 1 selvedge stitch

■ = Knit 1 stitch

○ = Make 1 yarn over

◢ = Knit 2 stitches together

◤ = Knit 2 stitches together left-leaning with passing over (skp): slip 1 stitch knitwise, knit the next stitch, and pass the slipped stitch over

◬ = Double left-leaning decrease with passing over (sk2p): slip 1 stitch knitwise, knit 2 stitches together, pass the slipped stitch over

## 227 DROPLET PATTERN

[multiple of 10 + 1 st + 2 selv sts]

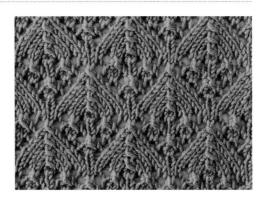

### Stitch Key

● = 1 selvedge stitch

■ = Knit 1 stitch

○ = Make 1 yarn over

◢ = Knit 2 stitches together

◣ = Knit 2 stitches together left-leaning with passing over (skp): slip 1 stitch knitwise, knit the next stitch, and pass the slipped stitch over

△ = Double left-leaning decrease with passing over (sk2p): slip 1 stitch knitwise, knit 2 stitches together, pass the slipped stitch over

Only RS rows are shown; in WS rows, purl all stitches and yarn overs. Begin with the sts before the pattern repeat, rep the marked pattern repeat (10 sts wide) widthwise continuously, and end with the sts after the pattern repeat. Repeat Rows 1–24 heightwise.

## 228 POTTERY PATTERN

[multiple of 10 + 1 st + 2 selv sts]

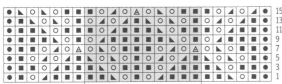

### Stitch Key

● = 1 selvedge stitch

■ = Knit 1 stitch

○ = Make 1 yarn over

◢ = Knit 2 stitches together

◣ = Knit 2 stitches together left-leaning with passing over (skp): slip 1 stitch knitwise, knit the next stitch, and pass the slipped stitch over

△ = Double left-leaning decrease with passing over (sk2p): slip 1 stitch knitwise, knit 2 stitches together, pass the slipped stitch over

Only RS rows are shown; in WS rows, purl all stitches and yarn overs. Begin with the sts before the pattern repeat, rep the marked pattern repeat (10 sts wide) widthwise continuously, and end with the sts after the pattern repeat. Repeat Rows 1–16 heightwise.

## 229 CANDLE PATTERN

[multiple of 12 + 1 st + 2 selv sts]

Only RS rows are shown; in WS rows, purl all stitches and yarn overs. Begin with the sts before the pattern repeat, rep the marked pattern repeat (12 sts wide) widthwise continuously, and end with the sts after the pattern repeat. Repeat Rows 1–20 heightwise.

Pattern Repeat = 12 stitches

### Stitch Key

• = 1 selvedge stitch

■ = Knit 1 stitch

O = Make 1 yarn over

◢ = Knit 2 stitches together

◤ = Knit 2 stitches together left-leaning with passing over (skp): slip 1 stitch knitwise, knit the next stitch, and pass the slipped stitch over

△ = Double left-leaning decrease with passing over (sk2p): slip 1 stitch knitwise, knit 2 stitches together, pass the slipped stitch over

## 230 EYELET-AND-CHEVRON PATTERN

[multiple of 10 + 3 sts + 2 selv sts]

Only RS rows are shown; in WS rows, purl all stitches and yarn overs. Begin with the sts before the pattern repeat, rep the marked pattern repeat (10 sts wide) widthwise continuously, and end with the sts after the pattern repeat. Repeat Rows 1–6 heightwise.

Pattern Repeat = 10 stitches

### Stitch Key

• = 1 selvedge stitch

■ = Knit 1 stitch

O = Make 1 yarn over

◢ = Knit 2 stitches together

◤ = Knit 2 stitches together left-leaning with passing over (skp): slip 1 stitch knitwise, knit the next stitch, and pass the slipped stitch over

△ = Double left-leaning decrease with passing over (sk2p): slip 1 stitch knitwise, knit 2 stitches together, pass the slipped stitch over

## FEATHER-AND-FAN PATTERN

[multiple of 17 + 2 selv sts]

Shown are both RS and WS rows. Begin with the selv st before the pattern repeat, rep the marked pattern repeat (17 sts wide) widthwise continuously, and end with the selv st after the pattern repeat. Repeat Rows 1–4 heightwise.

### Stitch Key

● = 1 selvedge stitch

■ = Knit 1 stitch

− = Purl 1 stitch

○ = Make 1 yarn over

◢ = Knit 2 stitches together

Pattern Repeat = 17 stitches

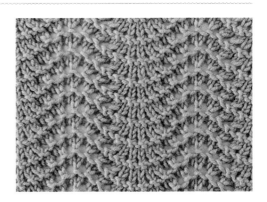

## FERN BANDS

[multiple of 16 + 2 selv sts]

Only RS rows are shown; in WS rows, knit the knits, and purl the purls. Begin with the selv st before the pattern repeat, rep the marked pattern repeat (16 sts wide) widthwise continuously, and end with the selv st after the pattern repeat. Repeat Rows 1–8 heightwise.

### Stitch Key

● = 1 selvedge stitch

■ = Knit 1 stitch

− = Purl 1 stitch

○ = Make 1 yarn over

◢ = Knit 2 stitches together

◤ = Knit 2 stitches together left-leaning with passing over (skp): slip 1 stitch knitwise, knit the next stitch, and pass the slipped stitch over

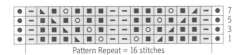

Pattern Repeat = 16 stitches

## MINI FEATHER-AND-FAN PATTERN

[multiple of 12 + 1 st + 2 selv sts]

Only RS rows are shown; in WS rows, knit the knits, and purl the purls. Begin with the selv st before the pattern repeat, rep the marked pattern repeat (12 sts wide) widthwise continuously, and end with the sts after the pattern repeat. Repeat Rows 1–8 heightwise.

### Stitch Key

● = 1 selvedge stitch

■ = Knit 1 stitch

− = Purl 1 stitch

○ = Make 1 yarn over

▲ = Double left-leaning decrease with passing over (sk2p): slip 1 stitch knitwise, knit 2 stitches together, pass the slipped stitch over

▲ = Knit 3 stitches together

Pattern Repeat = 12 stitches

## 234 ARROWHEAD PATTERN

[multiple of 10 + 1 st + 2 selv sts]

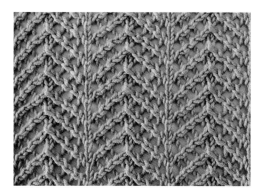

Only RS rows are shown; in WS rows, purl all stitches and yarn overs. Begin with the selv st before the pattern repeat, rep the marked pattern repeat (10 sts wide) widthwise continuously, and end with the sts after the pattern repeat. Repeat Rows 1–4 heightwise.

Pattern Repeat = 10 stitches

### Stitch Key

● = 1 selvedge stitch

■ = Knit 1 stitch

○ = Make 1 yarn over

◢ = Knit 2 stitches together

◣ = Knit 2 stitches together left-leaning with passing over (skp): slip 1 stitch knitwise, knit the next stitch, and pass the slipped stitch over

▲ = Double left-leaning decrease with passing over (sk2p): slip 1 stitch knitwise, knit 2 stitches together, pass the slipped stitch over

## 235 PLAITED LACE PATTERN

[multiple of 13 + 2 selv sts]

Only RS rows are shown; in WS rows, purl all stitches and yarn overs. Begin with the selv st before the pattern repeat, rep the marked pattern repeat (13 sts wide) widthwise continuously, and end with the selv st after the pattern repeat. Repeat Rows 1–12 heightwise.

Pattern Repeat = 13 stitches

### Stitch Key

● = 1 selvedge stitch

■ = Knit 1 stitch

○ = Make 1 yarn over

◢ = Knit 2 stitches together

◣ = Knit 2 stitches together left-leaning with passing over (skp): slip 1 stitch knitwise, knit the next stitch, and pass the slipped stitch over

## 236 BROKEN TRIANGLE PATTERN

[multiple of 13 + 2 selv sts]

Shown are both RS and WS rows. Begin with the selv st before the pattern repeat, rep the marked pattern repeat (13 sts wide) widthwise continuously, and end with the selv st after the pattern repeat. Repeat Rows 1–14 heightwise.

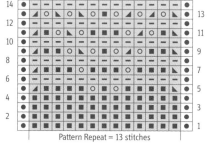

Pattern Repeat = 13 stitches

### Stitch Key

● = 1 selvedge stitch

■ = Knit 1 stitch

– = Purl 1 stitch

○ = Make 1 yarn over

◢ = Knit 2 stitches together

◣ = Knit 2 stitches together left-leaning with passing over (skp): slip 1 stitch knitwise, knit the next stitch, and pass the slipped stitch over

## BROKEN ZIGZAG COLUMNS

[multiple of 6 + 1 st + 2 selv sts]

Only RS rows are shown; in WS rows, purl all stitches and yarn overs. Begin with the sts before the pattern repeat, rep the marked pattern repeat (6 sts wide) widthwise continuously, and end with the sts after the pattern repeat. Repeat Rows 1–12 heightwise.

### Stitch Key

- ● = 1 selvedge stitch
- ■ = Knit 1 stitch
- ○ = Make 1 yarn over
- ◢ = Knit 2 stitches together
- ◥ = Knit 2 stitches together left-leaning with passing over (skp): slip 1 stitch knitwise, knit the next stitch, and pass the slipped stitch over

Pattern Repeat = 6 stitches

## POINTED-ARCH LACE PATTERN

[multiple of 10 + 1 st + 2 selv sts]

Only RS rows are shown; in WS rows, purl all stitches and yarn overs. Begin with the selv st before the pattern repeat, rep the marked pattern repeat (10 sts wide) widthwise continuously, and end with the sts after the pattern repeat. Repeat Rows 1–8 heightwise.

### Stitch Key

- ● = 1 selvedge stitch
- ■ = Knit 1 stitch
- ○ = Make 1 yarn over
- ⋂ = Knit 3 stitches together with center stitch on top (cdd): slip 2 stitches together knitwise, knit the next stitch, and pass the slipped stitches over

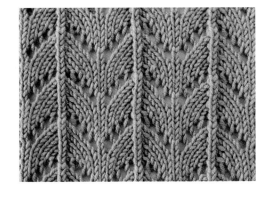

Pattern Repeat = 10 stitches

## 239 BUD PATTERN

[multiple of 10 + 1 st + 2 selv sts]

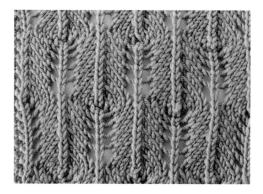

Pattern Repeat = 10 stitches

Only RS rows are shown; in WS rows, purl all stitches and yarn overs. Begin with the sts before the pattern repeat, rep the marked pattern repeat (10 sts wide) widthwise continuously, and end with the sts after the pattern repeat. Repeat Rows 1–24 heightwise.

### Stitch Key

● = 1 selvedge stitch

■ = Knit 1 stitch

○ = Make 1 yarn over

◢ = Knit 2 stitches together

◣ = Knit 2 stitches together left-leaning with passing over (skp): slip 1 stitch knitwise, knit the next stitch, and pass the slipped stitch over

∩ = Knit 3 stitches together with center stitch on top (cdd): slip 2 stitches together knitwise, knit the next stitch, and pass the slipped stitches over

## 240 SMALL DIAMOND PATTERN

[multiple of 10 + 1 st + 2 selv sts]

Pattern Repeat = 10 stitches

Only RS rows are shown; in WS rows, purl all stitches and yarn overs. Begin with the sts before the pattern repeat, rep the marked pattern repeat (10 sts wide) widthwise continuously, and end with the sts after the pattern repeat. Repeat Rows 1–12 heightwise.

### Stitch Key

● = 1 selvedge stitch

■ = Knit 1 stitch

○ = Make 1 yarn over

◢ = Knit 2 stitches together

◣ = Knit 2 stitches together left-leaning with passing over (skp): slip 1 stitch knitwise, knit the next stitch, and pass the slipped stitch over

▲ = Double left-leaning decrease with passing over (sk2p): slip 1 stitch knitwise, knit 2 stitches together, pass the slipped stitch over

# LACE PATTERN RIBBING

[multiple of 4 + 1 st + 2 selv sts]

Only RS rows are shown; in WS rows, knit the knits, and purl the purls and yarn overs. Begin with the sts before the pattern repeat, rep the marked pattern repeat (4 sts wide) widthwise continuously, and end with the sts after the pattern repeat. Repeat Rows 1–20 heightwise.

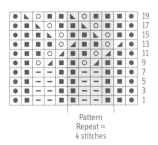

Pattern Repeat = 4 stitches

### Stitch Key

● = 1 selvedge stitch

■ = Knit 1 stitch

– = Purl 1 stitch

○ = Make 1 yarn over

◣ = Knit 2 stitches together

◥ = Knit 2 stitches together left-leaning with passing over (skp): slip 1 stitch knitwise, knit the next stitch, and pass the slipped stitch over

# LOTUS BLOSSOMS

[multiple of 12 + 1 st + 2 selv sts]

Only RS rows are shown; in WS rows, purl all stitches and yarn overs. Begin with the selv st before the pattern repeat, rep the marked pattern repeat (12 sts wide) widthwise continuously, and end with the sts after the pattern repeat. Repeat Rows 1–20 heightwise.

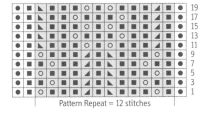

Pattern Repeat = 12 stitches

### Stitch Key

● = 1 selvedge stitch

■ = Knit 1 stitch

○ = Make 1 yarn over

◣ = Knit 2 stitches together

◥ = Knit 2 stitches together left-leaning with passing over (skp): slip 1 stitch knitwise, knit the next stitch, and pass the slipped stitch over

# FAN PATTERN

[multiple of 11 + 3 sts + 2 selv sts]

Only RS rows are shown; in WS rows, purl all stitches and yarn overs. Begin with the sts before the pattern repeat, rep the marked pattern repeat (11 sts wide) widthwise continuously, and end with the sts after the pattern repeat. Repeat Rows 1–26 heightwise.

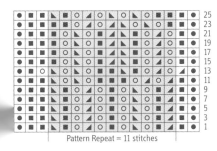

Pattern Repeat = 11 stitches

### Stitch Key

● = 1 selvedge stitch

■ = Knit 1 stitch

○ = Make 1 yarn over

◣ = Knit 2 stitches together

◥ = Knit 2 stitches together left-leaning with passing over (skp): slip 1 stitch knitwise, knit the next stitch, and pass the slipped stitch over

## 244 CAT'S HEADS
[multiple of 14 + 2 selv sts]

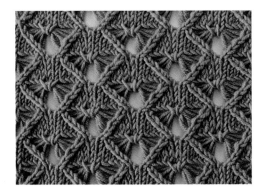

Shown are both RS and WS rows. Begin with the selv st before the pattern repeat, rep the marked pattern repeat (14 sts wide) widthwise continuously, and end with the selv st after the pattern repeat. In Rows 6 and 12, either knit or purl the yarn over of the previous row (see knitting chart). Repeat Rows 1–12 heightwise.

### Stitch Key

● = 1 selvedge stitch

■ = Knit 1 stitch

– = Purl 1 stitch

O = Make 1 yarn over

◢ = Knit 2 stitches together

◣ = Knit 2 stitches together left-leaning with passing over (skp): slip 1 stitch knitwise, knit the next stitch, and pass the slipped stitch over

◿ = Purl 2 stitches together

◹ = Purl 2 stitches together left-leaning (ssp): slip 2 stitches individually knitwise, return them to the left needle, then purl them together through the back loop

◆ = Knit 1 stitch through the back loop

☐ = No stitch, for better overview only

◠ = Slip the yarn over(s) of the previous row(s) purlwise together with an additional yarn over

Pattern Repeat = 14 stitches

## 245 VERTICAL LACE-AND-ZIGZAG PATTERN
[multiple of 24 + 1 st + 2 selv sts]

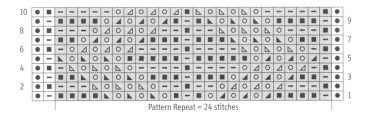

Pattern Repeat = 24 stitches

### Stitch Key

● = 1 selvedge stitch

■ = Knit 1 stitch

– = Purl 1 stitch

O = Make 1 yarn over

◢ = Knit 2 stitches together

◣ = Knit 2 stitches together left-leaning with passing over (skp): slip 1 stitch knitwise, knit the next stitch, and pass the slipped stitch over

◿ = Purl 2 stitches together

◹ = Purl 2 stitches together left-leaning (ssp): slip 2 stitches individually knitwise, return them to the left needle, then purl them together through the back loop

Shown are both RS and WS rows. Begin with the selv st before the pattern repeat, rep the marked pattern repeat (24 sts wide) widthwise continuously, and end with the sts after the pattern repeat. Repeat Rows 1–10 heightwise.

## HEXAGONAL ORNAMENTS

[multiple of 8 + 1 st + 2 selv sts]

### Stitch Key

● = 1 selvedge stitch

■ = Knit 1 stitch

○ = Make 1 yarn over

◢ = Knit 2 stitches together

◣ = Knit 2 stitches together left-leaning with passing over (skp): slip 1 stitch knitwise, knit the next stitch, and pass the slipped stitch over

△ = Double left-leaning decrease with passing over (sk2p): slip 1 stitch knitwise, knit 2 stitches together, pass the slipped stitch over

Pattern Repeat = 8 stitches

Only RS rows are shown; in WS rows, purl all stitches and yarn overs. Begin with the sts before the pattern repeat, rep the marked pattern repeat (8 sts wide) widthwise continuously, and end with the sts after the pattern repeat. Repeat Rows 1–32 heightwise.

## SPANISH LACE PATTERN

[multiple of 34 + 16 + 2 selv sts]

❱ Chart on page 322

Shown are both RS and WS rows. Begin with the sts before the pattern repeat, repeat the pattern repeat (34 sts wide) continuously, and end with the sts after the pattern repeat. Repeat Rows 1–24 heightwise.

# **Dropped-Stitch** Patterns

## 248 RIBBING WITH DROPPED STITCHES

[multiple of 8 + 2 sts + 2 selv sts]

Shown are both RS and WS rows. Begin with the selv st before the pattern repeat, rep the marked pattern repeat (8 sts wide) widthwise continuously, and end with the sts after the pattern repeat. Repeat Rows 1–16 heightwise.

### Stitch Key

| | |
|---|---|
| ● | = 1 selvedge stitch |
| ■ | = Knit 1 stitch |
| − | = Purl 1 stitch |
| ○ | = Make 1 yarn over |
| ☐ | = No stitch, for better overview only |
| ↓ | = Drop the stitch from the needle down to the yarn over |

Pattern Repeat = 8 stitches

## 249 SMALL SHELL PATTERN

[multiple of 10 + 5 sts + 2 selv sts]

Shown are both RS and WS rows. Begin with the selv st before the pattern repeat, rep the marked pattern repeat (10 sts wide) widthwise continuously, and end with the sts after the pattern repeat. Repeat Rows 3–6 heightwise.

Pattern Repeat = 10 stitches

### Stitch Key

| | |
|---|---|
| ● | = 1 selvedge stitch |
| ■ | = Knit 1 stitch |
| − | = Purl 1 stitch |
| ○ | = Make 1 yarn over |
| ☐ | = No stitch, for better overview only |

> > > > > = Slip 5 stitches purlwise, dropping the yarn overs from the previous row. Pull the stitches long, and place them back onto the left needle. Make 2 yarn overs onto the needle, knit the 5 elongated stitches together through the back loop, and make 2 yarn overs onto the needle.

## 250 GARTER STITCH WITH DROPPED STITCHES [multiple of 1 + 2 selv sts]

Shown are both RS and WS rows. Begin with the selv st before the pattern repeat, rep the marked pattern repeat (1 st wide) widthwise continuously, and end with the selv st after the pattern repeat. Repeat Rows 1–4 heightwise.

**Stitch Key**

● = 1 selvedge stitch

■ = Knit 1 stitch

⊙ = Knit 1 stitch, winding the working yarn around the needle twice, and pull both yarn overs through the stitch

▮ = Knit 1 stitch, dropping one of the two yarn overs from the previous row

Pattern
Repeat 1 =
1 stitch

## 251 ROWS OF DROPPED STITCHES [multiple of 2 + 1 st + 2 selv sts]

Shown are both RS and WS rows; in Row 2, drop the two yarn overs from Row 1. Begin with the selv st before the pattern repeat, rep the marked pattern repeat (2 sts wide) widthwise continuously, and end with the sts after the pattern repeat. Repeat Rows 1–4 heightwise.

**Stitch Key**

● = 1 selvedge stitch

■ = Knit 1 stitch

○ = Make 1 yarn over

② = Make 2 yarn overs

◣ = Knit 2 stitches together left-leaning with passing over (skp): slip 1 stitch knitwise, knit the next stitch, and pass the slipped stitch over

☐ = No stitch, for better overview only

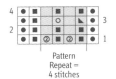

Pattern
Repeat =
4 stitches

## 252 DROPPED STITCHES WITH PASSED-OVER STITCHES [multiple of 4 + 2 selv sts]

Shown are both RS and WS rows. Begin with the selv st before the pattern repeat, rep the marked pattern repeat (4 sts wide) widthwise continuously, and end with the selv st after the pattern repeat. Repeat Rows 1–4 heightwise.

**Stitch Key**

● = 1 selvedge stitch

■ = Knit 1 stitch

− = Purl 1 stitch

○ = Make 1 yarn over

❭❭❭❭ = Drop the yarn over from the previous row, slip the first stitch knitwise, knit the following 3 stitches, and pass the slipped stitch over

☐ = No stitch, for better overview only

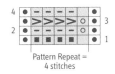

Pattern Repeat =
4 stitches

## 253 WAVES WITH DROPPED STITCHES

[multiple of 9 + 1 st + 2 selv sts]

Only RS rows are shown; in WS rows, knit all sts, and in Rows 2 and 5, always drop the yarn overs from the previous row. Begin with the selv st before the pattern repeat, rep the marked pattern repeat (9 sts wide) widthwise continuously, and end with the sts after the pattern repeat. Repeat Rows 1–8 heightwise.

### Stitch Key

● = 1 selvedge stitch

■ = Knit 1 stitch

○ = Make 1 yarn over

② = Make 2 yarn overs

③ = Make 3 yarn overs

☐ = No stitch, for better overview only

Pattern Repeat = 9 stitches

## 254 GROMMET PATTERN WITH DROPPED STITCHES

[multiple of 5 + 2 selv sts]

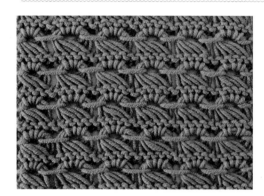

Shown are both RS and WS rows. Begin with the selv st before the pattern repeat, rep the marked pattern repeat (5 sts wide) widthwise continuously, and end with the selv st after the pattern repeat. Repeat Rows 1–4 heightwise.

### Stitch Key

● = 1 selvedge stitch

■ = Knit 1 stitch

③ = Make 3 yarn overs

☐ = No stitch, for better overview only

▊▊▊▊▊ = Slip 5 stitches purlwise, dropping the yarn overs from the previous row. Pull the stitches long, place them back onto the left needle, and knit them together through the back loop. Leaving the stitches on the left needle, make 1 yarn over onto the right needle, make 1 additional stitch by knitting the stitches through the back loop (twisted), make 1 additional yarn over onto the right needle, and make a third additional stitch knitwise twisted.

Pattern Repeat = 5 stitches

## 255 CROSSED DROPPED STITCHES

[multiple of 6 + 2 selv sts]

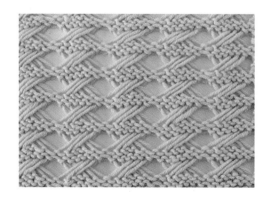

Shown are both RS and WS rows. Begin with the selv st before the pattern repeat, rep the marked pattern repeat (6 sts wide) widthwise continuously, and end with the selv st after the pattern repeat. In Row 3, when working off the stitches, observe the original stitch sequence, and first work the formerly 4th, 5th, and 6th stitches then the formerly 1st, 2nd, and 3rd stitches. Repeat Rows 1–4 heightwise.

### Stitch Key

● = 1 selvedge stitch

■ = Knit 1 stitch

③ = Make 3 yarn overs

☐ = No stitch, for better overview only

▷▷▷▷▷▷ = Slip 6 stitches purlwise, dropping the yarn overs from the previous row. Pull the stitches long, and place them back onto the left needle. Insert the right needle into the first 3 stitches, and pass them over the following 3 stitches. Return the 3 stitches from the right needle to the left needle, and knit all 6 stitches individually, one after another.

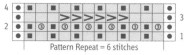

Pattern Repeat = 6 stitches

## 256 LARGE SHELL PATTERN  [multiple of 18 + 1 st + 2 selv sts]

### Stitch Key

- ● = 1 selvedge stitch
- ■ = Knit 1 stitch
- — = Purl 1 stitch
- ○ = Make 1 yarn over
- ② = Make 2 yarn overs
- ☐ = No stitch, for better overview only
- ◢ = Knit 2 stitches together
- ◣ = Knit 2 stitches together left-leaning with passing over (skp): slip 1 stitch knitwise, knit the next stitch, and pass the slipped stitch over
- ∼ = Drop the double yarn overs from the previous row from the needle, and purl 15 stitches together

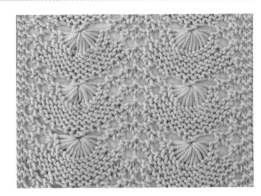

Pattern Repeat = 18 stitches

Shown are both RS and WS rows. Begin with the selv st before the pattern repeat, rep the marked pattern repeat (18 sts wide) widthwise continuously, and end with the sts after the pattern repeat. Repeat Rows 1–12 heightwise.

## 257 DAISY STITCH  [multiple of 6 + 1 st + 2 selv sts]

### Stitch Key

- ● = 1 selvedge stitch
- ■ = Knit 1 stitch
- — = Purl 1 stitch
- ② = Make 2 yarn overs
- ☐ = No stitch, for better overview only
- ■■■■ = Slip 3 stitches purlwise, dropping the yarn overs from the previous row. Pull the stitches long, place them back onto the left needle, and knit them together through the back loop. Leaving the stitches on the left needle, make 1 yarn over onto the right needle, then make 1 additional stitch by knitting the stitches through the back loop (twisted).
- ■■■■■■ = Slip 5 stitches purlwise, dropping the yarn overs from the previous row. Pull the stitches long, place them back onto the left needle, and knit them together through the back loop. Leaving the stitches on the left needle, make 1 yarn over onto the right needle, make 1 additional stitch by knitting the stitches through the back loop (twisted), make 1 additional yarn over onto the right needle, and make a third additional stitch knitwise twisted.

Shown are both RS and WS rows. Begin with Row 1 (WS), starting with the sts before the pattern repeat, rep the marked pattern repeat (6 sts wide) widthwise continuously, and end with the sts after the pattern repeat. Repeat Rows 1–4 heightwise.

Pattern Repeat = 6 stitches

# SLIPPED-STITCH PATTERNS

## 258 SMALL CATERPILLAR PATTERN

[multiple of 3 + 1 st + 2 selv sts]

Shown are both RS and WS rows. Begin with the selv st before the pattern repeat, rep the marked pattern repeat (3 sts wide) widthwise continuously, and end with the sts after the pattern repeat. Repeat Rows 1–4 heightwise.

Pattern Repeat = 3 stitches

### Stitch Key

- ● = 1 selvedge stitch in color A
- ● = 1 selvedge stitch in color B
- ■ = Knit 1 stitch in color A
- ■ = Knit 1 stitch in color B
- ▬ = Purl 1 stitch in color B
- CI = Slip 1 stitch in color B purlwise, with working yarn in back of work
- ID = Slip 1 stitch in color B purlwise, with working yarn in front of work

## 259 STAGGERED CATERPILLAR PATTERN

[multiple of 4 + 2 selv sts]

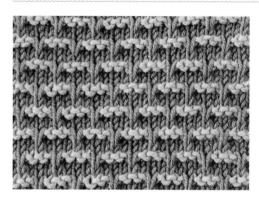

Shown are both RS and WS rows. Begin with the selv st before the pattern repeat, rep the marked pattern repeat (4 sts wide) widthwise continuously, and end with the selv st after the pattern repeat. Repeat Rows 1–8 heightwise.

Pattern Repeat = 4 stitches

### Stitch Key

- ● = 1 selvedge stitch in color A
- ● = 1 selvedge stitch in color B
- ■ = Knit 1 stitch in color A
- ■ = Knit 1 stitch in color B
- ▬ = Purl 1 stitch in color B
- CI = Slip 1 stitch in color B purlwise, with working yarn in back of work
- ID = Slip 1 stitch in color B purlwise, with working yarn in front of work

## 260 SMALL DOT PATTERN

[multiple of 2 + 1 st + 2 selv sts]

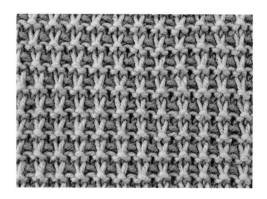

Shown are both RS and WS rows. Begin with the selv st before the pattern repeat, rep the marked pattern repeat (2 sts wide) widthwise continuously, and end with the sts after the pattern repeat. Repeat Rows 1–4 heightwise.

Pattern Repeat = 2 stitches

### Stitch Key

- ● = 1 selvedge stitch in color A
- ● = 1 selvedge stitch in color B
- ■ = Knit 1 stitch in color A
- ■ = Knit 1 stitch in color B
- CI = Slip 1 stitch in color A purlwise, with working yarn in back of work
- ID = Slip 1 stitch in color A purlwise, with working yarn in front of work

## 261 THREE-COLOR LADDER PATTERN [multiple of 4 + 3 sts + 2 selv sts]

### Stitch Key

⬤ = 1 selvedge stitch in color A

◉ = 1 selvedge stitch in color B

⬣ = 1 selvedge stitch in color C

▣ = Knit 1 stitch in color A

▩ = Knit 1 stitch in color B

▨ = Knit 1 stitch in color C

– = Purl 1 stitch in color A

Cl = Slip 1 stitch in color A purl-wise, with working yarn in back of work

Cl = Slip 1 stitch in color B purl-wise, with working yarn in back of work

Cl = Slip 1 stitch in color C purl-wise, with working yarn in back of work

ID = Slip 1 stitch in color A purlwise, with working yarn in front of work

ID = Slip 1 stitch in color B purlwise, with working yarn in front of work

ID = Slip 1 stitch in color C purlwise, with working yarn in front of work

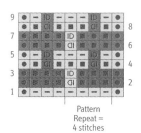

Pattern Repeat = 4 stitches

Shown are both RS and WS rows. Begin with the selv st before the pattern repeat, rep the marked pattern repeat (4 sts wide) widthwise continuously, and end with the sts after the pattern repeat. Work Rows 1–9 once, then repeat Rows 2–9 heightwise continuously.

## 262 THREE-COLOR STRIPE PATTERN [multiple of 3 + 2 selv sts]

### Stitch Key

⬤ = 1 selvedge stitch in color A

◉ = 1 selvedge stitch in color B

⬣ = 1 selvedge stitch in color C

▣ = Knit 1 stitch in color A

▨ = Knit 1 stitch in color B

▩ = Knit 1 stitch in color C

– = Purl 1 stitch in color A

– = Purl 1 stitch in color B

– = Purl 1 stitch in color C

Cl = Slip 1 stitch in color A knitwise, with working yarn in back of work

Cl = Slip 1 stitch in color B knitwise, with working yarn in back of work

Cl = Slip 1 stitch in color C knitwise, with working yarn in back of work

ID = Slip 1 stitch in color A purlwise, with working yarn in front of work

ID = Slip 1 stitch in color B purlwise, with working yarn in front of work

ID = Slip 1 stitch in color C purlwise, with working yarn in front of work

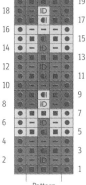

Pattern Repeat = 3 stitches

Shown are both RS and WS rows. Begin with the selv st before the pattern repeat, rep the marked pattern repeat (3 sts wide) widthwise continuously, and end with the selv st after the pattern repeat. In rows without slipped stitches (= Rows 1, 4, 7, 10, 13, 16, and 19), work the stitches more loosely. Work Rows 1–19 once, then repeat Rows 2–19 heightwise.

## 263 STAGGERED DIAGONAL STRIPE PATTERN
[multiple of 12 + 2 selv sts]

### Stitch Key

⬤ = 1 selvedge stitch in color A

⬤ = 1 selvedge stitch in color B

■ = Knit 1 stitch in color A

■ = Knit 1 stitch in color B

— = Purl 1 stitch in color A

— = Purl 1 stitch in color B

Ǫ| = Slip 1 stitch in color A purlwise, with working yarn in back of work

Ǫ| = Slip 1 stitch in color B purlwise, with working yarn in back of work

ID = Slip 1 stitch in color A purlwise, with working yarn in front of work

ID = Slip 1 stitch in color B purlwise, with working yarn in front of work

Shown are both RS and WS rows. Begin with the selv st before the pattern repeat, rep the marked pattern repeat (12 sts wide) widthwise continuously, and end with the selv st after the pattern repeat. Work Rows 1–26 once, then rep Rows 3–26 heightwise.

Pattern Repeat = 12 stitches

## 264 STAIR PATTERN
⟨⟩ [multiple of 4 + 2 selv sts]

Shown are both RS and WS rows. Begin with the selv st before the pattern repeat, rep the marked pattern repeat (4 sts wide) widthwise continuously, and end with the selv st after the pattern repeat. After having completed Row 1 (= RS) in color B, slide the stitches back to the right end of the needle, and work Row 2 (= RS) in color A. After having completed Row 3 (=WS) in color A, again, slide the stitches back to the right end of the needle, and work Row 4 (= WS) in color B. Repeat the sequence for Rows 7–10. In rows without slipped stitches (= Rows 1, 4, 7, and 10), work the stitches more loosely. Repeat Rows 1–12 heightwise.

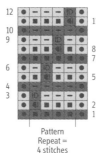

Pattern Repeat = 4 stitches

### Stitch Key

⬤ = 1 selvedge stitch in color A

⬤ = 1 selvedge stitch in color B

■ = Knit 1 stitch in color A

■ = Knit 1 stitch in color B

— = Purl 1 stitch in color A

— = Purl 1 stitch in color B

◢| = Slip 1 stitch in color B knitwise, with working yarn in back of work

ID = Slip 1 stitch in color B purlwise, with working yarn in front of work

## 265 RIBBING

[multiple of 2 + 1 st + 2 selv sts]

Shown are both RS and WS rows. Begin with the selv st before the pattern repeat, rep the marked pattern repeat (2 sts wide) widthwise continuously, and end with the sts after the pattern repeat. Repeat Rows 1 and 2 heightwise.

**Stitch Key**

● = 1 selvedge stitch

■ = Knit 1 stitch

− = Purl 1 stitch

ID = Slip 1 stitch purlwise, with working yarn in front of work

Pattern
Repeat =
2 stitches

## 266 WIDE RIBBING

[multiple of 5 + 2 sts + 2 selv sts]

Shown are both RS and WS rows. Begin with the st before the pattern repeat, rep the marked pattern repeat (5 sts wide) widthwise continuously, and end with the sts after the pattern repeat. Repeat Rows 1 and 2 heightwise.

**Stitch Key**

● = 1 selvedge stitch

■ = Knit 1 stitch

− = Purl 1 stitch

CI = Slip 1 stitch purlwise, with working yarn in back of work

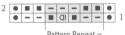

Pattern Repeat =
5 stitches

## 267 SMALL BASKETWEAVE RIBBING

[multiple of 2 + 1 st + 2 selv sts]

Shown are both RS and WS rows. Begin with the selv st before the pattern repeat, rep the marked pattern repeat (2 sts wide) widthwise continuously, and end with the sts after the pattern repeat. Repeat Rows 1–4 heightwise.

**Stitch Key**

● = 1 selvedge stitch in color A

● = 1 selvedge stitch in color B

■ = Knit 1 stitch in color A

■ = Knit 1 stitch in color B

− = Purl 1 stitch in color A

CI = Slip 1 stitch in color A purlwise, with working yarn in back of work

ID = Slip 1 stitch in color A purlwise, with working yarn in front of work

Pattern
Repeat =
2 stitches

## 268 TWO-COLOR BRICK PATTERN ⟨⟩ [multiple of 4 + 2 selv sts]

Shown are both RS and WS rows. Begin with the selv st before the pattern repeat, rep the marked pattern repeat (4 sts wide) widthwise continuously, and end with the selv st after the pattern repeat. After having completed Row 5 (= RS) in color A, slide the stitches back to the right end of the needle, and work Row 6 (= RS) in color B. After having completed Row 7 (= WS) in color B, again, slide the stitches back to the right end of the needle, and work Row 8 (= WS) in color A. In Rows 2 and 7, work the stitches more loosely. Repeat Rows 1–10 heightwise.

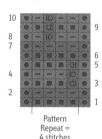

Pattern
Repeat =
4 stitches

### Stitch Key

● = 1 selvedge stitch in color A

● = 1 selvedge stitch in color B

■ = Knit 1 stitch in color A

■ = Knit 1 stitch in color B

— = Purl 1 stitch in color A

— = Purl 1 stitch in color B

QI = Slip 1 stitch in color A purlwise, with working yarn in back of work

ID = Slip 1 stitch in color B purlwise, with working yarn in front of work

## 269 THREE-COLOR PATTERN WITH CABLE STITCHES [multiple of 7 + 1 st + 2 selv sts]

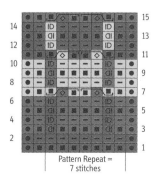

Shown are both RS and WS rows. Begin with the selv st before the pattern repeat, rep the marked pattern repeat (7 sts wide) widthwise continuously, and end with the sts after the pattern repeat. Work Rows 1–15 once, then repeat Rows 4–15 heightwise.

Pattern Repeat =
7 stitches

### Stitch Key

● = 1 selvedge stitch in color A

● = 1 selvedge stitch in color B

● = 1 selvedge stitch in color C

■ = Knit 1 stitch in color A

■ = Knit 1 stitch in color B

■ = Knit 1 stitch in color C

— = Purl 1 stitch in color A

— = Purl 1 stitch in color B

— = Purl 1 stitch in color C

QI = Slip 1 stitch in color A purlwise, with working yarn in back of work

QI = Slip 1 stitch in color B purlwise, with working yarn in back of work

QI = Slip 1 stitch in color C purlwise, with working yarn in back of work

ID = Slip 1 stitch in color A purlwise, with working yarn in front of work

ID = Slip 1 stitch in color B purlwise, with working yarn in front of work

ID = Slip 1 stitch in color C purlwise, with working yarn in front of work

= Hold 1 stitch on a cable needle in front of work, slip 1 stitch in color B purlwise, with working yarn in back of work, knit 1 stitch in color A, then knit the stitch from the cable needle in color A

= Hold 2 stitches on a cable needle behind work, knit 1 stitch in color A, then knit the first stitch from the cable needle in color A, and slip the second stitch from the cable needle in color B purlwise, with working yarn in back of work

= Hold 1 stitch on a cable needle in front of work, slip 1 stitch in color A purlwise, with working yarn in back of work, knit 1 stitch in color C, then knit the stitch from the cable needle in color C

= Hold 2 stitches on a cable needle behind work, knit 1 stitch in color C, then knit the first stitch from the cable needle in color C, and slip the second stitch from the cable needle in color A purlwise, with working yarn in back of work

= Hold 1 stitch on a cable needle in front of work, slip 1 stitch in color C purlwise, with working yarn in back of work, knit 1 stitch in color B, then knit the stitch from the cable needle in color B

= Hold 2 stitches on a cable needle behind work, knit 1 stitch in color B, then knit the first stitch from the cable needle in color B, and slip the second stitch from the cable needle in color C purlwise, with working yarn in back of work

## 270 STAGGERED BRICK PATTERN

[multiple of 6 + 3 sts + 2 selv sts]

Shown are both RS and WS rows. Begin with the selv st before the pattern repeat, rep the marked pattern repeat (6 sts wide) widthwise continuously, and end with the sts after the pattern repeat. Repeat Rows 1–12 heightwise.

### Stitch Key

● = 1 selvedge stitch in color A

◉ = 1 selvedge stitch in color B

■ = Knit 1 stitch in color A

▨ = Knit 1 stitch in color B

− = Purl 1 stitch in color A

▬ = Purl 1 stitch in color B

CI = Slip 1 stitch in color A purlwise, with working yarn in back of work

ID = Slip 1 stitch in color A purlwise, with working yarn in front of work

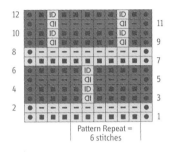

Pattern Repeat = 6 stitches

## 271 DOTTED RIDGES

[multiple of 2 + 1 st + 2 selv sts]

### Stitch Key

● = 1 selvedge stitch in color A

◉ = 1 selvedge stitch in color B

◉ = 1 selvedge stitch in color C

■ = Knit 1 stitch in color A

▨ = Knit 1 stitch in color B

▨ = Knit 1 stitch in color C

CI = Slip 1 stitch in color A purlwise, with working yarn in back of work

CI = Slip 1 stitch in color B purlwise, with working yarn in back of work

CI = Slip 1 stitch in color C purlwise, with working yarn in back of work

ID = Slip 1 stitch in color A purlwise, with working yarn in front of work

ID = Slip 1 stitch in color B purlwise, with working yarn in front of work

ID = Slip 1 stitch in color C purlwise, with working yarn in front of work

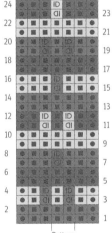

Pattern Repeat = 2 stitches

Shown are both RS and WS rows. Begin with the sts before the pattern repeat, rep the marked pattern repeat (2 sts wide) widthwise continuously, and end with the sts after the pattern repeat. Repeat Rows 1–24 heightwise.

## 272 TRELLIS PATTERN

[multiple of 6 + 5 sts + 2 selv sts]

Shown are both RS and WS rows. Begin with the sts before the pattern repeat, rep the marked pattern repeat (6 sts wide) widthwise continuously, and end with the sts after the pattern repeat. Repeat Rows 1–12 heightwise.

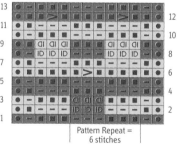

Pattern Repeat = 6 stitches

### Stitch Key

● = 1 selvedge stitch

■ = Knit 1 stitch

− = Purl 1 stitch

Cl = Slip 1 stitch purlwise, with working yarn in back of work

ID = Slip 1 stitch purlwise, with working yarn in front of work

> = Using the right needle, pick up the two floats in front of the 3 slipped stitches located 3–4 rows below, knit the next stitch, and pass the two floats over this stitch

## 273 TWO-COLOR TRELLIS PATTERN

[multiple of 6 + 5 sts + 2 selv sts]

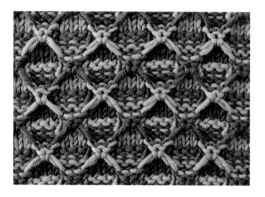

Shown are both RS and WS rows. Begin with the sts before the pattern repeat, rep the marked pattern repeat (6 sts wide) widthwise continuously, and end with the sts after the pattern repeat. Work Rows 1–13 once, then repeat Rows 2–13 heightwise.

Pattern Repeat = 6 stitches

### Stitch Key

● = 1 selvedge stitch in color A

● = 1 selvedge stitch in color B

■ = Knit 1 stitch in color A

■ = Knit 1 stitch in color B

− = Purl 1 stitch in color A

− = Purl 1 stitch in color B

> = Using the right needle, pick up the two floats in color A in front of the 3 slipped stitches located 3–4 rows below, knit the next stitch, and pass the two floats over this stitch

> = Using the right needle, pick up the two floats in color B in front of the 3 slipped stitches located 3–4 rows below, knit the next stitch, and pass the two floats over this stitch

## 274 BRICK PATTERN

[multiple of 4 + 1 st + 2 selv sts]

Shown are both RS and WS rows. Begin with the sts before the pattern repeat, rep the marked pattern repeat (4 sts wide) width-wise continuously, and end with the sts after the pattern repeat. Repeat Rows 1–16 heightwise.

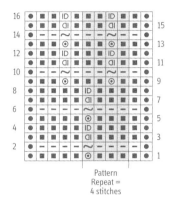

Pattern
Repeat =
4 stitches

### Stitch Key

● = 1 selvedge stitch

■ = Knit 1 stitch

– = Purl 1 stitch

∼ = Slip 1 stitch purlwise while dropping the additional loop from the needle

Ql = Slip 1 stitch purlwise, with working yarn in back of work

ID = Slip 1 stitch purlwise, with working yarn in front of work

⊙ = Insert the needle into the stitch as if to knit, lead the working yarn around the needle twice, and knit the stitch

## 275 TWO-COLOR BRICK PATTERN

[multiple of 4 + 1 st + 2 selv sts]

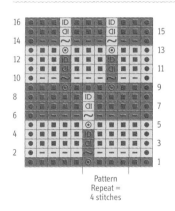

Pattern
Repeat =
4 stitches

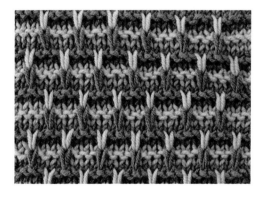

### Stitch Key

● = 1 selvedge stitch in color A

● = 1 selvedge stitch in color B

■ = Knit 1 stitch in color A

■ = Knit 1 stitch in color B

– = Purl 1 stitch in color A

– = Purl 1 stitch in color B

∼ = Slip 1 stitch in color A purlwise while dropping the additional loop from the needle

∼ = Slip 1 stitch in color B purlwise while dropping the additional loop from the needle

Ql = Slip 1 stitch in color A purlwise, with working yarn in back of work

Ql = Slip 1 stitch in color B purlwise, with working yarn in back of work

ID = Slip 1 stitch in color A purlwise, with working yarn in front of work

ID = Slip 1 stitch in color B purlwise, with working yarn in front of work

⊙ = Insert the needle into the stitch as if to knit, lead the working yarn in color A around the needle twice, and knit the stitch

⊙ = Insert the needle into the stitch as if to knit, lead the working yarn in color B around the needle twice, and knit the stitch

Shown are both RS and WS rows. Begin with the sts before the pattern repeat, rep the marked pattern repeat (4 sts wide) widthwise continuously, and end with the sts after the pattern repeat. Repeat Rows 1–16 heightwise.

144

## 276 HOUNDSTOOTH PATTERN

[multiple of 3 + 2 selv sts]

Shown are both RS and WS rows. Cast on in color B. Begin with the selv st before the pattern repeat, rep the marked pattern repeat (3 sts wide) widthwise continuously, and end with the selv st after the pattern repeat. Repeat Rows 1–4 heightwise.

Pattern
Repeat =
3 stitches

### Stitch Key

● = 1 selvedge stitch in color A
◉ = 1 selvedge stitch in color B
■ = Knit 1 stitch in color A
■ = Knit 1 stitch in color B
Cl = Slip 1 stitch in color A purlwise, with working yarn in back of work
Cl = Slip 1 stitch in color B purlwise, with working yarn in back of work

## 277 HOUNDSTOOTH PATTERN IN GARTER STITCH

[multiple of 3 + 2 selv sts]

Shown are both RS and WS rows. Cast on in color B. Begin with the selv st before the pattern repeat, rep the marked pattern repeat (3 sts wide) widthwise continuously, and end with the selv st after the pattern repeat. Repeat Rows 1–4 heightwise.

Pattern
Repeat =
3 stitches

### Stitch Key

● = 1 selvedge stitch in color A
◉ = 1 selvedge stitch in color B
■ = Knit 1 stitch in color A
■ = Knit 1 stitch in color B
— = Purl 1 stitch in color A
— = Purl 1 stitch in color B
Cl = Slip 1 stitch in color A purlwise, with working yarn in back of work
Cl = Slip 1 stitch in color B purlwise, with working yarn in back of work

## 278 ROSEHIP PATTERN

[multiple of 4 + 3 sts + 2 selv sts]

Shown are both RS and WS rows. Begin with the selv st before the pattern repeat, rep the marked pattern repeat (4 sts wide) widthwise continuously, and end with the sts after the pattern repeat. Repeat Rows 1–4 heightwise.

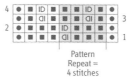

Pattern
Repeat =
4 stitches

### Stitch Key

● = 1 selvedge stitch
■ = Knit 1 stitch
Cl = Slip 1 stitch purlwise, with working yarn in back of work
ID = Slip 1 stitch purlwise, with working yarn in front of work

## 279 TEXTURED TWEED PATTERN

[multiple of 4 + 3 sts + 2 selv sts]

### Stitch Key

⬤ = 1 selvedge stitch in color A

⬤ = 1 selvedge stitch in color B

⬤ = 1 selvedge stitch in color C

■ = Knit 1 stitch in color A

■ = Knit 1 stitch in color B

■ = Knit 1 stitch in color C

Ⓠ = Slip 1 stitch in color A purlwise, with working yarn in back of work

Ⓠ = Slip 1 stitch in color B purlwise, with working yarn in back of work

Ⓠ = Slip 1 stitch in color C purlwise, with working yarn in back of work

ⒾⒹ = Slip 1 stitch in color A purlwise, with working yarn in front of work

ⒾⒹ = Slip 1 stitch in color B purlwise, with working yarn in front of work

ⒾⒹ = Slip 1 stitch in color C purlwise, with working yarn in front of work

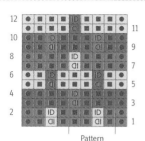

Pattern
Repeat =
4 stitches

Shown are both RS and WS rows. Cast on in color A. Begin with the selv st before the pattern repeat, rep the marked pattern repeat (4 sts wide) widthwise continuously, and end with the sts after the pattern repeat. Repeat Rows 1–12 heightwise.

## 280 THREE-COLOR BAND PATTERN

[multiple of 4 + 3 sts + 2 selv sts]

### Stitch Key

⬤ = 1 selvedge stitch in color A

⬤ = 1 selvedge stitch in color B

⬤ = 1 selvedge stitch in color C

■ = Knit 1 stitch in color A

■ = Knit 1 stitch in color B

■ = Knit 1 stitch in color C

— = Purl 1 stitch in color A

— = Purl 1 stitch in color B

— = Purl 1 stitch in color C

Ⓠ = Slip 1 stitch in color A purlwise, with working yarn in back of work

ⒾⒹ = Slip 1 stitch in color A purlwise, with working yarn in front of work

Shown are both RS and WS rows. Begin with the selv st before the pattern repeat, rep the marked pattern repeat (4 sts wide) widthwise continuously, and end with the sts after the pattern repeat. In Rows 2 and 6, work the stitches more loosely. Repeat Rows 1–10 heightwise.

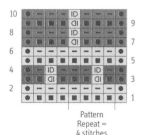

Pattern
Repeat =
4 stitches

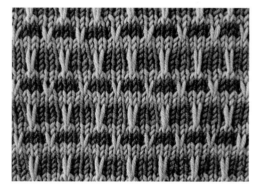

## 281 TWO-COLOR PATTERN WITH FLOATS

[multiple of 2 + 1 st + 2 selv sts]

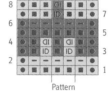

Pattern
Repeat =
2 stitches

### Stitch Key

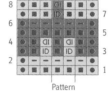 = 1 selvedge stitch in color A

= 1 selvedge stitch in color B

= Knit 1 stitch in color A

= Knit 1 stitch in color B

= Purl 1 stitch in color A

= Purl 1 stitch in color B

= Slip 1 stitch in color A purl-wise, with working yarn in back of work

= Slip 1 stitch in color B purl-wise, with working yarn in back of work

= Slip 1 stitch in color A purl-wise, with working yarn in front of work

= Slip 1 stitch in color B purl-wise, with working yarn in front of work

Shown are both RS and WS rows. Begin with the sts before the pattern repeat, rep the marked pattern repeat (2 sts wide) widthwise continuously, and end with the sts after the pattern repeat. Repeat Rows 1–8 heightwise.

## 282 THREE-COLOR PATTERN WITH FLOATS

[multiple of 2 + 1 st + 2 selv sts]

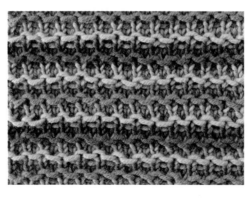

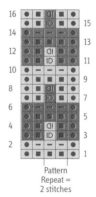

Pattern
Repeat =
2 stitches

Shown are both RS and WS rows. Begin with the selv st before the pattern repeat, rep the marked pattern repeat (2 sts wide) widthwise continuously, and end with the sts after the pattern repeat. Repeat Rows 1–16 heightwise.

### Stitch Key

= 1 selvedge stitch in color A

= 1 selvedge stitch in color B

= 1 selvedge stitch in color C

= Knit 1 stitch in color A

= Knit 1 stitch in color B

= Knit 1 stitch in color C

= Purl 1 stitch in color A

= Purl 1 stitch in color B

= Purl 1 stitch in color C

= Slip 1 stitch in color A purlwise, with working yarn in back of work

= Slip 1 stitch in color B purlwise, with working yarn in back of work

= Slip 1 stitch in color C purlwise, with working yarn in back of work

= Slip 1 stitch in color A purlwise, with working yarn in front of work

= Slip 1 stitch in color B purlwise, with working yarn in front of work

= Slip 1 stitch in color C purlwise, with working yarn in front of work

# 283 DIAGONAL ELONGATED-STITCH PATTERN [multiple of 4 + 1 st + 2 selv sts]

Shown are both RS and WS rows. Cast on in color A. Begin with the sts before the pattern repeat, rep the marked pattern repeat (4 sts wide) widthwise continuously, and end with the sts after the pattern repeat. Repeat Rows 1–8 heightwise.

Pattern Repeat = 4 stitches

## Stitch Key

- ● = 1 selvedge stitch in color A
- ◖ = 1 selvedge stitch in color B
- ■ = Knit 1 stitch in color A
- ▥ = Knit 1 stitch in color B
- ▬ = Purl 1 stitch in color A
- ▭ = Purl 1 stitch in color B
- ▣ = Slip 1 stitch in color A purlwise, with working yarn in back of work

- |ID| = Slip 1 stitch in color A purlwise, with working yarn in front of work
- ▮▮▮▙ = Hold 1 stitch on a cable needle in front of work, knit 2 stitches in color A, then knit the stitch from the cable needle in color A
- ▙▞▮▮ = Hold 2 stitches on a cable needle behind work, knit 1 stitch in color A, then knit the 2 stitches from the cable needle in color A

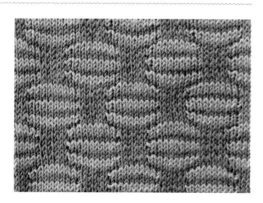

# 284 TRANSOM PATTERN [multiple of 14 + 1 st + 2 selv sts]

Shown are both RS and WS rows. Begin with the selv st before the pattern repeat, rep the marked pattern repeat (14 sts wide) widthwise continuously, and end with the sts after the pattern repeat. Repeat Rows 1–24 heightwise, fastening the long floats of the two rows below in the middle in every RS row without slipped stitches. For this, when knitting a stitch above the floats, insert the right needle first into the stitch, then underneath the two floats, wind the working yarn around the needle, and pull it through the stitch.

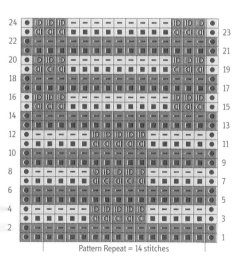

Pattern Repeat = 14 stitches

## Stitch Key

- ● = 1 selvedge stitch in color A
- ◖ = 1 selvedge stitch in color B
- ■ = Knit 1 stitch in color A
- ▥ = Knit 1 stitch in color B
- ▬ = Purl 1 stitch in color A
- ▭ = Purl 1 stitch in color B
- ▣ = Slip 1 stitch in color B purlwise, with working yarn in back of work
- |ID| = Slip 1 stitch in color B purlwise, with working yarn in front of work

## 285 DIAMOND PATTERN

[multiple of 10 + 3 sts + 2 selv sts]

Shown are both RS and WS rows. Begin with the sts before the pattern repeat, rep the marked pattern repeat (10 sts wide) widthwise continuously, and end with the sts after the pattern repeat. Work Rows 1–25 once, then repeat Rows 2–25 heightwise.

Pattern Repeat = 10 stitches

### Stitch Key

- ● = 1 selvedge stitch in color A
- ● = 1 selvedge stitch in color B
- ■ = Knit 1 stitch in color A
- ■ = Knit 1 stitch in color B
- – = Purl 1 stitch in color A
- ◨ = Slip 1 stitch in color A purlwise, with working yarn in back of work
- ◨ = Slip 1 stitch in color B purlwise, with working yarn in back of work
- ID = Slip 1 stitch in color A purlwise, with working yarn in front of work
- ID = Slip 1 stitch in color B purlwise, with working yarn in front of work

## 286 TWO-COLOR CROSSED-STITCH MOSAIC

[multiple of 6 + 2 selv sts]

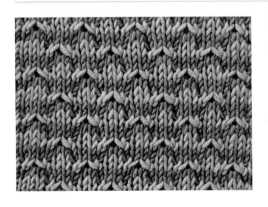

Shown are both RS and WS rows. Begin with the sts before the pattern repeat, rep the marked pattern repeat (6 sts wide) widthwise continuously, and end with the sts after the pattern repeat. Work Rows 1–10 once heightwise, then repeat only Rows 3–10 continuously.

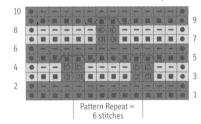

Pattern Repeat = 6 stitches

### Stitch Key

- ● = 1 selvedge stitch in color A
- ● = 1 selvedge stitch in color B
- ■ = Knit 1 stitch in color A
- ■ = Knit 1 stitch in color B
- – = Purl 1 stitch in color A
- ◨ = Purl 1 stitch in color B
- ◨ = Slip 1 stitch in color B purlwise, with working yarn in back of work

- ID = Slip 1 stitch in color B purlwise, with working yarn in front of work
- ◨/◨ = Hold 1 stitch on a cable needle behind work, knit 1 stitch in color B, then knit the stitch from the cable needle in color B
- ◨◨ = Hold 1 stitch on a cable needle in front of work, knit 1 stitch in color B, then knit the stitch from the cable needle in color B

## 287 VERTICAL STRIPES

[multiple of 4 + 2 selv sts]

Shown are both RS and WS rows. Begin with the sts before the pattern repeat, rep the marked pattern repeat (4 sts wide) widthwise continuously, and end with the sts after the pattern repeat. Work Rows 1–6 once, then repeat Rows 3–6 heightwise.

### Stitch Key

● = 1 selvedge stitch in color A

◼ = 1 selvedge stitch in color B

◼ = Knit 1 stitch in color A

◼ = Knit 1 stitch in color B

− = Purl 1 stitch in color A

− = Purl 1 stitch in color B

Ql = Slip 1 stitch in color A purl-wise, with working yarn in back of work

Ql = Slip 1 stitch in color B purl-wise, with working yarn in back of work

ID = Slip 1 stitch in color A purl-wise, with working yarn in front of work

ID = Slip 1 stitch in color B purl-wise, with working yarn in front of work

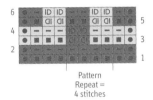

Pattern Repeat = 4 stitches

## 288 CHECKERBOARD PATTERN

[multiple of 4 + 2 selv sts]

Shown are both RS and WS rows. Begin with the sts before the pattern repeat, rep the marked pattern repeat (4 sts wide) widthwise continuously, and end with the sts after the pattern repeat. Repeat Rows 1–6 heightwise.

### Stitch Key

● = 1 selvedge stitch in color A

◉ = 1 selvedge stitch in color B

◉ = 1 selvedge stitch in color C

◼ = Knit 1 stitch in color A

◼ = Knit 1 stitch in color B

◼ = Knit 1 stitch in color C

− = Purl 1 stitch in color A

− = Purl 1 stitch in color B

− = Purl 1 stitch in color C

Ql = Slip 1 stitch in color A purl-wise, with working yarn in back of work

ID = Slip 1 stitch in color A purl-wise, with working yarn in front of work

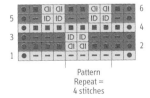

Pattern Repeat = 4 stitches

## 289 TWISTED LADDER PATTERN

[multiple of 6 + 2 selv sts]

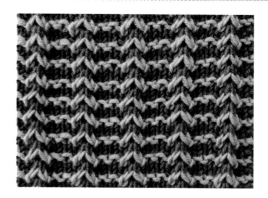

Shown are both RS and WS rows. Begin with the selv st before the pattern repeat, rep the marked pattern repeat (6 sts wide) widthwise continuously, and end with the selv st after the pattern repeat. Work Rows 1–6 once, then repeat Rows 3–6 heightwise.

### Stitch Key

◉ = 1 selvedge stitch in color A

◐ = 1 selvedge stitch in color B

■ = Knit 1 stitch in color A

▨ = Knit 1 stitch in color B

▬ = Purl 1 stitch in color A

▬ = Purl 1 stitch in color B

◫ = Slip 1 stitch in color B purl-wise, with working yarn in back of work

ID = Slip 1 stitch in color B purl-wise, with working yarn in front of work

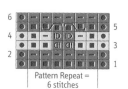

Pattern Repeat = 6 stitches

⊿ = Hold 1 stitch on a cable needle behind work, knit 1 stitch in color B, then knit the stitch from the cable needle in color B

⊾ = Hold 1 stitch on a cable needle in front of work, knit 1 stitch in color B, then knit the stitch from the cable needle in color B

## 290 MOSAIC AND CABLE PATTERN

[multiple of 6 + 2 selv sts]

Shown are both RS and WS rows. Begin with the selv st before the pattern repeat, rep the marked pattern repeat (6 sts wide) widthwise continuously, and end with the selv st after the pattern repeat. Work Rows 1–6 once, then repeat Rows 3–6 heightwise.

### Stitch Key

◉ = 1 selvedge stitch in color A

◐ = 1 selvedge stitch in color B

■ = Knit 1 stitch in color A

▨ = Knit 1 stitch in color B

▬ = Purl 1 stitch in color A

▬ = Purl 1 stitch in color B

◫ = Slip 1 stitch in color A purl-wise, with working yarn in back of work

ID = Slip 1 stitch in color A purl-wise, with working yarn in front of work

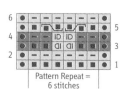

Pattern Repeat = 6 stitches

⊿ = Hold 1 stitch on a cable needle behind work, knit 1 stitch in color A, then knit the stitch from the cable needle in color A

⊾ = Hold 1 stitch on a cable needle in front of work, knit 1 stitch in color A, then knit the stitch from the cable needle in color A

## 291 CROSSED-STITCH RHOMBOID PATTERN [multiple of 4 + 2 sts + 2 selv sts]

Shown are both RS and WS rows. Begin with the selv st before the pattern repeat, rep the marked pattern repeat (4 sts wide) widthwise continuously, and end with the sts after the pattern repeat. Repeat Rows 1–12 heightwise.

### Stitch Key

● = 1 selvedge stitch

■ = Knit 1 stitch

– = Purl 1 stitch

CI = Slip 1 stitch purlwise, with working yarn in back of work

ID = Slip 1 stitch purlwise, with working yarn in front of work

⬛⬛ = Hold 1 stitch on a cable needle in front of work, knit the next stitch, then knit the stitch from the cable needle

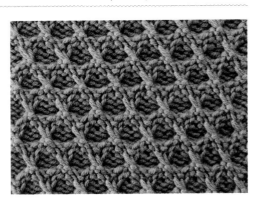

Pattern
Repeat =
4 stitches

## 292 SPRINKLED TWEED PATTERN [multiple of 4 + 3 sts + 2 selv sts]

Shown are both RS and WS rows. Cast on in color B. Begin with the selv st before the pattern repeat, rep the marked pattern repeat (4 sts wide) widthwise continuously, and end with the sts after the pattern repeat. Repeat Rows 1–4 heightwise.

### Stitch Key

● = 1 selvedge stitch in color A

● = 1 selvedge stitch in color B

■ = Knit 1 stitch in color A

■ = Knit 1 stitch in color B

– = Purl 1 stitch in color A

– = Purl 1 stitch in color B

CI = Slip 1 stitch in color A purlwise, with working yarn in back of work

CI = Slip 1 stitch in color B purlwise, with working yarn in back of work

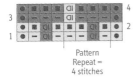

Pattern
Repeat =
4 stitches

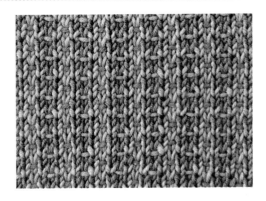

## 293 ZIGZAG PATTERN [multiple of 12 + 1 st + 2 selv sts]

Shown are both RS and WS rows. Begin with the selv st before the pattern repeat, rep the marked pattern repeat (12 sts wide) widthwise continuously, and end with the sts after the pattern repeat. Repeat Rows 1–16 heightwise.

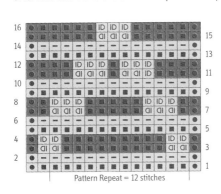

Pattern Repeat = 12 stitches

### Stitch Key

● = 1 selvedge stitch in color A

● = 1 selvedge stitch in color B

■ = Knit 1 stitch in color A

■ = Knit 1 stitch in color B

– = Purl 1 stitch in color A

CI = Slip 1 stitch in color A purlwise, with working yarn in back of work

ID = Slip 1 stitch in color A purlwise, with working yarn in front of work

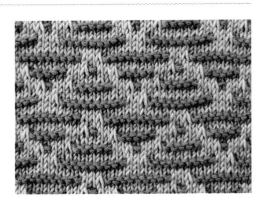

## 294 LARGE HONEYCOMB PATTERN

[multiple of 8 + 2 selv sts]

Shown are both RS and WS rows. Begin with the selv st before the pattern repeat, rep the marked pattern repeat (8 sts wide) widthwise continuously, and end with the selv st after the pattern repeat. Repeat Rows 1–12 heightwise.

Pattern Repeat = 8 stitches

### Stitch Key

- ● = 1 selvedge stitch in color A
- ◉ = 1 selvedge stitch in color B
- ■ = Knit 1 stitch in color A
- ▨ = Knit 1 stitch in color B
- — = Purl 1 stitch in color A
- ◖Ⅰ◗ = Slip 1 stitch in color B purlwise, with working yarn in back of work
- ⅠD = Slip 1 stitch in color B purlwise, with working yarn in front of work

## 295 TWO-COLOR DIAMOND PATTERN

[multiple of 10 + 2 selv sts]

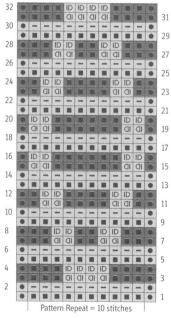

Pattern Repeat = 10 stitches

Shown are both RS and WS rows. Begin with the selv st before the pattern repeat, rep the marked pattern repeat (10 sts wide) widthwise continuously, and end with the selv st after the pattern repeat. Repeat Rows 1–32 heightwise.

### Stitch Key

- ● = 1 selvedge stitch in color A
- ◉ = 1 selvedge stitch in color B
- ■ = Knit 1 stitch in color A
- ▨ = Knit 1 stitch in color B
- — = Purl 1 stitch in color A
- ◖Ⅰ◗ = Slip 1 stitch in color A purlwise, with working yarn in back of work
- ⅠD = Slip 1 stitch in color A purlwise, with working yarn in front of work

## 296 RHOMBOID PATTERN

[multiple of 22 + 2 selv sts]

### Stitch Key

- ● = 1 selvedge stitch in color A
- ◉ = 1 selvedge stitch in color B
- ■ = Knit 1 stitch in color A
- ▣ = Knit 1 stitch in color B
- ▤ = Purl 1 stitch in color B
- QI = Slip 1 stitch in color B purlwise, with working yarn in back of work
- ID = Slip 1 stitch in color B purlwise, with working yarn in front of work

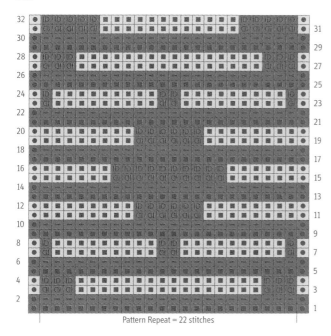

Shown are both RS and WS rows. Begin with the selv st before the pattern repeat, rep the marked pattern repeat (22 sts wide) widthwise continuously, and end with the selv st after the pattern repeat. Repeat Rows 1–32 heightwise, in Rows 5, 13, 17, 21, and 29, and in subsequent repeats of Row 1, fastening the long floats of the two rows below once in the middle. For this, when knitting a stitch above the floats, insert the right needle first into the stitch, then underneath the two floats, wind the working yarn around the needle, and pull it through the stitch.

Pattern Repeat = 22 stitches

## 297 BASKETWEAVE PATTERN

[multiple of 10 + 2 selv sts]

Shown are both RS and WS rows. Begin with the selv st before the pattern repeat, rep the marked pattern repeat (10 sts wide) widthwise continuously, and end with the selv st after the pattern repeat. Repeat Rows 1–16 heightwise.

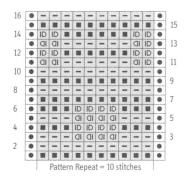

### Stitch Key

- ● = 1 selvedge stitch
- ■ = Knit 1 stitch
- — = Purl 1 stitch
- QI = Slip 1 stitch purlwise, with working yarn in back of work
- ID = Slip 1 stitch purlwise, with working yarn in front of work

Pattern Repeat = 10 stitches

## 298 SQUARE PATTERN

[multiple of 18 + 2 selv sts]

Shown are both RS and WS rows. Begin with the selv st before the pattern repeat, rep the marked pattern repeat (18 sts wide) widthwise continuously, and end with the selv st after the pattern repeat. Repeat Rows 1–32 heightwise.

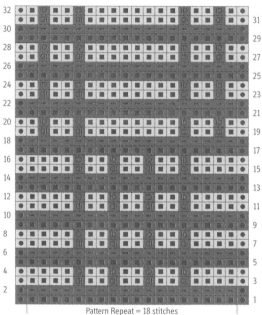

Pattern Repeat = 18 stitches

### Stitch Key

● = 1 selvedge stitch in color A

■ = 1 selvedge stitch in color B

■ = Knit 1 stitch in color A

■ = Knit 1 stitch in color B

■ = Purl 1 stitch in color B

Ql = Slip 1 stitch in color B purlwise, with working yarn in back of work

ID = Slip 1 stitch in color B purlwise, with working yarn in front of work

## 299 COLORFUL BASKETWEAVE PATTERN

[multiple of 2 + 1 st + 2 selv sts]

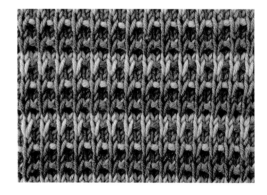

Shown are both RS and WS rows. Begin with the selv st before the pattern repeat, rep the marked pattern repeat (2 sts wide) widthwise continuously, and end with the sts after the pattern repeat. Repeat Rows 1–12 heightwise.

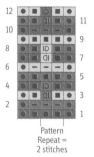

Pattern Repeat = 2 stitches

### Stitch Key

● = 1 selvedge stitch in color A

● = 1 selvedge stitch in color B

● = 1 selvedge stitch in color C

■ = Knit 1 stitch in color A

■ = Knit 1 stitch in color B

■ = Knit 1 stitch in color C

– = Purl 1 stitch in color A

– = Purl 1 stitch in color B

– = Purl 1 stitch in color C

Ql = Slip 1 stitch in color A purlwise, with working yarn in back of work

Ql = Slip 1 stitch in color B purlwise, with working yarn in back of work

Ql = Slip 1 stitch in color C purlwise, with working yarn in back of work

ID = Slip 1 stitch in color A purlwise, with working yarn in front of work

ID = Slip 1 stitch in color B purlwise, with working yarn in front of work

ID = Slip 1 stitch in color C purlwise, with working yarn in front of work

## 300 THREE-COLOR STAIR PATTERN

[multiple of 6 + 2 selv sts]

### Stitch Key

● = 1 selvedge stitch in color A

◐ = 1 selvedge stitch in color B

◑ = 1 selvedge stitch in color C

■ = Knit 1 stitch in color A

▣ = Knit 1 stitch in color B

▤ = Knit 1 stitch in color C

▬ = Purl 1 stitch in color A

▬ = Purl 1 stitch in color B

▬ = Purl 1 stitch in color C

QI = Slip 1 stitch in color A purl-wise, with working yarn in back of work

QI = Slip 1 stitch in color B purl-wise, with working yarn in back of work

QI = Slip 1 stitch in color C purl-wise, with working yarn in back of work

ID = Slip 1 stitch in color A purl-wise, with working yarn in front of work

ID = Slip 1 stitch in color B purl-wise, with working yarn in front of work

ID = Slip 1 stitch in color C purl-wise, with working yarn in front of work

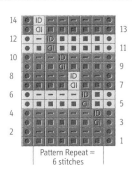

Pattern Repeat = 6 stitches

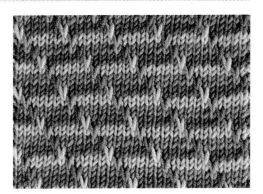

Shown are both RS and WS rows. Begin with the selv st before the pattern repeat, rep the marked pattern repeat (6 sts wide) widthwise continuously, and end with the selv st after the pattern repeat. Work Rows 1–14 once, then repeat Rows 3–14 heightwise.

## 301 VERTICAL STRIPES

[multiple of 10 + 1 st + 2 selv sts]

Shown are both RS and WS rows. Begin with the selv st before the pattern repeat, rep the marked pattern repeat (10 sts wide) widthwise continuously, and end with the sts after the pattern repeat. Work Rows 1–8 once, then repeat Rows 5–8 heightwise.

### Stitch Key

● = 1 selvedge stitch in color A

◐ = 1 selvedge stitch in color B

■ = Knit 1 stitch in color A

▣ = Knit 1 stitch in color B

▬ = Purl 1 stitch in color A

▬ = Purl 1 stitch in color B

QI = Slip 1 stitch in color A purl-wise, with working yarn in back of work

QI = Slip 1 stitch in color B purl-wise, with working yarn in back of work

ID = Slip 1 stitch in color A purl-wise, with working yarn in front of work

ID = Slip 1 stitch in color B purl-wise, with working yarn in front of work

= Hold 2 stitches on a cable needle in front of work, knit 1 stitch in color A, then knit the 2 stitches from the cable needle in color A

= Hold 1 stitch on a cable needle behind work, knit 2 stitches in color A, then knit the stitch from the cable needle in color A

= Hold 1 stitch on a cable needle in front of work, knit 2 stitches in color B, then knit the stitch from the cable needle in color B

= Hold 2 stitches on a cable needle behind work, knit 1 stitch in color B, then knit the 2 stitches from the cable needle in color B

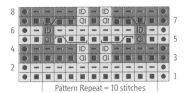

Pattern Repeat = 10 stitches

## 302 RHOMBOID LATTICE

[multiple of 6 + 2 selv sts]

### Stitch Key

- ● = 1 selvedge stitch
- ■ = Knit 1 stitch
- − = Purl 1 stitch
- O = Make 1 yarn over
- ↓ = Drop the yarn over from the previous row from the needle
- ☐ = No stitch, for better overview only
- ⊡ = Slip 1 stitch purlwise, with working yarn in back of work
- ⊡ = Slip 1 stitch purlwise, with working yarn in front of work
- ⬛⬛⬛ = Hold 1 stitch on a cable needle in front of work, knit 2 stitches, then knit the stitch from the cable needle

Shown are both RS and WS rows. Begin with the selv st before the pattern repeat, rep the marked pattern repeat (6 sts wide) widthwise continuously, and end with the selv st after the pattern repeat. Work Rows 1–13 once, then repeat Rows 2–13 heightwise.

(chart: Pattern Repeat = 6 stitches; rows 1–13)

⬛⧄⬛⬛ = Hold 2 stitches on a cable needle behind work, knit the next stitch, then knit the 2 stitches from the cable needle

## 303 INTERLOCKED STRIPE PATTERN

[multiple of 4 + 2 sts + 2 selv sts]

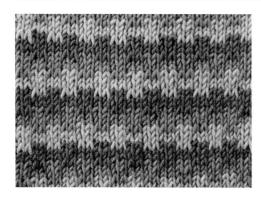

### Stitch Key

- ● = 1 selvedge stitch in color A
- ● = 1 selvedge stitch in color B
- ● = 1 selvedge stitch in color C
- ■ = Knit 1 stitch in color A
- ■ = Knit 1 stitch in color B
- ■ = Knit 1 stitch in color C
- − = Purl 1 stitch in color A
- − = Purl 1 stitch in color B
- − = Purl 1 stitch in color C
- ⊡ = Slip 1 stitch in color A purlwise, with working yarn in back of work
- ⊡ = Slip 1 stitch in color B purlwise, with working yarn in back of work
- ⊡ = Slip 1 stitch in color C purlwise, with working yarn in back of work
- ⊡ = Slip 1 stitch in color A purlwise, with working yarn in front of work

Shown are both RS and WS rows. Begin with the sts before the pattern repeat, rep the marked pattern repeat (4 sts wide) widthwise continuously, and end with the sts after the pattern repeat. Repeat Rows 1–24 heightwise.

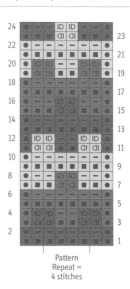

Pattern Repeat = 4 stitches

⊡ = Slip 1 stitch in color B purlwise, with working yarn in front of work

⊡ = Slip 1 stitch in color C purlwise, with working yarn in front of work

## 304 HORIZONTAL STRIPES

[multiple of 4 + 2 selv sts]

Shown are both RS and WS rows. Begin with the selv st before the pattern repeat, rep the marked pattern repeat (4 sts wide) widthwise continuously, and end with the selv st after the pattern repeat. After having completed Row 3 (= RS) in color B, slide the stitches back to the right end of the needle, and work Row 4 (= RS) in color A. After having completed Row 7 (= WS) in color A again, slide the stitches back to the right end of the needle, and work Row 8 (= WS) in color B. In Rows 3 and 8, work the stitches more loosely. Repeat Rows 1–10 heightwise.

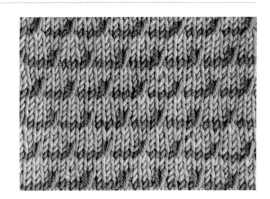

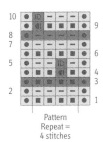

Pattern
Repeat =
4 stitches

### Stitch Key

⊙ = 1 selvedge stitch in color A

⊙ = 1 selvedge stitch in color B

■ = Knit 1 stitch in color A

■ = Knit 1 stitch in color B

− = Purl 1 stitch in color A

− = Purl 1 stitch in color B

⊡ = Slip 1 stitch in color B knitwise, with working yarn in back of work

ID = Slip 1 stitch in color B purlwise, with working yarn in front of work

## 305 LARGE BASKETWEAVE PATTERN

[multiple of 16 + 1 st + 2 selv sts]

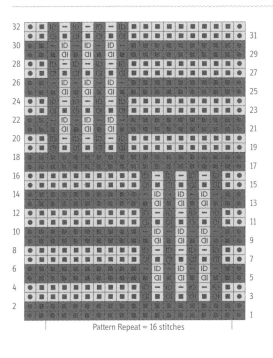

Pattern Repeat = 16 stitches

Shown are both RS and WS rows. Begin with the selv st before the pattern repeat, rep the marked pattern repeat (16 sts wide) widthwise continuously, and end with the sts after the pattern repeat. Repeat Rows 1–32 heightwise.

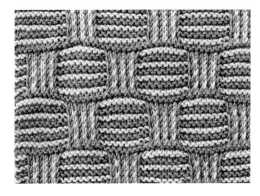

### Stitch Key

⊙ = 1 selvedge stitch in color A

⊙ = 1 selvedge stitch in color B

■ = Knit 1 stitch in color A

■ = Knit 1 stitch in color B

− = Purl 1 stitch in color A

− = Purl 1 stitch in color B

⊡ = Slip 1 stitch in color A purlwise, with working yarn in back of work

⊡ = Slip 1 stitch in color B purlwise, with working yarn in back of work

ID = Slip 1 stitch in color A purlwise, with working yarn in front of work

ID = Slip 1 stitch in color B purlwise, with working yarn in front of work

NUPPS

FLOWER
AND LEAF
PATTERNS

# **Nupp** Patterns

## 306 TINY NUPP PATTERN

[multiple of 2 + 1 st + 2 selv sts]

Only WS rows are shown; in RS rows, knit all sts. Begin with the sts before the pattern repeat, repeat the pattern repeat (2 sts wide) widthwise continuously, and end with the sts after the pattern repeat. Repeat Rows 1–4 heightwise.

### Stitch Key

● = 1 selvedge stitch

■ = Knit 1 stitch

N = Make 1 nupp: into the same stitch, work a total of 4 stitches (alternating [purl 1 stitch, knit 1 stitch]), and then, one after another, pass the 3rd, 2nd, and 1st stitch over the 4th stitch

Pattern
Repeat =
2 stitches

## 307 TWO-COLOR TINY NUPP PATTERN

[multiple of 2 + 1 st + 2 selv sts]

Only WS rows are shown; in RS rows, knit all sts. Begin with the sts before the pattern repeat, rep the marked pattern repeat (2 sts wide) widthwise continuously, and end with the sts after the pattern repeat. Change color at the beginning of every RS row. Repeat Rows 1–4 heightwise.

Pattern
Repeat =
2 stitches

### Stitch Key

■ = Knit 1 stitch in color A

■ = Knit 1 stitch in color B

● = 1 selvedge stitch in color A

● = 1 selvedge stitch in color B

N = Make 1 nupp in color A: into the following stitch, work a total of 4 stitches (alternating [purl 1 stitch, knit 1 stitch]), and then, one after another, pass the 3rd, 2nd, and 1st stitch over the 4th stitch

N = Make 1 nupp in color B: into the same stitch, work a total of 4 stitches (alternating [purl 1 stitch, knit 1 stitch]), and then, one after another, pass the 3rd, 2nd, and 1st stitch over the 4th stitch

## 308 EASY NUPP PATTERN

[multiple of 10 + 5 sts + 2 selv sts]

Only RS rows are shown; in WS rows, purl all sts. Begin with the sts before the pattern repeat, rep the marked pattern repeat (10 sts wide) widthwise continuously, and end with the sts after the pattern repeat. Repeat Rows 1–12 heightwise.

### Stitch Key

● = 1 selvedge stitch

■ = Knit 1 stitch

N = Make 1 nupp: into the same stitch, work a total of 3 stitches (knit 1 stitch, knit 1 stitch through the back loop, knit 1 stitch), turn work, knit 3 stitches, turn work, purl 3 stitches, turn work, knit 3 stitches, turn work, then double left-leaning decrease with passing over (sk2p)

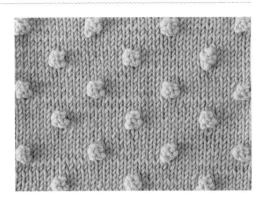

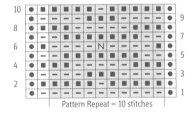

Pattern Repeat = 10 stitches

## 309 TEXTURED DIAMOND PATTERN WITH NUPPS

[multiple of 10 + 1 st + 2 selv sts]

Shown are both RS and WS rows. Begin with the selv st before the pattern repeat, rep the marked pattern repeat (10 sts wide) widthwise continuously, and end with the sts after the pattern repeat. Repeat Rows 1–10 heightwise.

### Stitch Key

● = 1 selvedge stitch

■ = Knit 1 stitch

─ = Purl 1 stitch

N = Make 1 nupp: into the same stitch, work a total of 3 stitches (knit 1 stitch, make 1 yarn over, knit 1 stitch), turn work, knit 3 stitches, turn work, purl 3 stitches, turn work, knit 3 stitches together, turn work, and slip the stitch purlwise

Pattern Repeat = 10 stitches

## 310 HAZELNUT PATTERN

[multiple of 4 + 1 st + 2 selv sts]

Shown are both RS and WS rows. Begin with the sts before the pattern repeat, rep the marked pattern repeat (4 sts wide) widthwise continuously, and end with the sts after the pattern repeat. Repeat Rows 1–12 heightwise.

### Stitch Key

● = 1 selvedge stitch

■ = Knit 1 stitch

─ = Purl 1 stitch

△ = Purl 3 stitches together.

3̌ = Work a total of 3 stitches into 1 stitch (knit 1, purl 1, knit 1)

☐ = No stitch, for better overview only

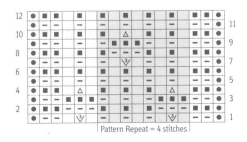

Pattern Repeat = 4 stitches

## 311 VERTICAL NUPP COLUMNS

[multiple of 8 + 3 sts + 2 selv sts]

Shown are both RS and WS rows. Begin with the selv st before the pattern repeat, rep the marked pattern repeat (8 sts wide) widthwise either once for a single vertical pattern column or continuously for an all-over pattern, and end with the sts after the pattern repeat. Repeat Rows 1–4 heightwise.

**Stitch Key**

● = 1 selvedge stitch

■ = Knit 1 stitch

– = Purl 1 stitch

N = Make 1 nupp: into the same stitch, work a total of 6 stitches (alternating [knit 1 stitch, knit 1 stitch through the back loop]), and then, one after another, pass the 5th, 4th, 3rd, 2nd, and 1st stitch over the 6th stitch

Pattern Repeat = 8 stitches

## 312 DIAGONAL NUPP ROWS

[multiple of 6 + 2 sts + 2 selv sts]

Only RS rows are shown; in WS rows, knit the knits, and purl the purls. Begin with the sts before the pattern repeat, rep the marked pattern repeat (6 sts wide) width-wise continuously, and end with the sts after the pattern repeat. Repeat Rows 1–12 heightwise.

**Stitch Key**

● = 1 selvedge stitch

■ = Knit 1 stitch

– = Purl 1 stitch

N = Make 1 nupp: into the same stitch, work a total of 6 stitches (alternating [knit 1 stitch, knit 1 stitch through the back loop]), and then, one after another, pass the 5th, 4th, 3rd, 2nd, and 1st stitch over the 6th stitch

Pattern Repeat = 6 stitches

## 313 CABLE-AND-NUPP COLUMNS

[multiple of 9 + 8 sts + 2 selv sts]

Only RS rows are shown; in WS rows, knit the knits, purl the purls, and knit the nupp stitches. Begin with the sts before the pattern repeat, rep the marked pattern repeat (9 sts wide) widthwise either once for a single verti-cal pattern column or continuously for an all-over pattern, and end with the sts after the pattern repeat. Repeat Rows 1–8 heightwise.

**Stitch Key**

● = 1 selvedge stitch

■ = Knit 1 stitch

– = Purl 1 stitch

▤▤▤▤ = Hold 2 stitches on a cable needle in front of work, knit 2 stitches, then knit the 2 stitches from the cable needle

N = Make 1 nupp: into the same stitch, work a total of 5 stitches (alternating [knit 1 stitch, make 1 yarn over]), turn work, purl 5 stitches, turn work, knit 5 stitches, turn work, purl 5 stitches, turn work, (knit 2 stitches together) twice, knit the next stitch, and then, one after another, pass the 2nd and 1st stitch over the 3rd stitch

Pattern Repeat = 9 stitches

## 314 ZIGZAG CORD WITH NUPPS

[multiple of 13 + 3 sts + 2 selv sts]

Only RS rows are shown; in WS rows, knit the knits, purl the purls, and purl the nupp stitches. Begin with the selv st before the pattern repeat, rep the marked pattern repeat (13 sts wide) either once for a single vertical pattern column or continuously for an all-over pattern, and end with the sts after the pattern repeat. Repeat Rows 1–24 heightwise.

### Stitch Key

● = 1 selvedge stitch

■ = Knit 1 stitch

– = Purl 1 stitch

= Hold 4 stitches on a cable needle in front of work, knit the next stitch, then knit the 4 stitches from the cable needle

= Hold 1 stitch on a cable needle behind work, knit 4 stitches, then knit the stitch from the cable needle

N = Make 1 nupp: into the same stitch, work a total of 5 stitches (alternating [knit 1 stitch, make 1 yarn over]), turn work, purl 5 stitches, turn work, knit 5 stitches, turn work, purl 5 stitches, turn work, (knit 2 stitches together) twice, knit the next stitch, and then, one after another, pass the 2nd and 1st stitch over the 3rd stitch

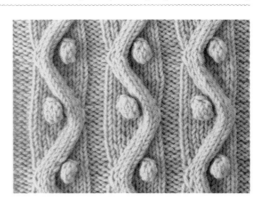

Pattern Repeat = 13 stitches

## 315 NUPP TREES

[multiple of 14 + 1 st + 2 selv sts]

Only RS rows are shown; in WS rows, knit the knits, purl the purls through the back loop, and knit the nupp stitches. Begin with the selv st before the pattern repeat, rep the marked pattern repeat (14 sts wide) widthwise continuously, and end with the sts after the pattern repeat. Repeat Rows 1–32 heightwise.

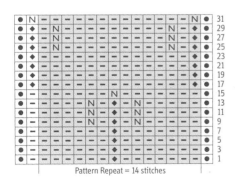

Pattern Repeat = 14 stitches

### Stitch Key

● = 1 selvedge stitch

◆ = Knit 1 stitch through the back loop

– = Purl 1 stitch

N = Make 1 nupp: into the same stitch, work a total of 5 stitches (alternating [knit 1 stitch, purl 1 stitch]), turn work, purl 5 stitches, turn work, and knit 5 stitches together through the back loop

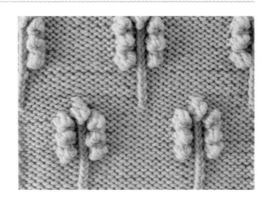

## 316 DOUBLE ZIGZAG CORD WITH NUPPS [multiple of 21 + 9 sts + 2 selv sts]

Only RS rows are shown; in WS rows, knit the knits, purl the purls, and purl the nupp stitches. Begin with the sts before the pattern repeat, rep the marked pattern repeat (21 sts wide) widthwise either once for a single vertical pattern column or continuously for an all-over pattern, and end with the sts after the pattern repeat. Repeat Rows 1–24 heightwise.

Pattern Repeat = 21 stitches

### Stitch Key

● = 1 selvedge stitch

■ = Knit 1 stitch

– = Purl 1 stitch

= Hold 3 stitches on a cable needle in front of work, knit the next stitch, then knit the 3 stitches from the cable needle

= Hold 1 stitch on a cable needle behind work, knit 3 stitches, then knit the stitch from the cable needle

N = Make 1 nupp: into the same stitch, work a total of 5 stitches (alternating [knit 1 stitch, make 1 yarn over]), turn work, purl 5 stitches, turn work, knit 5 stitches, turn work, purl 5 stitches, turn work, (knit 2 stitches together) twice, knit the next stitch, and then, one after another, pass the 2nd and 1st stitch over the 3rd stitch

## 317 ARGYLE PATTERN IN NUPPS [multiple of 12 + 5 sts + 2 selv sts]

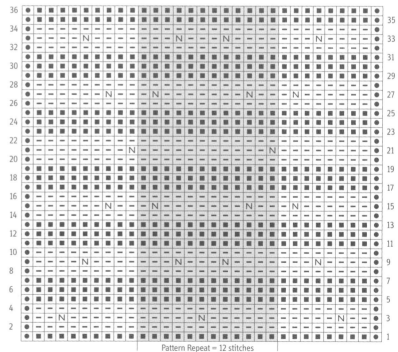

Pattern Repeat = 12 stitches

Shown are both RS and WS rows. Begin with the sts before the pattern repeat, rep the marked pattern repeat (12 sts wide) widthwise continuously, and end with the sts after the pattern repeat. Repeat Rows 1–36 heightwise.

### Stitch Key

● = 1 selvedge stitch

■ = Knit 1 stitch

– = Purl 1 stitch

N = Make 1 nupp: into the same stitch, work a total of 5 stitches (alternating [knit 1 stitch, make 1 yarn over]), turn work, purl 5 stitches, turn work, knit 5 stitches, turn work, purl 5 stitches, turn work, (knit 2 stitches together) twice, knit the next stitch, and then, one after another, pass the 2nd and 1st stitch over the 3rd stitch

## 318 PERSIAN PATTERN

[multiple of 2 + 2 selv sts]

Only WS rows are shown; in RS rows, purl all stitches. Begin with the sts before the pattern repeat, rep the marked pattern repeat (2 sts wide) widthwise continuously, and end with the sts after the pattern repeat. Repeat Rows 1–4 heightwise.

### Stitch Key

● = 1 selvedge stitch

■ = Knit 1 stitch

△ = Purl 3 stitches together

⑦ = Work a total of 3 stitches into 1 stitch (knit 1, purl 1, knit 1)

Pattern Repeat = 2 stitches

## 319 THREE-COLOR PERSIAN PATTERN

[multiple of 2 + 2 selv sts]

Only WS rows are shown; in RS rows, purl all stitches. Begin with the sts before the pattern repeat, rep the marked pattern repeat (2 sts wide) widthwise continuously, and end with the sts after the pattern repeat. Change color at the beginning of every WS row. Repeat Rows 1–12 heightwise.

### Stitch Key

● = 1 selvedge stitch in color A

● = 1 selvedge stitch in color B

● = 1 selvedge stitch in color C

■ = Knit 1 stitch in color A

■ = Knit 1 stitch in color B

■ = Knit 1 stitch in color C

⑦ = In color A, make 3 stitches from 1 by working (knit 1, purl 1, knit 1) into the same stitch

⑦ = In color B, make 3 stitches from 1 by working (knit 1, purl 1, knit 1) into the same stitch

⑦ = In color C, make 3 stitches from 1 by working (knit 1, purl 1, knit 1) into the same stitch

△ = Purl 3 stitches in color A together

△ = Purl 3 stitches in color B together

△ = Purl 3 stitches in color C together

Pattern Repeat = 2 stitches

## 320 ASTRAKHAN NUPPS

[multiple of 12 + 3 sts + 2 selv sts]

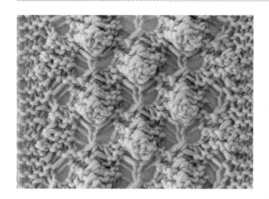

Shown are both RS and WS rows. Begin with the sts before the pattern repeat, rep the marked pattern repeat (12 sts wide) widthwise continuously, and end with the sts after the pattern repeat. Repeat Rows 1–12 heightwise.

### Stitch Key

- ● = 1 selvedge stitch
- ■ = Knit 1 stitch
- O = Make 1 yarn over
- △ = Purl 3 stitches together
- ⊿ = Purl 2 stitches together

Pattern Repeat = 12 stitches

## 321 NUPPS IN CABLED DIAMONDS

[multiple of 19 + 8 sts + 2 selv sts]

### Stitch Key

- ● = 1 selvedge stitch
- ■ = Knit 1 stitch
- – = Purl 1 stitch
- ◥■■■ = Hold 3 stitches on a cable needle in front of work, knit the next stitch, then knit the 3 stitches from the cable needle
- ■■■◢ = Hold 1 stitch on a cable needle behind work, knit 3 stitches, then knit the stitch from the cable needle
- –◥■■■ = Hold 3 stitches on a cable needle in front of work, purl 1 stitch, then knit the 3 stitches from the cable needle
- ■■■◢– = Hold 1 stitch on a cable needle behind work, knit 3 stitches, then purl the stitch from the cable needle

- ■■■◢◥■■■ = Hold 3 stitches on a cable needle in front of work, hold 1 stitch on a second cable needle behind work, knit 3 stitches, then knit the stitch from the second cable needle, then knit the 3 stitches from the first cable needle
- N = Make 1 nupp: into the same stitch, work a total of 5 stitches (alternating [knit 1 stitch, make 1 yarn over]), turn work, purl 5 stitches, turn work, knit 5 stitches, turn work, purl 5 stitches, turn work, (knit 2 stitches together) twice, knit the next stitch, and then, one after another, pass the 2nd and 1st stitch over the 3rd stitch

Only RS rows are shown; in WS rows, knit the knits, purl the purls, and purl the nupp stitches. For a single vertical pattern column begin with the sts before the pattern repeat, rep the marked pattern repeat (19 sts wide) once, and end with the sts after the pattern repeat. For an all-over pattern, begin with the first selv st, then skip the 3 knit stitches, and work only the purl stitch before the pattern repeat. Rep the marked pattern repeat (19 sts wide) continuously, and after the pattern repeat, purl 1 stitch, then skip the 3 knit stitches, and end with the selv st. Repeat Rows 1–26 heightwise.

Pattern Repeat = 19 stitches

## 322 INTERWOVEN LOZENGE PATTERN WITH NUPPS

[multiple of 10 + 2 sts + 2 selv sts]

Only RS rows are shown; in WS rows, knit the knits, purl the purls, and knit the nupp stitches. Begin with the sts before the pattern repeat, rep the marked pattern repeat (10 sts wide) (not including the temporary nupp in Row 1 and Row 9 into the stitch count) either once for a single vertical pattern column or continuously for an all-over pattern, and end with the sts after the pattern repeat. Repeat Rows 1–16 heightwise.

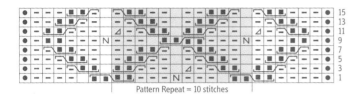

Pattern Repeat = 10 stitches

### Stitch Key

| ● | = 1 selvedge stitch |

| ■ | = Knit 1 stitch |

| − | = Purl 1 stitch |

| ⊿ | = Purl 2 stitches together |

| ☐ | = No stitch, for better overview only |

= Hold 2 stitches on a cable needle in front of work, purl 1 stitch, then knit the 2 stitches from the cable needle

= Hold 1 stitch on a cable needle behind work, knit 2 stitches, then purl the stitch from the cable needle

= Hold 2 stitches on a cable needle behind work, knit 2 stitches, then knit the 2 stitches from the cable needle

= Hold 2 stitches on a cable needle in front of work, knit 2 stitches, then knit the 2 stitches from the cable needle

N = Make 1 nupp: increase 5 stitches knitwise twisted from the bar between stitches (alternating [knit 1 stitch through the back loop, make 1 yarn over]), turn work, purl 5 stitches, turn work, knit 5 stitches, turn work, purl 5 stitches, turn work, (knit 2 stitches together) twice, knit the next stitch, and then, one after another, pass the 2nd and 1st stitch over the 3rd stitch

## 323 DIAMOND PATTERN FROM SMALL NUPPS

[multiple of 20 + 5 sts + 2 selv sts]

Only WS rows are shown; in RS rows, purl all stitches. Begin with the sts before the pattern repeat, rep the marked pattern repeat (20 sts wide) either once for a single vertical pattern column or continuously for an all-over pattern, and end with the sts after the pattern repeat. Work Rows 1–22 once, rep Rows 3–22 continuously, and end with Rows 23–24.

### Stitch Key

| ● | = 1 selvedge stitch |

| ■ | = Knit 1 stitch |

| △ | = Purl 3 stitches together |

| ⅋ | = Work a total of 3 stitches into 1 stitch (knit 1, purl 1, knit 1) |

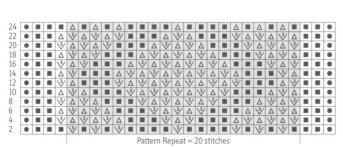

Pattern Repeat = 20 stitches

## 324 BLACKBERRY PATTERN
[multiple of 4 + 2 selv sts]

Shown are both RS and WS rows. Begin with the selv st before the pattern repeat, rep the marked pattern repeat (4 sts wide) widthwise continuously, and end with the selv st after the pattern repeat. Repeat Rows 1–4 heightwise.

**Stitch Key**

● = 1 selvedge stitch

■ = Knit 1 stitch

– = Purl 1 stitch

△ = Purl 3 stitches together

⦦ = Work a total of 3 stitches into 1 stitch (knit 1, purl 1, knit 1)

☐ = No stitch, for better overview only

Pattern Repeat = 4 stitches

## 325 NUPP TREES
[multiple of 18 + 15 sts + 2 selv sts]

Only RS rows are shown; in WS rows, knit the knits, purl the purls, and knit the nupp stitches. Begin with the sts before the pattern repeat, rep the marked pattern repeat (18 sts wide) widthwise continuously, and end with the sts after the pattern repeat. Repeat Rows 1–34 heightwise.

**Stitch Key**

● = 1 selvedge stitch

■ = Knit 1 stitch

– = Purl 1 stitch

= Hold 2 stitches on a cable needle in front of work, purl 1 stitch, then knit the 2 stitches from the cable needle

= Hold 1 stitch on a cable needle behind work, knit 2 stitches, then purl the stitch from the cable needle

= Hold 2 stitches on a cable needle in front of work, hold 1 stitch on a second cable needle behind work, knit 2 stitches, then purl the stitch from the second cable needle, then knit the 2 stitches from the first cable needle

N = Make 1 nupp: into the same stitch, work a total of 5 stitches (alternating [knit 1 stitch, make 1 yarn over]), turn work, purl 5 stitches, turn work, knit 5 stitches, turn work, purl 5 stitches, turn work, (knit 2 stitches together) twice, knit the next stitch, and then, one after another, pass the 2nd and 1st stitch over the 3rd stitch

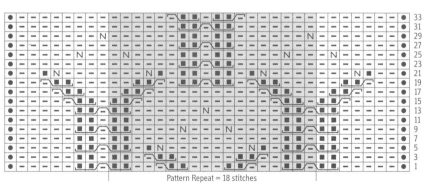

Pattern Repeat = 18 stitches

# Flower Patterns

## 326 FLOWER MOTIF

[multiple of 23 + 2 sts + 2 selv sts]

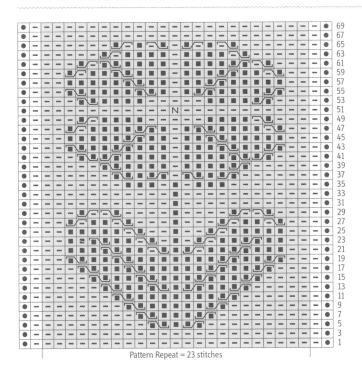

Pattern Repeat = 23 stitches

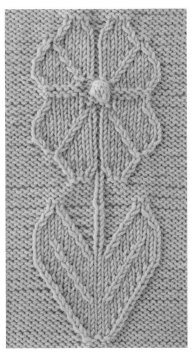

### Stitch Key

● = 1 selvedge stitch

■ = Knit 1 stitch

– = Purl 1 stitch

= Hold 1 stitch on a cable needle in front of work, knit the next stitch, then knit the stitch from the cable needle

= Hold 1 stitch on a cable needle behind work, knit the next stitch, then knit the stitch from the cable needle

= Hold 1 stitch on a cable needle in front of work, purl the next stitch, then knit the stitch from the cable needle

= Hold 1 stitch on a cable needle behind work, knit the next stitch, then purl the stitch from the cable needle

N = Make 1 nupp: into the same stitch, work a total of 5 stitches (alternating [knit 1 stitch, purl 1 stitch]), * turn work, purl 5 stitches, turn work, knit 5 stitches * , repeat from * to * once more, and then, one after another, pass the 4th, 3rd, 2nd, and 1st stitch over the 5th stitch

Only RS rows are shown; in WS rows, knit the knits, purl the purls, and knit the nupp stitches. Begin with the sts before the pattern repeat, rep the marked pattern repeat (23 sts wide) widthwise continuously, and end with the sts after the pattern repeat. Repeat Rows 1–70 heightwise.

## 327 IRIS PATTERN

[multiple of 18 + 1 st + 2 selv sts]

Only RS rows are shown; in WS rows, knit the knits, and purl the purls and yarn overs. Begin with the sts before the pattern repeat, rep the marked pattern repeat (18 sts wide) widthwise continuously, and end with the sts after the pattern repeat. Repeat Rows 1–36 heightwise.

### Stitch Key

● = 1 selvedge stitch

■ = Knit 1 stitch

– = Purl 1 stitch

O = Make 1 yarn over

◢ = Knit 2 stitches together

◣ = Knit 2 stitches together left-leaning with passing over (skp): slip 1 stitch knitwise, knit the next stitch, and pass the slipped stitch over

△ = Knit 3 stitches together left-leaning with passing over (sk2p): slip 1 stitch knitwise, knit 2 stitches together, and pass the slipped stitch over

Chart rows: 35, 33, 31, 29, 27, 25, 23, 21, 19, 17, 15, 13, 11, 9, 7, 5, 3, 1

Pattern Repeat = 18 stitches

## 328 ALL-OVER BLOSSOM PATTERN

[multiple of 13 + 2 selv sts]

Chart rows: 10, 8, 6, 4, 2 / 9, 7, 5, 3, 1

Pattern Repeat = 13 stitches

Shown are both RS and WS rows. Begin with the selv st before the pattern repeat, rep the marked pattern repeat (13 sts wide) widthwise continuously, and end with the selv st after the pattern repeat. Repeat Rows 1–10 heightwise.

### Stitch Key

● = 1 selvedge stitch

■ = Knit 1 stitch

– = Purl 1 stitch

O = Make 1 yarn over

◢ = Knit 2 stitches together

◢ = Purl 2 stitches together

☐ = No stitch, for better overview only

⋁ = Work a total of 6 stitches into 1 stitch: * knit the next stitch, leaving the stitch on the left needle, then purl the same stitch, and let it slip off the left needle. Repeat from * 2 times more.

## 329 TULIP WITH NUPPS

[multiple of 25 + 2 sts + 2 selv sts]

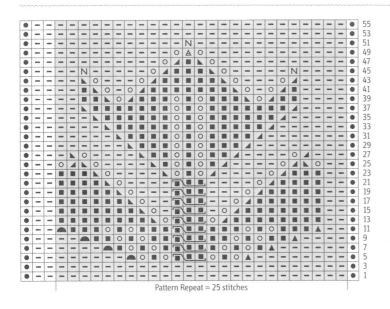

Pattern Repeat = 25 stitches

### Stitch Key

● = 1 selvedge stitch

■ = Knit 1 stitch

— = Purl 1 stitch

○ = Make 1 yarn over

◢ = Knit 2 stitches together

◣ = Knit 2 stitches together left-leaning with passing over (skp): slip 1 stitch knitwise, knit the next stitch, and pass the slipped stitch over

△ = Knit 3 stitches together left-leaning with passing over (sk2p): slip 1 stitch knitwise, knit 2 stitches together, and pass the slipped stitch over

◖ = Slip 2 stitches together knitwise through the back loop, knit 1 stitch, and pass the slipped stitches over

N = Make 1 nupp: work a total of 5 stitches into the same stitch (alternating [knit 1 stitch, purl 1 stitch]), * turn work, purl 5 stitches, turn work, knit 5 stitches * , repeat from * to * once more, and then, one after another, pass the 4th, 3rd, 2nd, and 1st stitch over the 5th stitch

◣■■ = Hold 2 stitches on a cable needle in front of work, knit the next stitch, then knit the stitches from the cable needle

Only RS rows are shown; in WS rows, knit the knits, and purl the purls and yarn overs. Begin with the selv st before the pattern repeat, rep the marked pattern repeat (25 sts wide) either once for a single motif or a single vertical pattern column or continuously for an all-over pattern, and end with the sts after the pattern repeat. Work Rows 1–55 either once for a single motif or a single vertical pattern column or continuously for an all-over pattern.

## 330 BED OF TULIPS

[multiple of 16 + 3 sts + 2 selv sts]

### Stitch Key

● = 1 selvedge stitch

■ = Knit 1 stitch

– = Purl 1 stitch

O = Make 1 yarn over

◢ = Knit 2 stitches together

◣ = Knit 2 stitches together left-leaning with passing over (skp): slip 1 stitch knitwise, knit the next stitch, and pass the slipped stitch over

∩ = Centered double decrease, knitting 3 stitches together with center stitch on top (cdd): slip 2 stitches together knitwise, knit 1 stitch, and pass the slipped stitches over

Only RS rows are shown; in WS rows, knit the knits, and purl the purls and yarn overs. Begin with the sts before the pattern repeat, rep the marked pattern repeat (16 sts wide) widthwise continuously, and end with the sts after the pattern repeat. Repeat Rows 1–48 heightwise.

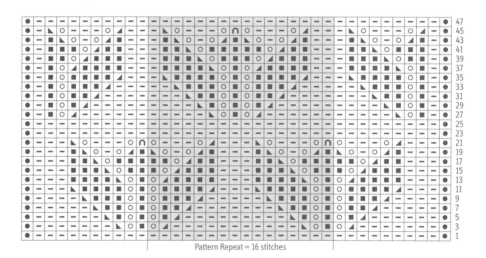

Pattern Repeat = 16 stitches

## 331 FLOWER BOUQUETS WITH NUPPS [multiple of 12 + 1 st + 2 selv sts]

### Stitch Key

⬤ = 1 selvedge stitch

◆ = Knit 1 stitch through the back loop

− = Purl 1 stitch

N = Make 1 nupp: into the same stitch, work a total of 3 stitches (knit 1, purl 1, knit 1), turn work, purl 3 stitches, turn work, knit 3 stitches, turn work, purl 3 stitches, turn work, then knit 3 stitches together left-leaning (sssk)

◆/− = Hold 1 stitch on a cable needle behind work, knit 1 stitch through the back loop, then purl the stitch from the cable needle

−\◆ = Hold 1 stitch on a cable needle in front of work, purl 1 stitch, then knit the stitch from the cable needle through the back loop

◆/◆\◆ = Hold 1 stitch on a cable needle in front of work, hold 1 stitch on a second cable needle behind work, knit 1 stitch through the back loop, then first knit the stitch from the second cable needle through the back loop, then knit the stitch from the first cable needle through the back loop

Only RS rows are shown; in WS rows, knit the knits, purl the purls through the back loop, and knit the nupp stitches. Begin with the sts before the pattern repeat, rep the marked pattern repeat (12 sts wide) widthwise continuously, and end with the sts after the pattern repeat. Repeat Rows 1–28 heightwise.

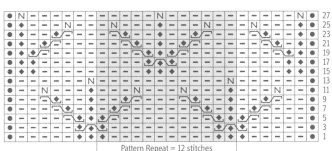

Pattern Repeat = 12 stitches

## 332 COLUMNS OF BLOSSOMS WITH NUPPS [multiple of 11 + 2 sts + 2 selv sts]

Only RS rows are shown; in WS rows, knit the knits, and purl the purls and yarn overs. Begin with the sts before the pattern repeat, rep the marked pattern repeat (11 sts wide) widthwise either once for a single vertical pattern column or continuously for an all-over pattern, and end with the sts after the pattern repeat. Repeat Rows 1–16 heightwise.

### Stitch Key

⬤ = 1 selvedge stitch

■ = Knit 1 stitch

− = Purl 1 stitch

O = Make 1 yarn over

◢ = Knit 2 stitches together

◣ = Knit 2 stitches together left-leaning with passing over (skp): slip 1 stitch knitwise, knit the next stitch, and pass the slipped stitch over

⋒ = Centered double decrease, knitting 3 stitches together with center

stitch on top (cdd): slip 2 stitches together knitwise, knit 1 stitch, and pass the slipped stitches over

N = Make 1 nupp: into the same stitch, work a total of 5 stitches (alternating [knit 1 stitch, make 1 yarn over]), turn work, purl 5 stitches, turn work, knit 5 stitches, turn work, purl 5 stitches, turn work, (knit 2 stitches together) twice, knit the next stitch, and then, one after another, pass the 2nd and 1st stitch over the 3rd stitch

Pattern Repeat = 11 stitches

# 333 SEA OF FLOWERS

[multiple of 22 + 3 sts + 2 selv sts]

Only RS rows are shown; in WS rows, knit the knits, and purl the purls. Begin with the sts before the pattern repeat, rep the marked pattern repeat (22 sts wide) widthwise continuously, and end with the sts after the pattern repeat. Repeat Rows 1–76 heightwise.

## Stitch Key

● = 1 selvedge stitch

■ = Knit 1 stitch

– = Purl 1 stitch

[3] = Work a total of 3 stitches into 1 stitch (knit 1, purl 1, knit 1)

▲ = Knit 3 stitches together left-leaning (sssk)

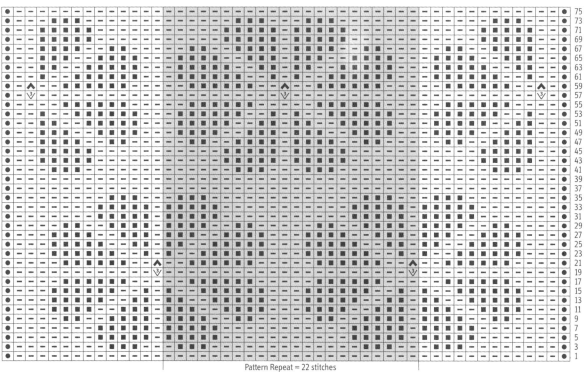

Pattern Repeat = 22 stitches

## 334 COLUMNS OF FILIGREE BLOSSOMS

[multiple of 14 + 2 sts + 2 selv sts]

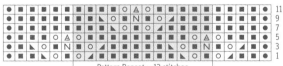

Pattern Repeat = 14 stitches

### Stitch Key

● = 1 selvedge stitch

■ = Knit 1 stitch

– = Purl 1 stitch

○ = Make 1 yarn over

◢ = Knit 2 stitches together

◣ = Knit 2 stitches together left-leaning with passing over (skp): slip 1 stitch knitwise, knit the next stitch, and pass the slipped stitch over

☐ = No stitch, for better overview only

✳ = Slip 6 stitches one after another knitwise, then knit them together

⊙ = Slip 6 stitches one after another purlwise, then knit them together

Only RS rows are shown; in WS rows, knit the knits, and purl the purls and yarn overs. Begin with the sts before the pattern repeat, rep the marked pattern repeat (14 sts wide) widthwise either once for a single vertical pattern column or continuously for an all-over pattern, and end with the sts after the pattern repeat. Repeat Rows 1—16 heightwise.

## 335 SMALL BLOSSOMS WITH NUPPS

[multiple of 12 + 9 sts + 2 selv sts]

Only RS rows are shown; in WS rows, purl all stitches and yarn overs. Begin with the sts before the pattern repeat, rep the marked pattern repeat (12 sts wide) widthwise continuously, and end with the sts after the pattern repeat. Repeat Rows 1—12 heightwise.

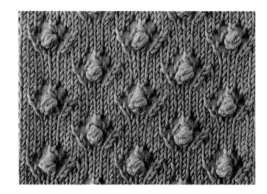

Pattern Repeat = 12 stitches

### Stitch Key

● = 1 selvedge stitch

■ = Knit 1 stitch

○ = Make 1 yarn over

◢ = Knit 2 stitches together

◣ = Knit 2 stitches together left-leaning with passing over (skp): slip 1 stitch knitwise, knit the next stitch, and pass the slipped stitch over

▲ = Knit 3 stitches together left-leaning with passing over (sk2p): slip 1 stitch knitwise, knit 2 stitches together, and pass the slipped stitch over

N = Make 1 nupp: into the same stitch, work a total of 6 stitches (alternating [knit 1 stitch, knit 1 stitch through the back loop]), turn work, purl all 6 stitches together, turn work, and knit 1 stitch

## 336 TRAVELING-STITCH BELL

[multiple of 13 + 5 sts + 2 selv sts]

Shown are both RS and WS rows. Begin with the sts before the pattern repeat, rep the marked pattern repeat (13 sts wide) either once for a single vertical pattern column or continuously for an all-over pattern, and end with the sts after the pattern repeat. Repeat Rows 1–18 heightwise.

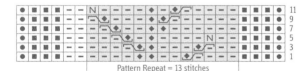

Pattern Repeat = 13 stitches

### Stitch Key

● = 1 selvedge stitch

■ = Knit 1 stitch

◆ = Knit 1 stitch through the back loop

◇ = Purl 1 stitch through the back loop

— = Purl 1 stitch

◆◆ = Hold 1 stitch on a cable needle in front of work, knit 1 stitch through the back loop, then knit the stitch from the cable needle through the back loop

◇◇ = Hold 1 stitch on a cable needle in front of work, purl 1 stitch through the back loop, then purl the stitch from the cable needle through the back loop

◆— = Hold 1 stitch on a cable needle behind work, knit 1 stitch through the back loop, then purl the stitch from the cable needle

—◆ = Hold 1 stitch on a cable needle in front of work, purl 1 stitch, then knit the stitch from the cable needle through the back loop

◇■ = Hold 1 stitch on a cable needle in front of work, purl 1 stitch through the back loop, then knit the stitch from the cable needle

■◇ = Hold 1 stitch on a cable needle behind work, knit the next stitch, then purl the stitch from the cable needle through the back loop

## 337 VINES WITH NUPP BLOSSOMS

[multiple of 13 + 8 sts + 2 selv sts]

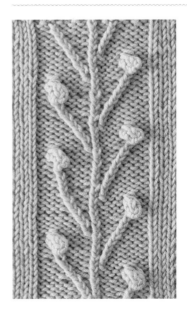

Only RS rows are shown; in WS rows, knit the knits, purl the purls, and purl those stitches through the back loop that had been previously knitted through the back loop, and knit the nupp stitches. For a single vine, begin with the stitches before the marked pattern repeat, rep the marked pattern repeat (13 sts wide) once, and end with the sts after the pattern repeat. For an all-over pattern, begin with the first selv st, then skip the 3 knit stitches, and rep the marked pattern repeat (13 sts wide) widthwise continuously. After the pattern repeat, purl 2 stitches, then skip the 3 knit stitches, and end with the selv st. Repeat Rows 1–12 heightwise.

Pattern Repeat = 13 stitches

### Stitch Key

● = 1 selvedge stitch

■ = Knit 1 stitch

◆ = Knit 1 stitch through the back loop

— = Purl 1 stitch

◆— = Hold 1 stitch on a cable needle behind work, knit 1 stitch through the back loop, then purl the stitch from the cable needle

—◆ = Hold 1 stitch on a cable needle in front of work, purl 1 stitch, then knit the stitch from the cable needle through the back loop

N = Make 1 nupp: into the same stitch, work a total of 3 stitches (knit 1, purl 1, knit 1), turn work, purl 3 stitches, turn work, knit 3 stitches, turn work, purl 3 stitches, turn work, then knit 3 stitches together left-leaning (sssk)

## 338 ROSE BUDS

[multiple of 14 + 5 sts + 2 selv sts]

### Stitch Key

● = 1 selvedge stitch

■ = Knit 1 stitch

◆ = Knit 1 stitch
through the back loop

◇ = Purl 1 stitch
through the back loop

− = Purl 1 stitch

☐ = No stitch, for better overview only

◆/− = Hold 1 stitch on a
cable needle behind work, knit
1 stitch through the back loop,
then purl the stitch from the
cable needle

−◆ = Hold 1 stitch on a
cable needle in front of work,
purl 1 stitch, then knit the
stitch from the cable needle
through the back loop

⑤ = Into the same stitch,
work a total of 5 stitches (knit
1 stitch, make 1 yarn over, knit
1 stitch, make 1 yarn over, knit
1 stitch)

⑤ = Knit 5 stitches together
as follows: knit the 1st
and 2nd stitches together
left-leaning (ssk), knit the 3rd,
4th, and 5th stitches together,
then pass the stitch resulting
from having worked ssk over
the stitch resulting from having worked k3tog

Shown are both RS and WS rows.
Begin with the sts before the
pattern repeat, rep the marked
pattern repeat (14 sts wide) widthwise continuously, and end with
the sts after the pattern repeat.
Repeat Rows 1–40 heightwise. For
better overview, the inserted buds
are charted separately in the
smaller chart at left.

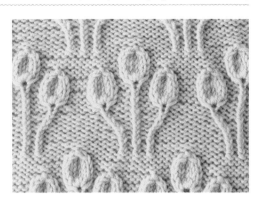

Pattern Repeat = 14 stitches

# **Leaf** Patterns

## 339 LEAFY VINE WITH STAGGERED LEAVES

[multiple of 26 + 7 sts + 2 selv sts]

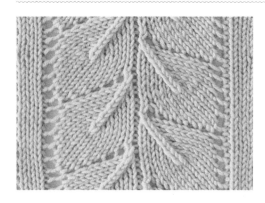

Only RS rows are shown; in WS rows, knit the knits, and purl the purls and yarn overs. Begin with the sts before the pattern repeat, rep the marked pattern repeat (26 sts wide) either once for a single vertical pattern column or continuously for an all-over pattern, and end with the sts after the pattern repeat. Repeat Rows 1–12 heightwise.

### Stitch Key

● = 1 selvedge stitch

■ = Knit 1 stitch

− = Purl 1 stitch

O = Make 1 yarn over

◢ = Knit 2 stitches together

◣ = Knit 2 stitches together left-leaning with passing over (skp): slip 1 stitch knitwise, knit the next stitch, and pass the slipped stitch over

∩ = Centered double decrease, knitting 3 stitches together with center stitch on top (cdd): slip 2 stitches together knitwise, knit 1 stitch, and pass the slipped stitches over

Pattern Repeat = 26 stitches

## 340 LEAF PATTERN STRIPS

[multiple of 23 + 8 sts + 2 selv sts]

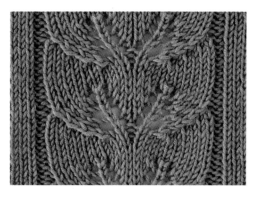

Only RS rows are shown; in WS rows, knit the knits, and purl the purls and yarn overs. Begin with the sts before the pattern repeat, rep the marked pattern repeat (23 sts wide) either once for a single vertical pattern column or continuously for an all-over pattern, and end with the sts after the pattern repeat. Repeat Rows 1–12 heightwise.

### Stitch Key

● = 1 selvedge stitch

■ = Knit 1 stitch

− = Purl 1 stitch

O = Make 1 yarn over

△ = Knit 3 stitches together left-leaning with passing over (sk2p): slip 1 stitch knitwise, knit 2 stitches together, and pass the slipped stitch over

▲ = Knit 3 stitches together

Pattern Repeat = 23 stitches

## 341 ALTERNATING FERN FRONDS

[multiple of 17 + 1 st + 2 selv sts]

Only RS rows are shown; in WS rows, knit the knits, and purl the purls and yarn overs. Begin with the selv st before the pattern repeat, rep the marked pattern repeat (17 sts wide) width-wise either once for a single vertical pattern column or continuously for an all-over pattern, and end with the sts after the pattern repeat. Repeat Rows 1–12 heightwise.

### Stitch Key

● = 1 selvedge stitch

■ = Knit 1 stitch

O = Make 1 yarn over

△ = Knit 3 stitches together left-leaning with passing over (sk2p): slip 1 stitch knitwise, knit 2 stitches together, and pass the slipped stitch over

▲ = Knit 3 stitches together

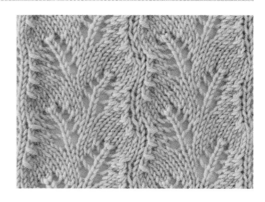

Pattern Repeat = 17 stitches

## 342 LEAF BOUQUETS

[multiple of 20 + 13 sts + 2 selv sts]

### Stitch Key

● = 1 selvedge stitch

■ = Knit 1 stitch

– = Purl 1 stitch

+ = Increase 1 stitch twisted from the bar be-tween stitches

✗ = Increase 1 stitch purlwise twisted from the bar between stitches

◢ = Knit 2 stitches together

◣ = Knit 2 stitches together left-leaning with passing over (skp): slip 1 stitch knitwise, knit the next stitch, and pass the slipped stitch over

◤ = Purl 2 stitches together

⑤ = Work a total of 5 stitches into 1 stitch: knit 1 stitch, leaving the stitch on the left needle, then purl the same stitch, then work another (knit 1 stitch, purl 1 stitch, knit 1 stitch) into the same stitch, and let it slip off the left needle

▲ = Knit 3 stitches together left-leaning with passing over (sk2p): slip 1 stitch knitwise, knit 2 stitches together, and pass the slipped stitch over

☐ = No stitch, for better overview only

■╱–╱ = Hold 1 stitch on a cable needle behind work, knit the next stitch, then purl the stitch from the cable needle

–╲■ = Hold 1 stitch on a cable needle in front of work, purl the next stitch, then knit the stitch from the cable needle

■╲■╲■ = Hold 2 stitches on a cable needle in front of work, knit the next stitch, then knit the stitches from the cable needle

Only RS rows are shown; in WS rows, knit the knits, and purl the purls. Begin with the sts before the pattern repeat, rep the marked pattern repeat (20 sts wide) either once for a single vertical pattern column or continuously for an all-over pattern, and end with the sts after the pattern repeat. Repeat Rows 1–28 heightwise. For better overview, the inserted leaves are charted separately in the smaller chart below.

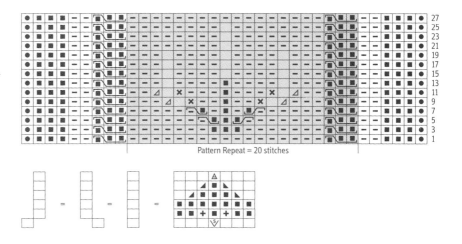

Pattern Repeat = 20 stitches

## 343 ALL-OVER LEAF PATTERN

[multiple of 10 + 1 st + 2 selv sts]

Only RS rows are shown; in WS rows, purl all stitches and yarn overs. Begin with the sts before the pattern repeat, rep the marked pattern repeat (10 sts wide) widthwise continuously, and end with the sts after the pattern repeat. Repeat Rows 1–16 heightwise.

### Stitch Key

● = 1 selvedge stitch

■ = Knit 1 stitch

○ = Make 1 yarn over

◢ = Knit 2 stitches together

◣ = Knit 2 stitches together left-leaning with passing over (skp): slip 1 stitch knitwise, knit the next stitch, and pass the slipped stitch over

∩ = Centered double decrease, knitting 3 stitches together with center stitch on top (cdd): slip 2 stitches together knitwise, knit 1 stitch, and pass the slipped stitches over

Chart rows: 15, 13, 11, 9, 7, 5, 3, 1

Pattern Repeat = 10 stitches

## 344 SHIFTED LEAF MOTIFS

[multiple of 6 + 1 st + 2 selv sts]

Only RS rows are shown; in WS rows, knit the knits, and purl the purls and yarn overs. Begin with the sts before the pattern repeat, rep the marked pattern repeat (6 sts wide) widthwise continuously, and end with the sts after the pattern repeat. Repeat Rows 1–28 heightwise.

### Stitch Key

● = 1 selvedge stitch

■ = Knit 1 stitch

– = Purl 1 stitch

○ = Make 1 yarn over

☐ = No stitch, for better overview only

◢ = Knit 2 stitches together

◣ = Knit 2 stitches together left-leaning with passing over (skp): slip 1 stitch knitwise, knit the next stitch, and pass the slipped stitch over

△ = Knit 3 stitches together left-leaning with passing over (sk2p): slip 1 stitch knitwise, knit 2 stitches together, and pass the slipped stitch over

Chart rows: 27, 25, 23, 21, 19, 17, 15, 13, 11, 9, 7, 5, 3, 1

Pattern Repeat = 6 stitches

## 345 LEAF-EYELET PATTERN

[multiple of 12 + 11 st + 2 selv sts]

Only RS rows are shown; in WS rows, knit the knits, and purl the purls and yarn overs. Begin with the sts before pattern repeat, rep the marked pattern repeat (12 sts wide) widthwise continuously, and end with the sts after the pattern repeat. Repeat Rows 1–16 heightwise.

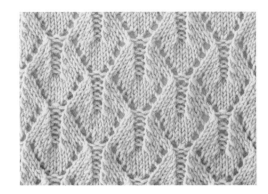

Pattern Repeat = 12 stitches

### Stitch Key

● = 1 selvedge stitch

■ = Knit 1 stitch

− = Purl 1 stitch

○ = Make 1 yarn over

◢ = Knit 2 stitches together

◣ = Knit 2 stitches together left-leaning with passing over (skp): slip 1 stitch knitwise, knit the next stitch, and pass the slipped stitch over

## 346 LACY LEAF PATTERN

[multiple of 22 + 1 st + 2 selv sts]

Only RS rows are shown; in WS rows, knit the knits, and purl the purls and yarn overs. Begin with the sts before the pattern repeat, rep the marked pattern repeat (22 sts wide) widthwise continuously, and end with the sts after the pattern repeat. Repeat Rows 1–32 heightwise.

### Stitch Key

● = 1 selvedge stitch        ■ = Knit 1 stitch        − = Purl 1 stitch

○ = Make 1 yarn over

◢ = Knit 2 stitches together

◣ = Knit 2 stitches together left-leaning with passing over (skp): slip 1 stitch knitwise, knit the next stitch, and pass the slipped stitch over

△ = Knit 3 stitches together left-leaning with passing over (sk2p): slip 1 stitch knitwise, knit 2 stitches together, and pass the slipped stitch over

Pattern Repeat = 22 stitches

## 347 ROWS OF SMALL LEAVES

[multiple of 8 + 2 selv sts]

Only RS rows are shown; in WS rows, knit the knits, purl the purls, and work (knit 1, purl 1) into double yarn overs. Begin with the selv st before the pattern repeat, rep the marked pattern repeat (8 sts wide) widthwise continuously, and end with the selv st after the pattern repeat. Repeat Rows 1–24 heightwise.

### Stitch Key

● = 1 selvedge stitch

■ = Knit 1 stitch

◆ = Knit 1 stitch through the back loop

– = Purl 1 stitch

○ = Make 1 yarn over

◢ = Knit 2 stitches together

◣ = Knit 2 stitches together left-leaning with passing over (skp): slip 1 stitch knitwise, knit the next stitch, and pass the slipped stitch over

✚ = Increase 1 stitch twisted from the bar between stitches

☐ = No stitch, for better overview only

Pattern Repeat = 8 stitches

## 348 DIMENSIONAL LEAF PATTERN

[multiple of 10 + 1 st + 2 selv sts]

Only RS rows are shown; in WS rows, knit the knits, and purl the purls and yarn overs. Begin with the sts before the pattern repeat, rep the marked pattern repeat (10 sts wide) widthwise continuously, and end with the sts after the pattern repeat. Work Rows 1–42 once, then repeat Rows 3–42 continuously, and end with Rows 1 and 2.

### Stitch Key

● = 1 selvedge stitch

■ = Knit 1 stitch

– = Purl 1 stitch

○ = Make 1 yarn over

◢ = Knit 2 stitches together

◣ = Knit 2 stitches together left-leaning with passing over (skp): slip 1 stitch knitwise, knit the next stitch, and pass the slipped stitch over

▲ = Knit 3 stitches together left-leaning with passing over (sk2p): slip 1 stitch knitwise, knit 2 stitches together, and pass the slipped stitch over

☐ = No stitch, for better overview only

Pattern Repeat = 10 stitches

## 349 PATTERN OF TINY LEAVES

[multiple of 12 + 1 st + 2 selv sts]

### Stitch Key

● = 1 selvedge stitch    ■ = Knit 1 stitch    − = Purl 1 stitch

○ = Make 1 yarn over

◢ = Knit 2 stitches together

◣ = Knit 2 stitches together left-leaning with passing over (skp): slip 1 stitch knitwise, knit the next stitch, and pass the slipped stitch over

△ = Knit 3 stitches together left-leaning with passing over (sk2p): slip 1 stitch knitwise, knit 2 stitches together, and pass the slipped stitch over

Pattern Repeat = 12 stitches

Only RS rows are shown; in WS rows, knit the knits, and purl the purls and yarn overs. Begin with the sts before the pattern repeat, rep the marked pattern repeat (12 sts wide) widthwise continuously, and end with the sts after the pattern repeat. Repeat Rows 1—12 heightwise.

## 350 LACE PATTERN WITH LEAVES

[multiple of 12 + 1 st + 2 selv sts]

### Stitch Key

● = 1 selvedge stitch    ■ = Knit 1 stitch    ○ = Make 1 yarn over

◢ = Knit 2 stitches together

◣ = Knit 2 stitches together left-leaning with passing over (skp): slip 1 stitch knitwise, knit the next stitch, and pass the slipped stitch over

∩ = Centered double decrease, knitting 3 stitches together with center stitch on top (cdd): slip 2 stitches together knitwise, knit 1 stitch, and pass the slipped stitches over

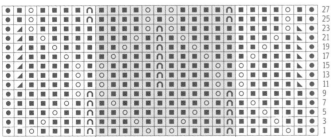

Pattern Repeat = 12 stitches

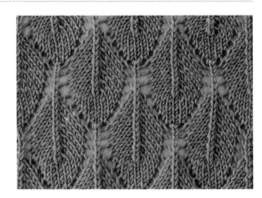

Only RS rows are shown; in WS rows, purl all stitches and yarn overs. Begin with the sts before the pattern repeat, rep the marked pattern repeat (12 sts wide) widthwise continuously, and end with the sts after the pattern repeat. Repeat Rows 1—28 heightwise.

## 351 LEAFY VINE WITH DECORATIVE HOLES [multiple of 25 + 8 sts + 2 selv sts]

Only RS rows are shown; in WS rows, knit the knits, purl the purls, and purl those stitches through the back loop that had been previously worked through the back loop. Begin with the sts before the pattern repeat, rep the marked pattern repeat (25 sts wide) either once for a single vertical pattern column or continuously for an all-over pattern, and end with the sts after the pattern repeat. Work Rows 1–36 heightwise once, then repeat Rows 13–36 continuously. For better overview, the inserted leaves are charted separately in the smaller chart at right.

### Stitch Key

● = 1 selvedge stitch

■ = Knit 1 stitch

◆ = Knit 1 stitch through the back loop

− = Purl 1 stitch

⌒ = Work a total of 7 stitches into 1 stitch: knit 1 stitch, purl 1 stitch, knit 1 stitch, purl 1 stitch, knit 1 stitch, purl 1 stitch, knit 1 stitch

☐ = No stitch, for better overview only

◆/− = Hold 1 stitch on a cable needle behind work, knit 1 stitch through the back loop, then purl the stitch from the cable needle

−/◆ = Hold 1 stitch on a cable needle in front of work, purl 1 stitch, then knit the stitch from the cable needle through the back loop

■■■■ = Hold 1 stitch on a cable needle in front of work, knit 3 stitches, then knit the stitch from the cable needle

■/■■■ = Hold 3 stitches on a cable needle behind work, knit the next stitch, then knit the 3 stitches from the cable needle

Pattern Repeat = 25 stitches

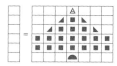

## 352 LEAFY VINE BAND [multiple of 15 + 7 sts + 2 selv sts]

### Stitch Key

● = 1 selvedge stitch

■ = Knit 1 stitch

− = Purl 1 stitch

○ = Make 1 yarn over

☐ = No stitch, for better overview only

◤ = Knit 2 stitches together

◣ = Knit 2 stitches together left-leaning with passing over (skp): slip 1 stitch knitwise, knit the next stitch, and pass the slipped stitch over

△ = Knit 3 stitches together left-leaning with passing over (sk2p): slip 1 stitch knitwise, knit 2 stitches together, and pass the slipped stitch over

Only RS rows are shown; in WS rows, knit the knits, and purl the purls and yarn overs. Begin with the sts before the pattern repeat, rep the marked pattern repeat (15 sts wide) widthwise either once for a single vertical pattern column or continuously for an all-over pattern, and end with the sts after the pattern repeat. Repeat Rows 1–10 heightwise.

Pattern Repeat = 15 stitches

## 353 EYELET LEAF COLUMNS

[multiple of 18 + 17 sts + 2 selv sts]

Only RS rows are shown; in WS rows, knit the knits, purl the purls, and purl those stitches through the back loop that had been previously knitted through the back loop. Begin with the sts before the pattern repeat, rep the marked pattern repeat (18 sts wide) widthwise continuously, and end with the sts after the pattern repeat. Repeat Rows 1–16 heightwise.

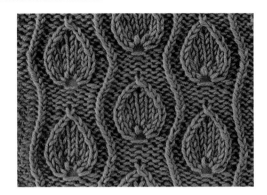

### Stitch Key

● = 1 selvedge stitch

■ = Knit 1 stitch

◆ = Knit 1 stitch through the back loop

– = Purl 1 stitch

✛ = Increase 1 stitch twisted from the bar between stitches

◢ = Knit 2 stitches together

◣ = Knit 2 stitches together left-leaning with passing over (skp): slip 1 stitch knitwise, knit the next stitch, and pass the slipped stitch over

◮ = Knit 3 stitches together left-leaning with passing over (sk2p): slip 1 stitch knitwise, knit 2 stitches together, and pass the slipped stitch over

⬚̄⁵ = Work a total of 5 stitches into 1 stitch: knit the next stitch, leaving the stitch on the left needle, then purl the same stitch, then work another (knit 1 stitch, purl 1 stitch, knit 1 stitch) into the same stitch, and let it slip off the left needle

☐ = No stitch, for better overview only

Pattern Repeat = 18 stitches

## 354 LEAF GARLAND

[multiple of 16 + 5 sts + 2 selv sts]

### Stitch Key

● = 1 selvedge stitch

■ = Knit 1 stitch

– = Purl 1 stitch

○ = Make 1 yarn over

◢ = Knit 2 stitches together

◣ = Knit 2 stitches together left-leaning with passing over (skp): slip 1 stitch knitwise, knit the next stitch, and pass the slipped stitch over

◮ = Knit 3 stitches together left-leaning with passing over (sk2p): slip 1 stitch knitwise, knit 2 stitches together, and pass the slipped stitch over

☐ = No stitch, for better overview only

Only RS rows are shown; in WS rows, knit the knits, and purl the purls and yarn overs. Begin with the selv st before the pattern repeat, rep the marked pattern repeat (16 sts wide) either once for a single vertical pattern column or continuously for an all-over pattern, and end with the sts after the pattern repeat. Repeat Rows 1–24 heightwise.

Pattern Repeat = 16 stitches

## 355 TEXTURED LEAF PATTERN

[multiple of 18 + 1 st + 2 selv sts]

### Stitch Key

● = 1 selvedge stitch

■ = Knit 1 stitch

– = Purl 1 stitch

○ = Make 1 yarn over

◢ = Knit 2 stitches together

◣ = Knit 2 stitches together left-leaning with passing over (skp): slip 1 stitch knit-wise, knit the next stitch, and pass the slipped stitch over

◿ = Purl 2 stitches together

◥ = Slip 2 stitches individually knitwise, return them to the left needle, then purl them together through the back loop (ssp)

▲ = Knit 3 stitches together left-leaning with passing over (sk2p): slip 1 stitch knit-wise, knit 2 stitches together, and pass the slipped stitch over

△ = Purl 3 stitches together

Only RS rows are shown; in WS rows, knit the knits, and purl the purls and yarn overs. Begin with the sts before the pattern repeat, rep the marked pattern repeat (18 sts wide) width-wise continuously, and end with the sts after the pattern repeat. Repeat Rows 1–24 heightwise.

Pattern Repeat = 18 stitches

Rows shown: 23, 21, 19, 17, 15, 13, 11, 9, 7, 5, 3, 1

## 356 ALL-OVER LEAF PATTERN

[multiple of 14 + 1 st + 2 selv sts]

### Stitch Key

● = 1 selvedge stitch

■ = Knit 1 stitch

– = Purl 1 stitch

○ = Make 1 yarn over

◢ = Knit 2 stitches together

◣ = Knit 2 stitches together left-leaning with passing over (skp): slip 1 stitch knit-wise, knit the next stitch, and pass the slipped stitch over

◿ = Purl 2 stitches together

◥ = Slip 2 stitches individually knitwise, return them to the left needle, then purl them together through the back loop (ssp)

▲ = Knit 3 stitches together left-leaning with passing over (sk2p): slip 1 stitch knit-wise, knit 2 stitches together, and pass the slipped stitch over

Only RS rows are shown; in WS rows, knit the knits, and purl the purls and yarn overs. Begin with the sts before the pattern repeat, rep the marked pattern repeat (14 sts wide) widthwise continuously, and end with the sts after the pattern repeat. Repeat Rows 1–40 heightwise.

Pattern Repeat = 14 stitches

Rows shown: 39, 37, 35, 33, 31, 29, 27, 25, 23, 21, 19, 17, 15, 13, 11, 9, 7, 5, 3, 1

## 357 FERN FROND PATTERN

[multiple of 25 + 1 st + 2 selv sts]

Only RS rows are shown; in WS rows, knit the knits, and purl the purls and yarn overs. Begin with the selv st before the pattern repeat, rep the marked pattern repeat (25 sts wide) either once for a single vertical pattern column or continuously for an all-over pattern, and end with the sts after the pattern repeat. Repeat Rows 1–10 heightwise.

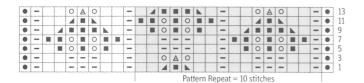

Pattern Repeat = 25 stitches

### Stitch Key

| | |
|---|---|
| ● = 1 selvedge stitch | ▲ = Knit 3 stitches together |
| ■ = Knit 1 stitch | ◮ = Knit 3 stitches together left-leaning with passing over (sk2p): slip 1 stitch knitwise, knit 2 stitches together, and pass the slipped stitch over |
| – = Purl 1 stitch | |
| ○ = Make 1 yarn over | |

## 358 MINI LEAF PATTERN

[multiple of 10 + 5 sts + 2 selv sts]

### Stitch Key

| | |
|---|---|
| ● = 1 selvedge stitch | ◤ = Knit 2 stitches together left-leaning with passing over (skp): slip 1 stitch knitwise, knit the next stitch, and pass the slipped stitch over |
| ■ = Knit 1 stitch | |
| – = Purl 1 stitch | |
| ○ = Make 1 yarn over | ◭ = Knit 3 stitches together left-leaning with passing over (sk2p): slip 1 stitch knitwise, knit 2 stitches together, and pass the slipped stitch over |
| ☐ = No stitch, for better overview only | |
| ◢ = Knit 2 stitches together | |

Only RS rows are shown; in WS rows, knit the knits, and purl the purls and yarn overs. Begin with the selv st before the pattern repeat, rep the marked pattern repeat (10 sts wide) widthwise continuously, and end with the sts after the pattern repeat. Repeat Rows 1–14 heightwise.

Pattern Repeat = 10 stitches

## 359 ASYMMETRIC LEAF MOTIFS

[multiple of 16 + 7 sts + 2 selv sts]

Only RS rows are shown; in WS rows, knit the knits, and purl the purls and yarn overs. Begin with the selv st before the pattern repeat, rep the marked pattern repeat (16 sts wide) widthwise continuously, and end with the sts after the pattern repeat. Repeat Rows 1–32 heightwise.

### Stitch Key

● = 1 selvedge stitch

■ = Knit 1 stitch

− = Purl 1 stitch

○ = Make 1 yarn over

◢ = Knit 2 stitches together

◤ = Knit 2 stitches together left-leaning with passing over (skp): slip 1 stitch knitwise, knit the next stitch, and pass the slipped stitch over

☐ = No stitch, for better overview only

Pattern Repeat = 16 stitches

## 360 LOZENGE WITH LEAF MOTIF

[multiple of 31 + 4 sts + 2 selv sts]

❯ Chart on page 323

Only RS rows are shown; in WS rows, knit the knits, purl the purls and single yarn overs, and purl those stitches through the back loop that had been knitted through the back loop before. Begin with the sts before the pattern repeat, work Pattern Repeat (31 sts wide) either once for a single motif or a single vertical pattern column or continuously for an all-over pattern, and end with the sts after the pattern repeat. Repeat Rows 1–58 heightwise either once for a single motif or for a vertical pattern column or continuously for an all-over pattern. For better overview, the inserted leaves are charted separately in the smaller chart.

# 361 CABLED LOZENGE WITH LEAF MOTIF [multiple of 23 + 3 sts + 2 selv sts]

## Stitch Key

● = 1 selvedge stitch

■ = Knit 1 stitch

– = Purl 1 stitch

+ = Increase 1 stitch twisted from the bar between stitches

◢ = Knit 2 stitches together

◣ = Knit 2 stitches together left-leaning with passing over (skp): slip 1 stitch knitwise, knit the next stitch, and pass the slipped stitch over

◿ = Purl 2 stitches together

▲ = Knit 3 stitches together left-leaning with passing over (sk2p): slip 1 stitch knitwise, knit 2 stitches together, and pass the slipped stitch over

□ = No stitch, for better overview only

= Hold 3 stitches on a cable needle in front of work, purl 1 stitch, then knit the 3 stitches from the cable needle

= Hold 1 stitch on a cable needle behind work, knit 3 stitches, then purl the stitch from the cable needle

= Hold 3 stitches on a cable needle in front of work, knit 3 stitches, then knit the 3 stitches from the cable needle

= Hold 3 stitches on a cable needle behind work, knit 3 stitches, then knit the 3 stitches from the cable needle

Only RS rows are shown; in WS rows, knit the knits, and purl the purls and yarn overs. Begin with the selv st before the pattern repeat, rep the marked pattern repeat (23 sts wide) either once for a single vertical pattern column or continuously for an all-over pattern, and end with the sts after the pattern repeat. Repeat Rows 1–28 heightwise. For better overview, the inserted leaf is charted separately in the smaller chart below.

Pattern Repeat = 23 stitches

# BRIOCHE PATTERNS

# MULTI-ROW PATTERNS

# **Brioche** Patterns

## 362 FULL BRIOCHE

[multiple of 2 + 1 st + 2 selv sts]

Shown are both RS and WS rows. Begin with the selv st before the pattern repeat, rep the marked pattern repeat (2 sts wide) widthwise continuously, and end with the sts after the pattern repeat. Work Rows 1–3 once, then repeat Rows 2 and 3 heightwise.

**Stitch Key**

● = 1 selvedge stitch

■ = Knit 1 stitch

🔒 = Knit 1 stitch together with the following yarn over

⊖ = Slip 1 stitch purlwise together with 1 yarn over

Pattern Repeat = 2 stitches

## 363 HALF-BRIOCHE

[multiple of 2 + 1 st + 2 selv sts]

Shown are both RS and WS rows. Begin with the selv st before the pattern repeat, rep the marked pattern repeat (2 sts wide) widthwise continuously, and end with the sts after the pattern repeat. Repeat Rows 1 and 2 heightwise.

**Stitch Key**

● = 1 selvedge stitch

■ = Knit 1 stitch

— = Purl 1 stitch

🔒 = Knit 1 stitch together with the following yarn over

⊖ = Slip 1 stitch purlwise together with 1 yarn over

Pattern Repeat = 2 stitches

## 364 FALSE BRIOCHE

[multiple of 4 + 3 sts + 2 selv sts]

Shown are both RS and WS rows. Begin with the selv st before the pattern repeat, rep the marked pattern repeat (4 sts wide) widthwise continuously, and end with the sts after the pattern repeat. Repeat Rows 1 and 2 heightwise.

**Stitch Key**

● = 1 selvedge stitch

■ = Knit 1 stitch

— = Purl 1 stitch

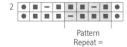

Pattern Repeat = 4 stitches

## 365 TWO-COLOR FULL BRIOCHE

➡ ◯ [multiple of 2 + 1 st + 2 selv sts]

Cast on the stitches using a circular needle and color B, do not turn the cast-on row, but slide the stitches back to the right end of the needle. Begin working Row 1 (RS) in color A. Shown are both RS and WS rows. Begin with the selv st before the pattern repeat, rep the marked pattern repeat (2 sts wide) widthwise continuously, and end with the sts after the pattern repeat. After having completed Row 2 (= first WS row) in color B, slide the stitches back to the right end of the needle, and work Row 3 (= second WS row) in color A. After having completed Row 4 (= first RS row) in color B again, slide the stitches back to the right end of the needle, and work Row 5 (= second RS row) in color A. Work Rows 1–5 once. Then rep Rows 2–5 heightwise, always alternating (2 WS rows, 2 RS rows).

Front

Back

Pattern Repeat = 2 stitches

### Stitch Key

⦿ = 1 selvedge stitch in color A

⦿ = 1 selvedge stitch in color B

■ = Knit 1 stitch in color A

■ = Knit 1 stitch in color B

⊖ = Slip 1 stitch in color A purlwise together with 1 yarn over

⊖ = Slip 1 stitch in color B purlwise together with 1 yarn over

⋒ = Knit 1 stitch in color A together with the following yarn over

⋒ = Knit 1 stitch in color B together with the following yarn over

⌂ = Purl 1 stitch in color A together with the following yarn over

⌂ = Purl 1 stitch in color B together with the following yarn over

## 366 TWO-COLOR STRIPED FULL BRIOCHE

➡ ◯ [multiple of 2 + 1 st + 2 selv sts]

Cast on the stitches using a circular needle and color A, then work Row 1 (= RS) in color A. Shown are both RS and WS rows. Begin with the sts before the pattern repeat, rep the marked pattern repeat (2 sts wide) widthwise continuously, and end with the sts after the pattern repeat. After having completed Row 1 (= first RS row) in color A, slide the stitches back to the right end of the needle, and work Row 2 (= second RS row) in color B. After having worked Row 3 (= first WS row) in color A again, slide the stitches back to the right end of the needle, and work Row 4 (= second RS row) in color B. Continue in the same manner, alternating (2 RS rows, 2 WS rows). Work Rows 1–24 once, changing colors in Rows 9 and 17. Then repeat Rows 9–24 heightwise.

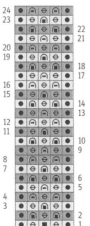

Pattern Repeat = 2 stitches

### Stitch Key

⦿ = 1 selvedge stitch in color A

⦿ = 1 selvedge stitch in color B

■ = Knit 1 stitch in color A

■ = Knit 1 stitch in color B

⊖ = Slip 1 stitch in color A purlwise together with 1 yarn over

⊖ = Slip 1 stitch in color B purlwise together with 1 yarn over

⋒ = Knit 1 stitch in color A together with the following yarn over

⋒ = Knit 1 stitch in color B together with the following yarn over

⌂ = Purl 1 stitch in color A together with the following yarn over

⌂ = Purl 1 stitch in color B together with the following yarn over

## 367 TWO-COLOR STAGGERED FULL BRIOCHE ➡ ◯ [multiple of 2 + 1 st + 2 selv sts]

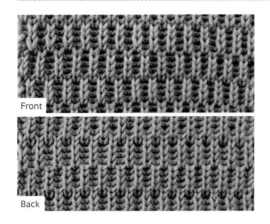

Front

Back

Cast on the stitches using a circular needle and color B, and work Row 1 (= RS) in color B. Shown are both RS and WS rows. Begin with the selv st before the pattern repeat, rep the marked pattern repeat (2 sts wide) widthwise continuously, and end with the sts after the pattern repeat. After having completed Row 1 (= first RS row) in color B, slide the stitches back to the right end of the needle, and work Row 2 (= second WS row) in color A. After having worked Row 3 (= first WS row) in color B again, slide the stitches back to the right end of the needle, and work Row 4 (= second WS row) in color A. Continue in the same manner, alternating (2 RS rows, 2 WS rows). Work Rows 1–24 once, changing colors in Rows 9 and 17. Then repeat Rows 9–24 heightwise.

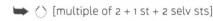

Pattern
Repeat =
2 stitches

### Stitch Key

● = 1 selvedge stitch in color A

● = 1 selvedge stitch in color B

■ = Knit 1 stitch in color A

■ = Knit 1 stitch in color B

⊖ = Slip 1 stitch in color A purlwise together with 1 yarn over

⊖ = Slip 1 stitch in color B purlwise together with 1 yarn over

⋒ = Knit 1 stitch in color A together with the following yarn over

⋒ = Knit 1 stitch in color B together with the following yarn over

⋒ = Purl 1 stitch in color A together with the following yarn over

⋒ = Purl 1 stitch in color B together with the following yarn over

## 368 STRIPED BRIOCHE ➡ [multiple of 9 + 2 selv sts]

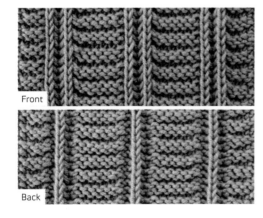

Front

Back

Shown are both RS and WS rows. Begin with the selv st before the pattern repeat, rep the marked pattern repeat (9 sts wide) widthwise continuously, and end with the selv st after the pattern repeat. Work Rows 1–6 once, then repeat Rows 3–6 heightwise.

Pattern Repeat = 9 stitches

### Stitch Key

● = 1 selvedge stitch

■ = Knit 1 stitch

– = Purl 1 stitch

⋒ = Knit 1 stitch together with the following yarn over

⊖ = Slip 1 stitch purlwise together with 1 yarn over

# 369 TWO-COLOR CABLED FULL BRIOCHE ➡ ◌ [multiple of 16 + 1 st + 2 selv sts]

Cast on the stitches using a circular needle and color B, and work Row 1 (= RS) in color B. Shown are both RS and WS rows. Begin with the selv st before the pattern repeat, rep the marked pattern repeat (16 sts wide) widthwise continuously, and end with the sts after the pattern repeat. After having completed Row 1 (= first RS row) in color B, slide the stitches back to the right end of the needle, and work Row 2 (= second RS row) in color A. After having worked Row 3 (= first WS row) in color B, slide the stitches back to the right end of the needle again, and work Row 4 (= second WS row) in color A. Continue in the same manner, alternating (2 RS rows, 2 WS rows). Work Rows 1–26 once, then rep Rows 3–26 heightwise.

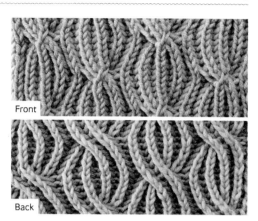

Front

Back

## Stitch Key

● = 1 selvedge stitch in color A

● = 1 selvedge stitch in color B

■ = Knit 1 stitch in color A

■ = Knit 1 stitch in color B

⊖ = Slip 1 stitch in color A purlwise together with 1 yarn over

⊖ = Slip 1 stitch in color B purlwise together with 1 yarn over

⋒ = Knit 1 stitch in color A together with the following yarn over

⋒ = Knit 1 stitch in color B together with the following yarn over

⋒ = Purl 1 stitch in color A together with the following yarn over

⋒ = Purl 1 stitch in color B together with the following yarn over

⌢⌢⌢⌢⌢⌢⌢▬ = Hold 3 stitches (1 stitch together with the following yarn over, 1 stitch, and 1 stitch together with the following yarn over) on a cable needle in front of work, hold 1 stitch on a second cable needle behind work, work 3 stitches in Brioche pattern in color A (alternating [knit 1 stitch together with the following yarn over, slip 1 stitch purlwise together with 1 yarn over]), then slip the stitch from the second cable needle purlwise together with 1 yarn over in color A, then work 3 stitches from the first cable needle in Brioche pattern in color A (alternating [knit 1 stitch together with the following yarn over, slip 1 stitch purlwise together with 1 yarn over]).

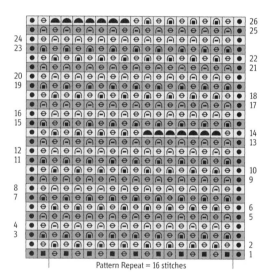

Pattern Repeat = 16 stitches

# 370 NET BRIOCHE

[multiple of 2 + 2 selv sts]

Shown are both RS and WS rows. Begin with the selv st before the pattern repeat, rep the marked pattern repeat (2 sts wide) widthwise continuously, and end with the selv st after the pattern repeat. Work Rows 1–5 once, then rep Rows 2–5 heightwise.

## Stitch Key

● = 1 selvedge stitch

■ = Knit 1 stitch

⋒ = Knit 1 stitch together with the following yarn over

⊖ = Slip 1 stitch purlwise together with 1 yarn over

> = Working the stitch and the yarn over separately: first, knit the stitch, then slip the yarn over purlwise with working yarn in back of yarn over

Pattern Repeat = 2 stitches

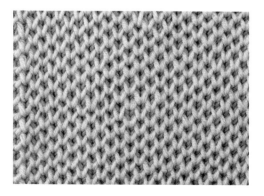

## 371 TWO-COLOR NET BRIOCHE [multiple of 2 + 2 selv sts]

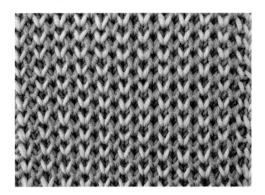

### Stitch Key

- ● = 1 selvedge stitch in color A
- ● = 1 selvedge stitch in color B
- ■ = Knit 1 stitch in color A
- ■ = Knit 1 stitch in color B
- ⊖ = Slip 1 stitch in color A purlwise together with 1 yarn over
- ⊖ = Slip 1 stitch in color B purlwise together with 1 yarn over
- ⋒ = Knit 1 stitch in color A together with the following yarn over
- ⋒ = Knit 1 stitch in color B together with the following yarn over
- ＞ = Working the stitch and the yarn over in color A separately: first, knit the stitch, then slip the yarn over purlwise with working yarn in back of yarn over
- ＞ = Working the stitch and the yarn over in color B separately: first, knit the stitch, then slip the yarn over purlwise with working yarn in back of yarn over

Shown are both RS and WS rows. Begin with the selv st before the pattern repeat, rep the marked pattern repeat (2 sts wide) widthwise continuously, and end with the selv st after the pattern repeat. Work Rows 1–5 once, then rep Rows 2–5 heightwise.

Pattern Repeat = 2 stitches

## 372 THREE-COLOR NET BRIOCHE [multiple of 2 + 2 selv sts]

### Stitch Key

- ● = 1 selvedge stitch in color A
- ● = 1 selvedge stitch in color B
- ● = 1 selvedge stitch in color C
- ■ = Knit 1 stitch in color A
- ■ = Knit 1 stitch in color B
- ■ = Knit 1 stitch in color C
- ⊖ = Slip 1 stitch in color A purlwise together with 1 yarn over
- ⊖ = Slip 1 stitch in color B purlwise together with 1 yarn over
- ⊖ = Slip 1 stitch in color C purlwise together with 1 yarn over
- ⋒ = Knit 1 stitch in color A together with the following yarn over
- ⋒ = Knit 1 stitch in color B together with the following yarn over
- ⋒ = Knit 1 stitch in color C together with the following yarn over
- ＞ = Working the stitch and the yarn over in color A separately: first, knit the stitch, then slip the yarn over purlwise with working yarn in back of yarn over
- ＞ = Working the stitch and the yarn over in color B separately: first, knit the stitch, then slip the yarn over purlwise with working yarn in back of yarn over
- ＞ = Working the stitch and the yarn over in color C separately: first, knit the stitch, then slip the yarn over purlwise with working yarn in back of yarn over

Shown are both RS and WS rows. Begin with the selv st before the pattern repeat, rep the marked pattern repeat (2 sts wide) widthwise continuously, and end with the selv st after the pattern repeat. Work Rows 1–13 once, then repeat Rows 2–13 heightwise.

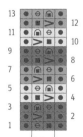

Pattern Repeat = 2 stitches

## 373 LADDER BRIOCHE

[multiple of 12 + 1 st + 2 selv sts]

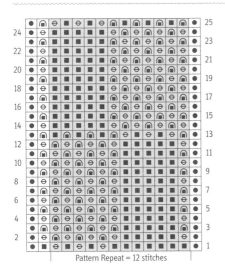

### Stitch Key

● = 1 selvedge stitch

■ = Knit 1 stitch

⌂ = Knit 1 stitch together with the following yarn over

⊖ = Slip 1 stitch purlwise together with 1 yarn over

Pattern Repeat = 12 stitches

Shown are both RS and WS rows. Begin with the selv st before the pattern repeat, rep the marked pattern repeat (12 sts wide) widthwise continuously, and end with the sts after the pattern repeat. Work Rows 1–25 once, then repeat Rows 2–25 heightwise.

## 374 BASKETWEAVE BRIOCHE

[multiple of 10 + 2 selv sts]

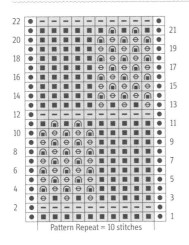

### Stitch Key

● = 1 selvedge stitch

■ = Knit 1 stitch

– = Purl 1 stitch

⌂ = Knit 1 stitch together with the following yarn over

⊖ = Slip 1 stitch purlwise together with 1 yarn over

Pattern Repeat = 10 stitches

Shown are both RS and WS rows. Begin with the selv st before the pattern repeat, rep the marked pattern repeat (10 sts wide) widthwise continuously, and end with the selv st after the pattern repeat. Work Rows 1–22 once, then rep Rows 3–22 continuously.

## 375 TWO-COLOR CHECKERBOARD BRIOCHE ○ [multiple of 24 + 2 selv sts]

Cast on the stitches using a circular needle and color B, and work Row 1 (= RS) in color B. Shown are both RS and WS rows. Begin with the selv st before the pattern repeat, rep the marked pattern repeat (24 sts wide) widthwise continuously, and end with the selv st after the pattern repeat. After having completed Row 1 (= first RS row) in color B, slide the stitches back to the right end of the needle, and work Row 2 (= second RS row) in color A. After having completed Row 3 (= first WS row) in color B again, slide the stitches back to the right end of the needle, and work Row 4 (= second WS row) in color A. Continue in the same manner, alternating (2 RS rows, 2 WS rows). Work Rows 1–57 once, then rep Rows 2–57 heightwise.

### Stitch Key

● = 1 selvedge stitch in color A

● = 1 selvedge stitch in color B

■ = Knit 1 stitch in color A

■ = Knit 1 stitch in color B

⊖ = Slip 1 stitch in color A purlwise together with 1 yarn over

⊖ = Slip 1 stitch in color B purlwise together with 1 yarn over

⋒ = Knit 1 stitch in color A together with the following yarn over

⋒ = Knit 1 stitch in color B together with the following yarn over

⌒ = Purl 1 stitch in color A together with the following yarn over

⌒ = Purl 1 stitch in color B together with the following yarn over

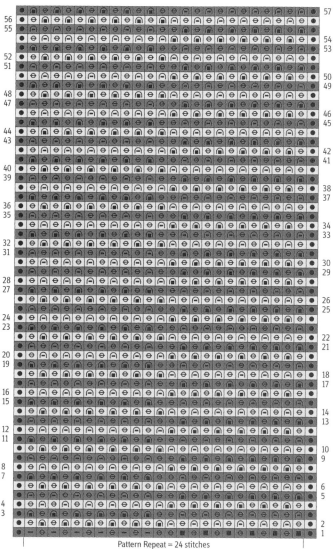

Pattern Repeat = 24 stitches

## 376 CHECKERBOARD PATTERN

[multiple of 12 + 2 selv sts]

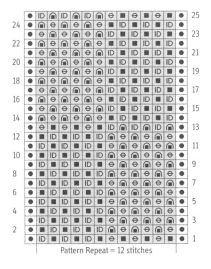

Pattern Repeat = 12 stitches

### Stitch Key

● = 1 selvedge stitch

■ = Knit 1 stitch

ID = Slip 1 stitch purlwise, with working yarn in front of work

⌂ = Knit 1 stitch together with the following yarn over

⊖ = Slip 1 stitch purlwise together with 1 yarn over

Shown are both RS and WS rows. Begin with the selv st before the pattern repeat, rep the marked pattern repeat (12 sts wide) widthwise continuously, and end with the selv st after the pattern repeat. Work Rows 1–25 once, then repeat Rows 2–25 heightwise.

## 377 BEAD PATTERN BRIOCHE

[multiple of 16 + 1 st + 2 selv sts]

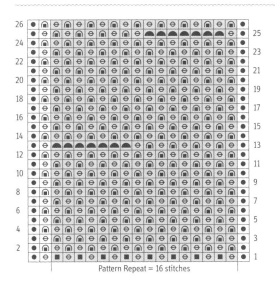

Pattern Repeat = 16 stitches

Shown are both RS and WS rows. Begin with the selv st before the pattern repeat, rep the marked pattern repeat (16 sts wide) widthwise continuously, and end with the sts after the pattern repeat. Work Rows 1–26 once, then rep Rows 3–26 heightwise.

### Stitch Key

● = 1 selvedge stitch

⊖ = Slip 1 stitch purlwise together with 1 yarn over

⌂ = Knit 1 stitch together with the following yarn over

■ = Knit 1 stitch

⌂⌂⌂⌂⌂⌂⌂ = Hold 1 stitch together with the following yarn over on a cable needle in front of work, hold 5 stitches with the accompanying yarn overs (2 sts, 1 yo, 2 sts, 1 yo, 1 st) on a second cable needle behind work, knit 1 stitch together with the following yarn over, then work the 5 stitches from the second cable needle in Brioche pattern (alternating [slip 1 stitch purlwise together with 1 yarn over, knit 1 stitch together with the following yarn over]), then knit the stitch from the first cable needle together with the following yarn over

## 378 STAGGERED BRIOCHE

[multiple of 2 + 1 st + 2 selv sts]

Shown are both RS and WS rows. Begin with the selv st before the pattern repeat, rep the marked pattern repeat (2 sts wide) widthwise continuously, and end with the sts after the pattern repeat. Work Rows 1–18 once heightwise, then repeat only Rows 3–18 continuously.

### Stitch Key

● = 1 selvedge stitch

■ = Knit 1 stitch

– = Purl 1 stitch

⋒ = Knit 1 stitch together with the following yarn over

⊖ = Slip 1 stitch purlwise together with 1 yarn over

Pattern Repeat = 2 stitches

## 379 BRIOCHE WITH HORIZONTAL STRIPES

[multiple of 2 + 1 st + 2 selv sts]

Shown are both RS and WS rows. Begin with the selv st before the pattern repeat, rep the marked pattern repeat (2 sts wide) widthwise continuously, and end with the sts after the pattern repeat. Repeat Rows 1–12 heightwise.

### Stitch Key

● = 1 selvedge stitch

■ = Knit 1 stitch

⋒ = Knit 1 stitch together with the following yarn over

⊖ = Slip 1 stitch purlwise together with 1 yarn over

Pattern Repeat = 2 stitches

## 380 BRIOCHE-AND-CABLE RIBBING

[multiple of 6 + 3 sts + 2 selv sts]

Shown are both RS and WS rows. Begin with the selv st before the pattern repeat, rep the marked pattern repeat (6 sts wide) widthwise continuously, and end with the sts after the pattern repeat. Work Rows 1–11 once heightwise, then repeat Rows 2–11 heightwise.

Pattern Repeat = 6 stitches

### Stitch Key

● = 1 selvedge stitch

■ = Knit 1 stitch

⋒ = Knit 1 stitch together with the following yarn over

⊖ = Slip 1 stitch purlwise together with 1 yarn over

◖◗◖ = Hold 1 stitch together with the following yarn over on a cable needle in front of work, hold 1 stitch on a second cable needle behind work, knit 1 stitch together with the following yarn over, then slip the stitch from the second cable needle purlwise together with the yarn over, then knit the stitch from the first cable needle together with the following yarn over

## 381 CABLED BRIOCHE PATTERN

[multiple of 18 + 2 sts + 2 selv sts]

Shown are both RS and WS rows. Begin with the selv st before the pattern repeat, rep the marked pattern repeat (18 sts wide) widthwise continuously, and end with the sts after the pattern repeat. Work Rows 1–38 once heightwise, then repeat only Rows 3–38 continuously.

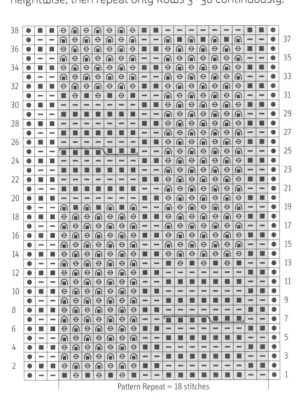

Pattern Repeat = 18 stitches

### Stitch Key

● = 1 selvedge stitch

■ = Knit 1 stitch

– = Purl 1 stitch

⋒ = Knit 1 stitch together with the following yarn over

⊖ = Slip 1 stitch purlwise together with 1 yarn over

⌐■■■■■■■⌐ = Hold 3 stitches on a cable needle in front of work, knit 4 stitches, then knit the 3 stitches from the cable needle

# **Multi-Row** Patterns

## 382 BRIOCHE PATTERN [multiple of 2 + 1 st + 2 selv sts]

Shown are both RS and WS rows. Begin with the selv st before the pattern repeat, rep the marked pattern repeat (2 sts wide) widthwise continuously, and end with the sts after the pattern repeat. Repeat Rows 1–4 heightwise.

Pattern
Repeat =
2 stitches

### Stitch Key

● = 1 selvedge stitch

■ = Knit 1 stitch

− = Purl 1 stitch

◉ = Insert the needle knit-wise into the stitch one row below, and knit this stitch, undoing the stitch above it in the current row

## 383 ALL-OVER PATTERN [multiple of 8 + 2 selv sts]

Shown are both RS and WS rows. Begin with the sts before the pattern repeat, rep the marked pattern repeat (8 sts wide) widthwise continuously, and end with the sts after the pattern repeat. Repeat Rows 1–10 heightwise.

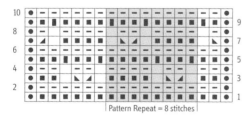

Pattern Repeat = 8 stitches

### Stitch Key

● = 1 selvedge stitch

■ = Knit 1 stitch

− = Purl 1 stitch

◢ = Knit 2 stitches together

◣ = Knit 2 stitches to-gether left-leaning with passing over (skp): slip 1 stitch knitwise, knit the next stitch, and pass the slipped stitch over

▮ = Insert the right needle knitwise into the stitch in Row 3 or Row 7 respectively, place the working yarn around the needle, and pull the stitch into a long loop. Alternatively, a crochet hook can be used for this maneuver.

☐ = No stitch, for better overview only

## 384 DIAGONAL LOOP PATTERN

Shown are both RS and WS rows. Begin with the selv st before the pattern repeat, rep the marked pattern repeat (6 sts wide) widthwise continuously, and end with the sts after the pattern repeat. Repeat Rows 1–8 heightwise.

### Stitch Key

● = 1 selvedge stitch

■ = Knit 1 stitch

– = Purl 1 stitch

~ = Insert the right needle knitwise between the following 3rd and 4th stitch 2 rows below, place the working yarn around the needle, and pull the stitch into a long loop

◿ = Purl the long loop from the previous row together with the next stitch of the current row

☐ = No stitch, for better overview only

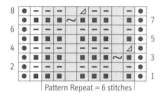

## 385 STAGGERED BRIOCHE

Shown are both RS and WS rows. Begin with the sts before the pattern repeat, rep the marked pattern repeat (2 sts wide) widthwise continuously, and end with the sts after the pattern repeat. Work Rows 1–11 once heightwise, then repeat Rows 2–11 heightwise.

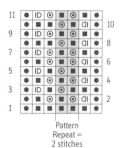

### Stitch Key

● = 1 selvedge stitch

■ = Knit 1 stitch

⊙ = Insert the needle knitwise into the stitch one row below, and knit this stitch, undoing the stitch above it in the current row

ID = Slip 1 stitch purlwise, with working yarn in front of work

CI = Slip 1 stitch purlwise, with working yarn in back of work

## 386 SMALL GATHERED-STITCH PATTERN

Shown are both RS and WS rows. Begin with the selv st before the pattern repeat, rep the marked pattern repeat (4 sts wide) widthwise continuously, and end with the sts after the pattern repeat. Work Rows 1–13 once, then repeat Rows 2–13 heightwise.

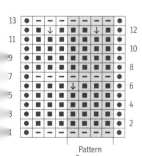

### Stitch Key

● = 1 selvedge stitch

■ = Knit 1 stitch

– = Purl 1 stitch

↓ = Insert the needle knitwise into the stitch 4 rows below, and undo the stitches above it. Alternatively, you can first drop the stitch 4 rows, then catch it with the right needle. After this, insert the right needle under the 4 resulting floats, place the working yarn around the needle, and knit the next stitch, enclosing the 4 floats.

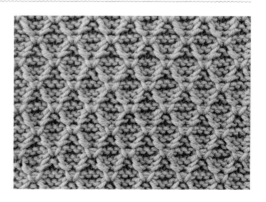

## 387 SHELL PATTERN

[multiple of 12 + 3 sts + 2 selv sts]

Only RS rows are shown. First, work the sts before the pattern repeat, rep the marked pattern repeat (12 sts wide) widthwise continuously, and end with the sts after the pattern repeat. In WS rows, knit all stitches. Begin with Row 1 (WS), repeat Rows 1–22 continuously, ending with a RS row.

### Stitch Key

● = 1 selvedge stitch

− = Purl 1 stitch

⊿ = Purl 2 stitches together

＋ = Increase 1 stitch twisted from the bar between stitches

⊙ = Insert the needle knitwise into the stitch one row below, and knit this stitch, undoing the stitch above it in the current row

Pattern Repeat = 12 stitches

## 388 TWEED PATTERN

[multiple of 2 + 1 st + 2 selv sts]

Shown are both RS and WS rows. Begin with the selv st before the pattern repeat, rep the marked pattern repeat (2 sts wide) widthwise continuously, and end with the sts after the pattern repeat. Work Rows 1–6 once, then repeat Rows 3–6 heightwise.

Pattern Repeat = 2 stitches

### Stitch Key

● = 1 selvedge stitch in color A

⊙ = 1 selvedge stitch in color B

■ = Knit 1 stitch in color A

■ = Knit 1 stitch in color B

⊙ = Insert the needle into the stitch one row below as if to knit, and knit the stitch in color A, undoing the stitch above it in the current row

⊙ = Insert the needle into the stitch one row below as if to knit, and knit the stitch in color B, undoing the stitch above it in the current row

## 389 GATHERED-STITCH DIAMOND PATTERN

[multiple of 6 + 5 sts + 2 selv sts]

Shown are both RS and WS rows. Begin with the selv st before the pattern repeat, rep the marked pattern repeat (6 sts wide) widthwise continuously, and end with the sts after the pattern repeat. Repeat Rows 1–12 heightwise.

Pattern Repeat = 6 stitches

### Stitch Key

● = 1 selvedge stitch

■ = Knit 1 stitch

− = Purl 1 stitch

↓ = Insert the needle knitwise into the stitch 4 rows below, and undo the stitches above it. Alternatively, you can first drop the stitch 4 rows, then catch it with the right needle. After this, insert the right needle under the 4 resulting floats, place the working yarn around the needle, and knit the next stitch, enclosing the 4 floats.

## 390 CLUSTER STITCH PATTERN

[multiple of 8 + 3 sts + 2 selv sts]

Shown are both RS and WS rows. Begin with the sts before the pattern repeat, rep the marked pattern repeat (8 sts wide) widthwise continuously, and end with the sts after the pattern repeat. Repeat Rows 1–8 heightwise.

### Stitch Key

● = 1 selvedge stitch

■ = Knit 1 stitch

— = Purl 1 stitch

ID = Slip 1 stitch purlwise, with working yarn in front of work

~ = Purl 1 stitch, then insert the right needle knitwise into the knit stitch below it in Row 3, place the working yarn around the needle, and pull the stitch into a long loop

◢ = Knit the long loop from the previous row together with the next stitch of the current row

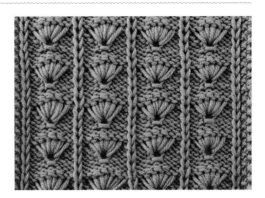

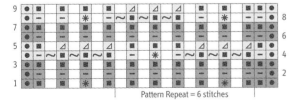

Pattern Repeat = 8 stitches

## 391 TWO-COLOR CLUSTER STITCH PATTERN

[multiple of 6 + 5 sts + 2 selv sts]

### Stitch Key

● = 1 selvedge stitch in color A

● = 1 selvedge stitch in color B

■ = Knit 1 stitch in color A

■ = Knit 1 stitch in color B

— = Purl 1 stitch in color A

— = Purl 1 stitch in color B

◢ = Purl the long loop from the previous row together with the next stitch of the current row in color A

~ = Insert the right needle knitwise into the stitch below it marked with ✳, place the working yarn in color A around the needle, and pull the stitch into a long loop

✳ = Purl the stitch in color A in every 4th and 8th row

✳ = Knit the stitch in Row 1 in color B

☐ = No stitch, for better overview only

Shown are both RS and WS rows. Begin with the sts before the pattern repeat, rep the marked pattern repeat (6 sts wide) widthwise continuously, and end with the sts after the pattern repeat. Work Rows 1–9 once, then repeat Rows 2–9 heightwise continuously. If desired, the pattern can be worked in one color only.

Pattern Repeat = 6 stitches

## 392 BUBBLE PATTERN  [multiple of 4 + 3 sts + 2 selv sts]

### Stitch Key

● = 1 selvedge stitch

■ = Knit 1 stitch

− = Purl 1 stitch

↓ = Insert the needle knitwise into the stitch 4 rows below, and undo the stitches above it. Alternatively, you can first drop the stitch 4 rows, then catch it with the right needle. After this, insert the right needle under the 4 resulting floats, place the working yarn around the needle, and knit the next stitch, enclosing the 4 floats.

Pattern Repeat = 4 stitches

Shown are both RS and WS rows. Begin with the selv st before the pattern repeat, rep the marked pattern repeat (4 sts wide) widthwise continuously, and end with the sts after the pattern repeat. Work Rows 1–13 once, then repeat Rows 2–13 heightwise.

## 393 THREE-COLOR BUBBLE PATTERN  [multiple of 4 + 3 sts + 2 selv sts]

### Stitch Key

● = 1 selvedge stitch in color A

● = 1 selvedge stitch in color B

● = 1 selvedge stitch in color C

■ = Knit 1 stitch in color A

■ = Knit 1 stitch in color B

■ = Knit 1 stitch in color C

− = Purl 1 stitch in color A

− = Purl 1 stitch in color B

− = Purl 1 stitch in color C

Pattern Repeat = 4 stitches

↓ = Insert the needle knitwise into the stitch 4 rows below, and undo the stitches above it. Alternatively, you can first drop the stitch 4 rows, then catch it with the right needle. After this, insert the right needle under the 4 resulting floats, place the working yarn around the needle, and knit the next stitch, enclosing the 4 floats.

Shown are both RS and WS rows. Begin with the selv st before the pattern repeat, rep the marked pattern repeat (4 sts wide) widthwise continuously, and end with the sts after the pattern repeat. Work Rows 1–13 once, then repeat Rows 2–13 heightwise.

## 394 THREE-COLOR CANDY PATTERN [multiple of 4 + 3 sts + 2 selv sts]

### Stitch Key

- ⬤ = 1 selvedge stitch in color A
- ⬤ = 1 selvedge stitch in color B
- ⬤ = 1 selvedge stitch in color C
- ▪ = Knit 1 stitch in color A
- ▪ = Knit 1 stitch in color B
- ▪ = Knit 1 stitch in color C
- ▬ = Purl 1 stitch in color B
- ▬ = Purl 1 stitch in color C

↓ = Insert the needle knitwise into the stitch 4 rows below, and undo the stitches above it. Alternatively, you can first drop the stitch 4 rows, then catch it with the right needle. After this, insert the right needle under the 4 resulting floats, place the working yarn around the needle, and knit the next stitch, enclosing the 4 floats.

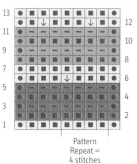

Pattern Repeat = 4 stitches

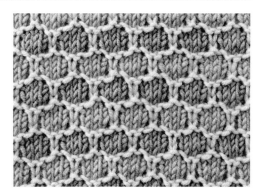

Shown are both RS and WS rows. Begin with the selv st before the pattern repeat, rep the marked pattern repeat (4 sts wide) widthwise continuously, and end with the sts after the pattern repeat. Work Rows 1–13 once, then repeat Rows 2–13 heightwise.

## 395 FOUR-COLOR CLOUD PATTERN [multiple of 6 + 1 st + 2 selv sts]

### Stitch Key

- ⬤ = 1 selvedge stitch in color A
- ⬤ = 1 selvedge stitch in color B
- ⬤ = 1 selvedge stitch in color C
- ⬤ = 1 selvedge stitch in color D
- ▪ = Knit 1 stitch in color A
- ▪ = Knit 1 stitch in color B
- ▪ = Knit 1 stitch in color C
- ▪ = Knit 1 stitch in color D
- ▬ = Purl 1 stitch in color A
- ▬ = Purl 1 stitch in color B
- ▬ = Purl 1 stitch in color C
- ▬ = Purl 1 stitch in color D

↓ ↓ ↓ ↓ = Insert the needle knitwise into the stitch 4 rows below, and undo the stitches above it. Alternatively, you can first drop the stitch 4 rows, then catch it with the right needle. After this, insert the right needle under the 4 resulting floats, place the working yarn around the needle, and knit the next stitch, enclosing the 4 floats.

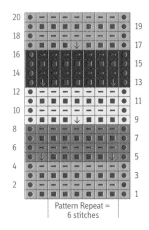

Pattern Repeat = 6 stitches

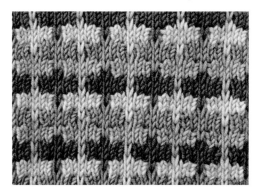

Shown are both RS and WS rows. Begin with the selv st before the pattern repeat, rep the marked pattern repeat (6 sts wide) widthwise continuously, and end with the sts after the pattern repeat. Work Rows 1–20 once, then repeat Rows 5–20 heightwise.

## 396 CLUSTER STITCH FLOWER PATTERN

[multiple of 10 + 1 st + 2 selv sts]

Shown are both RS and WS rows. Begin with the sts before the pattern repeat, rep the marked pattern repeat (10 sts wide) widthwise continuously, and end with the sts after the pattern repeat. Repeat Rows 1–20 heightwise.

Pattern Repeat = 10 stitches

### Stitch Key

● = 1 selvedge stitch

■ = Knit 1 stitch

− = Purl 1 stitch

➤ = Purl the 6 loops from the previous row together with the stitch in between

⋁ = Insert the right needle knitwise into each of the 3 holes below resulting from yarn overs in the previous rows, place the working yarn around the needle, then pull out a long loop from each hole (= 3 loops). Alternatively, a crochet hook can be used for this maneuver.

⋀ = Purl the stitch together with the 3 loops from the previous row

☐ = No stitch, for better overview only

## 397 TWO-COLOR CLUSTER STITCH FLOWER PATTERN

[multiple of 10 + 1 st + 2 selv sts]

Shown are both RS and WS rows. Begin with the selv st before the pattern repeat, rep the marked pattern repeat (10 sts wide) widthwise continuously, and end with the sts after the pattern repeat. Repeat Rows 1–10 heightwise.

### Stitch Key

● = 1 selvedge stitch in color A

● = 1 selvedge stitch in color B

■ = Knit 1 stitch in color A

■ = Knit 1 stitch in color B

− = Purl 1 stitch in color A

− = Purl 1 stitch in color B

○ = Make 1 yarn over in color B

◢ = Knit 2 stitches together in color B

◣ = Knit 2 stitches together left-leaning with passing over (skp) in color B: slip 1 stitch knitwise, knit the next stitch, and pass the slipped stitch over

➤ = Purl the 6 loops from the previous row together with the stitch in between in color A

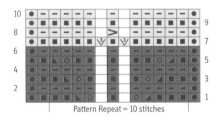

Pattern Repeat = 10 stitches

⋁ = Insert the right needle knitwise into each of the 3 holes below resulting from yarn overs in the previous rows, place the working yarn in color A around the needle, and pull out a long loop from each hole (= 3 loops). Alternatively, a crochet hook can be used for this maneuver.

☐ = No stitch, for better overview only

## 398 DIAGONAL STRIPE PATTERN [multiple of 32 + 1 st + 2 selv sts]

Only RS rows are shown. First, work the selvedge stitch before the pattern repeat, repeat the pattern repeat (32 sts wide) continuously, and end with the sts after the pattern repeat. In WS rows, knit all stitches. Begin with Row 1 (WS), repeat Rows 1–4 heightwise, and end with a RS row.

### Stitch Key

● = 1 selvedge stitch

− = Purl 1 stitch

+ = Increase 1 stitch twisted from the bar between stitches

◿ = Purl 2 stitches together

◉ = Insert the needle knitwise into the stitch one row below, and knit this stitch, undoing the stitch above it in the current row

Pattern Repeat = 32 stitches

## 399 STAGGERED WELT PATTERN [multiple of 16 + 2 sts + 2 selv sts]

### Stitch Key

● = 1 selvedge stitch      − = Purl 1 stitch

✽ = Insert the right needle into the purl bump of the stitch 10 rows below, and lift it onto the left needle. Then purl the lifted stitch together with the following stitch on the left needle.

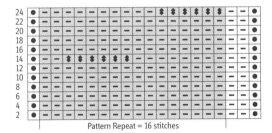

Pattern Repeat = 16 stitches

Only WS rows are shown; in RS rows, knit all sts. Begin with the selv st before the pattern repeat, rep the marked pattern repeat (16 sts wide) widthwise continuously, and end with the sts after the pattern repeat. Work Rows 1–24 once, then repeat Rows 5–24 heightwise.

## 400 SMOCKED WELT PATTERN

[multiple of 14 + 2 selv sts]

Only RS rows are shown; in WS rows, purl all sts. Begin with the selv st before the pattern repeat, rep the marked pattern repeat (14 sts wide) widthwise continuously, and end with the selv st after the pattern repeat. Repeat Rows 1–26 heightwise.

Pattern Repeat = 14 stitches

### Stitch Key

⬤ = 1 selvedge stitch

◼ = Knit 1 stitch

◈ = On the wrong side of the fabric, insert the right needle into the purl bump of the purl stitch 12 rows below, and lift it onto the left needle. Then knit the lifted stitch together with the following stitch on the left needle.

## 401 TWO-COLOR WELT PATTERN

[multiple of 12 + 2 selv sts]

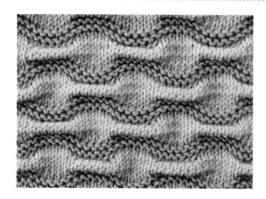

Shown are both RS and WS rows. Begin with the selv st before the pattern repeat, rep the marked pattern repeat (12 sts wide) widthwise continuously, and end with the selv st after the pattern repeat. Repeat Rows 1–24 heightwise.

### Stitch Key

⬤ = 1 selvedge stitch in color A

⬤ = 1 selvedge stitch in color B

◼ = Knit 1 stitch in color A

◼ = Knit 1 stitch in color B

— = Purl 1 stitch in color A

— = Purl 1 stitch in color B

↕ = Insert the right needle into the purl bump of the purl stitch 7 rows below, and lift it onto the left needle. Then purl the lifted stitch together with the following stitch on the left needle in color A.

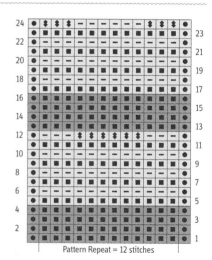

Pattern Repeat = 12 stitches

## 402 THREE-COLOR WELT PATTERN

[multiple of 12 + 2 selv sts]

Shown are both RS and WS rows. Begin with the selv st before the pattern repeat, rep the marked pattern repeat (12 sts wide) widthwise continuously, and end with the selv st after the pattern repeat. Repeat Rows 1–48 heightwise.

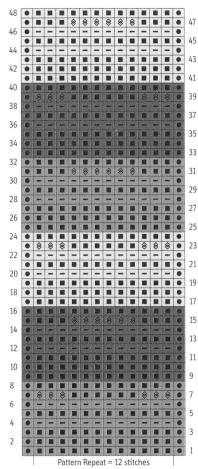

Pattern Repeat = 12 stitches

### Stitch Key

⬤ = 1 selvedge stitch in color A

⬤ = 1 selvedge stitch in color B

⬤ = 1 selvedge stitch in color C

■ = Knit 1 stitch in color A

■ = Knit 1 stitch in color B

■ = Knit 1 stitch in color C

— = Purl 1 stitch in color A

— = Purl 1 stitch in color B

— = Purl 1 stitch in color C

⬧ = Insert the right needle into the purl bump of the purl stitch 6 rows below, and lift it onto the left needle. Then purl the lifted stitch together with the following stitch on the left needle in color A.

⬧ = Insert the right needle into the purl bump of the purl stitch 6 rows below, and lift it onto the left needle. Then purl the lifted stitch together with the following stitch on the left needle in color B.

⬧ = Insert the right needle into the purl bump of the purl stitch 6 rows below, and lift it onto the left needle. Then purl the lifted stitch together with the following stitch on the left needle in color C.

DECORATIVE
EDGINGS

# **Beginning** Borders

## 403 ZIGZAG EYELET PATTERN EDGING

[multiple of 20 + 1 st + 2 selv sts]

Cast on the stitches using the cable cast-on method, and knit 2 rows. Then continue from chart. Only RS rows are shown; in WS rows, knit the knits, and purl the purls and yarn overs. Begin with the selv st before the pattern repeat, rep the marked pattern repeat (20 sts wide) widthwise continuously, and end with the sts after the pattern repeat. Work Rows 1–30 once.
**Combining:** Work this edging at the beginning of the piece, then continue in a different stitch pattern. If needed, add in another 2–4 rows in stockinette for the transition before beginning the other stitch pattern.

### Stitch Key

- **●** = 1 selvedge stitch
- **■** = Knit 1 stitch
- **−** = Purl 1 stitch
- **O** = Make 1 yarn over
- **◢** = Knit 2 stitches together

- **◤** = Knit 2 stitches together left-leaning with passing over (skp): slip 1 stitch knitwise, knit the next stitch, and pass the slipped stitch over

- **⋔** = Centered double decrease, knitting 3 stitches together with center stitch on top (cdd): slip 2 stitches together knitwise, knit 1 stitch, and pass the slipped stitches over

Pattern Repeat = 20 stitches

29 27 25 23 21 19 17 15 13 11 9 7 5 3 1

## 404 FEATHER-AND-FAN BORDER

[multiple of 17 + 2 selv sts]

Cast on the stitches using the cable cast-on method. Shown are both RS and WS rows. Begin with the selv st before the pattern repeat, rep the marked pattern repeat (17 sts wide) widthwise continuously, and end with the selv st after the pattern repeat. Work Rows 1–6 once, then repeat only Rows 3–6 twice more, and work Rows 15–24 once.
**Combining:** Work this edging at the beginning of the piece, then continue in a different stitch pattern. If needed, add in another 2–4 rows in stockinette for the transition before beginning the other stitch pattern.

### Stitch Key

- **●** = 1 selvedge stitch
- **■** = Knit 1 stitch
- **−** = Purl 1 stitch
- **O** = Make 1 yarn over
- **◢** = Knit 2 stitches together

**◤** = Knit 2 stitches together left-leaning with passing over (skp): slip 1 stitch knitwise, knit the next stitch, and pass the slipped stitch over

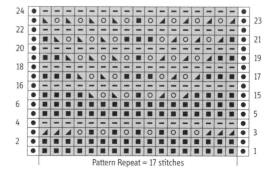

Pattern Repeat = 17 stitches

## 405 DROPLET ARCS

[multiple of 10 + 1 st + 2 selv sts]

Cast on the stitches using the cable cast-on method. Only RS rows are shown; in WS rows, purl all stitches and yarn overs. Begin with the sts before the pattern repeat, rep the marked pattern repeat (10 sts wide) widthwise continuously, and end with the sts after the pattern repeat. Work Rows 1–20 once.

**Combining:** Work this edging at the beginning of the piece, then continue in a different stitch pattern. If needed, add in another 2–4 rows in stockinette for the transition before beginning the other stitch pattern.

### Stitch Key

● = 1 selvedge stitch

O = Make 1 yarn over

■ = Knit 1 stitch

◢ = Knit 2 stitches together

◣ = Knit 2 stitches together left-leaning with passing over (skp): slip 1 stitch knitwise, knit the next stitch, and pass the slipped stitch over

▲ = Knit 3 stitches together left-leaning with passing over (sk2p): slip 1 stitch knitwise, knit 2 stitches together, and pass the slipped stitch over

Pattern Repeat = 10 stitches

## 406 DIAMOND LACE PATTERN BORDER

[multiple of 12 + 7 sts + 2 selv sts]

Cast on the stitches using the cable cast-on method, and knit 2 rows. Then continue from chart. Only RS rows are shown; in WS rows, purl all stitches and yarn overs. Begin with the sts before the pattern repeat, rep the marked pattern repeat (12 sts wide) widthwise continuously, and end with the sts after the pattern repeat. Work Rows 1–18 once heightwise.

**Combining:** Work this edging at the beginning of the piece, then continue in a different stitch pattern. If needed, add in another 2–4 rows in stockinette for the transition before beginning the other stitch pattern.

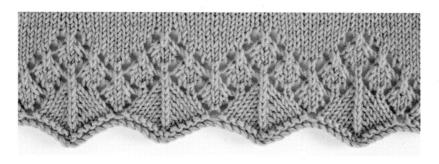

Pattern Repeat = 12 stitches

### Stitch Key

● = 1 selvedge stitch

■ = Knit 1 stitch

O = Make 1 yarn over

◢ = Knit 2 stitches together

◣ = Knit 2 stitches together left-leaning with passing over (skp): slip 1 stitch knitwise, knit the next stitch, and pass the slipped stitch over

⋂ = Centered double decrease, knitting 3 stitches together with center stitch on top (cdd): slip 2 stitches together knitwise, knit 1 stitch, and pass the slipped stitches over

## 407 VINE BORDER

[multiple of 10 + 1 st + 2 selv sts]

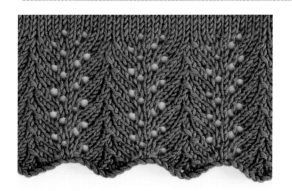

Cast on the stitches using the cable cast-on method. Only RS rows are shown; in WS rows, purl all stitches and yarn overs. Begin with the selv st before the pattern repeat, rep the marked pattern repeat (10 sts wide) widthwise continuously, and end with the sts after the pattern repeat. Work Rows 1–4 multiple times until the desired height has been reached (pictured: worked 6 times total).

**Combining:** Work this edging at the beginning of the piece, then continue in a different stitch pattern. If needed, add in another 2–4 rows in stockinette for the transition before beginning the other stitch pattern.

### Stitch Key

● = 1 selvedge stitch

■ = Knit 1 stitch

O = Make 1 yarn over

◢ = Knit 2 stitches together

◣ = Knit 2 stitches together left-leaning with passing over (skp): slip 1 stitch knitwise, knit the next stitch, and pass the slipped stitch over

Pattern Repeat = 10 stitches

## 408 ZIGZAG FLOWER BORDER

[multiple of 20 + 1 st + 2 selv sts]

Cast on the stitches using the cable cast-on method, and knit 2 rows. Then continue from chart. Only RS rows are shown; in WS rows, purl all stitches and yarn overs. Begin with the sts before the pattern repeat, rep the marked pattern repeat (20 sts wide) widthwise continuously, and end with the sts after the pattern repeat. Work Rows 1–28 once.

**Combining:** Work this edging at the beginning of the piece, then continue in a different stitch pattern.

### Stitch Key

● = 1 selvedge stitch

■ = Knit 1 stitch

O = Make 1 yarn over

◢ = Knit 2 stitches together

◣ = Knit 2 stitches together left-leaning with passing over (skp): slip 1 stitch knitwise, knit the next stitch, and pass the slipped stitch over

▲ = Knit 3 stitches together left-leaning with passing over (sk2p): slip 1 stitch knitwise, knit 2 stitches together, and pass the slipped stitch over

∩ = Centered double decrease, knitting 3 stitches together with center stitch on top (cdd): slip 2 stitches together knitwise, knit 1 stitch, and pass the slipped stitches over

Pattern Repeat = 20 stitches

## 409 WOVEN CABLE BORDER

[24 sts]

The border is worked sideways without selvedge stitches. Only RS rows are shown; in WS rows, purl all sts. Repeat Rows 1–8 until the desired length has been reached.

**Combining:** Bind off the stitches in a RS row, leaving the last stitch on the right needle. Now, pick up stitches along the long side from the outermost sts, and continue using the picked-up stitches. Alternatively, work the cabled border separately, and sew it onto the main piece later.

### Stitch Key

■ = Knit 1 stitch

= Hold 3 stitches on a cable needle in front of work, knit 3 stitches, then knit the 3 stitches from the cable needle

= Hold 3 stitches on a cable needle behind work, knit 3 stitches, then knit the 3 stitches from the cable needle

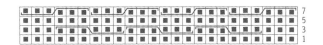

## 410 BEAR PAW BORDER

[multiple of 22 + 1 st + 2 selv sts]

Cast on the stitches using the cable cast-on method, and knit 2 rows. Then continue from chart. Only RS rows are shown; in WS rows, knit the knits, and purl the purls and yarn overs. Begin with the selv st before the pattern repeat, rep the marked pattern repeat (22 sts wide) widthwise continuously, and end with the sts after the pattern repeat. Repeat Rows 1–12 multiple times until the desired height has been reached (pictured: worked 3 times).

**Combining:** Work this edging at the beginning of the piece, then continue in a different stitch pattern. If needed, add in another 2–4 rows in stockinette for the transition before beginning the other stitch pattern.

Pattern Repeat = 22 stitches

### Stitch Key

● = 1 selvedge stitch

○ = Make 1 yarn over

■ = Knit 1 stitch

◢ = Knit 2 stitches together

– = Purl 1 stitch

◿ = Purl 2 stitches together

◣ = Knit 2 stitches together left-leaning with passing over (skp): slip 1 stitch knitwise, knit the next stitch, and pass the slipped stitch over

∩ = Centered double decrease, knitting 3 stitches together with center stitch on top (cdd): slip 2 stitches together knitwise, knit 1 stitch, and pass the slipped stitches over

# Borders as Side Edge Finishing

## 411 LEAFY VINE EDGING

[multiple of 17 sts + 2 selv sts]

### LEFT EDGE

Only RS rows are shown; in WS rows, knit the knits, and purl the purls and yarn overs. In RS rows, slip the selv st at the beginning of the row knitwise, and knit the selv st at the end of the row. In WS rows, slip the selv st at the beginning of the row purlwise, and knit the selv st at the end of the row. Repeat Rows 1–12 heightwise.

**Combining:** Knit up the leaf border separately, and sew it on later, or omit the selv sts at the right edge of the piece, and combine the vine with another stitch pattern. Alternatively, when the desired length has been reached, BO the sts in a WS row, leaving the last stitch on the right needle. Along the long right edge, pick up the required number of stitches, and continue using the picked-up stitches.

### Stitch Key

● = 1 selvedge stitch

■ = Knit 1 stitch

– = Purl 1 stitch

○ = Make 1 yarn over

◢ = Knit 2 stitches together

◣ = Knit 2 stitches together left-leaning with passing over (skp): slip 1 stitch knitwise, knit the next stitch, and pass the slipped stitch over

▲ = Knit 3 stitches together left-leaning with passing over (sk2p): slip 1 stitch knitwise, knit 2 stitches together, and pass the slipped stitch over

### RIGHT EDGE

Only RS rows are shown; in WS rows, knit the knits, and purl the purls and yarn overs. In RS rows, slip the selv st at the beginning of the row purlwise, and knit the selv st at the end of the row. In WS rows, slip the selv st at the beginning of the row knitwise, and knit the selv st at the end of the row. Repeat Rows 1–12 heightwise.

**Combining:** Knit up the leaf border separately, and sew it on later, or omit the selv sts at the left edge of the piece, and combine the vine with another stitch pattern. Alternatively, when the desired length has been reached, BO the sts in a RS row, leaving the last stitch on the right needle. Along the long left edge, pick up the required number of stitches, and continue using the picked-up stitches.

### Stitch Key

● = 1 selvedge stitch

■ = Knit 1 stitch

– = Purl 1 stitch

○ = Make 1 yarn over

◢ = Knit 2 stitches together

◣ = Knit 2 stitches together left-leaning with passing over (skp): slip 1 stitch knitwise, knit the next stitch, and pass the slipped stitch over

▲ = Knit 3 stitches together left-leaning with passing over (sk2p): slip 1 stitch knitwise, knit 2 stitches together, and pass the slipped stitch over

## 412 LEAF EDGING

[multiple of 6 sts + 1 selv st (before beginning of Row 1)]

### LEFT EDGE

Shown are both RS and WS rows. In RS rows, slip the selv sts knitwise, and in WS rows, knit the selv sts. Repeat Rows 1–18 heightwise.

**Combining:** Knit up the border separately, and sew it on later, or omit the selv sts, and combine the border with another stitch pattern. Alternatively, when the desired length has been reached, BO the sts in a WS row, leaving the last stitch on the right needle. Along the long right edge, pick up the required number of stitches, and continue using the picked-up stitches.

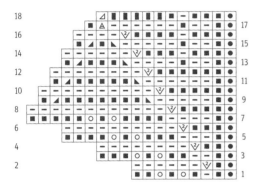

### Stitch Key

● = 1 selvedge stitch

■ = Knit 1 stitch

− = Purl 1 stitch

○ = Make 1 yarn over

◢ = Knit 2 stitches together

◣ = Knit 2 stitches together left-leaning with passing over (skp): slip 1 stitch knitwise, knit the next stitch, and pass the slipped stitch over

▮ = Bind off 1 stitch knitwise

ᐯ = Make 2 stitches from 1 (kfb): first, knit 1 stitch, but leave it on the left needle, then knit the same stitch again through the back loop

▲ = Knit 3 stitches together left-leaning with passing over (sk2p): slip 1 stitch knitwise, knit 2 stitches together, and pass the slipped stitch over

### RIGHT EDGE

Shown are both RS and WS rows. In RS rows, knit the selv sts, and in WS rows, slip the selv sts knitwise. Repeat Rows 1–18 heightwise.

**Combining:** Knit up the border separately, and sew it on later, or omit the selv sts, and combine the border with another stitch pattern. Alternatively, when the desired length has been reached, BO the sts in a RS row, leaving the last stitch on the right needle. Along the long left edge, pick up the required number of stitches, and continue using the picked-up stitches.

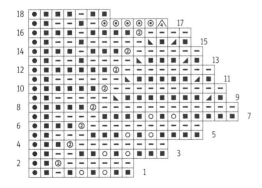

### Stitch Key

● = 1 selvedge stitch

■ = Knit 1 stitch

− = Purl 1 stitch

○ = Make 1 yarn over

◢ = Knit 2 stitches together

◣ = Knit 2 stitches together left-leaning with passing over (skp): slip 1 stitch knitwise, knit the next stitch, and pass the slipped stitch over

⊙ = Bind off 1 stitch purlwise

◭ = Slip 2 stitches individually knitwise, knit 2 stitches, then pass the two slipped stitches over

② = Make 2 stitches from 1 (kbf): first, knit 1 stitch through the back loop, but leave it on the left needle, knit it once more through the front leg

## 413 LACE PATTERN EDGING   [multiple of 12 sts + 1 selv st (before beginning of Row 1]

### LEFT EDGE

Shown are both RS and WS rows. In RS rows, slip the selv sts knitwise, and in WS rows, knit the selv sts. Repeat Rows 1–14 heightwise.

**Combining:** Knit up the border separately, and sew it on later, or omit the selv sts, and combine the border at the side with another stitch pattern. Alternatively, when the desired length has been reached, BO the sts in a WS row, leaving the last stitch on the right needle. Along the long right edge, pick up the required number of stitches, and continue using the picked-up stitches.

### Stitch Key

● = 1 selvedge stitch

■ = Knit 1 stitch

– = Purl 1 stitch

O = Make 1 yarn over

◢ = Knit 2 stitches together

◣ = Knit 2 stitches together left-leaning with passing over (skp): slip 1 stitch knitwise, knit the next stitch, and pass the slipped stitch over

▲ = Knit 3 stitches together left-leaning with passing over (sk2p): slip 1 stitch knitwise, knit 2 stitches together, and pass the slipped stitch over

### RIGHT EDGE

Shown are both RS and WS rows. In RS rows, knit the selv sts, and in WS rows, slip the selv sts knitwise. Repeat Rows 1–14 heightwise.

**Combining:** Knit up the border separately, and sew it on later, or omit the selv sts, and combine the border at the side with another stitch pattern. Alternatively, when the desired length has been reached, BO the sts in a RS row, leaving the last stitch on the right needle. Along the left long edge, pick up the required number of stitches, and continue using the picked-up stitches.

### Stitch Key

● = 1 selvedge stitch

■ = Knit 1 stitch

– = Purl 1 stitch

O = Make 1 yarn over

◢ = Knit 2 stitches together

◣ = Knit 2 stitches together left-leaning with passing over (skp): slip 1 stitch knitwise, knit the next stitch, and pass the slipped stitch over

▲ = Knit 3 stitches together

## 414 ARROW LEAF BORDER [multiple of 8 sts + 2 selv sts (before beginning of Row 1)]

### LEFT EDGE

Only RS rows are shown; in WS rows, knit the knits, and purl the purls and yarn overs. In RS rows, slip the selv st at the beginning of the row knitwise, and knit the selv st at the end of the row. In WS rows, slip the selv st at the beginning of the row purlwise, and knit the selv st at the end of the row. Repeat Rows 1–60 heightwise.

**Combining:** Knit up the leaf border separately, and sew it on later, or omit the selv sts at the right edge of the piece, and combine the border at the side with another stitch pattern. Alternatively, when the desired length has been reached, BO the sts in a WS row, leaving the last stitch on the right needle. Along the long right edge, pick up the required number of stitches, and continue using the picked-up stitches.

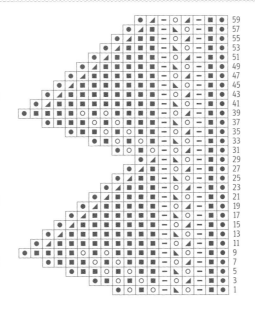

#### Stitch Key

● = 1 selvedge stitch

■ = Knit 1 stitch

– = Purl 1 stitch

○ = Make 1 yarn over

◢ = Knit 2 stitches together

◣ = Knit 2 stitches together left-leaning with passing over (skp): slip 1 stitch knitwise, knit the next stitch, and pass the slipped stitch over

### RIGHT EDGE

Only RS rows are shown; in WS rows, knit the knits, and purl the purls and yarn overs. In RS rows, slip the selv st at the beginning of the row purlwise, and knit the selv st at the end of the row. In WS rows, slip the selv st at the beginning of the row knitwise, and knit the selv st at the end of the row. Repeat Rows 1–60 heightwise.

**Combining:** Knit up the leaf border separately, and sew it on later, or omit the selv sts at the left edge of the piece, and combine the border at the side with another stitch pattern. Alternatively, when the desired length has been reached, BO the sts in a RS row, leaving the last stitch on the right needle. Along the long left edge, pick up the required number of stitches, and continue using the picked-up stitches.

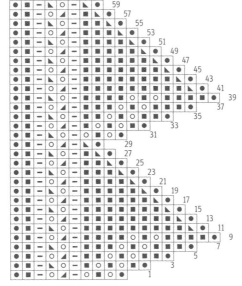

#### Stitch Key

● = 1 selvedge stitch

■ = Knit 1 stitch

– = Purl 1 stitch

○ = Make 1 yarn over

◢ = Knit 2 stitches together

◣ = Knit 2 stitches together left-leaning with passing over (skp): slip 1 stitch knitwise, knit the next stitch, and pass the slipped stitch over

## 415 DELICATE LACE EDGING

[multiple of 7 sts + 1 selv st (before beginning of Row 1)]

### LEFT EDGE

Shown are both RS and WS rows. In RS rows, slip the selv sts knitwise, and in WS rows, knit the selv sts. Repeat Rows 1–4 heightwise.

**Combining:** Knit up the border separately, and sew it on later, or omit the selv sts, and combine the border at the side with another stitch pattern. Alternatively, when the desired length has been reached, BO the sts in a WS row, leaving the last stitch on the right needle. Along the long right edge, pick up the required number of stitches, and continue using the picked-up stitches.

### Stitch Key

- ● = 1 selvedge stitch
- ■ = Knit 1 stitch
- O = Make 1 yarn over
- ⊿ = Purl 2 stitches together
- ⱱ = Work a total of 3 stitches into 1 stitch (kfbf): knit 1 stitch, but leave it on the left needle. Now, knit the stitch through the back loop, still leaving it on the left needle, then knit it through the front leg, and let it slip off the left needle.
- ⋀ = Knit 3 stitches, and then, one after another, pass the 2nd and 1st stitch over the 3rd stitch
- ☐ = No stitch, for better overview only

### RIGHT EDGE

Shown are both RS and WS rows. In RS rows, knit the selv sts, and in WS rows, slip the selv sts knitwise. Repeat Rows 1–4 heightwise.

**Combining:** Knit up the border separately, and sew it on later, or omit the selv sts, and combine the border at the side with another stitch pattern. Alternatively, when the desired length has been reached, BO the sts in a RS row, leaving the last stitch on the right needle. Along the long left edge, pick up the required number of stitches, and continue using the picked-up stitches.

### Stitch Key

- ● = 1 selvedge stitch
- ■ = Knit 1 stitch
- O = Make 1 yarn over
- ⊿ = Purl 2 stitches together
- ⱱ = Work a total of 3 stitches into 1 stitch (kfbf): knit 1 stitch, but leave it on the left needle. Now, knit the stitch through the back loop, still leaving it on the left needle, then knit it through the front leg, and let it slip off the left needle.
- ⋀ = Knit 3 stitches, and then, one after another, pass the 2nd and 1st stitch over the 3rd stitch
- ☐ = No stitch, for better overview only

## 416 CABLE PATTERN EDGING

[multiple of 15 sts + 1 selv st]

### LEFT EDGE

Only RS rows are shown; in WS rows, knit the knits, and purl the purls. In RS rows, slip the selv sts knitwise, and in WS rows, knit the selv sts. Repeat Rows 1–16 heightwise.

**Combining:** Knit up the border separately, and sew it on later, or omit the selv sts at the right edge of the piece, and combine the border at the side with another stitch pattern (pictured: Moss stitch). Alternatively, when the desired length has been reached, BO the sts in a WS row, leaving the last stitch on the right needle. Along the long right edge, pick up the required number of stitches, and continue using the picked-up stitches.

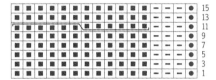

### Stitch Key

$\bullet$ = 1 selvedge stitch

$\blacksquare$ = Knit 1 stitch

$-$ = Purl 1 stitch

= Hold 6 stitches on a cable needle in front of work, knit 6 stitches, then knit the 6 stitches from the cable needle

### RIGHT EDGE

Only RS rows are shown; in WS rows, knit the knits, and purl the purls. In RS rows, knit the selv sts, and in WS rows, slip the selv sts knitwise. Repeat Rows 1–16 heightwise.

**Combining:** Knit up the border separately, and sew it on later, or omit the selv sts at the left edge of the piece, and combine the border at the side with another stitch pattern (pictured: Moss stitch). Alternatively, when the desired length has been reached, BO the sts in a RS row, leaving the last stitch on the right needle. Along the long left edge, pick up the required number of stitches, and continue using the picked-up stitches.

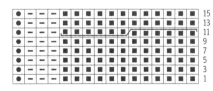

### Stitch Key

$\bullet$ = 1 selvedge stitch

$\blacksquare$ = Knit 1 stitch

$-$ = Purl 1 stitch

= Hold 6 stitches on a cable needle behind work, knit 6 stitches, then knit the 6 stitches from the cable needle

## 417 ZIGZAG EDGING

[multiple of 19 sts + 2 selv sts (before beginning of Row 1)]

### LEFT EDGE

Only RS rows are shown; in WS rows, purl all stitches and yarn overs. In RS rows, slip the selv st at the beginning of the row knitwise, and knit the selv st at the end of the row. In WS rows, slip the selv st at the beginning of the row purlwise, and knit the selv st at the end of the row. Repeat Rows 1–32 heightwise.

**Combining:** Knit up the border separately, and sew it on later, or omit the selv sts at the right edge of the piece, and combine the border at the side with another stitch pattern. Alternatively, when the desired length has been reached, BO the sts in a WS row, leaving the last stitch on the right needle. Along the long right edge, pick up the required number of stitches, and continue using the picked-up stitches.

### Stitch Key

● = 1 selvedge stitch

■ = Knit 1 stitch

○ = Make 1 yarn over

◢ = Knit 2 stitches together

◣ = Knit 2 stitches together left-leaning with passing over (skp): slip 1 stitch knitwise, knit the next stitch, and pass the slipped stitch over

### RIGHT EDGE

Only RS rows are shown; in WS rows, purl all stitches and yarn overs. In RS rows, slip the selv st at the beginning of the row purlwise, and knit the selv st at the end of the row. In WS rows, slip the selv st at the beginning of the row knitwise, and knit the selv st at the end of the row. Repeat Rows 1–32 heightwise.

**Combining:** Knit up the border separately, and sew it on later, or omit the selv sts at the left edge of the piece, and combine the border at the side with another stitch pattern. Alternatively, when the desired length has been reached, BO the sts in a RS row, leaving the last stitch on the right needle. Along the long left edge, pick up the required number of stitches, and continue using the picked-up stitches.

### Stitch Key

● = 1 selvedge stitch

■ = Knit 1 stitch

○ = Make 1 yarn over

◢ = Knit 2 stitches together

◣ = Knit 2 stitches together left-leaning with passing over (skp): slip 1 stitch knitwise, knit the next stitch, and pass the slipped stitch over

# **Ending** Borders

## CHEVRON MESH ENDING BORDER

[multiple of 10 + 1 st + 2 selv sts]

Only RS rows are shown; in WS rows, purl all stitches and yarn overs. Begin with the selv st before the pattern repeat, rep the marked pattern repeat (10 sts wide) widthwise continuously, and end with the sts after the pattern repeat. Work Rows 1–16 once, then bind off the stitches according to the chart, using the elastic bind-off method.

**Combining:** Add at the end of another finished piece, adding in another 2–4 rows in stockinette for the transition before beginning the edging. Alternatively, knit up the border separately, and sew it on later.

### Stitch Key

● = 1 selvedge stitch

■ = Knit 1 stitch

O = Make 1 yarn over

☐ = No stitch, for better overview only

◢ = Knit 2 stitches together

◣ = Knit 2 stitches together left-leaning with passing over (skp): slip 1 stitch knitwise, knit the next stitch, and pass the slipped stitch over

△ = Knit 3 stitches together left-leaning with passing over (sk2p): slip 1 stitch knitwise, knit 2 stitches together, and pass the slipped stitch over

∼ = Bind off 1 stitch using elastic bind-off method

> = First, bind off 1 stitch using elastic bind-off method, then pull the working yarn through the stitch a second time, creating a chain as in crochet. This creates a point at the edge.

⬔ = Knit 3 stitches together, then bind off using elastic bind-off method

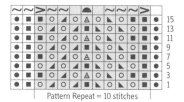

Pattern Repeat = 10 stitches

# 226

## 419 FLOWER MOTIF BORDER

[multiple of 16 + 1 st + 2 selv sts]

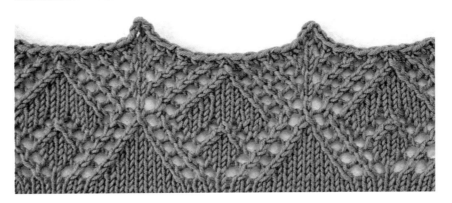

Pattern Repeat = 16 stitches

Only RS rows are shown; in WS rows, purl all stitches and yarn overs. Begin with the sts before the pattern repeat, rep the marked pattern repeat (16 sts wide) widthwise continuously, and end with the sts after the pattern repeat. Work Rows 1–20 once, then bind off the stitches according to the chart, using the elastic bind-off method.
**Combining:** Add at the end of another finished piece, adding in another 2–4 rows in stockinette for the transition before beginning the edging. Alternatively, knit up the border separately, and sew it on later. The flowers are worked from the top down, making this pattern a good final section at the end of a scarf, shawl or collar.

### Stitch Key

• = 1 selvedge stitch

■ = Knit 1 stitch

O = Make 1 yarn over

◢ = Knit 2 stitches together

◣ = Knit 2 stitches together left-leaning with passing over (skp): slip 1 stitch knitwise, knit the next stitch, and pass the slipped stitch over

△ = Knit 3 stitches together left-leaning with passing over (sk2p): slip 1 stitch knitwise, knit 2 stitches together, and pass the slipped stitch over

~ = Bind off 1 stitch using elastic bind-off method

➤ = First, bind off 1 stitch using elastic bind-off method, then pull the working yarn through the stitch a second time, creating a chain as in crochet. This creates a point at the edge.

◖ = Knit 3 stitches together, then bind off using elastic bind-off method

☐ = No stitch, for better overview only

## 420 ZIGZAG LACE ENDING BORDER

[multiple of 12 + 1 st + 2 selv sts]

Only RS rows are shown; in WS rows, purl all stitches and yarn overs. Begin with the sts before the pattern repeat, rep the marked pattern repeat (12 sts wide) widthwise continuously, and end with the sts after the pattern repeat. Work Rows 1–10 once heightwise, then bind off the stitches according to the chart, using the elastic bind-off method.

**Combining:** Add at the end of another finished piece, adding in another 2–4 rows in stockinette for the transition before beginning the edging. Alternatively, knit up the border separately, and sew it on later.

### Stitch Key

⬛ = 1 selvedge stitch

⬛ = Knit 1 stitch

◯ = Make 1 yarn over

◢ = Knit 2 stitches together

◣ = Knit 2 stitches together left-leaning with passing over (skp): slip 1 stitch knitwise, knit the next stitch, and pass the slipped stitch over

△ = Knit 3 stitches together left-leaning with passing over (sk2p): slip 1 stitch knitwise, knit 2 stitches together, and pass the slipped stitch over

~ = Bind off 1 stitch using elastic bind-off method

> = First, bind off 1 stitch using elastic bind-off method, then pull the working yarn through the stitch a second time, creating a chain as in crochet. This creates a point at the edge.

◖ = Knit 3 stitches together, then bind off using elastic bind-off method

☐ = No stitch, for better overview only

Pattern Repeat = 12 stitches

# STRANDED COLORWORK AND INTARSIA PATTERNS

## 421 SMALL FLAGSTONE PATTERN [multiple of 3 + 1 st (+ 2 selv sts when worked in rows)]

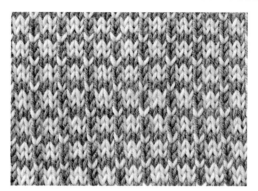

Work in stranded colorwork technique. Row numbers for odd rows are shown in the chart. Even-numbered rows are read from right to left when working in rounds, and from left to right when working in turned rows. In Row 1, begin with the pattern repeat, rep the marked pattern repeat (3 sts wide) widthwise continuously, and end with the stitch after the pattern repeat. Work Rows 1–7 once, then repeat Rows 2–7 heightwise continuously.

### Stitch Key

☐ = 1 stitch in natural white

■ = 1 stitch in light gray

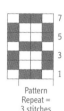

Pattern
Repeat =
3 stitches

## 422 DOT-STRIPE PATTERN [multiple of 3 + 2 sts (+ 2 selv sts when worked in rows)]

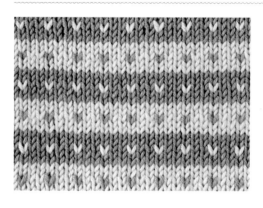

Work in stranded colorwork technique. Row numbers for odd rows are shown in the chart. Even-numbered rows are read from right to left when working in rounds, and from left to right when working in turned rows. In Row 1, begin with the pattern repeat, rep the marked pattern repeat (3 sts wide) widthwise continuously, and end with the sts after the pattern repeat. Repeat Rows 1–10 heightwise.

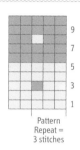

Pattern
Repeat =
3 stitches

### Stitch Key

☐ = 1 stitch in linen          ▨ = 1 stitch in dusty rose

## 423 THREE-COLOR ZIGZAG STRIPE PATTERN
[multiple of 6 + 1 st (+ 2 selv sts when worked in rows)]

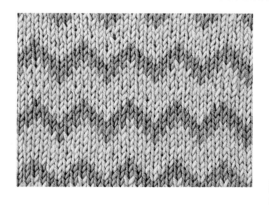

Work in stranded colorwork technique. Row numbers for odd rows are shown in the chart. Even-numbered rows are read from right to left when working in rounds, and from left to right when working in turned rows. In Row 1, begin with the pattern repeat, rep the marked pattern repeat (6 sts wide) widthwise continuously, and end with the stitch after the pattern repeat. Repeat Rows 1–18 heightwise.

### Stitch Key

☐ = 1 stitch in lilac          ■ = 1 stitch in plum blue

▨ = 1 stitch in pink

Pattern Repeat =
6 stitches

## 424 DOT PATTERN [multiple of 6 + 1 st (+ 2 selv sts when worked in rows)]

Work in stranded colorwork technique. Row numbers for odd rows are shown in the chart. Even-numbered rows are read from right to left when working in rounds, and from left to right when working in turned rows. In Row 1, begin with the pattern repeat, rep the marked pattern repeat (6 sts wide) widthwise continuously, and end with the stitch after the pattern repeat. Repeat Rows 1–8 heightwise.

**Stitch Key**

☐ = 1 stitch in lime
▨ = 1 stitch in medium blue

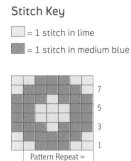

Pattern Repeat =
6 stitches

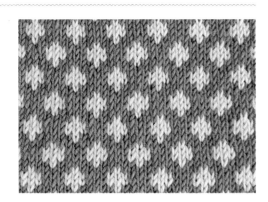

## 425 SMALL TILE PATTERN [multiple of 8 + 1 st (+ 2 selv sts when worked in rows)]

Work in stranded colorwork technique. Row numbers for odd rows are shown in the chart. Even-numbered rows are read from right to left when working in rounds, and from left to right when working in turned rows. In Row 1, begin with the pattern repeat, rep the marked pattern repeat (8 sts wide) widthwise continuously, and end with the stitch after the pattern repeat. Work Rows 1–9 once, then repeat Rows 2–9 heightwise continuously.

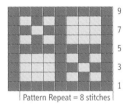

Pattern Repeat = 8 stitches

**Stitch Key**

☐ = 1 stitch in powder pink
▨ = 1 stitch in purple

## 426 SMALL CHECKERBOARD PATTERN

[multiple of 6 (+ 2 selv sts when worked in rows)]

Work in stranded colorwork technique. Row numbers for odd rows are shown in the chart. Even-numbered rows are read from right to left when working in rounds, and from left to right when working in turned rows. Rep the marked pattern repeat (6 sts wide) widthwise, and repeat Rows 1–6 heightwise continuously.

**Stitch Key**

☐ = 1 stitch in camel
▨ = 1 stitch in chestnut

Pattern Repeat =
6 stitches

## 427 SMALL GRAPHIC PATTERN [multiple of 8 (+ 2 selv sts when worked in rows)]

Work in stranded colorwork technique. Row numbers for odd rows are shown in the chart. Even-numbered rows are read from right to left when working in rounds, and from left to right when working in turned rows. Rep the marked pattern repeat (8 sts wide) widthwise, and repeat Rows 1–8 heightwise continuously.

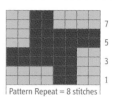

Pattern Repeat = 8 stitches

### Stitch Key

☐ = 1 stitch in apricot

■ = 1 stitch in chocolate brown

## 428 CLASSIC ARGYLE PATTERN [multiple of 12 + 1 st (+ 2 selv sts when worked in rows)]

Work in stranded colorwork technique. Row numbers for odd rows are shown in the chart. Even-numbered rows are read from right to left when working in rounds, and from left to right when working in turned rows. In Row 1, begin with the pattern repeat, rep the marked pattern repeat (12 sts wide) widthwise continuously, and end with the stitch after the pattern repeat. Work Rows 1–11 once heightwise, then repeat Rows 2–11 heightwise continuously.

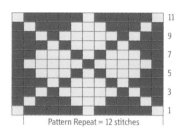

Pattern Repeat = 12 stitches

### Stitch Key

☐ = 1 stitch in yellow

■ = 1 stitch in pine green

## 429 TWO-COLOR FILLED LOZENGE PATTERN [multiple of 12 + 1 st (+ 2 selv sts when worked in rows)]

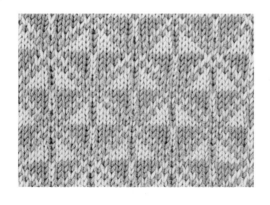

Work in stranded colorwork technique. Row numbers for odd rows are shown in the chart. Even-numbered rows are read from right to left when working in rounds, and from left to right when working in turned rows. In Row 1, begin with the pattern repeat, rep the marked pattern repeat (12 sts wide) widthwise continuously, and end with the stitch after the pattern repeat. Repeat Rows 1–12 heightwise continuously.

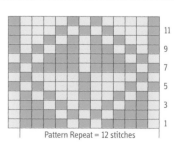

Pattern Repeat = 12 stitches

### Stitch Key

☐ = 1 stitch in yellow

■ = 1 stitch in apple green

## 430 NORDIC DIAMOND PATTERN
[multiple of 22 + 1 st (+ 2 selv sts when worked in rows)]

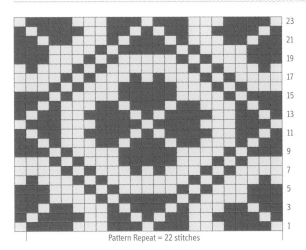

Pattern Repeat = 22 stitches

Work in stranded colorwork technique. Row numbers for odd rows are shown in the chart. Even-numbered rows are read from right to left when working in rounds, and from left to right when working in turned rows. In Row 1, begin with the pattern repeat, rep the marked pattern repeat (22 sts wide) widthwise continuously, and end with the stitch after the pattern repeat. Work Rows 1–23 once, then repeat Rows 2–23 heightwise continuously.

**Stitch Key**

☐ = 1 stitch in lime

■ = 1 stitch in pine green

## 431 ALTERNATING SQUARE PATTERN
[multiple of 16 + 1 st (+ 2 selv sts when worked in rows)]

Work in stranded colorwork technique. Row numbers for odd rows are shown in the chart. Even-numbered rows are read from right to left when working in rounds, and from left to right when working in turned rows. In Row 1, begin with the pattern repeat, rep the marked pattern repeat (16 sts wide) widthwise continuously, and end with the stitch after the pattern repeat. Work Rows 1–17 once, then repeat Rows 2–17 heightwise continuously.

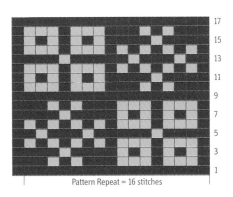

Pattern Repeat = 16 stitches

**Stitch Key**

☐ = 1 stitch in golden yellow

■ = 1 stitch in chocolate brown

## 432 DIAMOND-SQUARE PATTERN [multiple of 10 + 1 st (+ 2 selv sts when worked in rows)]

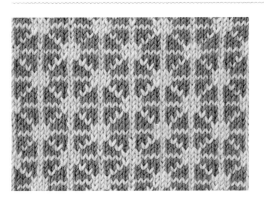

Work in stranded colorwork technique. Row numbers for odd rows are shown in the chart. Even-numbered rows are read from right to left when working in rounds, and from left to right when working in turned rows. In Row 1, begin with the pattern repeat, rep the marked pattern repeat (10 sts wide) widthwise continuously, and end with the stitch after the pattern repeat. Work Rows 1–11 once heightwise, then repeat Rows 2–11 heightwise continuously.

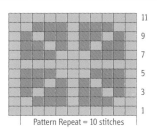

Pattern Repeat = 10 stitches

### Stitch Key

☐ = 1 stitch in mint ▇ = 1 stitch in medium blue

## 433 RHOMBOID PATTERN [multiple of 10 (+ 2 selv sts when worked in rows)]

Work in stranded colorwork technique. Row numbers for odd rows are shown in the chart. Even-numbered rows are read from right to left when working in rounds, and from left to right when working in turned rows. Rep the marked pattern repeat (10 sts wide) widthwise, and repeat Rows 1–10 heightwise continuously.

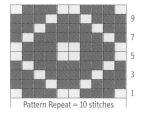

Pattern Repeat = 10 stitches

### Stitch Key

☐ = 1 stitch in linen
▇ = 1 stitch in denim blue

## 434 BROKEN RHOMBOID PATTERN [multiple of 8 + 1 st (+ 2 selv sts when worked in rows)]

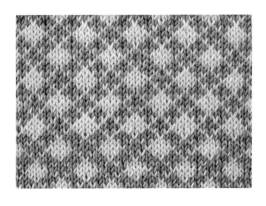

Work in stranded colorwork technique. Row numbers for odd rows are shown in the chart. Even-numbered rows are read from right to left when working in rounds, and from left to right when working in turned rows. In Row 1, begin with the pattern repeat, rep the marked pattern repeat (8 sts wide) widthwise continuously, and end with the stitch after the pattern repeat. Work Rows 1–9 once, then repeat Rows 2–9 heightwise continuously.

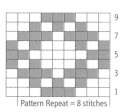

Pattern Repeat = 8 stitches

### Stitch Key

☐ = 1 stitch in natural white
▇ = 1 stitch in pink

## 435 BROKEN CHEVRON PATTERN [multiple of 12 + 1 st (+ 2 selv sts when worked in rows)]

Work in stranded colorwork technique. Row numbers for odd rows are shown in the chart. Even-numbered rows are read from right to left when working in rounds, and from left to right when working in turned rows. In Row 1, begin with the pattern repeat, rep the marked pattern repeat (12 sts wide) widthwise continuously, and end with the stitch after the pattern repeat. Repeat Rows 1–10 heightwise continuously.

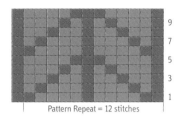

Pattern Repeat = 12 stitches

**Stitch Key**

= 1 stitch in coral

= 1 stitch in burgundy

## 436 MOCK WOVEN PATTERN [multiple of 12 + 1 st (+ 2 selv sts when worked in rows)]

Work in stranded colorwork technique. Row numbers for odd rows are shown in the chart. Even-numbered rows are read from right to left when working in rounds, and from left to right when working in turned rows. In Row 1, begin with the pattern repeat, rep the marked pattern repeat (12 sts wide) widthwise continuously, and end with the stitch after the pattern repeat. Repeat Rows 1–12 heightwise continuously.

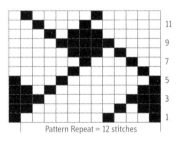

Pattern Repeat = 12 stitches

**Stitch Key**

= 1 stitch in white

= 1 stitch in black

## 437 CUBE ILLUSION PATTERN [multiple of 8 + 2 sts (+ 2 selv sts when worked in rows)]

Work in stranded colorwork technique. Row numbers for odd rows are shown in the chart. Even-numbered rows are read from right to left when working in rounds, and from left to right when working in turned rows. In Row 1, begin with the stitch before the pattern repeat, rep the marked pattern repeat (8 sts wide) widthwise continuously, and end with the stitch after the pattern repeat. Repeat Rows 1–14 heightwise continuously.

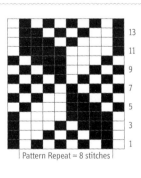

Pattern Repeat = 8 stitches

**Stitch Key**

= 1 stitch in white          = 1 stitch in black

## 438 STRIPED DIAMONDS

[multiple of 18 + 1 st (+ 2 selv sts when worked in rows)]

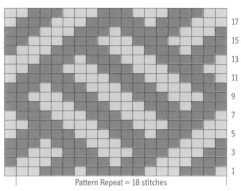

Pattern Repeat = 18 stitches

Work in stranded colorwork technique. Row numbers for odd rows are shown in the chart. Even-numbered rows are read from right to left when working in rounds, and from left to right when working in turned rows. In Row 1, begin with the pattern repeat, rep the marked pattern repeat (18 sts wide) widthwise continuously, and end with the stitch after the pattern repeat. Repeat Rows 1–18 heightwise continuously.

**Stitch Key**

☐ = 1 stitch in light salmon
■ = 1 stitch in coral

## 439 GRAPHIC ORNAMENTS

[multiple of 24 + 1 st (+ 2 selv sts when worked in rows)]

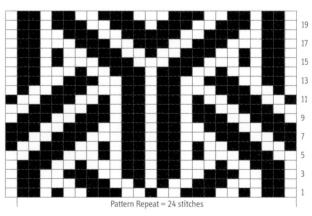

Pattern Repeat = 24 stitches

Work in stranded colorwork technique. Row numbers for odd rows are shown in the chart. Even-numbered rows are read from right to left when working in rounds, and from left to right when working in turned rows. In Row 1, begin with the pattern repeat, rep the marked pattern repeat (24 sts wide) widthwise continuously, and end with the stitch after the pattern repeat. Repeat Rows 1–20 heightwise continuously.

**Stitch Key**

☐ = 1 stitch in white
■ = 1 stitch in black

## 440 SMALL DOTS

[multiple of 4 + 3 (+ 2 selv sts when worked in rows)]

Work in stranded colorwork technique. Row numbers for odd rows are shown in the chart. Even-numbered rows are read from right to left when working in rounds, and from left to right when working in turned rows. In Row 1, begin with the pattern repeat, rep the marked pattern repeat (4 sts wide) widthwise continuously, and end with the sts after the pattern repeat. Repeat Rows 1–6 heightwise.

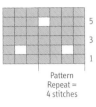

Pattern
Repeat =
4 stitches

### Stitch Key

☐ = 1 stitch in natural white

▨ = 1 stitch in pastel blue

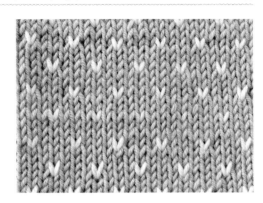

## 441 SHIFTED VERTICAL STRIPES

[multiple of 2 (+ 2 selv sts when worked in rows)]

Work in stranded colorwork technique. Row numbers for odd rows are shown in the chart. Even-numbered rows are read from right to left when working in rounds, and from left to right when working in turned rows. Rep the marked pattern repeat (2 sts wide) widthwise continuously, then repeat Rows 1–10 heightwise continuously.

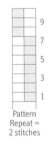

Pattern
Repeat =
2 stitches

### Stitch Key

☐ = 1 stitch in natural white       ▨ = 1 stitch in powder pink

## 442 STRIPES WITH COLOR REPEAT

[multiple of 4 + 2 sts (+ 2 selv sts when worked in rows)]

Work in stranded colorwork technique. Row numbers for odd rows are shown in the chart. Even-numbered rows are read from right to left when working in rounds, and from left to right when working in turned rows. In Row 1, begin with the pattern repeat, rep the marked pattern repeat (4 sts wide) widthwise continuously, and end with the sts after the pattern repeat. Work Rows 1–25 once, then repeat Rows 6–25 heightwise continuously.

### Stitch Key

▨ = 1 stitch in mint

▨ = 1 stitch in aqua blue

▨ = 1 stitch in medium blue

■ = 1 stitch in nautical blue

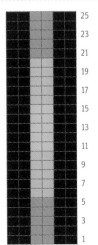

Pattern
Repeat =
4 stitches

## 443 SNOWFLAKES [multiple of 12 + 1 st (+ 2 selv sts when worked in rows)]

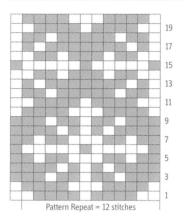

Pattern Repeat = 12 stitches

**Stitch Key**

☐ = 1 stitch in white

▧ = 1 stitch in pastel blue

Work in stranded colorwork technique. Row numbers for odd rows are shown in the chart. Even-numbered rows are read from right to left when working in rounds, and from left to right when working in turned rows. In Row 1, begin with the pattern repeat, rep the marked pattern repeat (12 sts wide) widthwise continuously, and end with the stitch after the pattern repeat. Work Rows 1–20 once, then repeat Rows 3–20 heightwise continuously.

## 444 ICE CRYSTAL BORDER [multiple of 16 + 1 st (+ 2 selv sts when worked in rows)]

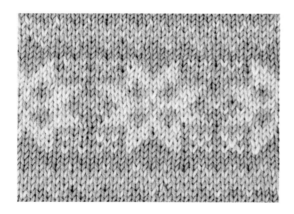

Work in stranded colorwork technique. Row numbers for odd rows are shown in the chart. Even-numbered rows are read from right to left when working in rounds, and from left to right when working in turned rows. In Row 1, begin with the pattern repeat, rep the marked pattern repeat (16 sts wide) widthwise continuously, and end with the stitch after the pattern repeat. Work Rows 1–32 once.

Pattern Repeat = 16 stitches

**Stitch Key**

☐ = 1 stitch in white     ▧ = 1 stitch in pastel blue

## 445 FLOWER BORDER [multiple of 18 + 1 st (+ 2 selv sts when worked in rows)]

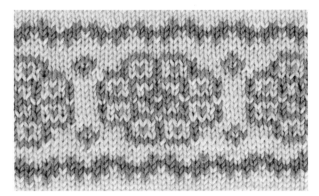

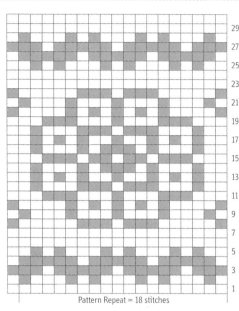

Pattern Repeat = 18 stitches

Work in stranded colorwork technique. Row numbers for odd rows are shown in the chart. Even-numbered rows are read from right to left when working in rounds, and from left to right when working in turned rows. In Row 1, begin with the pattern repeat, rep the marked pattern repeat (18 sts wide) widthwise continuously, and end with the stitch after the pattern repeat. Work Rows 1–30 once.

### Stitch Key

☐ = 1 stitch in natural white      ▨ = 1 stitch in pink

## 446 STAR BORDER [multiple of 16 + 1 st (+ 2 selv sts when worked in rows)]

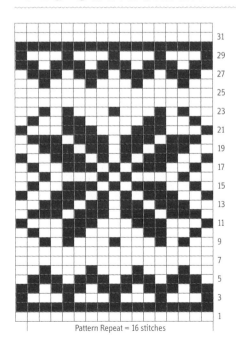

Pattern Repeat = 16 stitches

Work in stranded colorwork technique. Row numbers for odd rows are shown in the chart. Even-numbered rows are read from right to left when working in rounds, and from left to right when working in turned rows. In Row 1, begin with the pattern repeat, rep the marked pattern repeat (16 sts wide) widthwise continuously, and end with the stitch after the pattern repeat. Work Rows 1–32 once.

### Stitch Key

☐ = 1 stitch in natural white      ■ = 1 stitch in cherry red

## 447 LARGE STAR BORDER

[multiple of 20 + 3 (+ 2 selv sts when worked in rows)]

Work in stranded colorwork technique. Row numbers for odd rows are shown in the chart. Even-numbered rows are read from right to left when working in rounds, and from left to right when working in turned rows. In Row 1, begin with the stitch before the pattern repeat, rep the marked pattern repeat (20 sts wide) widthwise continuously, and end with the sts after the pattern repeat. Work Rows 1–32 once.

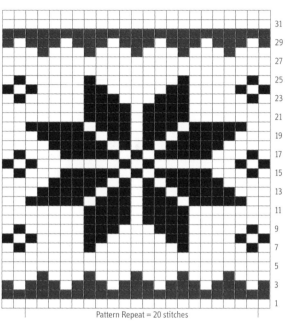

Pattern Repeat = 20 stitches

### Stitch Key

☐ = 1 stitch in natural white     ◼ = 1 stitch in cherry red     ■ = 1 stitch in nautical blue

## 448 ELK BORDER

[multiple of 18 (+ 2 selv sts when worked in rows)]

Pattern Repeat = 18 stitches

Work in stranded colorwork technique. Row numbers for odd rows are shown in the chart. Even-numbered rows are read from right to left when working in rounds, and from left to right when working in turned rows. In Row 1, begin with the pattern repeat, rep the marked pattern repeat (18 sts wide) widthwise continuously, and work Rows 1–26 once.

### Stitch Key

☐ = 1 stitch in natural white     ◼ = 1 stitch in cherry red     ■ = 1 stitch in nautical blue

## 449 LARGE DIAMOND PATTERN [multiple of 38 + 1 st (+ 2 selv sts when worked in rows)]

Work in stranded colorwork technique. Row numbers for odd rows are shown in the chart. Even-numbered rows are read from right to left when working in rounds, and from left to right when working in turned rows. In Row 1, begin with the pattern repeat, work Pattern Repeat (38 sts wide) widthwise continuously, and end with the stitch after the pattern repeat. Work Rows 1–39 once, then repeat Rows 2–39 heightwise continuously.

### Stitch Key

☐ = 1 stitch in natural white

■ = 1 stitch in anthracite

Pattern Repeat = 38 stitches

242

## 450 CLASSIC BORDER

[multiple of 24 + 1 st (+ 2 selv sts when worked in rows)]

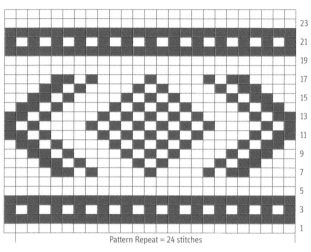

Pattern Repeat = 24 stitches

Work in stranded colorwork technique. Row numbers for odd rows are shown in the chart. Even-numbered rows are read from right to left when working in rounds, and from left to right when working in turned rows. In Row 1, begin with the pattern repeat, rep the marked pattern repeat (24 sts wide) widthwise continuously, and end with the stitch after the pattern repeat. Work Rows 1–24 once.

### Stitch Key

☐ = 1 stitch in natural white   ■ = 1 stitch in anthracite

## 451 DIAMOND BORDER

[multiple of 4 + 1 st (+ 2 selv sts when worked in rows)]

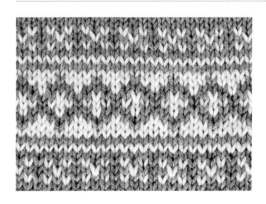

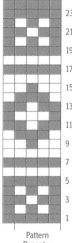

Pattern Repeat = 4 stitches

Work in stranded colorwork technique. Row numbers for odd rows are shown in the chart. Even-numbered rows are read from right to left when working in rounds, and from left to right when working in turned rows. In Row 1, begin with the pattern repeat, rep the marked pattern repeat (4 sts wide) widthwise continuously, and end with the stitch after the pattern repeat. Work Rows 1–24 once.

### Stitch Key

☐ = 1 stitch in natural white
■ = 1 stitch in light gray

## 452 TILE PATTERN

[multiple of 34 + 2 sts (+ 2 selv sts when worked in rows)]

Work in stranded colorwork technique. Row numbers for odd rows are shown in the chart. Even-numbered rows are read from right to left when working in rounds, and from left to right when working in turned rows. In Row 1, begin with the pattern repeat, repeat the pattern repeat (34 sts wide) continuously, and end with the sts after the pattern repeat. Work Rows 1–40 once, then repeat Rows 3–40 heightwise continuously.

### Stitch Key

☐ = 1 stitch in natural white

■ = 1 stitch in royal blue

Pattern Repeat = 34 stitches

## 453 DIAMOND BORDER
[multiple of 12 + 1 st (+ 2 selv sts when worked in rows)]

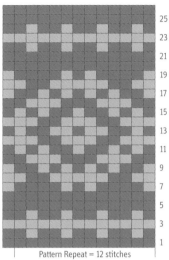

Pattern Repeat = 12 stitches

### Stitch Key

☐ = 1 stitch in pastel blue

■ = 1 stitch in denim blue

Work in stranded color-work technique. Row numbers for odd rows are shown in the chart. Even-numbered rows are read from right to left when working in rounds, and from left to right when working in turned rows. In Row 1, begin with the pattern repeat, rep the marked pattern repeat (12 sts wide) widthwise continuously, and end with the stitch after the pattern repeat. Work Rows 1–26 once.

## 454 PLAYFUL BORDER
[multiple of 8 + 1 st (+ 2 selv sts when worked in rows)]

Work in stranded colorwork technique. Row numbers for odd rows are shown in the chart. Even-numbered rows are read from right to left when working in rounds, and from left to right when working in turned rows. In Row 1, begin with the pattern repeat, rep the marked pattern repeat (8 sts wide) widthwise continuously, and end with the stitch after the pattern repeat. Work Rows 1–24 once.

### Stitch Key

☐ = 1 stitch in mint

■ = 1 stitch in medium blue

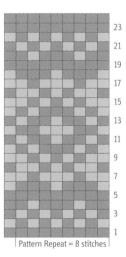

Pattern Repeat = 8 stitches

## 455 TRADITIONAL BORDER

[multiple of 12 + 1 st (+ 2 selv sts when worked in rows)]

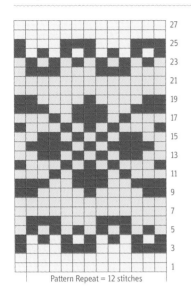

Pattern Repeat = 12 stitches

### Stitch Key

☐ = 1 stitch in linen

☐ = 1 stitch in lime

■ = 1 stitch in pine green

Work in stranded colorwork technique. Row numbers for odd rows are shown in the chart. Even-numbered rows are read from right to left when working in rounds, and from left to right when working in turned rows. In Row 1, begin with the pattern repeat, rep the marked pattern repeat (12 sts wide) widthwise continuously, and end with the stitch after the pattern repeat. Work Rows 1 and 2 until the desired height has been reached, and then, for the border, first work Rows 3–25 once, then repeat Rows 26 and 27 to the desired height.

## 456 X-O BORDER

[multiple of 24 + 1 st (+ 2 selv sts when worked in rows)]

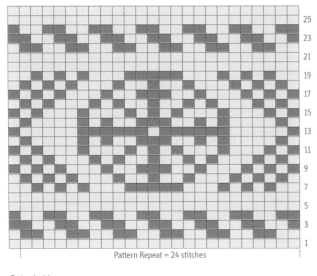

Pattern Repeat = 24 stitches

### Stitch Key

☐ = 1 stitch in lilac          ■ = 1 stitch in purple

Work in stranded colorwork technique. Row numbers for odd rows are shown in the chart. Even-numbered rows are read from right to left when working in rounds, and from left to right when working in turned rows. In Row 1, begin with the pattern repeat, rep the marked pattern repeat (24 sts wide) widthwise continuously, and end with the stitch after the pattern repeat. Work Rows 1–26 once.

## 457 SMALL EDGINGS AND BORDERS
[multiple of 6 + 1 st (+ 2 selv sts when worked in rows)]

Work in stranded colorwork technique. Row numbers for odd rows are shown in the chart. Even-numbered rows are read from right to left when working in rounds, and from left to right when working in turned rows. In Row 1, begin with the pattern repeat, rep the marked pattern repeat (6 sts wide) widthwise continuously, and end with the stitch after the pattern repeat. Repeat Rows 1–72 heightwise continuously.

### Stitch Key

☐ = 1 stitch in natural white       ■ = 1 stitch in cherry red

☐ = 1 stitch in yellow              ■ = 1 stitch in royal blue

☐ = 1 stitch in grass green

Pattern Repeat = 6 stitches

## 458 BUTTERFLY
[multiple of 11 + 2 for each motif]

Work in Intarsia technique, and embroider individual stitches in Powder Pink in duplicate stitch afterward. Row numbers for odd rows are shown in the chart. Read even-numbered rows from left to right. Work Rows 1–14 once.

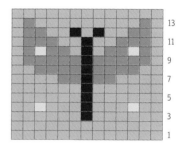

### Stitch Key

☐ = 1 stitch in pastel blue

☐ = 1 stitch in powder pink

☐ = 1 stitch in pink

☐ = 1 stitch in azalea

■ = 1 stitch in red-brown

## 459 LADYBUGS

[multiple of 12 + 2 sts (+ 2 selv sts when worked in rows)]

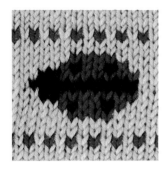

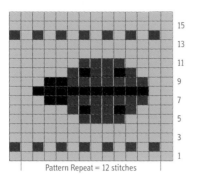

Pattern Repeat = 12 stitches

Work in stranded colorwork technique. Row numbers for odd rows are shown in the chart. Even-numbered rows are read from right to left when working in rounds, and from left to right when working in turned rows. In Row 1, begin with the stitch before the pattern repeat, rep the marked pattern repeat (12 sts wide) widthwise continuously, and end with the stitch after the pattern repeat. Work Rows 1–16 once.

### Stitch Key

☐ = 1 stitch in grass green     ■ = 1 stitch in black

■ = 1 stitch in cherry red

## 460 RUGGED BORDER

[multiple of 6 + 1 st (+ 2 selv sts when worked in rows)]

Work in stranded colorwork technique. Row numbers for odd rows are shown in the chart. Even-numbered rows are read from right to left when working in rounds, and from left to right when working in turned rows. In Row 1, begin with the pattern repeat, rep the marked pattern repeat (6 sts wide) widthwise continuously, and end with the stitch after the pattern repeat. Work Rows 1–14 once.

### Stitch Key

☐ = 1 stitch in natural white

■ = 1 stitch in nautical blue

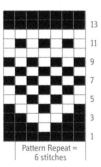

Pattern Repeat = 6 stitches

## 461 ZIGZAG BORDER

[multiple of 16 + 1 st (+ 2 selv sts when worked in rows)]

Work in stranded colorwork technique. Row numbers for odd rows are shown in the chart. Even-numbered rows are read from right to left when working in rounds, and from left to right when working in turned rows. In Row 1, begin with the pattern repeat, rep the marked pattern repeat (16 sts wide) widthwise continuously, and end with the stitch after the pattern repeat. Work Rows 1–24 once.

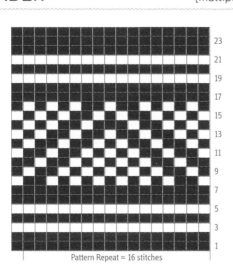

Pattern Repeat = 16 stitches

### Stitch Key

☐ = 1 stitch in natural white

■ = 1 stitch in cherry red

## 462 MINI-COLORWORK PATTERN [multiple of 12 (+ 2 selv sts when worked in rows)]

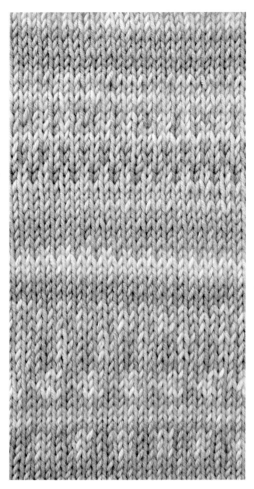

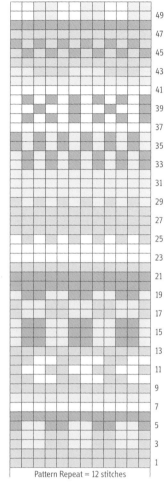

Pattern Repeat = 12 stitches

Work in stranded color-work technique. Row numbers for odd rows are shown in the chart. Even-numbered rows are read from right to left when working in rounds, and from left to right when working in turned rows. In Row 1, begin with the pattern repeat, work the marked pattern repeat (12 sts wide) widthwise continuously, and repeat Rows 1–50 heightwise continuously.

### Stitch Key

☐ = 1 stitch in natural white
☐ = 1 stitch in linen
☐ = 1 stitch in powder pink
☐ = 1 stitch in pastel blue

## 463 HEARTS [multiple of 20 + 1 st (+ 2 selv sts when worked in rows)]

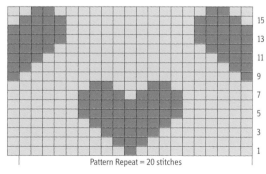

Pattern Repeat = 20 stitches

Either work in Intarsia technique or embroider in duplicate stitch afterward. Row numbers for odd rows are shown in the chart. Even-numbered rows are read from right to left when working in rounds, and from left to right when working in turned rows. In Row 1, begin with the pattern repeat, rep the marked pattern repeat (20 sts wide) widthwise continuously, and end with the stitch after the pattern repeat. Repeat Rows 1–16 heightwise.

### Stitch Key

☐ = 1 stitch in powder pink
☐ = 1 stitch in azalea

## 464 ROSE MOTIF

[multiple of 36 + 2 for each motif]

Work the motif in Intarsia technique, and embroider small interior areas within the rose and the lower left leaf in duplicate stitch afterward. Row numbers for odd rows are shown in the chart. Read even-numbered rows from left to right. Work Rows 1–28 once.

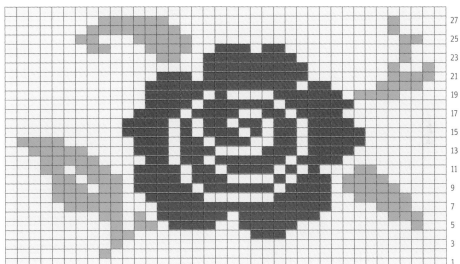

### Stitch Key

☐ = 1 stitch in linen

■ = 1 stitch in cardinal red

▨ = 1 stitch in apple green

## 465 SEA OF FLOWERS

[multiple of 10 + 1 st (+ 2 selv sts when worked in rows)]

Work in stranded colorwork technique. Row numbers for odd rows are shown in the chart. Even-numbered rows are read from right to left when working in rounds, and from left to right when working in turned rows. In Row 1, begin with the pattern repeat, rep the marked pattern repeat (10 sts wide) widthwise continuously, and end with the stitch after the pattern repeat. Repeat Rows 1–18 heightwise.

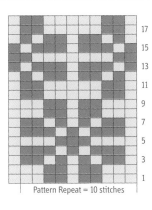

Pattern Repeat = 10 stitches

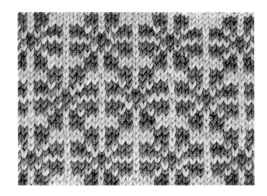

### Stitch Key

☐ = 1 stitch in lime

■ = 1 stitch in plum blue

## 466 MULTI-COLOR BLOSSOMS [multiple of 20 + 1 st (+ 2 selv sts when worked in rows)]

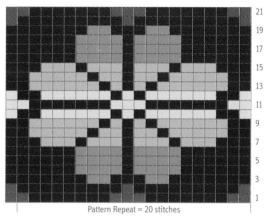

Pattern Repeat = 20 stitches

Work in stranded colorwork technique. Row numbers for odd rows are shown in the chart. Even-numbered rows are read from right to left when working in rounds, and from left to right when working in turned rows. In Row 1, begin with the pattern repeat, rep the marked pattern repeat (20 sts wide) widthwise continuously, and end with the stitch after the pattern repeat. Work Rows 1–21 once, then repeat Rows 2–21 heightwise continuously.

**Stitch Key**

◻ = 1 stitch in powder pink    ▨ = 1 stitch in cardinal red
◻ = 1 stitch in pink           ■ = 1 stitch in burgundy
▨ = 1 stitch in azalea

## 467 FLOWER BORDER [multiple of 20 + 1 st (+ 2 selv sts when worked in rows)]

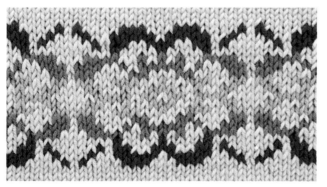

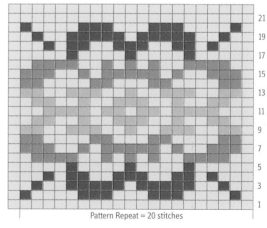

Pattern Repeat = 20 stitches

Work in stranded colorwork technique. Row numbers for odd rows are shown in the chart. Even-numbered rows are read from right to left when working in rounds, and from left to right when working in turned rows. In Row 1, begin with the pattern repeat, rep the marked pattern repeat (20 sts wide) widthwise continuously, and end with the stitch after the pattern repeat. For a single border, work Rows 1–22 once; for an all-over pattern, repeat Rows 1–20 heightwise continuously.

**Stitch Key**

◻ = 1 stitch in lime     ▨ = 1 stitch in azalea
◻ = 1 stitch in pink     ■ = 1 stitch in cardinal red

## 468 LEAFY TENDRILS [multiple of 20 + 1 st (+ 2 selv sts when worked in rows)]

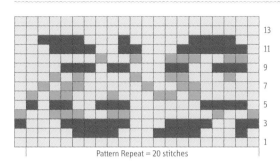

Pattern Repeat = 20 stitches

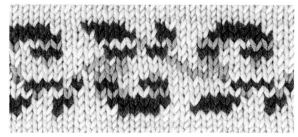

### Stitch Key

☐ = 1 stitch in lime

▨ = 1 stitch in apple green

■ = 1 stitch in pine green

Work in stranded colorwork technique. Row numbers for odd rows are shown in the chart. Even-numbered rows are read from right to left when working in rounds, and from left to right when working in turned rows. In Row 1, begin with the pattern repeat, rep the marked pattern repeat (20 sts wide) widthwise continuously, and end with the stitch after the pattern repeat. For a single border, work Rows 1–14 once; for an all-over pattern, repeat Rows 1–14 heightwise continuously.

## 469 STRAWBERRIES [multiple of 16 + 1 st (+ 2 selv sts when worked in rows)]

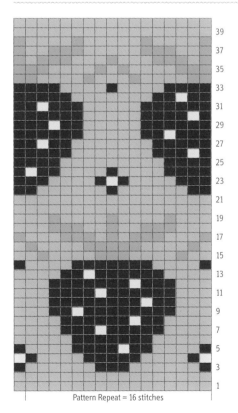

Pattern Repeat = 16 stitches

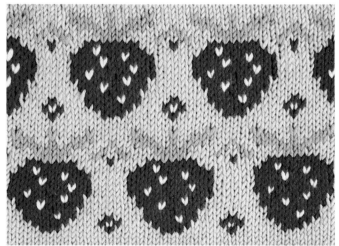

Work in stranded colorwork technique, and embroider individual yellow dots in duplicate stitch afterward. Row numbers for odd rows are shown in the chart. Even-numbered rows are read from right to left when working in rounds, and from left to right when working in turned rows. In Row 1, begin with the pattern repeat, rep the marked pattern repeat (16 sts wide) widthwise continuously, and end with the stitch after the pattern repeat. Work Rows 1–40 once, then repeat Rows 3–40 heightwise continuously.

### Stitch Key

☐ = 1 stitch in sun yellow          ▨ = 1 stitch in apple green

■ = 1 stitch in cherry red          ▨ = 1 stitch in aqua blue

## 470 SMALL BLOSSOM PATTERN
[multiple of 12 + 1 st (+ 2 selv sts when worked in rows)]

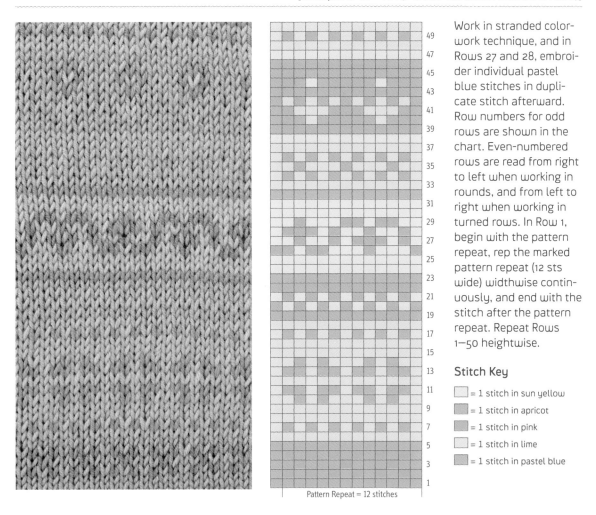

Pattern Repeat = 12 stitches

Work in stranded colorwork technique, and in Rows 27 and 28, embroider individual pastel blue stitches in duplicate stitch afterward. Row numbers for odd rows are shown in the chart. Even-numbered rows are read from right to left when working in rounds, and from left to right when working in turned rows. In Row 1, begin with the pattern repeat, rep the marked pattern repeat (12 sts wide) widthwise continuously, and end with the stitch after the pattern repeat. Repeat Rows 1–50 heightwise.

**Stitch Key**

☐ = 1 stitch in sun yellow
☐ = 1 stitch in apricot
☐ = 1 stitch in pink
☐ = 1 stitch in lime
☐ = 1 stitch in pastel blue

## 471 SMALL HEART BORDER [multiple of 9 + 2 sts (+ 2 selv sts when worked in rows)]

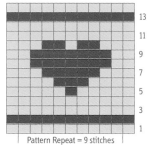

Pattern Repeat = 9 stitches

Work in stranded colorwork technique. Row numbers for odd rows are shown in the chart. Even-numbered rows are read from right to left when working in rounds, and from left to right when working in turned rows. In Row 1, begin with the stitch before the pattern repeat, rep the marked pattern repeat (9 sts wide) widthwise continuously, and end with the stitch after the pattern repeat. Work Rows 1–14 once.

**Stitch Key**

☐ = 1 stitch in powder pink
■ = 1 stitch in cardinal red

## 472 TEDDY BEAR [multiple of 33 + 2 for each motif]

Work in Intarsia technique, and embroider small black areas in duplicate stitch afterward. Row numbers for odd rows are shown in the chart. Read even-numbered rows from left to right. Work Rows 1–42 once.

### Stitch Key

= 1 stitch in light salmon

= 1 stitch in golden yellow

= 1 stitch in chestnut

= 1 stitch in black

## 473 ANCHOR

[multiple of 13 + 2 for each motif]

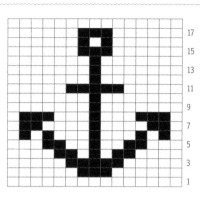

**Stitch Key**

☐ = 1 stitch in natural white

■ = 1 stitch in nautical blue

Either work the motif in Intarsia technique or first work the background in White, and embroider the anchor in duplicate stitch afterward. Row numbers for odd rows are shown in the chart. Even-numbered rows are read from right to left when working in rounds, and from left to right when working in turned rows. Work Rows 1–18 once.

## 474 STEERING WHEEL

[multiple of 19 + 2 for each motif]

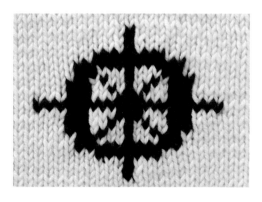

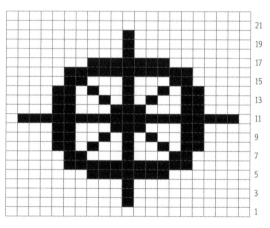

Either work the motif in Intarsia technique or first work the background in White, and embroider the wheel in duplicate stitch afterward. Row numbers for odd rows are shown in the chart. Even-numbered rows are read from right to left when working in rounds, and from left to right when working in turned rows. Work Rows 1–22 once.

**Stitch Key**

☐ = 1 stitch in natural white

■ = 1 stitch in nautical blue

## 475 WAVES

[multiple of 6 + 2 sts (+ 2 selv sts when worked in rows)]

Work in stranded colorwork technique. Row numbers for odd rows are shown in the chart. Even-numbered rows are read from right to left when working in rounds, and from left to right when working in turned rows. In Row 1, begin with the stitches before the pattern repeat, then rep the marked pattern repeat (6 sts wide) widthwise continuously. For a single border, work Rows 1–10 once; for an all-over pattern, repeat Rows 1–10 heightwise continuously.

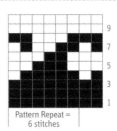

Pattern Repeat = 6 stitches

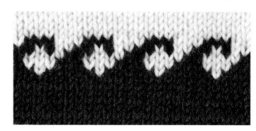

### Stitch Key

☐ = 1 stitch in natural white

■ = 1 stitch in nautical blue

## 476 SAILBOAT

[multiple of 24 + 2 selv sts when worked in rows]

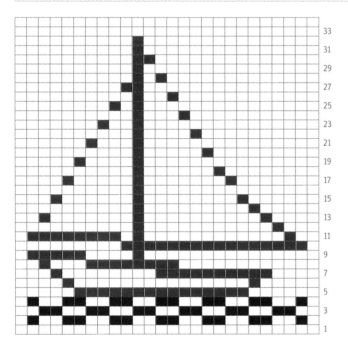

### Stitch Key

☐ = 1 stitch in natural white

■ = 1 stitch in cherry red

■ = 1 stitch in nautical blue

Either work the motif in Intarsia technique, embroidering the mast and individual stitches at the sides of the sails in duplicate stitch afterward, or, first, work the background in White, and embroider the boat and the waves in duplicate stitch afterward. Row numbers for odd rows are shown in the chart. Even-numbered rows are read from right to left when working in rounds, and from left to right when working in turned rows. Work Rows 1–34 once.

## 477 SMALL NUMBERS

[multiple of 2–3 + 2 for each number]

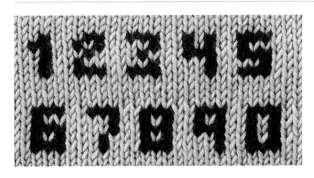

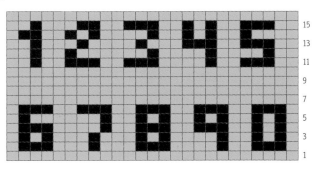

Either work in stranded colorwork or Intarsia technique or embroider in duplicate stitch afterward. Row numbers for odd rows are shown in the chart. Even-numbered rows are read from right to left when working in rounds, and from left to right when working in turned rows.

**Stitch Key**

■ = 1 stitch in golden yellow

■ = 1 stitch in black

## 478 LARGER NUMBERS

[multiple of 3–5 + 2 for each number]

Either work in stranded colorwork or Intarsia technique or embroider in duplicate stitch afterward. Row numbers for odd rows are shown in the chart. Even-numbered rows are read from right to left when working in rounds, and from left to right when working in turned rows.

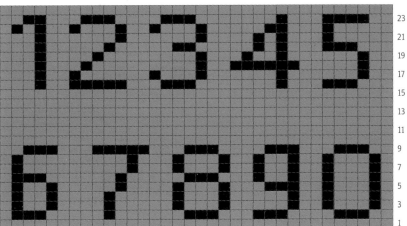

**Stitch Key**

■ = 1 stitch in coral

■ = 1 stitch in black

## 479 SMALL ALPHABET

[multiple of 3–5 + 2 for each letter]

Either work in stranded colorwork or Intarsia technique or embroider in duplicate stitch afterward. Row numbers for odd rows are shown in the chart. Even-numbered rows are read from right to left when working in rounds, and from left to right when working in turned rows.

### Stitch Key

☐ = 1 stitch in golden yellow

■ = 1 stitch in black

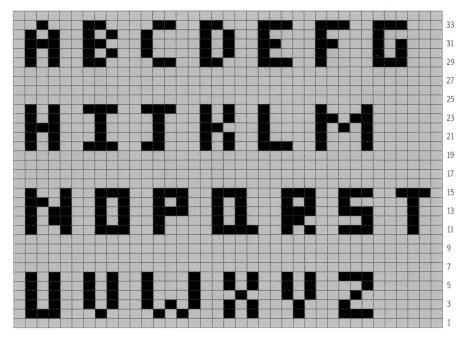

## 480 LARGER ALPHABET

[multiple of 4–7 + 2 for each letter]

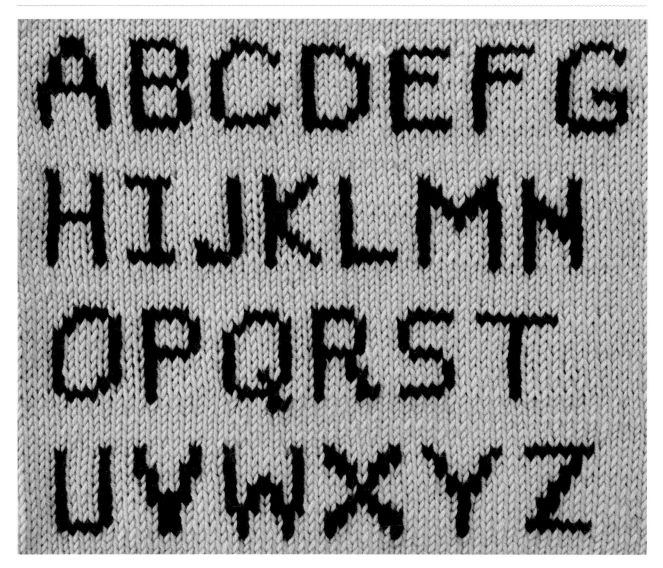

Either work in stranded colorwork or Intarsia technique or embroider in duplicate stitch afterward. Row numbers for odd rows are shown in the chart. Even-numbered rows are read from right to left when working in rounds, and from left to right when working in turned rows.

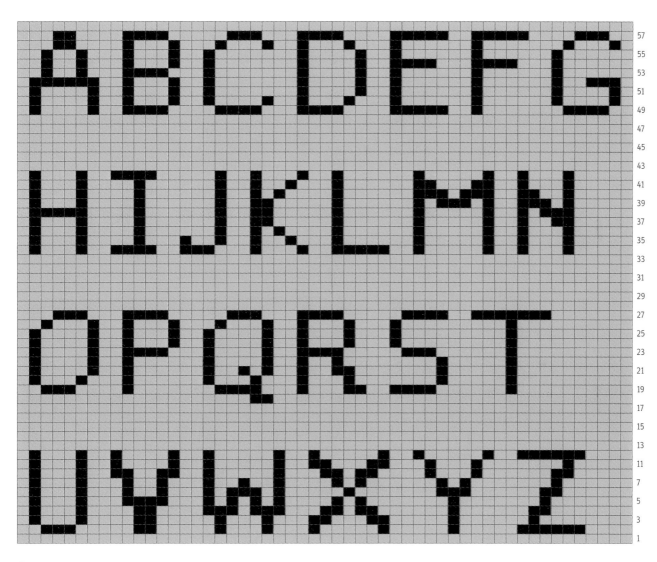

57
55
53
51
49
47
45
43
41
39
37
35
33
31
29
27
25
23
21
19
17
15
13
11
7
5
3
1

## Stitch Key

☐ = 1 stitch in apricot

■ = 1 stitch in black

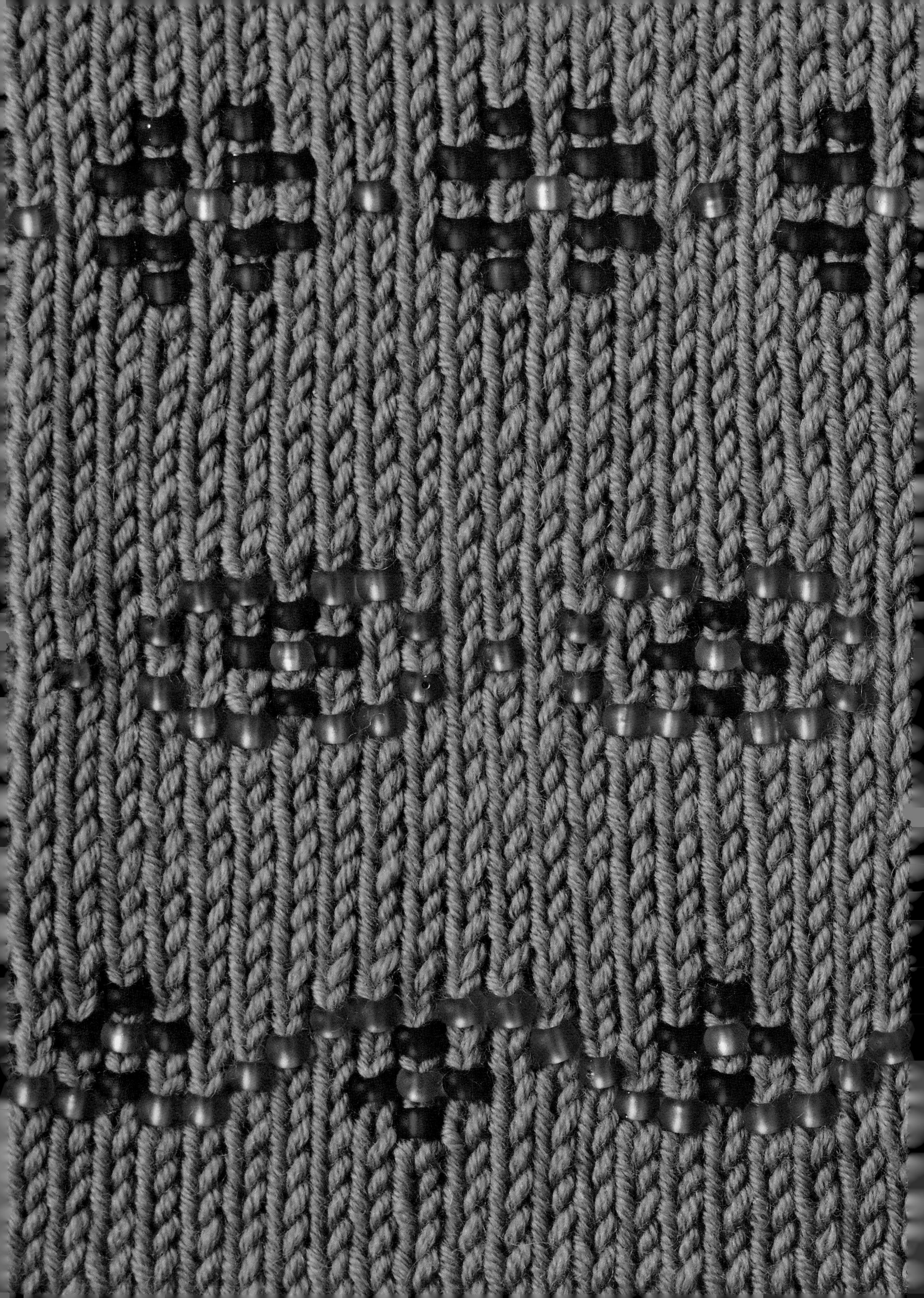

# PATTERNS USING SPECIAL TECHNIQUES

## 481 STAR PATTERN

[multiple of 4 + 1 st + 2 selv sts]

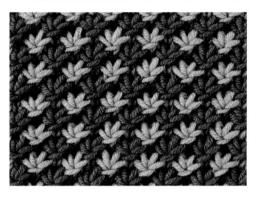

Only WS rows are shown; in RS rows, knit all sts. Begin with the sts before the pattern repeat, rep the marked pattern repeat (4 sts wide) widthwise continuously, and end with the sts after the pattern repeat. Repeat Rows 1–4 heightwise.

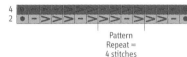

Pattern
Repeat =
4 stitches

### Stitch Key

● = 1 selvedge stitch in color A

■ = 1 selvedge stitch in color B

– = Purl 1 stitch in color A

■ = Purl 1 stitch in color B

>>> = Purl 3 stitches together in color A, but leave the stitch on the left needle, make 1 yarn over in color A, and purl the 3 stitches on the left needle together once more in color A

■ = Purl 3 stitches together in color B, but leave the stitch on the left needle, make 1 yarn over in color B, purl the 3 stitches on the left needle together once more in color B

## 482 CHEVRON PATTERN

[multiple of 14 + 1 st + 2 selv sts]

Cast on the stitches using the cable cast-on method, and knit 2 rows. Then continue from chart. Only RS rows are shown; in WS rows, purl all sts. Begin with the sts before the pattern repeat, rep the marked pattern repeat (14 sts wide) widthwise continuously, and end with the sts after the pattern repeat. Repeat Rows 1 and 2 heightwise, changing colors after every 6 rows. For the ragged finishing border, in Row 6 (= WS) after the last color change, knit all sts, repeat Row 1 once more, and work another WS row in knit. Then bind off the stitches according to the chart, using the elastic bind-off method.

Pattern Repeat = 14 stitches

### Stitch Key

● = 1 selvedge stitch

■ = Knit 1 stitch

◢ = Knit 2 stitches together

◣ = Knit 2 stitches together left-leaning with passing over (skp): slip 1 stitch knitwise, knit the next stitch, and pass the slipped stitch over

+ = Increase 1 stitch twisted from the bar between stitches

∩ = Centered double decrease, knitting 3 stitches together with center stitch on top (cdd): slip 2 stitches together knitwise, knit 1 stitch, and pass the slipped stitches over

~ = Bind off 1 stitch using elastic bind-off method

> = First, bind off 1 stitch using elastic bind-off method, then pull the working yarn through the stitch a second time, creating a chain as in crochet. This creates a point at the edge.

▲ = Knit 2 stitches together, then bind off using elastic bind-off method

◿ = Knit 2 stitches together left-leaning with passing over (skp), then bind off using elastic bind-off method

◓ = Knit 3 stitches together with center stitch on top (cdd), then bind off using elastic bind-off method

☐ = No stitch, for better overview only

## 483 GATHERED PATTERN

[multiple of 1 + 2 selv sts]

Shown are both RS and WS rows. Begin with the selv st before the pattern repeat, rep the marked pattern repeat (1 st wide) widthwise continuously, and end with the selv st after the pattern repeat. Work Rows 1–14 once, then repeat Rows 5–14 heightwise continuously.

Pattern
Repeat =
1 stitch

### Stitch Key

● = 1 selvedge stitch

■ = Knit 1 stitch

− = Purl 1 stitch

◢ = Knit 2 stitches together

🆅 = Make 2 stitches from 1 (kfb): first, knit 1 stitch, but leave it on the left needle, then knit the same stitch again through the back loop

☐ = No stitch, for better over-view only

## 484 PLAITED BASKETWEAVE STITCH

[multiple of 2 + 2 selv sts]

Shown are both RS and WS rows. Begin with the sts before the pattern repeat, rep the marked pattern repeat (2 sts wide) widthwise continuously, and end with the sts after the pattern repeat. Repeat Rows 1 and 2 heightwise.

Pattern
Repeat =
2 stitches

### Stitch Key

● = 1 selvedge stitch

− = Purl 1 stitch

■■ = Lead the right needle behind the first stitch on the left needle, bypassing it, and knit the second stitch, but leave it on the left needle, then knit the first stitch on the left needle the regular way. Now release both stitches from the left needle.

−/− = Lead the right needle in front of the first stitch on the left needle, bypassing it, and purl the second stitch, but leave it on the left needle, then purl the first stitch on the left needle the regular way. Now release both stitches from the left needle.

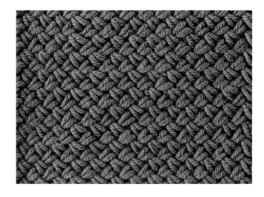

## 485 SMALL LAZY LINKS STITCH

[multiple of 8 + 2 sts + 2 selv sts]

Only RS rows are shown; in WS rows, knit the knits, and purl the purls. Begin with the sts before the pattern repeat, rep the marked pattern repeat (8 sts wide) widthwise continuously, and end with the sts after the pattern repeat. Repeat Rows 1–8 heightwise.

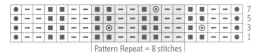

Pattern Repeat = 8 stitches

### Stitch Key

● = 1 selvedge stitch

■ = Knit 1 stitch

− = Purl 1 stitch

⊙ = Bring the working yarn to the back of the work, and insert the right needle between the 6th and 7th stitch on the left needle. Pull the working yarn through as a long loop between the stitches, and place it on the left needle before the first stitch. Then knit the long loop and the following stitch together.

## 486 LARGE LAZY LINKS STITCH

[multiple of 16 + 14 sts + 2 selv sts]

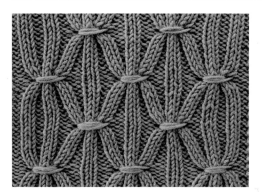

Only RS rows are shown; in WS rows, knit the knits, and purl the purls. Begin with the sts before the pattern repeat, rep the marked pattern repeat (16 sts wide) widthwise continuously, and end with the sts after the pattern repeat. Repeat Rows 1–20 heightwise.

Pattern Repeat = 16 stitches

19
17
15
13
11
9
7
5
3
1

### Stitch Key

⦿ = 1 selvedge stitch

■ = Knit 1 stitch

▬ = Purl 1 stitch

▷▷▷▷▷▷▷▷ = Place the next 10 stitches on an auxiliary needle, and wind the working yarn from front to back 3 times around the group of stitches on the auxiliary needle. Then work the 10 stitches from the auxiliary needle as (knit 2 stitches, purl 2 stitches, knit 2 stitches, purl 2 stitches, knit 2 stitches).

## 487 SHIFTING SQUARES

[multiple of 8 + 7 sts + 2 selv sts]

Shown are both RS and WS rows. Begin with the sts before the pattern repeat, rep the marked pattern repeat (8 sts wide) widthwise continuously, and end with the sts after the pattern repeat. Work Rows 1–10 once, then repeat Rows 3–10 continuously, and end with working Rows 1–2 once.

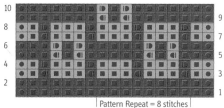

Pattern Repeat = 8 stitches

### Stitch Key

⦿ = 1 selvedge stitch in color A

▨ = 1 selvedge stitch in color B

■ = Knit 1 stitch in color A

▨ = Knit 1 stitch in color B

◧ = Slip 1 stitch in color A knitwise, with working yarn in back of work

◨ = Slip 1 stitch in color A knitwise, with working yarn in front of work

◧ = Slip 1 stitch in color B knitwise, with working yarn in back of work

▨ = Slip 1 stitch in color B knitwise, with working yarn in front of work

## 488 TWO-COLOR TRAVELING STITCH

[multiple of 2 + 1 st + 2 selv sts]

Only RS rows are shown; in WS rows, purl all stitches in the same color as in the RS row. Begin with the sts before the pattern repeat, rep the marked pattern repeat (2 sts wide) widthwise continuously, and end with the sts after the pattern repeat. Repeat Rows 1–4 continuously, changing colors in every right-side row.

### Stitch Key

= 1 selvedge stitch in color A

= 1 selvedge stitch in color B

= Knit 1 stitch in color A

= Knit 1 stitch in color B

= Slip 1 stitch in color A purlwise, with working yarn in back of work. Knit 1 stitch and 1 yarn over in color A, then pass the slipped stitch over the knit stitch and the yarn over.

= Slip 1 stitch in color B purlwise, with working yarn in back of work. Knit 1 stitch and 1 yarn over in color B, then pass the slipped stitch over the knit stitch and the yarn over.

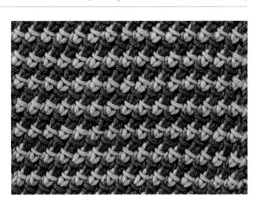

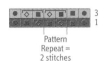

Pattern
Repeat =
2 stitches

## 489 CHEVRON-AND-EYELET PATTERN

[multiple of 15 + 2 selv sts]

Cast on the stitches using the cable cast-on method, and knit 2 rows. Then continue from chart. Only RS rows are shown; in WS rows, purl all sts. Begin with the selv st before the pattern repeat, rep the marked pattern repeat (15 sts wide) widthwise continuously, and end with the selv st after the pattern repeat. Repeat Rows 1 and 2 continuously, always alternating 6 rows in the first color and 2 rows in the second color.
For the ragged final border, in Row 6 (= WS) knit all sts, repeat Row 1 once more, and work another WS row in knit. Then bind off the stitches according to the chart, using the elastic bind-off method.

Pattern Repeat = 15 stitches

### Stitch Key

= 1 selvedge stitch

= Knit 1 stitch

= Knit 2 stitches together

= Knit 2 stitches together left-leaning with passing over (skp): slip 1 stitch knitwise, knit the next stitch, and pass the slipped stitch over

= Make 1 yarn over

= Bind off 1 stitch using elastic bind-off method

= First, bind off 1 stitch using elastic bind-off method, then pull the working yarn through the stitch a second time, creating a chain as in crochet. This creates a point at the edge.

= Knit 2 stitches together, then bind off using elastic bind-off method

= Knit 2 stitches together left-leaning with passing over (skp), then bind off using elastic bind-off method

= Knit 3 stitches together with center stitch on top (cdd), then bind off using elastic bind-off method

= No stitch, for better overview only

## 490 MOSAIC BORDER

[multiple of 12 + 2 selv sts]

Shown are both RS and WS rows. Begin with the selv st before the pattern repeat, rep the marked pattern repeat (12 sts wide) widthwise continuously, and end with the selv st after the pattern repeat. Work Rows 1–62 once.

### Stitch Key

● = 1 selvedge stitch in color A

▨ = 1 selvedge stitch in color B

▪ = Knit 1 stitch in color A

▪ = Knit 1 stitch in color B

◨ = Slip 1 stitch in color A knitwise with working yarn in back of work

▯ = Slip 1 stitch in color A knitwise with working yarn in front of work

▨ = Slip 1 stitch in color B knitwise with working yarn in back of work

▨ = Slip 1 stitch in color B knitwise with working yarn in front of work

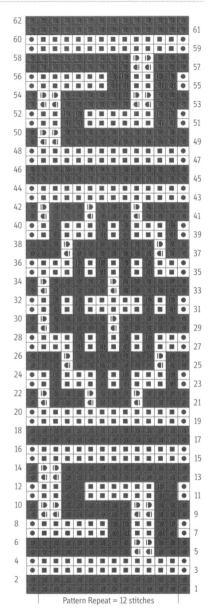

Pattern Repeat = 12 stitches

## 491 ILLUSION PATTERN WITH ZIGZAG STRIPES [multiple of 6 + 1 st + 2 selv sts]

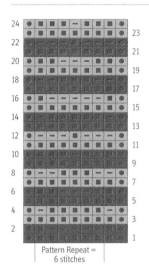

Pattern Repeat =
6 stitches

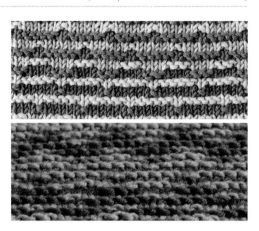

Shown are both RS and WS rows. Begin with the sts before the pattern repeat, rep the marked pattern repeat (6 sts wide) widthwise continuously, and end with the sts after the pattern repeat. Repeat Rows 1–24 heightwise, changing colors in every right-side row.

### Stitch Key

⬤ = 1 selvedge stitch in background color

▨ = 1 selvedge stitch in motif color

▪ = Knit 1 stitch in background color

▨ = Knit 1 stitch in motif color

▬ = Purl 1 stitch in background color

▨ = Purl 1 stitch in motif color

## 492 ILLUSION PATTERN WITH LOZENGES [multiple of 8 + 1 st + 2 selv sts]

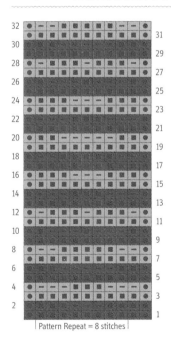

Pattern Repeat = 8 stitches

Shown are both RS and WS rows. Begin with the sts before the pattern repeat, rep the marked pattern repeat (8 sts wide) widthwise continuously, and end with the sts after the pattern repeat. Repeat Rows 1–32 heightwise, changing colors in every right-side row.

### Stitch Key

⬤ = 1 selvedge stitch in background color

▨ = 1 selvedge stitch in motif color

▪ = Knit 1 stitch in background color

▨ = Knit 1 stitch in motif color

▬ = Purl 1 stitch in background color

▨ = Purl 1 stitch in motif color

# Decorative Borders with Beads Stitches

NOTE: For tutorial on working stitches with beads, see "Incorporating Beads" in chapter "Knitting Basics."

## 493 SMALL MULTI-COLOR BLOSSOMS AND VINES

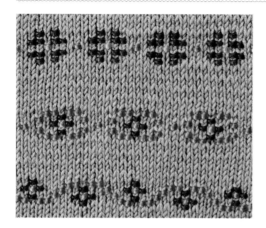

### Stitch Key

⬤ = 1 selvedge stitch

◼ = Knit 1 stitch

▬ = Purl 1 stitch

⌂ = Knit the next stitch, place it back onto the left needle, and, with the help of a thread loop, thread a bead in color A onto the stitch

⌂ = Purl 1 stitch, place it back onto the left needle, and, with the help of a thread loop, thread a bead in color A onto the stitch

⌂ = Knit the next stitch, place it back onto the left needle, and, with the help of a thread loop, thread a bead in color B onto the stitch

⌂ = Purl 1 stitch, place it back onto the left needle, and, with the help of a thread loop, thread a bead in color B onto the stitch

⌂ = Knit the next stitch, place it back onto the left needle, and, with the help of a thread loop, thread a bead in color C onto the stitch

⌂ = Purl 1 stitch, place it back onto the left needle, and, with the help of a thread loop, thread a bead in color C onto the stitch

### SMALL MULTI-COLOR BLOSSOMS
[8 + 1 st + 2 selv sts]

Shown are both RS and WS rows. Begin with the selv st before the pattern repeat, rep the marked pattern repeat (8 sts wide) widthwise continuously, and end with the sts after the pattern repeat. Work Rows 1–5 once.

Pattern Repeat = 8 stitches

### MULTI-COLOR BLOSSOM BORDER
[10 + 1 st + 2 selv sts]

Shown are both RS and WS rows. Begin with the selv st before the pattern repeat, rep the marked pattern repeat (10 sts wide) widthwise continuously, and end with the sts after the pattern repeat. Work Rows 1–5 once.

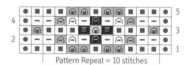

Pattern Repeat = 10 stitches

### VINE WITH MULTI-COLOR BLOSSOMS
[14 + 5 sts + 2 selv sts]

Shown are both RS and WS rows. Begin with the selv st before the pattern repeat, rep the marked pattern repeat (14 sts wide) widthwise continuously, and end with the sts after the pattern repeat. Work Rows 1–4 once.

Pattern Repeat = 14 stitches

## 494 BOWS AND LOZENGES

### LOZENGE BORDER   [6 + 1 st + 2 selv sts]

Shown are both RS and WS rows. Begin with the selv st before the pattern repeat, rep the marked pattern repeat (6 sts wide) widthwise continuously, and end with the sts after the pattern repeat. Work Rows 1–5 once.

### SMALL BOWS   [7 + 2 selv sts]

Shown are both RS and WS rows. Begin with the selv st before the pattern repeat, rep the marked pattern repeat (7 sts wide) widthwise continuously, and end with the selv st after the pattern repeat. Work Rows 1–5 once.

### ORNAMENTS   [14 + 1 st + 2 selv sts]

Shown are both RS and WS rows. Begin with the selv st before the pattern repeat, rep the marked pattern repeat (14 sts wide) widthwise continuously, and end with the sts after the pattern repeat. Work Rows 1–5 once.

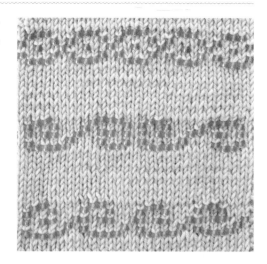

Pattern Repeat = 6 stitches

Pattern Repeat = 7 stitches

Pattern Repeat = 14 stitches

### Stitch Key

● = 1 selvedge stitch

■ = Knit 1 stitch

– = Purl 1 stitch

⌂ = Knit the next stitch, place it back onto the left needle, and, with the help of a thread loop, thread a bead onto the stitch

⌂ = Purl 1 stitch, place it back onto the left needle, and, with the help of a thread loop, thread a bead onto the stitch

## 495 FLOWER BORDER                    [multiple of 18 + 1 st + 2 selv sts]

Shown are both RS and WS rows. Begin with the selv st before the pattern repeat, rep the marked pattern repeat (18 sts wide) widthwise continuously, and end with the sts after the pattern repeat. Repeat Rows 1 and 2 to the desired height of the border, then work Rows 3–28 once, then repeat Rows 27–28 continuously to the desired height of the knitted piece.

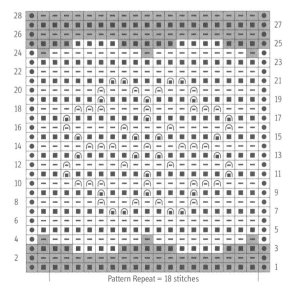

Pattern Repeat = 18 stitches

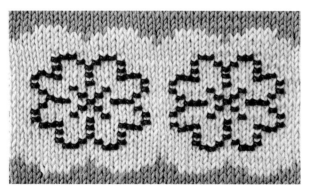

### Stitch Key

● = 1 selvedge stitch in color A

● = 1 selvedge stitch in color B

■ = Knit 1 stitch in color A

■ = Knit 1 stitch in color B

– = Purl 1 stitch in color A

– = Purl 1 stitch in color B

⌂ = Knit 1 stitch in color A, place it back onto the left needle, and, with the help of a thread loop, thread a bead onto the stitch

⌂ = Purl 1 stitch in color A, place it back onto the left needle, and, with the help of a thread loop, thread a bead onto the stitch

NOTE: For tutorial on working stitches with beads, see "Incorporating Beads" in chapter "Knitting Basics."

# Shape-retaining Woven-look Patterns

## 496 LINEN STITCH PATTERN WITH WOVEN LOOK [multiple of 2 + 2 selv sts]

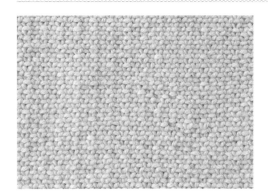

Shown are both RS and WS rows. Begin with the selv st before the pattern repeat, rep the marked pattern repeat (2 sts wide) widthwise continuously, and end with the selv st after the pattern repeat. Repeat Rows 1 and 2 heightwise.

Pattern Repeat = 2 stitches

### Stitch Key

● = 1 selvedge stitch

■ = Knit 1 stitch

— = Purl 1 stitch

ID = Slip 1 stitch purlwise, with working yarn in front of work

CI = Slip 1 stitch purlwise, with working yarn in back of work

## 497 HERRINGBONE PATTERN [multiple of 10 + 2 selv sts]

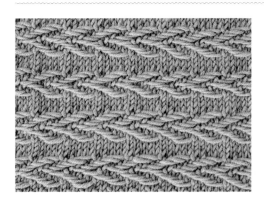

Shown are both RS and WS rows. Begin with the selv st before the pattern repeat, rep the marked pattern repeat (10 sts wide) widthwise continuously, and end with the selv st after the pattern repeat. Repeat Rows 1–14 heightwise.

Pattern Repeat = 10 stitches

### Stitch Key

● = 1 selvedge stitch

■ = Knit 1 stitch

— = Purl 1 stitch

ID = Slip 1 stitch purlwise, with working yarn in front of work

CI = Slip 1 stitch purlwise, with working yarn in back of work

## 498 HORIZONTAL TUNISIAN PATTERN

[multiple of 1 + 2 selv sts]

Shown are both RS and WS rows. Begin with the selv st before the pattern repeat, rep the marked pattern repeat (1 st wide) widthwise continuously, and end with the selv st after the pattern repeat. Repeat Rows 1 and 2 heightwise.

Pattern Repeat = 1 stitch

### Stitch Key

● = 1 selvedge stitch

○ = Make 1 yarn over

◖ = Slip 1 stitch knitwise with working yarn in back of work

⬥ = Knit 1 yarn over together with the following stitch through the back loop (as in ssk)

▢ = No stitch, for better overview only

## 499 VERTICAL TUNISIAN PATTERN

[multiple of 1 + 2 selv sts]

Shown are both RS and WS rows. Begin with the selv st before the pattern repeat, rep the marked pattern repeat (1 st wide) widthwise continuously, and end with the selv st after the pattern repeat. Repeat Rows 1 and 2 heightwise.

Pattern Repeat = 1 stitch

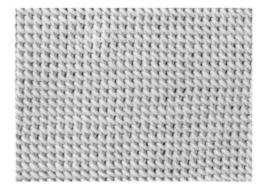

### Stitch Key

● = 1 selvedge stitch

○ = Make 1 yarn over

◖ = Slip 1 stitch knitwise with working yarn in back of work

▮ = Knit 1 stitch together with the following yarn over through the back loop (as in ssk)

▢ = No stitch, for better overview only

## 500 FALSE TUNISIAN PATTERN

[multiple of 1 + 2 selv sts]

Shown are both RS and WS rows. Begin with the selv st before the pattern repeat, rep the marked pattern repeat (1 st wide) widthwise continuously, and end with the selv st after the pattern repeat. Repeat Rows 1 and 2 heightwise.

Pattern Repeat = 1 stitch

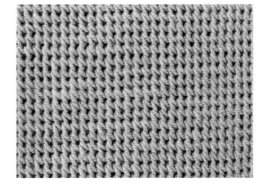

### Stitch Key

● = 1 selvedge stitch

⊖ = Slip 1 stitch purlwise together with 1 yarn over

⬥ = Knit 1 yarn over together with the following stitch through the back loop (as in ssk)

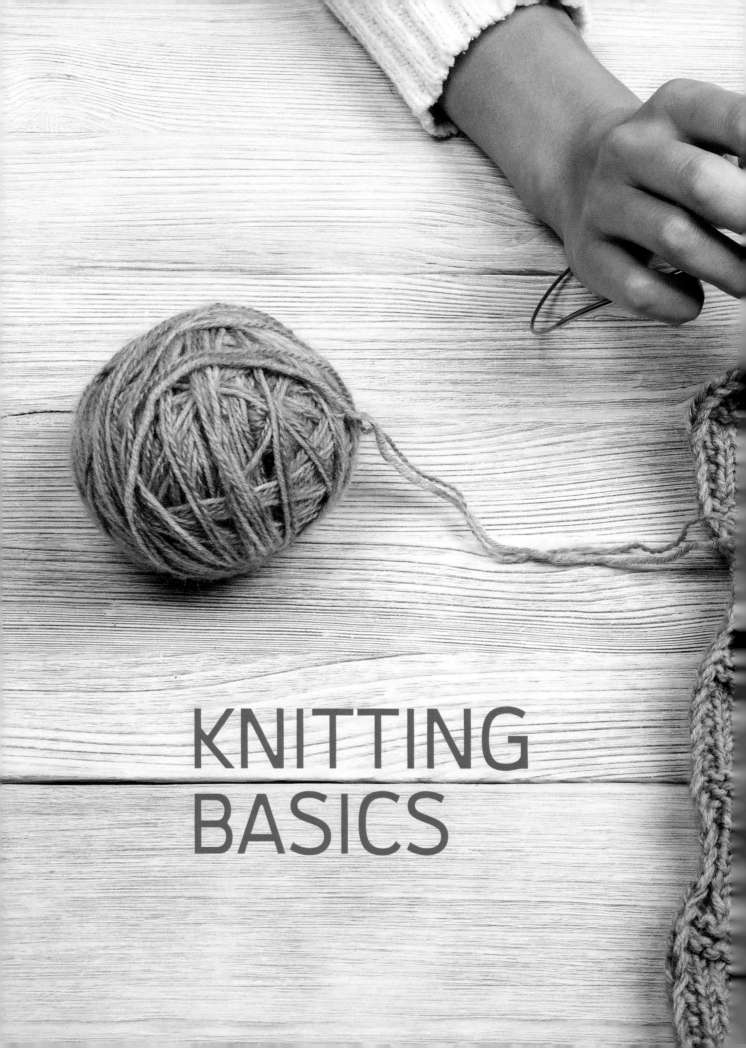

# KNITTING
# BASICS

## ABBREVIATIONS

**BO =** bind off

**cdd =** knit 3 stitches together with center stitch on top: slip 2 stitches together knitwise, knit the next stitch, and pass the slipped stitches over

**CO =** cast on

**k2tog =** knit 2 stitches together

**k3tog =** knit 3 stitches together

**kfb =** make 2 stitches from 1: first, knit 1 stitch, but leave it on the left needle, then knit the same stitch again through the back loop

**kfbf =** work a total of 3 stitches into 1 stitch: knit 1 stitch, but leave it on the left needle. Now, knit the stitch through the back loop, still leaving it on the left needle, then knit it through the front leg, and let it slip off the left needle

**rep =** repeat

**RS =** right side (row)

**selv st(s) =** selvedge stitch(es)

**sk2p =** knit 3 stitches together left-leaning with passing over: slip 1 stitch knitwise, knit 2 stitches together, and pass the slipped stitch over

**skp =** knit 2 stitches together left-leaning with passing over: slip 1 stitch knitwise, knit the next stitch, and pass the slipped stitch over

**ssk =** knit 2 stitches together left-leaning: slip 2 stitches individually knitwise, return them to the left needle, then knit them through the back loop

**ssp =** purl 2 stitches together left-leaning: slip 2 stitches individually knitwise, return them to the left needle, then purl them together through the back loop

**sssk =** knit 3 stitches together left-leaning: slip 3 stitches individually knitwise, return them to the left needle, then knit them through the back loop

**st(s) =** stitch(es)

**WS =** wrong side (row)

**yo =** yarn over

## SYMBOLS

↔  stitch pattern is adjustable widthwise

↕  stitch pattern is adjustable heightwise

◯  requires circular knitting needles

➡  stitch pattern is reversible

[ ]  Numbers in square brackets listed at the beginning of each stitch pattern indicate the total stitch count to cast on for the stitch pattern. The total stitch count will be a multiple of the first number plus the listed number of additional stitches and selvedge stitches. Example: "[multiple of 16 + 3 sts + 2 selv sts]" means that the total stitch count to be cast on will be the sum of: a number which is a multiple of 16, plus 3 stitches, plus 2 selvedge stitches.

## BEGINNING SLIPKNOT

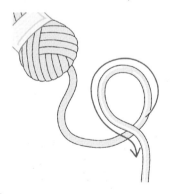

1 Arrange the working yarn in a loop.

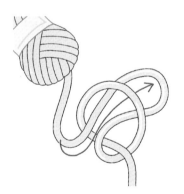

2 Pull the end of the yarn that is connected to the ball (= working yarn), as a loop through the initial loop.

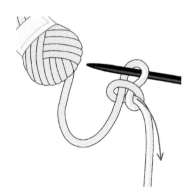

3 Place the resulting loop onto a knitting needle, and tighten on the needle.

# CASTING ON STITCHES

## LONG-TAIL CAST-ON

The long-tail cast-on is one of the most common cast-on methods. It produces a sturdy but still elastic cast-on edge.

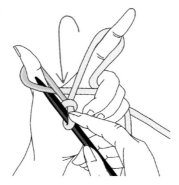

1 Leave a beginning tail at least 3 times as long as the intended width of the cast-on row. Make a beginning slip-knot, and tighten it on the needle. Using thumb and index finger of your left hand, reach between the two strands of yarn, then lead the working yarn connected to the skein over your index finger, and the unattached yarn end over the thumb. Hold the two strands of yarn to your palm with the remaining three fingers.

2 Make a downward motion with the needle, so that a loop forms around the thumb. Insert the needle into this thumb loop from below.

3 Lead the needle tip in the direction of the arrow around the working yarn . . .

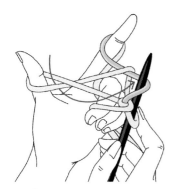

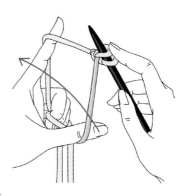

4 . . . and pull the working yarn through the thumb loop.

5 Pull your thumb out of the loop, and gently tug at the yarn to tighten the loop on the needle—not too tight and not too loose.

6 Lift the thumb to return to the initial position, and repeat steps 2–6 to cast on more stitches.

TIP: For a not-too-tight and especially even cast-on edge, the stitches can also be cast onto two needles held together. Remove the second needle after all stitches have been cast on.

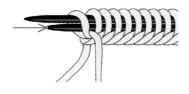

## CABLE CAST-ON

The cable cast-on method produces an especially stretchy cast-on edge that is suitable for all patterns with a curved or zigzagging edge.

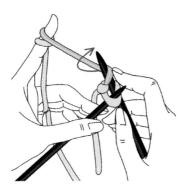

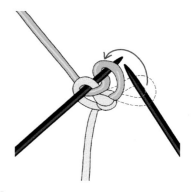

1 Make a beginning slipknot, and tighten it on the needle. Leave the unattached yarn end short; it only needs to be long enough to be woven in later. The cast-on is worked with the working yarn coming from the ball. Hold the knitting needle bearing the beginning slipknot in your left hand, and wind the working yarn around the index finger. Insert the right needle from right to left through the loop, and lead the yarn around the needle in the direction of the arrow.

2 Pull the yarn through the loop . . .

3 . . . and move the newly formed stitch from the right to the left needle.

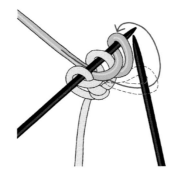

4 For the third stitch, insert the right needle between the first and second stitch on the left needle, and lead the yarn around the needle in the direction of the arrow.

5 Pull the working yarn through between the two needles, and move the newly formed stitch from the right to the left needle. To cast on additional stitches, repeat steps 4 and 5, always inserting the needle between the two newest cast-on stitches.

# WORKING STITCHES

## KNIT STITCHES

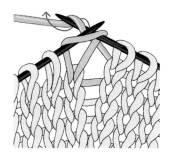 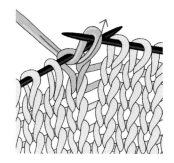 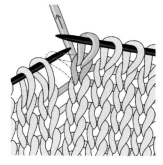

1 Insert the tip of the right needle from the left and the front to the back and the right into the stitch. Move the needle around the working yarn in the direction of the arrow . . .

2 . . . and pull the working yarn through the stitch.

3 Let the stitch slip off the left needle, and gently tighten it on the right needle.

## PURL STITCHES

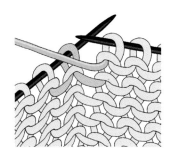 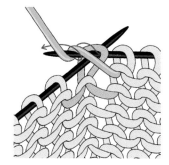 

1 Move the working yarn to the front of the work, and place it in front of the needle and the next stitch.

2 Insert the right needle from right to left into the stitch, staying behind the working yarn. Move the needle in the direction of the arrow around the working yarn . . .

3 . . . pull the working yarn through the stitch, and let the stitch slip off the left needle.

KNITTING THROUGH THE BACK LOOP

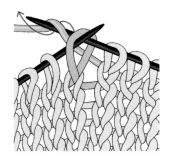

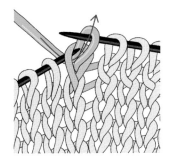

1 Insert the right needle from right to left into the stitch, with working yarn in back of needle.

2 Grasp the working yarn as described for the knit stitch, and pull it through the stitch. Let the old stitch slip off the left needle.

PURLING THROUGH THE BACK LOOP

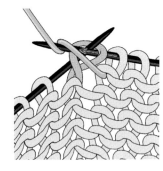

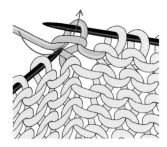

1 Move the working yarn to the front of the work, and insert the right needle in back of work from left to right under the back leg of the stitch.

2 Grasp the working yarn as described for the purl stitch, and pull it through the stitch. Let the old stitch slip off the left needle.

# SLIPPING STITCHES

## KNITWISE (AS IF TO KNIT), WITH WORKING YARN IN BACK OF WORK

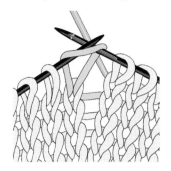

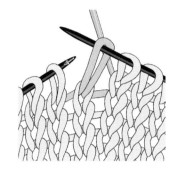

1 Insert the needle into the stitch as if to knit. The working yarn is located in back of work.

2 Do not pull the working yarn through, but move the stitch from the left to the right needle without working it.

## PURLWISE (AS IF TO PURL), WITH WORKING YARN IN FRONT OF WORK

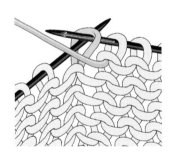

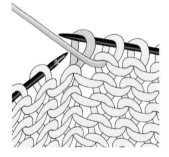

1 Insert the needle into the stitch as if to purl. The working yarn is located in front of work.

2 Do not pull the working yarn through, but move the stitch from the left to the right needle without working it.

## AS IF TO PURL (PURLWISE), WITH WORKING YARN IN BACK OF WORK

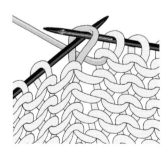

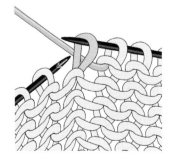

1 Insert the needle into the stitch as if to purl. The working yarn is located in back of work.

2 Do not pull the working yarn through, but move the stitch from the left to the right needle unworked.

# INCREASING STITCHES

### INCREASING THROUGH YARN OVERS

Place the working yarn in front of work as if to purl, then lead it over the right needle to the back.

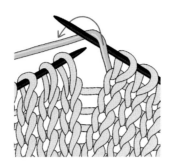

### INCREASING KNITWISE TWISTED FROM THE BAR BETWEEN STITCHES

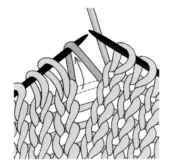

1 Insert the left needle from front to back under the bar between stitches, and lift it onto the needle.

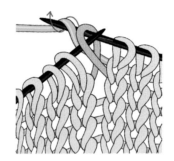

2 Insert the right needle from right to left into the loop created by the bar between stitches, grasp the working yarn . . .

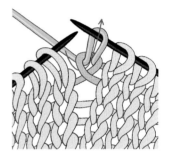

3 . . . and pull it through the loop. Let the stitch slip off the left needle.

## MAKING MULTIPLE STICHES FROM ONE

### ALTERNATING KNITTING THROUGH THE FRONT AND BACK LEG OF THE STITCH (KFB)

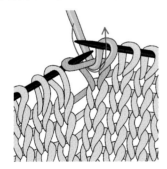

1 Insert the needle into the next stitch from left to right as if to knit, grasp the working yarn, pull it through, and place this loop onto the right needle. Leave the old stitch on the left needle.

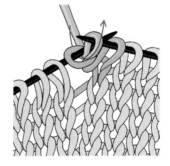

2 Now, insert the needle from right to left through the back loop as if to knit into the same stitch once more, grasp the working yarn, pull it through, and place this loop onto the right needle. Still leave the old stitch on the left needle.

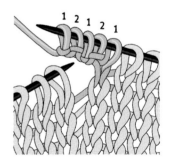

3 Repeat, alternating steps 1 and 2, until the required number of stitches has been created, then let the old stitch slip off the left needle.

## ALTERNATING KNITWISE INCREASES WITH YARN OVERS

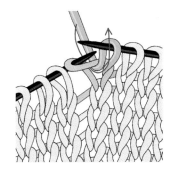

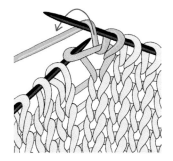

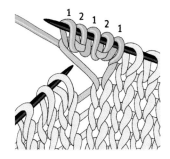

1  Insert the needle into the next stitch from left to right as if to knit, grasp the working yarn, pull it through, and place this loop onto the right needle. Leave the old stitch on the left needle.

2  Move the working yarn to the front of the work, then place it over the right needle to the back as done for a yarn over. Still leave the old stitch on the left needle.

3  Repeat, alternating steps 1 and 2, until the required number of stitches has been created, ending with step 1, then let the old stitch slip off the left needle.

## ALTERNATING KNITWISE AND PURLWISE INCREASES

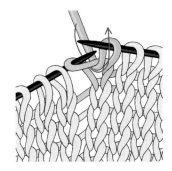

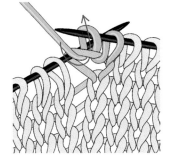

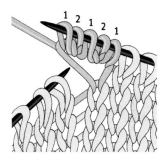

1  Insert the needle into the next stitch from left to right as if to knit, grasp the working yarn, pull it through, and place this loop onto the right needle. Leave the old stitch on the left needle.

2  Now, insert the right needle from right to left into this stitch as if to purl, grasp the working yarn, pull it through, and place this loop onto the right needle. Still leave the old stitch on the left needle.

3  Repeat, alternating steps 1 and 2, until the required number of stitches has been created, then let the old stitch slip off the left needle.

# DECREASING STITCHES

## KNITTING TWO STITCHES TOGETHER RIGHT-LEANING (K2TOG)

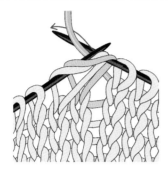

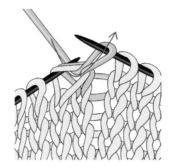

1 Insert the right needle as if to knit into the two following stitches together, grasp the working yarn . . .

2 . . . and knit both stitches together as one.

## KNITTING TWO STITCHES TOGETHER LEFT-LEANING

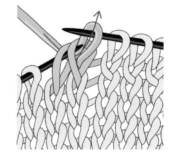

1 Insert the right needle as if to knit through the back loops into the two following stitches together, grasp the working yarn . . .

2 . . . and knit both stitches together as one through the back loop.

## KNITTING TWO STITCHES TOGETHER LEFT-LEANING WITH PASSING OVER (SKP)

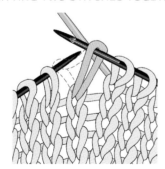

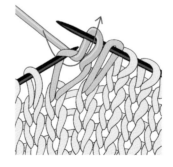

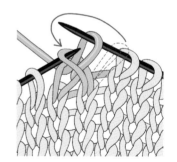

1 Slip one stitch as if to knit.

2 Knit the next stitch . . .

3 . . . and, using the left needle, pass the slipped stitch over the previously knitted stitch and the right needle. Let the old stitch slip off the left needle.

PLEASE NOTE: Alternatively, you can slip the two stitches one after another as if to knit, return both together to the left needle, then knit them together through the back loop (ssk).

## PURLING TWO STITCHES TOGETHER (WILL BE RIGHT-LEANING ON THE RIGHT SIDE OF THE FABRIC)

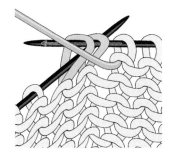

1 Move the working yarn to the front of the work. Insert the right needle into the following two stitches together as if to purl . . .

2 . . . grasp the working yarn, and purl both stitches together as one.

## PURLING TWO STITCHES TOGETHER (WILL BE LEFT-LEANING ON THE RIGHT SIDE OF THE FABRIC)

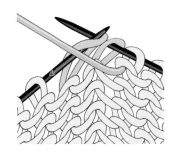

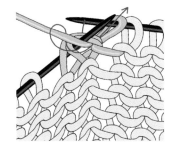

1 Move the working yarn to the front of the work. Slip two stitches one after another as if to knit . . .

2 . . . return them to the left needle, and purl both stitches together through the back loop.

## KNITTING THREE STITCHES TOGETHER RIGHT-LEANING (K3TOG)

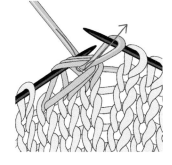

1 Insert the right needle as if to knit into the three following stitches together, grasp the working yarn . . .

2 . . . and knit all three stitches together as one.

## KNITTING THREE STITCHES TOGETHER LEFT-LEANING WITH PASSING OVER (SK2P)

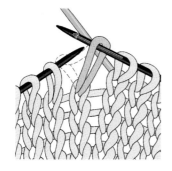

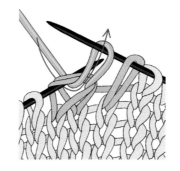

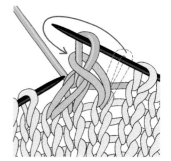

1 Slip one stitch as if to knit.

2 Knit the next two stitches together . . .

3 . . . and, using the left needle, pass the slipped stitch over the two previously knit stitches and the right needle. Let the old stitch slip off the left needle.

## KNITTING THREE STITCHES TOGETHER WITH CENTER STITCH ON TOP (CENTERED DOUBLE DECREASE; CDD)

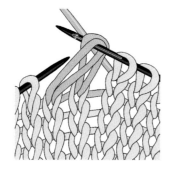

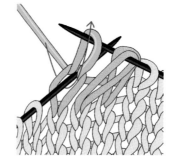

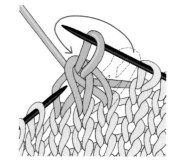

1 Slip two stitches together as if to knit.

2 Knit the next stitch . . .

3 . . . and, using the left needle, pass the two slipped stitches over the previously knitted stitch and the right needle. Let the old stitch slip off the left needle.

## PURLING THREE STITCHES TOGETHER

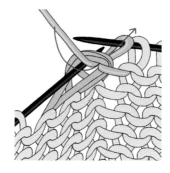

1 Move the working yarn to the front of the work. Insert the right needle into the following three stitches together as if to purl . . .

2 . . . grasp the working yarn, and purl all three stitches together.

# SELVEDGE STITCHES

### CHAIN SELVEDGE
In both right-side and wrong-side rows, always slip the first stitch purlwise with yarn in front of work, and knit the last stitch.

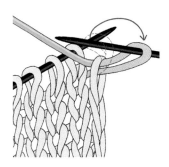 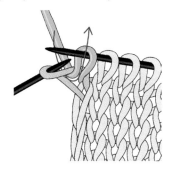

### KNOTTED SELVEDGE
In both right-side and wrong-side rows, always slip the first stitch knitwise with yarn in back of work, and knit the last stitch.

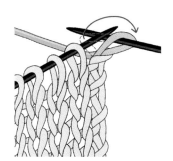 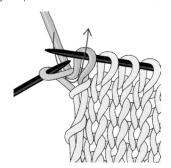

### BRIOCHE SELVEDGE
Used for pieces worked in back-and-forth rows in Brioche patterns.
In both right-side and wrong-side rows, always work the first and last three stitches of the row as follows: knit the knit stitches, and slip the purl stitches purlwise, with working yarn in front of work, without working them.

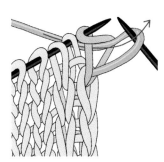 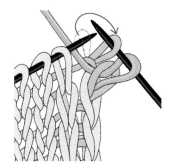 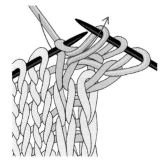

# BINDING OFF

## BINDING OFF KNITWISE

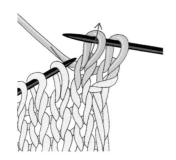

1 Knit two stitches.

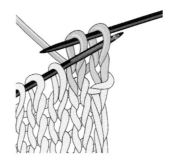

2 Insert the left needle from left to right into the first one of the two stitches . . .

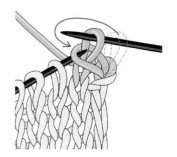

3 . . . pass this stitch over the second stitch and the right needle, then let it slip off the left needle. Knit the next stitch, and repeat steps 2 and 3.

## ELASTIC BIND-OFF

This method produces an especially stretchy edge for all stitch patterns with curved or zigzagging bind-off edges.

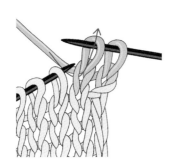

1 Knit two stitches.

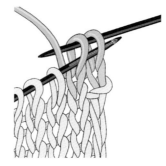

2 Insert the left needle from left to right into the two stitches on the right needle together. Lead the working yarn over the right needle . . .

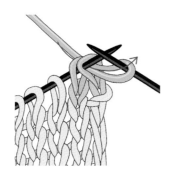

3 . . . pull it through both stitches at once, and let the stitches slip off the left needle.

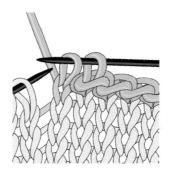

4 Knit the next stitch, and repeat steps 2 and 3.

# CABLE PATTERNS

For less experienced knitters, it is recommended to first practice cabling with a cable needle before trying out cabling without one.

## CABLING STITCHES TO THE LEFT

### WITH ONE CABLE NEEDLE

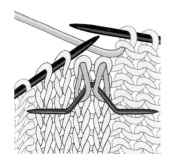

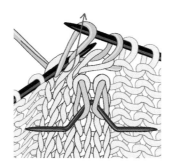

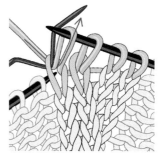

1 Place the required number of stitches (in pictured example, two stitches) onto a cable needle as if to purl, and hold the cable needle in front of work.

2 Work the remaining cable stitches (in pictured example, two stitches) in the stitch pattern listed for the cable.

3 Then work the stitches from the cable needle in the stitch pattern listed for the cable.

### WITH TWO CABLE NEEDLES

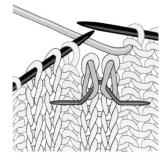

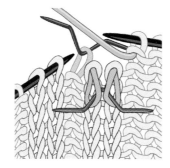

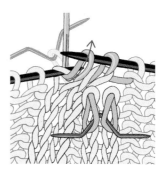

1 Place the required number of stitches for the first group of stitches (in pictured example, two stitches) onto the first cable needle as if to purl, and hold the cable needle in front of work.

2 Now, place the second group of stitches (in pictured example, one stitch) onto the second cable needle as if to purl, and hold the cable needle behind work.

3 Work the remaining stitches of the third group of stitches in the stitch pattern listed for the cable.

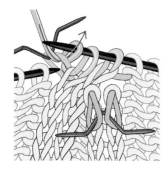

4 First, work the stitches from the second cable needle in the stitch pattern listed for the cable (in pictured example, purl) . . .

5 . . . then work the stitches from the first cable needle in the stitch pattern listed for the cable.

WITHOUT CABLE NEEDLE

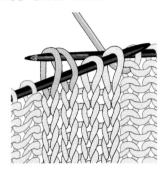

1 Insert the right needle behind the stated number of stitches (in pictured example, two stitches), bypassing them, into the stated number of following stitches (in pictured example, two stitches) on the left needle as if to purl. The working yarn is located behind the stitches.

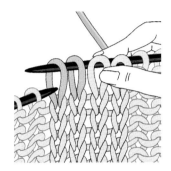

2 Pull the left needle out of the stitches to be cabled. The stitches of the right needle stay on the needle, and the remaining stitches stay unsecured in front of the needle. Secure the live stitches by lightly pressing them with your thumb against the right needle.

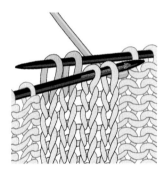

3 Insert the left needle into the open stitches in front of work from left to right to catch them.

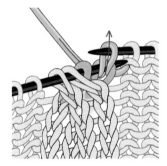

4 Return the stitches from the right needle to the left needle as if to knit, and work the cable stitches in the new order.

## CABLING STITCHES TO THE RIGHT

### WITH ONE CABLE NEEDLE

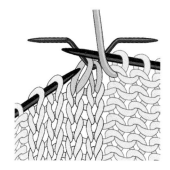 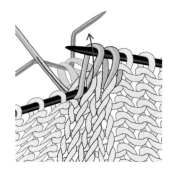 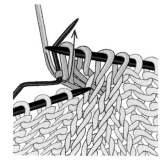

1 Place the required number of stitches (in pictured example, two stitches) onto a cable needle as if to purl, and hold the cable needle behind work.

2 Work the remaining stitches (in pictured example, two stitches) in the stitch pattern listed for the cable.

3 Then work the stitches from the cable needle in the stitch pattern listed for the cable.

### WITH TWO CABLE NEEDLES

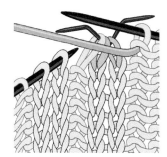 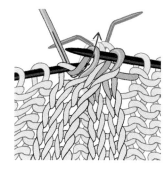

1 Place the required number of stitches (in pictured example, three stitches) first onto a cable needle as if to purl, and hold the cable needle behind work.

2 Work the remaining stitches in the stitch pattern listed for the cable.

 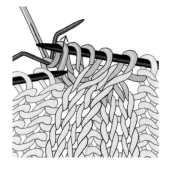

3 Then take up a second cable needle, and slip the required number of stitches (in pictured example, two stitches) from the first cable needle to the second as if to purl, and hold in front of work. Work the remaining stitches from the first cable needle in the listed pattern (in pictured example, purl one stitch) . . .

4 . . . then work the stitches from the second cable needle in the stitch pattern listed for the cable.

WITHOUT CABLE NEEDLE

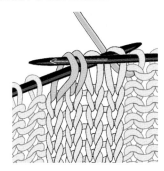

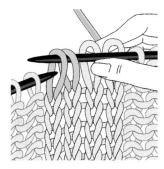

1 Insert the right needle in front of the listed number of stitches (in pictured example, two stitches), bypassing them, into the stated number of following stitches (in pictured example, two stitches) on the left needle as if to purl. The working yarn is located behind the stitches.

2 Pull the left needle out of the stitches to be cabled. The stitches of the right needle stay on the needle, and the remaining stitches stay unsecured behind the needle. Secure the live stitches by lightly pressing them with your thumb against the right needle.

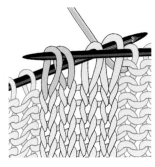

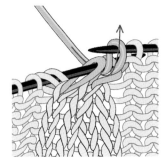

3 Insert the left needle into the open stitches behind work from left to right to catch them.

4 Return the stitches from the right needle to the left needle as if to knit, and work the cable stitches in the new order.

# CROSSED STITCHES

Crossed stitches are stitches, either knitted or knitted through the back loop, that are arranged into decorative patterns by crossing them with each other, or pulling them across other stitches. For less experienced knitters, it is recommended to first practice using a cable needle before trying out crossing stitches without one (see "cabling stitches").

## CROSSING TWO STITCHES TO THE LEFT

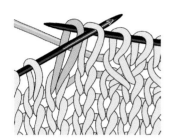

1 Slip both stitches to be crossed onto the right needle as if to purl, with yarn in back of work. Insert the left needle in front of the first stitch (counted from the tip of the needle), bypassing it, into the second stitch on the right needle as if to knit.

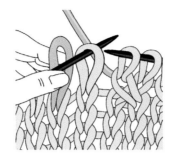

2 Pull the right needle out of both stitches. The second stitch remains on the left needle, and the first stitch stays unsecured behind the needle. Secure the live stitch by lightly pressing it with your thumb against the left needle.

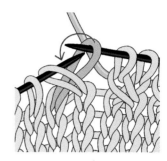

3 Insert the right needle into the live stitch behind work to catch it, and place it onto the left needle as if to purl.

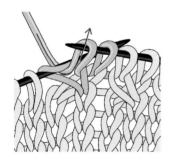

4 Work both stitches individually according to the instructions, either knitting them or knitting them through the back loop.

## CROSSING TWO STITCHES TO THE RIGHT

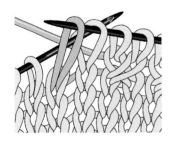

1 Slip both stitches to be crossed onto the right needle as if to purl, with yarn in back of work. Insert the left needle behind the first stitch (counted from the tip of the needle), bypassing it, into the second stitch on the right needle as if to knit.

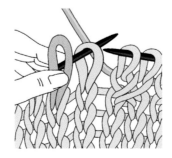

2 Pull the right needle out of both stitches. The second stitch remains on the left needle, and the first stitch stays unsecured in front of the needle. Secure the live stitch by lightly pressing it with your thumb against the left needle.

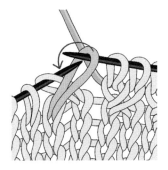

3 Insert the right needle into the open stitch in front of work to catch it, and place it onto the left needle as if to purl.

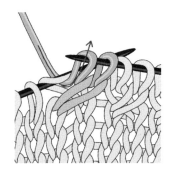

4 Work both stitches individually according to the instructions, either knitting them or knitting them through the back loop.

## STITCH TRAVELING TO THE LEFT

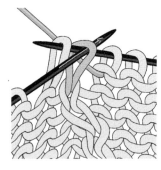

1 Place the traveling stitch and the following purl stitch onto the right needle as if to purl, with yarn in back of work. Insert the left needle in front of the purl stitch (= first stitch as counted from the tip of the needle), bypassing it, into the traveling stitch (= second stitch) on the right needle as if to knit.

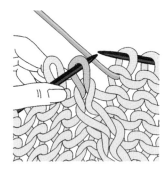

2 Pull the right needle out of both stitches. The traveling stitch remains on the left needle, and the purl stitch stays unsecured behind the needle. Secure the live stitch by lightly pressing it with your finger against the left needle.

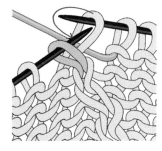

3 Insert the right needle into the live stitch behind work to catch it, and place it onto the left needle as if to purl.

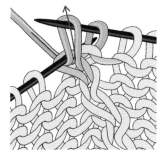

4 Purl the purl stitch, and work the traveling stitch according to the instructions, either knitting it or knitting it through the back loop.

STITCH TRAVELING TO THE RIGHT

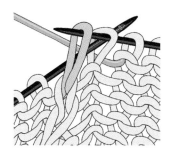

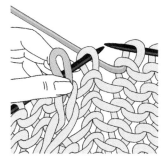

1 Slip the purl stitch and the following traveling stitch as if to purl with yarn in back of work onto the right needle. Insert the left needle behind the traveling stitch (= first stitch as counted from the tip of the needle), bypassing it, then into the purl stitch (= second stitch) on the right needle as if to knit.

2 Pull the right needle out of both stitches. The purl stitch remains on the left needle, and the traveling stitch stays unsecured in front of the needle. Secure the live stitch by lightly pressing it with your thumb against the left needle.

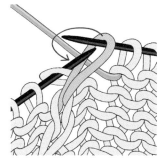

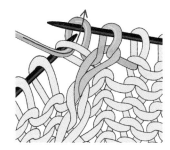

3 Insert the right needle into the open stitch in front of work to catch it, then place it onto the left needle as if to purl.

4 Work the traveling stitch according to the pattern, either knitting it or knitting it through the back loop, and purl the purl stitch.

## BRIOCHE STITCHES

### SLIPPING A STITCH PURLWISE TOGETHER WITH ITS ACCOMPANYING YARN OVER

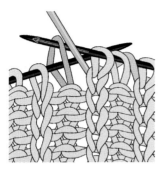

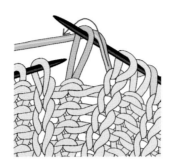

1 Move the working yarn to the front of the work. Behind the working yarn, insert the needle into the following stitch as if to purl, and place the working yarn from front to back over the stitch like a yarn over.

2 Slip the stitch together with the yarn over onto the right needle without working it.

### KNITTING A STITCH TOGETHER WITH THE FOLLOWING YARN OVER

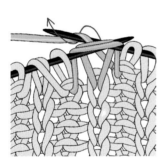

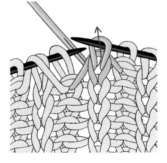

1 Insert the right needle into the following stitch and the yarn over across it together as if to knit, grasp the working yarn . . .

2 . . . and knit the stitch and the yarn over together.

### PURLING A STITCH TOGETHER WITH THE FOLLOWING YARN OVER

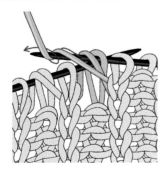

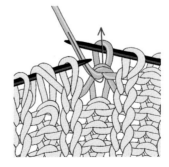

1 Move the working yarn to the front of the work. Insert the right needle into the following stitch and the yarn over across it together as if to purl . . .

2 . . . and pull the working yarn through, purling the stitch and the yarn over together.

# MULTI-ROW PATTERNS (KNITTED SPIKE STITCHES)

## ONE ROW BELOW

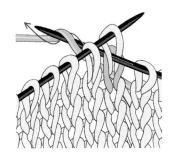

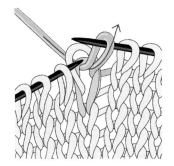

1 Insert the right needle into the stitch one row below as if to knit . . .

2 . . . pull the working yarn through the stitch, and let the stitch slip off the left needle. This undoes the stitch above it. Treating the undone stitch as you would a yarn over, knit it together with the stitch.

## SEVERAL ROWS BELOW

In the same way, insert the needle into stitches several rows below, and undo the column of stitches above it.

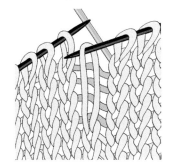

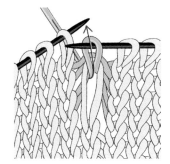

1 Alternatively, undo the column of stitches down to the desired stitch, then insert the right needle into it as if to knit to catch it.

2 After this, insert the right needle under the bars of undone stitches, place the working yarn around the needle, and knit 1 stitch, catching all bars in the process.

# SPECIAL COLORWORK TECHNIQUES

## INTARSIA

For larger areas or motifs in one color, each section is worked from a separate ball of yarn to avoid very long strands of yarn carried behind work. When changing colors, the strands of yarn are crossed with each other.
Work in back-and-forth rows up to the color change spot, and cross the two strands of yarn counterclockwise around each other.

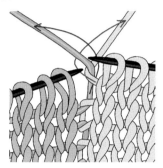

## STRANDED COLORWORK

In the stranded colorwork technique, in every row or round, two or more colors are used. One or more strands in unused colors are carried loosely in back of work, called floats.
There are different ways of holding the strands:

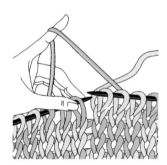
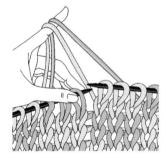
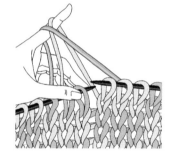

1 Only the current working yarn rests on the index finger; the other strands hang down loosely in back of work, and the active color always changes. This method is suitable for beginners.

2 Two parallel strands of yarn go over the index finger in the same direction.

3 Two strands of yarn are crossed over the index finger: one strand runs from back to front, the second one from front to back over the index finger.

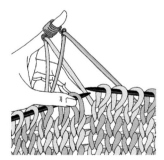
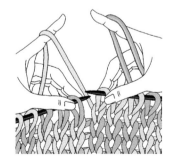

4 A yarn guide (Fair-Isle ring) worn on the index finger, available in specialty stores in versions for 2 to 4 colors, holds the strands of yarn. This prevents unintentional twisting of the strands.

5 The yarns are held using two hands, each color over one index finger. This method requires practice.

PLEASE NOTE: The floats should be as even as possible and held neither too tightly nor too loosely. For longer spans needing to be bridged, the unused color should be twisted once with the active color halfway through the float to avoid annoying loops on the wrong side of the work. When working in back-and-forth rows, strands should always be crossed at the end of the row before turning. Working in the round will produce especially neat and even stitches.

## EMBROIDERING IN DUPLICATE STITCH

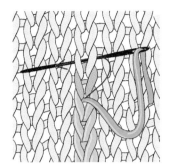

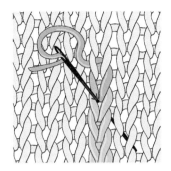

1 First, insert a tapestry needle from the wrong side of the work through the stitch below the stitch to be embroidered, and pull the yarn through to the right side of the work. Now, go back through to the wrong side to the right and above the stitch to be embroidered, lead the yarn in back of work 1 stitch to the left, and come out again on the right side of work.

2 Move the needle down to the base of the stitch, go through to the wrong side of the work again, and pull the yarn through to the wrong side of the work.

## INCORPORATING BEADS

Thread a piece of sewing thread into a beading needle or thin sewing needle, and secure with a knot a short way below the eye. First, knit the stitch to which the bead will be added, then return it to the left needle.

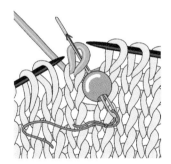

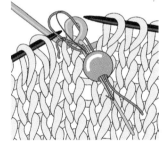

1 Now, thread a bead onto the needle, then use the beading needle to lift the stitch from the knitting needle.

2 Pull the needle through the stitch, then lead it back through the threaded bead.

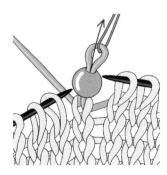

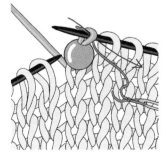

3 Now, pull the stitch through the bead with the help of the thread loop, placing the bead on the stitch.

4 Place the stitch onto the right needle with the help of the thread loop, then remove the thread.

# READING KNITTING CHARTS

For ease of reading, knitting patterns are presented in the form of special illustrations, called charts. These charts show which stitches need to be next to and atop each other. Every box in the chart stands for one action.

If only right-side rows (= rows with an odd row number placed at the right of the chart) are worked in pattern, wrong-side rows will not be shown in the chart; how to work them will be stated in the written instructions.

Knitting charts are read in the direction the row is worked, from right to left and from bottom to top. If wrong-side rows (= rows with an even row number placed at the left of the chart) are depicted, too, they will be read in the opposite direction, from left to right.

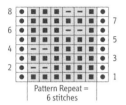

Pattern Repeat =
6 stitches

The symbols in the chart are explained in a **Stitch Key**.

● = 1 selvedge stitch

■ = Knit 1 stitch

– = Purl 1 stitch

The framed pattern repeat has to be worked as often as stated in the instructions. Stitch markers to divide individual pattern repeats make orientation within the pattern much easier.

In some stitch patterns, the stitch count changes within the row. Here, either the chart will become accordingly wider or narrower at the edges or, within the chart, boxes without symbols, which require no action, are inserted as placeholders for better orientation.

Pattern
Repeat =
4 stitches

With some of the patterns (such as leaf and flower patterns), additional charts have been included. For these, at the marked spots, change from the main chart to the additional chart, and after having worked the stitches of the additional chart, resume working from the main chart.

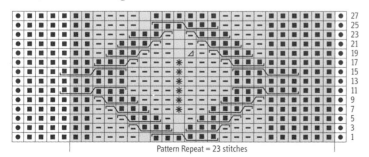

Pattern Repeat = 23 stitches

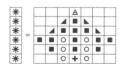

Knitting charts for Intarsia or stranded colorwork patterns are presented with boxes of differently colored backgrounds. They are read the same way as charts for textured patterns, working stockinette stitch and changing colors as shown in the chart. Each box represents a stitch in the indicated color. When working in back-and-forth rows with turning, these stitches are to be knit in right-side rows and purled in wrong-side rows. As with other knitting charts, right-side rows are worked from right to left, and wrong-side rows in the opposite direction from left to right. When working in the round, all stitches in all rounds are always knitted, and the chart is always read from right to left.

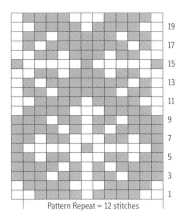

Pattern Repeat = 12 stitches

## Stitch Key

☐ = 1 stitch in white

▨ = 1 stitch in pastel blue

# FROM PATTERN TO FINISHED OBJECT

# PLANNING YOUR PROJECT

Every project starts with planning. What type of item do you want to knit? A fashionable accessory, such as a scarf, hat, arm- or legwarmers, or a bag? Those always come in handy. A trendy pullover, a snuggly cardigan, or a comfy poncho for the new season? Or should it be something decorative for your home? A pretty pillowcase, a soft blanket, a lampshade, or a flowerpot cozy?

### DRAWING A GARMENT PATTERN

Once you have decided what item to knit, it's time to think about how to approach making it. Existing garment patterns or finished articles of clothing or accessories can be used as a starting point. Do you intend to knit the garment seamlessly in one piece, or will it be in multiple pieces and seamed? First, draw a rough shape of the garment. If it consists of multiple parts, an outline of each piece to be knitted will need to be drawn. For a pullover, for instance, you will need one piece for the front, one for the back, and one sleeve. (Identical parts, such as sleeves, need to be drawn only once.) Cuffs, if applicable, should be drawn together with the piece to which they are attached. For parts to be knitted onto existing pieces, such as facings or a collar, make a note, or draw a schematic.

Now, measurements have to be filled in the schematic. For rectangular pieces, such as scarves, length and width are sufficient. A pullover or a cardigan, however, in addition to length and width for each piece, will need armhole and neckline depth as well as shoulder, neckline, and armhole width.

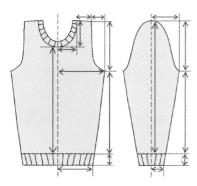

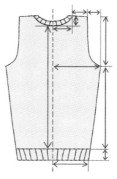

These measurements can be taken from an existing well-fitting garment but should be checked against the actual body measurements and corrected if needed. Is there enough ease to allow for movement? Do neckline circumference and head circumference match? For pillowcases and lampshades or cozies for flowerpots, the stretch factor has to be considered and the item knit up slightly smaller for a snug fit.

### CHOOSING A STITCH PATTERN

After you have decided on the type of item and its shape, it's now time to think about the stitch pattern. Do you intend to knit the whole item in one pattern, or do you want to combine several of them?

Classic designs often combine an all-over pattern with a different border at the beginning and the end. On account of their inherent stretchiness, ribbing or cable patterns are ideally suited for cuffs, neckline, and button bands. Since cable patterns pull in noticeably, it helps to first cast on fewer stitches, increasing the remainder, evenly distributed, during the first row worked in pattern. This approach yields a straight cast-on row without pulling in. The same is true for binding off cable patterns. Here, in the last pattern row, a few stitches need to be decreased before binding off all stitches during the bind-off row.

Edgings and borders (see pages 212 and following) are ideally suited as decorative finishings. Some of them, such as droplet arcs edging, vine border, feather-and-fan border, or chevron lace edging, make good beginning borders for accessories such as scarves, arm- or legwarmers, ponchos and lampshades, or decorative edges for front, back, and sleeves of pullovers and cardigans.

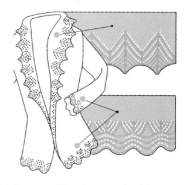

Edgings and borders worked in one piece with the main part are used as finishing for side edges on scarves, shawls, and open-front cardigans. Other edgings and borders, such as lace edgings, chevron-lace finishing, or the flower motif border, create a decorative finishing for the ends of scarves, shawls, or collars.

Individual decorative edgings can be combined heightwise as desired with garter stitch fabric, repeated multiple times, or paired with each other. Sequences of different edgings are another option.

Individual pattern strips can be combined widthwise as well. Examples for these can be found in chapters Aran and Alpine patterns (see pages 70 and following) as well as in lace-and-cable patterns (see pages 86 and following). For these patterns, the different width of individual pattern columns needs to be taken into account and, if needed, filled in to the desired width with knit or purl stitches.

## PICKING A SUITABLE YARN

Stitch patterns can have completely different looks depending on the type of yarn used. For instance, the same lace pattern, worked using the same needle size, will look entirely different if worked in a delicate mohair yarn or a thicker merino wool or cotton yarn. Fluffy or textured yarns will often swallow a stitch patten. Smooth yarns, however, improve the stitch definition. This also applies to solid-colored versus multi-color yarns. The way the yarn is plied plays a role too. Yarns plied more tightly will produce a better stitch definition.

When deciding on a yarn, the purpose of the future item must be factored in. Coarse sock yarn, for instance, is not suitable next to delicate baby or toddler skin, while it is the right choice for hard-wearing and durable socks. A coat knit in pure silk would lose its shape very quickly. Knit in fluffy mohair, however, the same coat is bound to serve and delight for a long time. For airy summer garments, linen and cotton yarns are best, while for warm winter things, wool yarns or wool blends are a better choice. Care instructions for the fiber come into play too. Garments that will be subjected to frequent washings should be worked in easy-care yarns.

## MAKING AND EVALUATING A GAUGE SWATCH

After the stitch pattern has been picked, the next important step is making a gauge swatch. Should you feel tempted to skip it and want to start knitting right away, don't give in to this urge. For a perfect result, a carefully prepared and blocked gauge swatch is simply indispensable. It is the only way to avoid disappointment in an ill-fitting garment later.

To prepare the gauge swatch, using the actual project yarn with a matching needle size, knit a square of about 6 x 6 in (15 x 15 cm) in the desired stitch pattern or patterns. The yarn wrapper will give an approximate idea about needle size and the required number of stitches to cast on. If the stitch count on the ball band is given for a 4 x 4 in

(10 x 10 cm) square, increase the stitch count by half for your larger intended swatch size. For cable and ribbing patterns, a few stitches more need to be cast on, since fabric in these patterns will pull in noticeably. If needed, adjust the needle size until the fabric turns out to your liking.

For stranded colorwork patterns, too, the gauge swatch should be worked in the actual pattern, not just in stockinette in one color, since stranded colorwork patterns with multiple colors will turn out differently than a piece worked in plain stockinette in just one color. For projects to be knit in the round, the gauge swatch should be worked in the round, too, since the gauge for rows with all knit stitches will be different from that for knit and purl rows. To measure a gauge swatch knit in the round, either work the swatch two times as wide as needed and pat it flat to measure or secure the stitches with two parallel columns of stitches, as shown, and then cut open the swatch lengthwise between the seams.

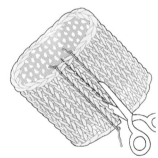

After having bound off, either moisten the gauge swatch or wash it briefly, and then block it carefully (see page 305). A stockinette stitch gauge swatch worked in pure wool or cotton may instead be gently blocked with a steam iron from the wrong side of the fabric while covered with a moist cloth. After the gauge swatch has been thoroughly dried, remove it from the blocking surface, and measure it only after it has been detached, since it might further shrink after having been lifted. Using a tape measure or ruler, mark a square of 4 x 4 in (10 x 10 cm) in the middle of the swatch with tailor pins; then count the stitches and rows within the marked area, and write down the numbers.

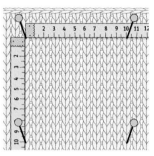

Alternatively, place a knitting gauge ruler on top of the swatch, and count the stitches and rows within the framed area.

## CALCULATING STITCH COUNTS

For further calculations, a pocket calculator is very useful. First, count the number of stitches over a width of 4 in (10 cm), and then divide it by 4. This gives you the stitch count for a width of 1 in (2.5 cm). Now, multiply this stitch count by the desired width of the piece to be knitted in inches (cm). This yields the stitch count to be cast on for the desired width. For knitting in back-and-forth rows with turning, add two extra stitches as selvedge stitches. Write the calculated number of stitches into the schematic or garment pattern, and then repeat the calculations for the width of each part of the piece.

EXAMPLE: 15 stitches widthwise were counted in 4 in (10 cm). Dividing 15 stitches by 4 in (10 cm) results in a stitch count of 3.75 stitches for every 1 in (1.5 stitches for every 1 cm) widthwise. For the desired width of 16 in (40 cm), multiply the stitch count of 3.75 by 16 in (1.5 by 40 cm). This results in 60 stitches being needed for your example with a width of 16 in (40 cm).

## CALCULATING THE ROW COUNT

The number of rows is calculated the same way. Count the number of rows needed for a height of 4 in (10 cm), and divide it by 4. This is the row count for a height of 1 in (2.5 cm). Now, multiply this row count with the desired height of the knitted piece. This yields the number of rows needed for the desired height. Write the calculated number of rows into the schematic or pattern, and repeat the calculations for the heights of all respective parts of the piece.

EXAMPLE: A gauge swatch of 4 in (10 cm) contains 20 rows heightwise. Dividing 20 rows by 4 in (10 cm) gives a row count of 5 rows for every 1 in (2 rows for every 1 cm) heightwise. For a desired height of 16 in (40 cm), the row count of 5 needs to be multiplied by 16 in (2 rows by 40 cm). This results in 80 rows being needed for this example with a height of 16 in (40 cm).

### CALCULATING INCREASES AND DECREASES

For pieces that are not straight rectangles, increases and decreases have to be additionally calculated. If all stitches will be increased or decreased within the same row, the number of stitches to be increased or decreased is calculated over the width only, using the method described above. If increases or decreases are to be distributed over a certain height, the number of rows has to be factored in as well. For this step, first determine the number of stitches for the width to be increased or decreased. Then, based on the height over which these stitches are to be increased or decreased, calculate the number of rows as described above. Finally, divide the number of rows by the number of stitches.

EXAMPLE: 10 stitches are to be increased over 80 rows. 80 divided by 10 yields 8. In this example, accordingly, in every 8th row, 1 stitch will be added a total of 10 times.
If dividing produces decimal places instead of a whole number, first, the number of remaining rows has to be determined. To do this, the number before the decimal point needs to be multiplied by the number of stitches. Subtracting the result from the total number of rows gives the number of

remaining rows. These will now be distributed as evenly as possible over the appropriate height.

EXAMPLE: 10 stitches are to be increased over a height of 86 rows. 86 divided by 10 yields 8.6. 8 multiplied by 10 yields 80. 86 rows minus 80 rows yields 6 remaining rows. In this example, 1 stitch will be increased first in every 8th row 4 times total, then in every 9th row 6 times total.
For an especially even distribution, 1 stitch can be increased in every 8th row twice, then in every 9th row 3 times; then repeat the whole sequence once.
When increases and decreases occur not over a straight slant, they have to be distributed differently, following the shape in the schematic. For armholes and necklines with a curved shape, first more stitches have to be decreased over fewer rows, and then the remaining stitches over more rows to create a curved line.

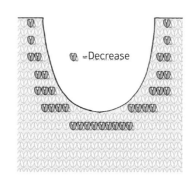

When stitch patterns with different gauges are combined, stitches need to be increased or decreased depending on the respective gauge.

### ESTIMATING THE TOTAL YARN AMOUNT NEEDED

Based on the total yardage listed on the yarn label and the gauge swatch, the approximate total yardage for the desired project can be estimated.
To do this, first work a gauge swatch of at least 50 or, better yet, 100 stitches, in the actual stitch pattern and with the needle size that will later be used for the project. Mark beginning and end of this section on the yarn in the swatch; then unravel the stitches, and measure the length of yarn between the two marked spots. This will be the length of yarn needed to work 50 or 100 stitches. Dividing this length by 50 or 100, respectively, yields the length of yarn needed for 1 stitch. Now, calculate the total stitch count for the piece on the basis of the schematic by multiplying the number of rows by the number of stitches per row. Then multiply the total stitch count by the length of yarn required for 1 stitch. This yields the total yardage needed for the whole project. Finally, this now needs to be divided by the yardage per skein to determine the total number of skeins required for the project.

EXAMPLE: 100 stitches used up 1.6 yd (1.5 m) of yarn. 1.6 yd divided by 100 stitches yields 0.016 yd per stitch (1.5 m divided by 100 stitches yields 0.015 m per stitch). For a small scarf with 40 stitches per row and a length of 350 rows, you would need 350 times 40; thus, the whole scarf would have 14,000 stitches in all. The yarn amount needed is calculated as follows: 14,000 times 0.016 yd = 224 yds (14,000 times 0.015 m = 210 m) of yarn. With a yardage of 93 yd (85 m) per skein, you would need 224 yd divided by 93 yd (210 m divided by 85 m), amounting to about 2.5 skeins.
A little buffer should always be added to this calculated amount since cast-on and bind-off rows use up more yarn

than regular rows; the beginning and ending tail also need to be accounted for, and a small reserve for knots in the skein (if any) should be factored in as well. Additional yarn might be needed for seaming and, if applicable, for finishing elements added afterward, such as button bands, ties, fringe, etc.

## ADJUSTING THE PATTERN REPEAT TO THE STITCH COUNT

If the calculated number of stitches does not match the stitch count of the selected stitch pattern, adjustments have to be made. First check, on the basis of the stitch count of the selected stitch pattern, how many stitches are left over or would be additionally needed for another full repeat of the pattern repeat (always stated in this book). For small differences, the calculated number of stitches can be increased or reduced or, depending on the pattern, 1–2 extra stitches in knit or purl can be added at the edges. In case of larger discrepancies, the beginning of the row or round needs to be shifted to within the pattern repeat. To keep the symmetry of the pattern, count off half the number of extra stitches from the end of the pattern repeat, and mark this spot as the new beginning of the row or round. The end of the row or round also needs to be moved accordingly. Continue working the pattern repeat until all stitches—or, when working in back-and-forth rows, all stitches except for the selvedge stitch—have been worked, and mark this spot as the new end of the row or round.

EXAMPLE: Discrepancy of 4 extra stitches

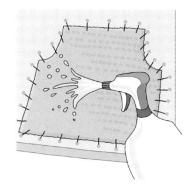

Pattern Repeat = 8 stitches

## BLOCKING KNITTED PIECES

After knitting and before seaming, all parts should be wet blocked. Blocking creates an even and neat stitch definition. Side edges won't roll as much and will be easier to seam.

Either moisten the knitted pieces or wash them briefly, roll them up in a towel, and gently press out excess water. Then, using rust-proof tailor pins, pin them out on a suitable flat surface according to the measurements in the schematic. Alternatively, the pieces can first be pinned while still dry and then moistened with a spray bottle or covered with a wet cloth.

Good choices for surfaces are special blocking mats, soft ironing mats, or a styrofoam board covered with fabric. Larger pieces can be blocked on the carpet as well. Ribbing should not be stretched too much, so it will retain its elasticity.

Pieces worked in the round can be blocked especially easily with the help of two metal or fiberglass rods or wooden dowels. For this, first insert the rods into and through the knitted tube, then pull them apart, and pin them in place with tailor or blocking pins.

Pieces from pure wool or cotton worked in stockinette stitch or stranded colorwork and Intarsia patterns can also be gently blocked with a steam iron from the wrong side of the fabric while covered with a moist cloth.

Let all pieces dry thoroughly, and then sew them together. For garments featuring button bands, facings, or a collar, these will be either knitted onto the main piece directly after seaming by picking up the required number of stitches from the edge or first knitted separately and sewn on later.

ADDITIONAL
CHARTS

155 MAGIC KNOT ▸ page 84

Pattern Repeat 1 = 4 stitches

Pattern Repeat 2 = 4 stitches

## Stitch Key

● = 1 selvedge stitch

■ = Knit 1 stitch

⁃ = Purl 1 stitch

+ = Increase 1 stitch from the bar between stitches twisted

☐ = No stitch, for better over-view only

↘⁵ = Into the following stitch, work a total of 5 stitches (alter-nating "knit 1 stitch, make 1 yarn over")

◀ = Sextuple passing-over, starting at left: * On the left needle, pass the second stitch over the first stitch. Slip the first stitch from the right needle purlwise to the left needle; there, pass the second stitch over the first needle, and on the right needle, pass the second stitch (counted from the tip of the needle) over the first stitch (counted from the tip of the nee-dle). Now, return the first stitch to the left needle. Repeat from *

2 = Sextuple passing-over, starting at right: Slip 4 stitches purlwise to the right needle. * On the right needle, pass the second stitch (counted from the tip of the needle) over the first stitch (counted from the tip of the needle). Then slip the first stitch from the right needle purlwise to the left needle; there, pass the second stitch over the first stitch. Now, return the first stitch to the right nee-dle. Repeat from * twice more. Then return the stitch to the left needle, and purl it.

▨■ = Hold 1 stitch on a cable needle behind work,

knit the next stitch, then knit the stitch from the cable needle

▨■ = Hold 1 stitch on a cable needle behind work, knit the next stitch, then knit the stitch from the cable needle

◢◣ = Hold 1 stitch on a cable needle behind work, knit 2 stitches together, then knit the stitch from the cable needle

▨■■ = Hold 3 stitches on a cable needle in front of work, purl 1 stitch, then knit the 3 stitches from the cable needle

▨⁃ = Hold 1 stitch on a cable needle behind work,

knit 3 stitches, then knit the stitch from the cable needle

▨■■ = Hold 3 stitches on a cable needle in front of work, knit the next stitch, then knit the 3 stitches from the cable needle

▨■■ = Hold 1 stitch on a cable needle behind work, knit 3 stitches, then knit the stitch from the cable needle

⁃▨ = Hold 3 stitches on a cable needle in front of work, knit 2 stitches, then knit the 3 stitches from the cable needle

⁃▨ = Hold 3 stitches on a cable needle in front of work, purl 2 stitches, then knit the 3 stitches from the cable needle

▨⁃ = Hold 3 stitches on a cable needle in

front of work, hold 1 stitch on a second cable needle behind work, knit 3 stitches, then purl the stitch from the second ca-ble needle, then knit the 3 stitches from the first cable needle

▨⁃▨■ = Hold 4 stitches on the first cable nee-dle behind work, knit 3 stitches, then place the second stitch from the first cable nee-dle onto a second cable needle, and hold in front of work. Purl the remaining stitch from the first cable needle, then knit the 3 stitches from the second ca-ble needle.

## 150 CELTIC KNOT ❯ page 82

Pattern
Repeat 1 =
2 stitches

Pattern
Repeat 2 =
2 stitches

55 53 51 49 47 45 43 41 39 37 35 33 31 29 27 25 23 21 19 17 15 13 11 9 7 5 3 1

## Stitch Key

● = 1 selvedge stitch

■ = Knit 1 stitch

– = Purl 1 stitch

✛ = Increase 1 stitch from the bar between stitches twisted

☐ = No stitch, for better overview only

◀ = Quadruple passing-over, starting at left: Slip 2 stitches purlwise to the right needle. On the left needle, pass the second stitch over the first stitch. Slip the first stitch on the left needle purlwise to the right needle, and on the right needle, pass the second stitch (counted from the tip of the needle) over the first stitch (counted from the tip of the needle). Now, return the first stitch to the left needle, and again, pass the second stitch over the first stitch. Return the first stitch to the right needle, and once again, pass the second stitch over the first stitch. Place the first stitch back onto the left needle, then purl it.

◀ = Quadruple passing-over, starting at right: Slip 3 stitches purlwise to the right needle; there, pass the second stitch (counted from the tip of the needle) over the first stitch (counted from the tip of the needle). Now, slip the first stitch from the right needle purlwise onto the left needle. On the left needle, pass the second stitch over the first stitch, then slip the first stitch back to the right needle. There, again, pass the second stitch over the first stitch, and slip the first stitch back to the left needle. On the left needle, once more, pass the second stitch over the first stitch, then purl the stitch.

▷ = Into the following stitch, work a total of 3 stitches (kfbf = knit the stitch first through the front leg, then through the back loop, and through the front leg again)

☐–☐ ■☐ = Hold 2 stitches on a cable needle in front of work, purl 2 stitches, then knit the 2 stitches from the cable needle

■☐ –☐ = Hold 2 stitches on a cable needle behind work, knit 2 stitches, then purl the 2 stitches from the cable needle

■ ■ – ■ ■ = Hold 2 stitches on a cable needle in front of work, hold 1 stitch on a second cable needle behind work, knit 2 stitches, then purl the stitch from the second cable needle, then knit the 2 stitches from the first cable needle

■ ■ – ■ ■ ■ = Hold 3 stitches on the first cable needle behind work, knit 2 stitches, then place the first and second stitch from the first cable needle onto a second cable needle and hold in front of work. Purl the remaining stitch from the first cable needle, then knit the 2 stitches from the second cable needle.

## 139  TRADITIONAL ARAN PATTERN  › page 75

Pattern Repeat 1 = 1 stitch

Pattern Repeat 2 = 8 stitches

Pattern Repeat 3 = 1 stitch

23 21 19 17 15 13 11 9 7 5 3 1

### Stitch Key

● = 1 selvedge stitch

■ = Knit 1 stitch

| = Purl 1 stitch

= Hold 3 stitches on a cable needle in front of work, knit the next stitch, then knit the 3 stitches from the cable needle

= Hold 1 stitch on a cable needle behind work, knit 3 stitches, then knit the stitch from the cable needle

= Hold 3 stitches on a cable needle in front of work, purl 1 stitch, then knit the 3 stitches from the cable needle

= Hold 1 stitch on a cable needle behind work, knit 3 stitches, then purl the stitch from the cable needle

= Hold 2 stitches on a cable needle in front of work, knit 2 stitches, then knit the 2 stitches from the cable needle

= Hold 2 stitches on a cable needle in front of work, knit 2 stitches, then knit the 2 stitches from the cable needle

= Hold 2 stitches on a cable needle behind work, knit 2 stitches, then purl the 2 stitches from the cable needle

= Hold 3 stitches on a cable needle behind work, knit 3 stitches, then knit the 3 stitches from the cable needle

## 146  IRISH PATTERN COMBINATION  › page 80

9 7 5 3 1

Pattern Repeat 1 = 14 stitches

Pattern Repeat 2 = 10 stitches

Pattern Repeat 3 = 14 stitches

### Stitch Key

● = 1 selvedge stitch

■ = Knit 1 stitch

| = Purl 1 stitch

= Hold 1 stitch on a cable needle in front of work, knit the next stitch, then knit the stitch from the cable needle

= Hold 2 stitches on a cable needle in front of work, knit 2 stitches, then knit the 2 stitches from the cable needle

= Hold 2 stitches on a cable needle behind work, knit 2 stitches, then knit the 2 stitches from the cable needle

= Hold 3 stitches on a cable needle in front of work, purl 2 stitches, then knit the 3 stitches from the cable needle

= Hold 2 stitches on a cable needle behind work, knit 3 stitches, then purl the 2 stitches from the cable needle

= Hold 3 stitches on a cable needle in front of work, knit 3 stitches, then knit the 3 stitches from the cable needle

= Hold 3 stitches on a cable needle behind work, knit 3 stitches, then knit the 3 stitches from the cable needle

## 133 CABLE PATTERN WITH HEART GARLAND  ❱ page 72

19 17 15 13 11 9 7 5 3 1

Pattern Repeat = 41 stitches

### Stitch Key

● = 1 selvedge stitch

■ = Knit 1 stitch

I = Purl 1 stitch

= Hold 2 stitches on a cable needle in front of work, purl 1 stitch, then knit the 2 stitches from the cable needle

= Hold 1 stitch on a cable needle behind work, knit 2 stitches, then purl the stitch from the cable needle

= Hold 1 stitch on a cable needle in front of work, knit 2 stitches, then knit the stitch from the cable needle

= Hold 2 stitches on a cable needle behind work, knit 2 stitches, then knit the 2 stitches from the cable needle

= Hold 2 stitches on a cable needle in front of work, knit 2 stitches, then knit the 2 stitches from the cable needle

= Hold 2 stitches on a cable needle in front of work, purl 2 stitches, then knit the 2 stitches from the cable needle

= Hold 2 stitches on a cable needle behind work, knit 2 stitches, then purl the 2 stitches from the cable needle

= Hold 1 stitch on a cable needle in front of work, knit 3 stitches, then knit the stitch from the cable needle

= Hold 3 stitches on a cable needle behind work, knit the next stitch, then knit the 3 stitches from the cable needle

## 140 TRAVELING-STITCH COMBINATION  ❱ page 75

15 13 11 9 7 5 3 1

Pattern Repeat 1 = 2 stitches

Pattern Repeat 2 = 4 stitches

Pattern Repeat 3 = 2 stitches

### Stitch Key

● = 1 selvedge stitch

◆ = Knit 1 stitch through the back loop

I = Purl 1 stitch

= Hold 1 stitch on a cable needle behind work, knit 1 stitch through the back loop, then knit the stitch from the cable needle through the back loop

= Hold 1 stitch on a cable needle in front of work, knit 1 stitch through the back loop, then knit the stitch from the cable needle through the back loop

= Hold 1 stitch on a cable needle behind work, knit 1 stitch through the back loop, then purl the stitch from the cable needle

= Hold 1 stitch on a cable needle in front of work, purl 1 stitch, then knit the stitch from the cable needle through the back loop

## 137 LAID-BACK CABLE DIAMONDS  ❯ page 74

23
21
19
17
15
13
11
9
7
5
3
1

Pattern Repeat = 40 stitches

### Stitch Key

- ● = 1 selvedge stitch
- ■ = Knit 1 stitch
- − = Purl 1 stitch
- = Hold 2 stitches on a cable needle in front of work, knit 2 stitches, then knit the 2 stitches from the cable needle
- = Hold 2 stitches on a cable needle behind work, knit 2 stitches, then knit the 2 stitches from the cable needle
- = Hold 3 stitches on a cable needle in front of work, knit 3 stitches, then knit the 3 stitches from the cable needle
- = Hold 3 stitches on a cable needle behind work, knit 3 stitches, then knit the 3 stitches from the cable needle
- = Hold 6 stitches on a cable needle in front of work, hold 1 stitch on a second cable needle behind work, knit 6 stitches, then purl the stitch from the second cable needle, then knit the stitches from the first cable needle

## 136 TEXTURED CABLE PATTERN  ❯ page 73

25
23
21
19
17
15
13
11
9
7
5
3
1

Pattern Repeat 1 = 2 stitches

Pattern Repeat 2 = 2 stitches

### Stitch Key

- ● = 1 selvedge stitch
- ■ = Knit 1 stitch
- − = Purl 1 stitch
- = Hold 1 stitch on a cable needle in front of work, knit the next stitch, then knit the stitch from the cable needle
- = Hold 1 stitch on a cable needle behind work, knit the next stitch, then knit the stitch from the cable needle
- = Hold 1 stitch on a cable needle in front of work, knit 2 stitches, then purl the stitch from the cable needle
- = Hold 2 stitches on a cable needle behind work, knit 3 stitches, then purl the stitch from the cable needle
- = Hold 2 stitches on a cable needle in front of work, knit 2 stitches, then knit the 2 stitches from the cable needle
- = Hold 2 stitches on a cable needle behind work, knit 2 stitches, then knit the 2 stitches from the cable needle
- = Hold 3 stitches on a cable needle in front of work, purl 1 stitch, then knit the 3 stitches from the cable needle
- = Hold 3 stitches on a cable needle in front of work, knit 4 stitches, then knit the 3 stitches from the cable needle
- = Hold 3 stitches on a cable needle in front of work, hold 1 stitch on a second cable needle behind work, knit 3 stitches, then purl the stitch from the second cable needle, then knit the stitches from the first cable needle

134 NORDIC CABLE PATTERN ❯ page 72

29
27
25
23
21
19
17
15
13
11
9
7
5
3
1

Pattern
Repeat 1 =
1 stitch

Pattern Repeat 2 = 12 stitches

Pattern Repeat 3 = 12 stitches

Pattern
Repeat 4 =
1 stitch

## Stitch Key

⬤ = 1 selvedge stitch

▦ = Knit 1 stitch

— = Purl 1 stitch

= Hold 1 stitch on a cable needle in front of work, knit the next stitch, then knit the stitch from the cable needle

= Hold 1 stitch on a cable needle behind work, knit the next stitch, then knit the stitch from the cable needle

= Hold 2 stitches on a cable needle in front of work, knit the next stitch, then knit the 2 stitches from the cable needle

= Hold 1 stitch on a cable needle behind work, knit 2 stitches, then knit the stitch from the cable needle

= Hold 2 stitches on a cable needle behind work, knit the next stitch, then knit the 2 stitches from the cable needle

= Hold 1 stitch on a cable needle in front of work, then knit the 2 stitches from the first cable needle

= Hold 4 stitches on a cable needle behind work, knit 3 stitches, and purl 1 stitch, then work the stitches from the cable needle as (knit 3 stitches, purl 1 stitch)

= Hold 4 stitches on a cable needle in front of work, knit 3 stitches, and purl 1 stitch, then work the stitches from the cable needle as (knit 3 stitches, purl 1 stitch)

## 142 CELTIC ORNAMENT ❱ page 76

35 33 31 29 27 25 23 21 19 17 15 13 11 9 7 5 3 1

Pattern
Repeat 1 =
1 stitch

Pattern
Repeat 2 =
1 stitch

## Stitch Key

● = 1 selvedge stitch

■ = Knit 1 stitch

| = Purl 1 stitch

+ = Increase 1 stitch from the bar between stitches twisted

☐ = No stitch, for better overview only

◀ = Quadruple passing-over, starting at left: Slip 2 stitches purlwise to the right needle. * On the left needle, pass the second stitch over the first stitch. Slip the first stitch on the left needle purlwise to the right needle, and on the right needle, pass the second stitch (counted from the tip of the needle) over the first stitch (counted from the tip of the needle). Now, return the first stitch to the left needle. Repeat from * once, then purl the stitch.

◀ = Quadruple passing-over, starting at right: Slip 3 stitches purlwise to the right needle. * On the right needle, pass the second stitch (counted from the tip of the needle) over the first stitch (counted from the tip of the needle). Then slip the first stitch from the right needle purlwise to the left needle; there, pass the second stitch over the first stitch. Now, return the first stitch to the right needle. Repeat from * once. Then return the stitch to the left needle, and purl it.

ᐯ = Into the following stitch, work a total of 3 stitches (kfbf = knit the stitch first through the front leg, then through the back loop, and through the front leg again)

☐—☐■☐ = Hold 2 stitches on a cable needle in front of work, purl 2 stitches, then knit the 2 stitches from the cable needle

☐☐/—☐☐ = Hold 2 stitches on a cable needle behind work, knit 2 stitches, then purl the 2 stitches from the cable needle

■☐/☐■■ = Hold 2 stitches on a cable needle behind work, knit 2 stitches, then knit the 2 stitches from the cable needle

■☐/—☐■ = Hold 2 stitches on a cable needle in front of work, hold 1 stitch on a second cable needle behind work, knit 2 stitches, then purl the stitch from the second cable needle, then knit the 2 stitches from the first cable needle.

## 151 QUADRUPLE KNOT  ❯ page 82

Pattern
Repeat 2 =
4 stitches

Pattern
Repeat 1 =
4 stitches

### Stitch Key

● = 1 selvedge stitch

■ = Knit 1 stitch

– = Purl 1 stitch

+ = Increase 1 stitch from the bar between stitches twisted

◿ = Purl 2 stitches together

⋀ = Quadruple passing-over, starting at left: Slip 2 stitches purlwise to the right needle. * On the left needle, pass the second stitch over the first stitch. Slip the first stitch on the left needle purlwise to the right needle, and on the right needle, pass the second stitch (counted from the tip of the needle) over the first stitch (counted from the tip of the needle). Now, return the first stitch to the left needle. Repeat from * once, then purl the stitch.

3̌ = Into the following stitch, work a total of 3 stitches (kfbf = knit the stitch first through the front leg, then through the back loop, and through the front leg again)

☐ = No stitch, for better overview only

= Hold 2 stitches on a cable needle in front of work, purl 2 stitches, then knit the 2 stitches from the cable needle

= Hold 2 stitches on a cable needle behind work, knit 2 stitches, then purl the 2 stitches from the cable needle

= Hold 2 stitches on a cable needle in front of work, hold 1 stitch on a second cable needle behind work, knit 2 stitches, then purl the stitch from the second cable needle, then knit the 2 stitches from the first cable needle

= Hold 3 stitches on the first cable needle behind work, knit 2 stitches, then place the first and second stitch from the first cable needle onto a second cable needle and hold in front of work. Purl the remaining stitch from the first cable needle, then knit the 2 stitches from the second cable needle.

## 135 ALPINE PATTERN WITH TRAVELING STITCHES ❭ page 73

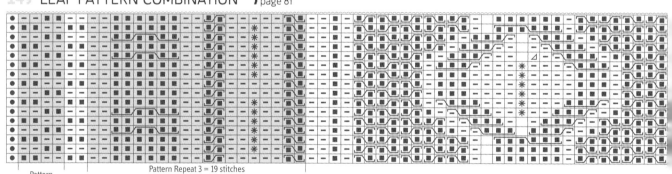

Pattern
Repeat 2 =
1 stitch

### Stitch Key

⬤ = 1 selvedge stitch

◆ = Knit 1 stitch through the back loop

— = Purl 1 stitch

◆⬤ = Hold 1 stitch on a cable needle in front of work, knit 1 stitch through the back loop, then knit the stitch from the cable needle through the back loop

◆— = Hold 1 stitch on a cable needle behind work, knit 1 stitch through the back loop, then purl the stitch from the cable needle

—⬤ = Hold 1 stitch on a cable needle in front of work, purl 1 stitch, then knit the stitch from the cable needle through the back loop

◆◆◆ = Hold 1 stitch on a cable needle behind work, knit 2 stitches through the back loop, then knit the stitch from the cable needle through the back loop

◆⬤⬤ = Hold 2 stitches on a cable needle in front of work, knit 1 stitch through the back loop, then knit the 2 stitches from the cable needle through the back loop

◆◆— = Hold 1 stitch on a cable needle behind work, knit 2 stitches through the back loop, then purl the stitch from the cable needle

—⬤◆ = Hold 2 stitches on a cable needle in front of work, purl 1 stitch, then knit the 2 stitches from the cable needle through the back loop

## 149 LEAF PATTERN COMBINATION ❭ page 81

Pattern Repeat 3 = 19 stitches

Pattern
Repeat 4 =
4 stitches

### Stitch Key

⬤ = 1 selvedge stitch

■ = Knit 1 stitch

— = Purl 1 stitch

◢ = Purl 2 stitches together

◣ = Knit 2 stitches together

◣ = Knit 2 stitches together left-leaning with passing over (skp): slip 1 stitch knitwise, knit the next stitch, and pass the slipped stitch over

◭ = Knit 3 stitches together left-leaning with passing over (sk2p): slip 1 stitch knitwise, knit 2 stitches together, and pass the slipped stitch over

☐ = No stitch, for better overview only

⌂ = Work a total of 7 stitches into 1 stitch (alternating [knit 1 stitch, purl 1 stitch], ending with [knit 1 stitch])

■■ = Hold 1 stitch on a cable needle in front of work, knit the next stitch, then knit the stitch from the cable needle

■□ = Hold 1 stitch on a cable needle behind work, knit the next stitch, then knit the stitch from the cable needle

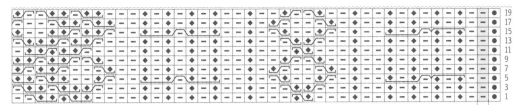

Pattern
Repeat 1 =
1 stitch

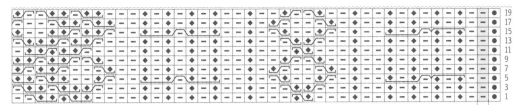 = Hold 3
stitches on a cable needle in front of
work, hold 1 stitch on a second cable
needle behind work, knit 1 stitch
through the back loop, purl 1 stitch,
and knit 1 stitch through the back
loop, then purl the stitch from the
second cable needle, then work the
stitches from the first cable needle
as: knit 1 stitch through the back
loop, purl 1 stitch, and knit 1 stitch
through the back loop

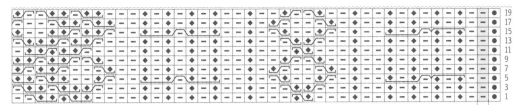 = Hold 4
stitches on the first cable needle be-
hind work, knit 1 stitch through the
back loop, purl 1 stitch, and knit 1
stitch through the back loop, then
place the 1st, 2nd, and 3rd stitch from
the first cable needle onto a second
cable needle, and hold in front of
work. Purl the remaining stitch from
the first cable needle, then work the 3
stitches from the second cable needle
as: knit 1 stitch through the back loop,
purl 1 stitch, and knit 1 stitch through
the back loop.

Pattern Repeat 2 = 19 stitches

Pattern
Repeat 1 =
4 stitches

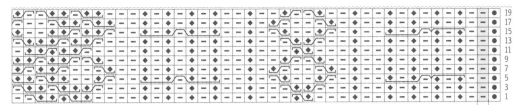 = Hold 3 stitches on a cable needle in front
of work, purl 1 stitch, then knit the 3 stitches from the
cable needle

 = Hold 1 stitch on a cable needle behind
work, knit 3 stitches, then purl the stitch from the cable
needle

 = Hold 3 stitches on a cable needle in front
of work, knit 3 stitches, then knit the 3 stitches from
the cable needle

 = Hold 2 stitches on a cable needle in
front of work, hold 2 stitches on a second cable needle
behind work, knit 2 stitches, then knit the stitches from
the second cable needle, then knit the 2 stitches from the
first cable needle

## 152 CLASSIC ALPINE PATTERN ❯ page 83

Pattern
Repeat 3 =
1 stitch

Pattern Repeat 2 =
8 stitches

### Stitch Key

⬤ = 1 selvedge stitch

■ = Knit 1 stitch

− = Purl 1 stitch

▮▮ = Hold 1 stitch on a cable needle in front of work, knit the next stitch, then knit the stitch from the cable needle

▮▮ = Hold 1 stitch on a cable needle behind work, knit the next stitch, then knit the stitch from the cable needle

▮▮ = Hold 1 stitch on a cable needle in front of work, purl the next stitch, then knit the stitch from the cable needle

▮▮ = Hold 1 stitch on a cable needle behind work, knit the next stitch, then purl the stitch from the cable needle

## 148 CLASSIC ARAN PATTERN ❯ page 81

Pattern
Repeat 2 =
4 stitches

### Stitch Key

⬤ = 1 selvedge stitch

■ = Knit 1 stitch

− = Purl 1 stitch

▮▮ = Hold 1 stitch on a cable needle in front of work, knit the next stitch, then knit the stitch from the cable needle

▮▮ = Hold 1 stitch on a cable needle behind work, knit the next stitch, then knit the stitch from the cable needle

▮▮▮ = Hold 2 stitches on a cable needle in front of work, knit the next stitch, then knit the 2 stitches from the cable needle

▮▮▮ = Hold 1 stitch on a cable needle behind work, knit 2 stitches, then knit the stitch from the cable needle

▮▮▮ = Hold 1 stitch on a cable needle in front of work, knit 2 stitches, then knit the stitch from the cable needle

▮▮▮ = Hold 2 stitches on a cable needle behind work, knit the next stitch, then knit the 2 stitches from the cable needle

## 153 CABLE PATTERN COMBINATION ❯ page 83

Pattern
Repeat 3 =
3 stitches

Pattern Repeat 2 =
8 stitches

### Stitch Key

⬤ = 1 selvedge stitch

■ = Knit 1 stitch

− = Purl 1 stitch

▮▮ = Hold 1 stitch on a cable needle in front of work, knit the next stitch, then knit the stitch from the cable needle

▮▮ = Hold 1 stitch on a cable needle behind work, knit the next stitch, then knit the stitch from the cable needle

▮▮▮▮ = Hold 2 stitches on a cable needle in front of work, knit 2 stitches, then knit the 2 stitches from the cable needle

Pattern
Repeat 1 =
1 stitch

= Hold 1 stitch on a cable needle behind work, knit the next stitch, then purl the stitch from the cable needle

= Hold 2 stitches on a cable needle in front of work, knit the next stitch, then knit the 2 stitches from the cable needle

= Hold 1 stitch on a cable needle in front of work, knit 2 stitches, then knit the stitch from the cable needle

= Hold 2 stitches on a cable needle behind work, knit the next stitch, then knit the 2 stitches from the cable needle

= Hold 2 stitches on a cable needle in front of work, knit 2 stitches, then knit the 2 stitches from the cable needle

Pattern
Repeat 4 =
4 stitches

= Hold 2 stitches on a cable needle in front of work, purl 1 stitch, then knit the 2 stitches from the cable needle

= Hold 1 stitch on a cable needle behind work, knit 2 stitches, then purl the stitch from the cable needle

= Hold 2 stitches on a cable needle in front of work, knit 2 stitches, then knit the 2 stitches from the cable needle

= Hold 2 stitches on a cable needle behind work, knit 2 stitches, then knit the 2 stitches from the cable needle

= Hold 2 stitches on a cable needle in front of work, purl 2 stitches, then knit the 2 stitches from the cable needle

= Hold 2 stitches on a cable needle behind work, knit 2 stitches, then purl the 2 stitches from the cable needle

Pattern
Repeat 1 =
3 stitches

= Hold 2 stitches on a cable needle behind work, knit 2 stitches, then knit the 2 stitches from the cable needle

= Hold 2 stitches on a cable needle in front of work, purl 2 stitches, then knit the 2 stitches from the cable needle

= Hold 2 stitches on a cable needle behind work, knit 2 stitches, then purl the 2 stitches from the cable needle

## 144 FESTIVE ALPINE PATTERN  ❯ page 79

Pattern
Repeat 2 =
1 stitch

### Stitch Key

● = 1 selvedge stitch

■ = Knit 1 stitch

− = Purl 1 stitch

◆ = Knit 1 stitch through the back loop

N = Make 1 nupp: into the following stitch, work a total of 6 stitches (alternating [knit 1 stitch, knit 1 stitch through the back loop]), and then, one after another, pass the 5th, 4th, 3rd, 2nd, and 1st stitch over the 6th stitch

◉ = Make 1 nupp: into the following stitch, work a total of 5 stitches (alternating [knit 1 stitch, knit 1 stitch through the back loop]), turn work, purl 5 stitches, turn work, knit 5 stitches, turn work, purl 2 stitches together, purl 1 stitch, purl 2 stitches together, turn work, slip 1 stitch knitwise, knit 2 stitches together, and pass the slipped stitch over

⬛⬛ = Hold 1 stitch on a cable needle in front of work, knit the next stitch, then knit the stitch from the cable needle

## 145 CABLE-AND-NUPP PATTERN  ❯ page 79

Pattern Repeat 2 =
8 stitches

### Stitch Key

● = 1 selvedge stitch

■ = Knit 1 stitch

− = Purl 1 stitch

◉ = Make 1 nupp: into the following bar between stitches, work a total of 7 stitches (alternating "increase 1 stitch from the bar between stitches twisted, make 1 yarn over"), turn work, purl 7 stitches, turn work, knit 7 stitches together through the back loop (sssssssk), and pass the preceding stitch over the stitch

N = Make 1 nupp: into the following stitch, work a total of 7 stitches (alternating "knit 1 stitch, make 1 yarn over"), turn work, purl 7 stitches, turn work, knit 7 stitches together through the back loop (sssssssk)

☐ = No stitch, for better overview only

⬜⬛ = Hold 1 stitch on a cable needle in front of work, purl the next stitch, then knit the stitch from the cable needle

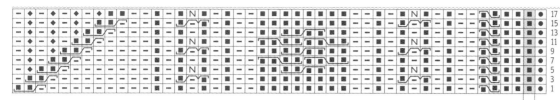

Pattern
Repeat 1 =
1 stitch

![cable needle symbol] = Hold 1 stitch on a cable needle behind work, knit the next stitch, then knit the stitch from the cable needle

![cable needle symbol] = Hold 2 stitches on a cable needle in front of work, purl 1 stitch, then knit the 2 stitches from the cable needle

![cable needle symbol] = Hold 1 stitch on a cable needle behind work, knit 2 stitches, then purl the stitch from the cable needle

![cable needle symbol] = Hold 2 stitches on a cable needle behind work, knit the next stitch, then place the 2nd stitch from the cable needle onto the left needle, and hold the cable needle with the first stitch in front of work. Purl the stitch on the left needle, then knit the stitch from the cable needle.

![cable needle symbol] = Hold 2 stitches on a cable needle in front of work, knit 2 stitches, then knit the 2 stitches from the cable needle

![cable needle symbol] = Hold 2 stitches on a cable needle behind work, knit 2 stitches, then knit the 2 stitches from the cable needle

Pattern Repeat 1 =
8 stitches

![cable needle symbol] = Hold 1 stitch on a cable needle behind work, knit the next stitch, then purl the stitch from the cable needle

![cable needle symbol] = Hold 2 stitches on a cable needle in front of work, purl 1 stitch, then knit the 2 stitches from the cable needle

![cable needle symbol] = Hold 1 stitch on a cable needle behind work, knit 2 stitches, then purl the stitch from the cable needle

![cable needle symbol] = Hold 3 stitches on a cable needle in front of work, knit 3 stitches, then knit the 3 stitches from the cable needle

![cable needle symbol] = Hold 3 stitches on a cable needle in front of work, purl 3 stitches, then knit the 3 stitches from the cable needle

![cable needle symbol] = Hold 3 stitches on a cable needle behind work, knit 3 stitches, then purl the 3 stitches from the cable needle

![cable needle symbol] = Hold 5 stitches on the first cable needle behind work, knit the next stitch, place the first stitch from the first cable onto the second cable needle, and hold in front of work. Knit the remaining 4 stitches from the first cable needle, then knit the stitch from the second cable needle.

## 180 ZIGZAG EYELET-AND-CABLE PATTERN BORDER  ❯ page 100

Pattern Repeat = 34 stitches

**Stitch Key**

▨ = 1 selvedge stitch
■ = Knit 1 stitch
▬ = Purl 1 stitch
○ = Make 1 yarn over

◤ = Knit 2 stitches together
◢ = Knit 2 stitches together left-leaning with passing over (skp): slip 1 stitch knitwise, knit the next stitch, and pass the slipped stitch over

knit 2 stitches, then knit the 2 stitches from the cable needle

▨▨▨▨ = Hold 2 stitches on a cable needle in front of work, knit 2 stitches, then knit the 2 stitches from the cable needle

▨▨▨▨ = Hold 2 stitches on a cable needle behind work, knit 2 stitches, then knit the 2 stitches from the cable needle

## 247 SPANISH LACE PATTERN  ❯ page 129

Pattern Repeat = 34 stitches

**Stitch Key**

● = 1 selvedge stitch
■ = Knit 1 stitch
▬ = Purl 1 stitch
○ = Make 1 yarn over

◤ = Knit 2 stitches together
◣ = Knit 2 stitches together left-leaning with passing over (skp): slip 1 stitch knitwise, knit the next stitch, and pass the slipped stitch over
◹ = Purl 2 stitches together
◺ = Purl 2 stitches together left-leaning (sspl): slip 2 stitches individually knitwise, return them to the left needle, then purl them together through the back loop

## 360 LOZENGE WITH LEAF MOTIF ❯ page 188

(chart grid, rows numbered 1–57 odd on the right side)

Pattern Repeat = 31 stitches

## Stitch Key

● = 1 selvedge stitch

■ = Knit 1 stitch

◆ = Knit 1 stitch through the back loop

− = Purl 1 stitch

○ = Make 1 yarn over

◢ = Knit 2 stitches together

◣ = Knit 2 stitches together left-leaning with passing over (skp): slip 1 stitch knitwise, knit the next stitch, and pass the slipped stitch over

△ = Knit 3 stitches together left-leaning with passing over (sk2p): slip 1 stitch knitwise, knit 2 stitches together, and pass the slipped stitch over

☐ = No stitch, for better overview only

◆/− = Hold 1 stitch on a cable needle behind work, knit 1 stitch through the back loop, then purl the stitch from the cable needle

−/◆ = Hold 1 stitch on a cable needle in front of work, purl 1 stitch, then knit the stitch from the cable needle through the back loop

−/■ ■ = Hold 2 stitches on a cable needle in front of work, purl 1 stitch, then knit the 2 stitches from the cable needle

■ ■/− = Hold 1 stitch on a cable needle behind work, knit 2 stitches, then purl the stitch from the cable needle

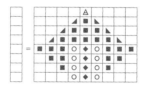

■/■ ■ = Hold 2 stitches on a cable needle in front of work, knit the next stitch, then knit the stitches from the cable needle

■ ■/■ = Hold 1 stitch on a cable needle behind work, knit 2 stitches, then knit the stitch from the cable needle

■ ■/■ ■ = Hold 3 stitches on a cable needle in front of work, knit 2 stitches, then knit the 3 stitches from the cable needle

# INDEX

## KNIT-PURL PATTERNS

# CABLE PATTERNS · TRAVELING-STITCH PATTERNS

# ARAN PATTERNS · ALPINE PATTERNS · CELTIC PATTERNS

# LACE-AND-CABLE PATTERNS

# LACE PATTERNS · DROPPED-STITCH PATTERNS

# SLIPPED-STITCH PATTERNS

# NUPPS · FLOWER AND LEAF PATTERNS

# BRIOCHE PATTERNS · MULTI-ROW PATTERNS

# DECORATIVE EDGINGS

# STRANDED COLORWORK AND INTARSIA PATTERNS

# PATTERNS USING SPECIAL TECHNIQUES

# ABOUT THE AUTHOR

**Lydia Klös** is a passionate knitter and, in addition to her work as a book author and jewelry designer, frequently travels the lecturing circuit as a presenter and workshop instructor.